# THE WORLD ENCYCLOPEDIA OF
# AMPHIBIOUS
# WARFARE VESSELS

# THE WORLD ENCYCLOPEDIA OF
# AMPHIBIOUS
# WARFARE VESSELS

## AN ILLUSTRATED GUIDE TO AMPHIBIOUS WARFARE AND THE LANDING CRAFTS USED BY SEABORNE FORCES, FROM THE GALLIPOLI CAMPAIGN TO THE PRESENT DAY

## BERNARD IRELAND WITH FRANCIS CROSBY

LORENZ BOOKS

# Contents

# A DIRECTORY OF LANDING CRAFT

# Introduction

In the 14th century, small expeditions of determined men could achieve great things – Cortés and Pizarro waded ashore with battalion-sized forces and overthrew established civilizations in the name of gold and religion, resulting in the mainly Spanish-speaking subcontinent of South America. Since then, empires have been built and have collapsed, and colonies have been won and lost.

European colonial powers emerged, each with its own "sphere of influence". Each new colony developed fortified and garrisoned settlements and, as the new wealth was extracted, the hidden arm of seapower supplied the forces of administration and protection. Like tectonic plates, the spheres of influence tended to overlap to create great frictional forces along their boundaries. Great Britain, France, Spain and the Netherlands waged new-style wars, not on each other's sovereign territory but in lands far away. These, necessarily, were expeditionary wars and, as fortified settlements became better defended, so grew the requirement for the seaborne movement of military forces.

By more recent standards, however, numbers remained relatively small: Rooke's 2,000 marines sealed the fate of Gibraltar; Clive triumphed at Plassey with under 3,000 troops, while the disastrous capitulation of Cornwallis at Yorktown involved a force of only 7,000.

Ever-ambitious as a colonial power, Britain remained vulnerable to defeat by invasion. Unlike France, a rival and foe, Britain maintained no great standing army and the first, and effectively only, line of defence was the Royal Navy. This service also policed and protected a growing empire and trade routes; each ship on station was an amphibious force in miniature, able to field a self-contained "naval brigade" to calm any colonial uprising.

The South African ("Boer") War at the turn of the 20th century demanded considerable numbers of merchant ships, chartered to transport the horses upon which the mobility of the British Army depended. It really marked the end of the old-style colonial war, heralding a new era of alliances pitted against alliances, mechanization and modern weapons capable of inflicting death on a massive scale. With conflict in a worldwide arena, armies expanded, with constant movement not of thousands, but millions of troops.

A new front involved not only infantry but also transport and equipment. To rely on landing all this through established ports was to compromise the advantage of surprise.

The operations at Gallipoli thus showed the way forward with the landing over the beach of an initial one and a half divisions. The resulting casualties and variable pace of the operation demonstrated the need for, among much else, more specialist craft. Stalemate caused by a resolute defence resulted in valuable shipping being positioned offshore until enemy submarines arrived to make the situation untenable.

Between the wars Gallipoli was studied in detail, the lessons learned being tempered with the widely held opinion that the added dimension of air power might make such future operations impossible.

The 1930s nonetheless saw the development of the great assault fleet. Although operations were still envisaged on a relatively small scale, a clear requirement was apparent for two major categories of vessel, namely "ships" for shore-to-shore movement, possibly over considerable distances, and "craft" for ship-to-shore movement, the critical phase whereby the military component was landed.

The development complete, it needed only the requirements of World War II to initiate a combination of design ingenuity and industry to realize a large fleet, the likes of which the world had truly never seen.

Amphibious warfare is again receiving considerable attention and investment by governments around the globe, and this book is, perhaps, a timely reminder of that fact.

The book is divided into three sections, the first sketching the historical development of amphibious warfare, the second a directory of landing ships that transport personnel, cargo or vehicles, and the third a directory of landing craft. Specification panels are included for each vessel, giving information about country of origin, displacement, dimensions, armament, machinery, power and endurance.

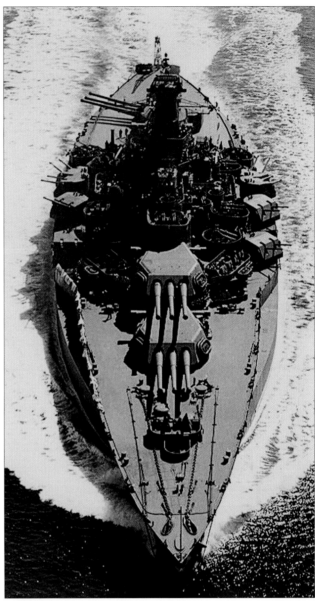

RIGHT: **A vital element in amphibious operations in World War II was the pre-landing naval bombardment of enemy postions. Ships such as USS** *Tennessee* **(BB-43) would provide this massive firepower.**

ABOVE: **Japan successfully overran South-east Asia in 1942 with almost no specialist amphibious equipment, by boldly exploiting the unpreparedness and low morale of the poorly equipped defending forces.**

ABOVE: **The speed of the Landing Craft, Air Cushion (LCAC) permits, for the first time, Over-The-Horizon (OTH) operations, greatly reducing the vulnerability of valuable multi-purpose amphibious warfare ships.**

# A History of Amphibious Warfare

In conventional warfare, the deciding factor has to be "boots on the ground". To comprehensively defeat an opponent, an army needs to occupy territory. In observing that "the Army was a missile to be fired by the Navy", Admiral of the Fleet Sir John ("Jacky") Fisher was acknowledging just that and, in effect, naval operations are largely only a means to an end. The army will, ultimately, decide the issue.

It is no coincidence, therefore, that navies down the ages have been involved in transporting armies to (usually) hostile shores. Resupply came by sea and the force would be available for any evacuation.

During World War II, special types of vessel had to be designed and developed for the campaign to recapture the Far East from Imperial Japanese forces. Many of the types, particularly the Landing Craft, Tank (LCT), were used for the massive amphibious landings on D-Day (June 6, 1944) to free Europe from many years of German occupation.

At the end of the war, much of this vast fleet was placed in reserve or scrapped. The advent of the Korean War (June 25, 1950) saw a sudden and urgent requirement for assault vessels of all types. There began the development and building of vessels to serve with the many powerful amphibious warfare fleets deployed by many navies around the world. This chapter details the development of amphibious forces through many theatres of combat.

LEFT: A prototype of what became the Landing Craft, Vehicle, Personnel (LCVP) undergoing trials with members of the US Navy and staff of the Higgins Boat Company in January 1940. A Higgins LCPL Mk 1, the type it was designed to replace, can be seen to the right.

LEFT: **Marines and sailors from cutters landing at New Providence in the Bahamas on March 3, 1776. This was the first amphibious landing by American forces and was made to capture desperately needed munitions for use in the War of Independence, 1775–83. A force of 250 overran the British Fort Montague and later captured Fort Nassau along with 88 cannon, 15 mortars and a large amount of gunpowder.**

# Categories of amphibious warfare

Current theory recognizes five categories of amphibious operation, namely assault, raids, demonstrations, feints and withdrawal. We naturally tend to think of these in the context of our own times, particularly of World War II, but the history of any traditional naval power will yield examples of how our forebears found solutions to relevant problems.

An assault is the primary form of operation, the objective of which is simply to establish a force on a hostile shore. This, in itself, has little point unless it is the precursor to occupation. This might well be the opening of a campaign but, although Normandy (1944) is easily remembered, Gallipoli (1915) or even the Norman Conquest (1066) are just as important.

An assault may have the alternative objective to seize a permanent base, from where more operations may be mounted. Numerous examples can be found during the war in the Pacific (1941–45); Gibraltar (1704) or Minorca (1708) were earlier examples of this type of operation.

A further assault objective may be occupation simply to deny a location to an enemy. During World War II the Azores, Iceland and Madagascar were all occupied, but an earlier parallel is seen in the British seizure of Trincomalee, Ceylon (Sri Lanka) from the Dutch in 1795. This was in order to deny the city and peninsula to the French, the new ally of the Dutch.

Raids are also an assault, but are of a size and configuration suited to a designated objective. There is also a time element involved, for once the objective has been achieved, the raiding force will need to be withdrawn. Local sea control, even if temporary, is thus a prerequisite. Raids, typically, are expensive in terms of casualties, as objectives tend to be well defended. Singular acts of personal courage also feature, but the chances of failure are relatively high. Modern successes include Pebble Island (Falklands, 1982) and St. Nazaire (1942); failures, Zeebrugge and Ostend (1918). Historically, Drake's brief occupation of Cadiz (1587), cost Spain dearly in materiel

RIGHT: **Royal Marines returning to Britain after the raid on Zeebrugge, April 1918. Of the 1,700 troops deployed, some 170 were killed and 300 injured. Eight of the raiding force were awarded the Victoria Cross. The operation was promoted as a British success by government propaganda.**

ABOVE: **Two Mulberry harbours were constructed, one at Omaha Beach (Mulberry "A") and the other at Arromanches (Mulberry "B") after the D-Day landings, June 6, 1944. Both were completed on June 9, but on June 19 a violent storm destroyed the harbour at Omaha. The remaining harbour at Arromanches (Port Winston) continued to be used for a further 10 months.**

and treasure. Numerous later skirmishing expeditions were brilliant examples of small-scale raids, adding many useful prize ships to the strength of the Royal Navy.

A modern variation on the raid is to use sea and shoreline in manoeuvre warfare, undertaking "leapfrog" landings, known as "desants", to insert a small force in a strategically important location behind enemy lines until relieved by advancing friendly forces. This type of assault can be very destabilizing for an entrenched opponent; examples include those of the Soviet Union in the Black Sea, US and Australian forces in New Guinea and the British landing at Termoli on the Adriatic coast in 1943.

Demonstrations and feints are similar since both are calculated to confuse an opponent. A demonstration is staged with the objective of deceiving the opposition into shifting from a favourable to a less-favourable position, while a feint is designed to distract the enemy from the real danger. Because of the slow means of communication in earlier days, demonstrations and feints were applicable on a local level to military operations rather than to an amphibious assault.

Loading for an amphibious landing is a skilled and protracted operation and not practicable under fire. Large-scale withdrawals, therefore, tend to involve only personnel, with supplies and equipment being destroyed or abandoned. The withdrawals from Gallipoli (1915) and Dunkirk (1940) are modern examples, with others, such as Toulon (1793) and Corunna/Vigo (1809), featuring in history.

Withdrawal necessarily follows raids, with which heavy equipment is not usually associated. Most raids, such as those on Zeebrugge and St. Nazaire, require only what

might be termed man-portable equipment. An obvious and disastrous exception was the assault on Dieppe (1942). This operation suffered from problems that included the slow speed of Landing Craft, Tank (LCT), and the abandonment of all of the 29 Churchill tanks landed due to the shingle and the slope of the beach.

RIGHT: **Armoured Amphibious Vehicles (AAV) of the US Marine Corps landing on Sattahip beach in eastern Thailand during exercise "Cobra Gold" on May 19, 2006. On the horizon is a US Navy Landing Ship, Dock (LSD).**

# Gallipoli

The experience of Gallipoli was so awful that many were convinced that opposed landings were no longer feasible in the face of modern weaponry. As First Lord of the Admiralty, Winston S. Churchill conceived the notion of the Royal Navy forcing the Dardanelles, positioning off Constantinople (Istanbul) and threatening bombardment, forcing Turkey out of World War I.

With German advisers, however, the Turks had carefully mined the waterway, covering the minefields with shore-based artillery and searchlights. Following several attempts, resulting in both loss of life and ships, the Royal Navy had to admit defeat.

The adopted solution was to militarily seize the Gallipoli peninsula, which formed the northern side of the Dardanelles, thus allowing the fleet to pass. Gallipoli was suited to defence, being rugged, with parched hills cut by deep, dry gullies. The steep beach line offered few landing sites other than restricted coves, dominated by high ground.

ABOVE: Naval and requisitioned commercial shipping was able to anchor off the Gallipoli beachhead only until the arrival of German U-boats.

Commanding the Turkish forces was General Otto Liman von Sanders, a German officer who, to the Turks' natural bravery and fortitude, had imposed much-needed efficiency and discipline. Travelling the terrain thoroughly, he had identified and fortified all possible landing places. Barbed wire lined every beach, above and below water. Electrically controlled mines were buried in the beaches, all of which were covered by well-positioned machine-guns, providing enfilading fire over each cove from the high ground. Artillery, located further inland, was carefully directed on to intended target areas.

British planning was plagued by inter-service lack of contact, the Admiralty and War Office having differing aims. Personnel familiar with the terrain were not consulted, planning relying on out-of-date maps. To minimize casualties, the Army wanted a night landing; the Navy refused, citing

ABOVE: HMS *Perdita*, a Royal Navy minelayer, leaving Mudros harbour to operate in the Dardanelles, 1916. RIGHT: With so much reliance placed upon ships' boats for troop movement, steam-powered picket boats from major warships were of crucial importance for towing lighters and other craft.

inaccurate charts and possible mining. Preparations and stockpiling were lengthy and widespread, hopelessly compromising secrecy.

Around Cape Helles, at the tip of the peninsula, five beaches would be assaulted simultaneously by the British 29th Division. Fully equipped troops would be packed into open ships' boats, towed ashore in lines by steam pinnaces. At "V" beach only, the assault would be spearheaded by troops landing from *River Clyde*, a purposely modified Glasgow-built collier, which would be run ashore. Simultaneously, 32km/20 miles along the coast at Suvla Bay, the 3rd Australian Brigade would go ashore just before dawn to seize enemy positions and allow the landing of the 1st Australian Division and the New Zealand Brigade.

The operation was set for April 25, 1915. The ANZAC forces were landed at the wrong location, and hit by a determined Turkish counter-attack. Confined to a shallow beachhead the troops dug in and were not able to move forward.

At Helles, the *River Clyde* grounded too far out, her troops being cut down even as they struggled ashore. Troops packed in wooden boats were killed by machine-gun fire as the boats were impeded by underwater barbed wire. Beachheads were won, however, at all five locations, but at a dreadful price.

ABOVE LEFT: **Anzac Cove (Gaba Tepe) on the Gallipoli peninsula.** ABOVE: **HMT** *River Clyde* **ashore at "V" beach. Note the lack of damage, as all Turkish fire was of low calibre and mainly directed at moving troops and equipment.**

Great numbers of wounded died for lack of immediate surgical facilities, while medical evacuation was hopelessly inadequate. All areas were vulnerable to enemy fire, even the provision of water proving almost impossible. Naval support gunfire was available, but not effective against an enemy located in deep gullies. Heavy howitzers were required.

On the night of August 6/7, the British IX Corps was landed at Suvla to break the deadlock but leadership and motivation were poor. The situation remained static as before. This persisted, and disease began to claim as many lives as the Turkish bullets.

At home, there was a change of government and Churchill was removed from office. The Army commander, General Sir Ian Hamilton, was then replaced. Field Marshal Kitchener visited and, appalled by what he saw, decided to abandon the campaign which, in any case, had become rather irrelevant to the conduct of the overall war effort. During the night of January 8/9, 1916, some 17,000 men were evacuated by the Royal Navy in the only efficiently run part of the campaign.

LEFT: **Following the initial landings, most reinforcements could be brought ashore unopposed. Landing techniques had advanced little since the Napoleonic Wars.**

# Operation "ZO", Zeebrugge and Ostend

The Belgian inland-waterway port of Bruges is connected to the sea, via canals, at Zeebrugge and Ostend. Occupied by Germany throughout World War I, Bruges was home to both destroyers and coastal submarines. Located so close on the flank of British shipping in the Strait of Dover, this presence was a continuous menace. In April 1918, the new Senior Naval Officer of Dover Command, Acting Vice-Admiral Sir Roger Keyes, revived a long-delayed plan to block both exits of the Bruges canal. Rather unimaginatively entitled "ZO", the operational plan was to use five small and obsolete cruisers as blockships, three at Zeebrugge, two at Ostend.

To this day, Zeebrugee lock entrance lays within the structure of the massive stone-built mole, which curves out to sea for over 1.6km/1 mile. On the outer side the mole forms a high, continuous wall; on the inner side it is a working quay. To permit water flow, the inshore 300 yards of the structure was built as an open, steel-framed viaduct.

Both ashore and on the mole extension were powerful batteries of guns. Those on the mole menaced the blockships at very close range, so Keyes proposed to neutralize them with a diversionary attack. An old submarine would first be expended to blow up the viaduct, preventing enemy reinforcement. Simultaneously, the old cruiser HMS *Vindictive*, modified for the occasion, would be lain alongside the outer wall, hard by the mole battery, which would be captured by a landing party. The blockships, meanwhile, would round the mole and be scuttled in the canal entrance. Their crews would be rescued by accompanying Motor Launches (ML).

The MLs would also lay a continuous chemical smoke screen. This was essential, though the night was moonless and it was high water. A first attempt at the raid, on the night of April 11/12, 1918, was abandoned due to a sudden shift in wind direction. In extricating the 70-odd craft from a point in mid-Channel, one small craft became detached. Running ashore, her papers were recovered by the enemy, thus compromising Keyes' plan. Ignoring this possibility, Keyes sailed again on the night of April 22/23.

In drizzling rain, HMS *Vindictive* emerged from the smoke screen rather short of the mole, just before midnight. Topside, awaiting orders to land, were 700 marines and 200 bluejackets. Swept by close-range fire, these suffered heavy casualties, including their leaders. Anxious to get alongside, the commanding officer of HMS *Vindictive* placed the ships 340 yards too far down the mole. The vessel was pinned in by a Mersey ferry, brought for the task, and the soldiers swarmed ashore over specially designed brows. Courage was never lacking, but human flesh was never a match for machine-guns and barbed wire. The gun battery on the mole was never taken.

ABOVE: **Acting Vice-Admiral Sir Roger Keyes with Earl Haig. In 1943, Keyes was created Baron Keyes of Zeebrugge and Dover.**

Just 55 minutes after landing, the assault party was recalled as the blockships arrived. The first, heavily hit by artillery at close range, staggered through a net boom and, her propellers fouled, she was scuttled clear of the entrance. The second, in contrast, was barely damaged and was carefully aligned for sinking, only to be hit by the third vessel. Both were then scuttled with explosives, the crews being safely taken off.

Aerial photographs taken the following day indicated that the latter pair of blockships had been well placed. Unfortunately, banks of silt had accumulated due to the

ABOVE: **The reason for the raid: a German submarine, based at Bruges, departing for a patrol against British shipping in the Channel or North Sea.**

ABOVE: **A navigable channel with a minimum low water depth of 4m/13ft existed to the right of the wrecks of HMS** *Intrepid* **(left) and HMS** *Iphigenia*.
RIGHT: **Motor Launches (ML) were used to lay a smoke screen to cover the attack, then to rescue the crews of the blockading vessels.**

neglect of the war years and the Germans experienced little difficulty in dredging a channel around the hulks, which, largely filled with concrete, were beyond easy salvage.

The Ostend part of "ZO" was a total failure. Shrewdly acting on information in the captured papers, the enemy simply moved navigation buoys. This elementary precaution was sufficient to see both blockships scuttled in entirely the wrong position. Three weeks later, the battered HMS *Vindictive* was expended in a second, but still only partially successful attempt, to blockade Ostend.

Operation "ZO" gave the British a moral boost but, with Bruges still working, was a failure. Eight of the force received the Victoria Cross; Keyes was knighted and 170 died.

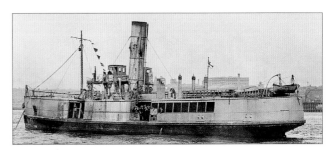

ABOVE: **HMS** *Iris II*, **one of the Mersey ferries at Liverpool docks after the raid. The other was HMS** *Daffodil*.
LEFT: **An aerial photograph of the canal entrance after the raid. Note HMS** *Thetis* **at the entrance with HMS** *Intrepid* **and HMS** *Iphigenia* **across the waterway.**

# Plan Orange and a new rationale for the US Marine Corps

In the early years of the 20th century, an accomplished small-boat sailor/gunrunner published a work of fiction that, myth has it, finally alerted the British establishment to the dangers inherent in burgeoning German naval power. Erskine Childers, author of "Riddle of the Sands", was something of a maverick and, having written the work by which he is remembered, came to a sad end, being executed during the Irish "troubles".

The parallels between Childers' progress and that of Lieutenant Colonel Earle H. Ellis, US Marine Corps, are interesting. Having written his prescient "Advanced Base Operations in Micronesia" in 1921 he applied for, and was granted, permission to travel incognito throughout the Japanese "Mandates" in an extraordinary role as a virtual freelance spy. Despite his service background, Ellis was also an intensely private individual who quickly "went native", marrying locally, and drank himself to an early death. First interred in Micronesia, his remains were exhumed and repatriated to the USA for burial. Because of official resistance to acknowledge the unorthodoxy of his odyssey, the truth emerged slowly and reluctantly, his fate becoming garlanded in myth and generally being attributed to the activities of the Japanese secret police. Nothing of further significance is believed to have resulted from his Micronesian wanderings, but his earlier book is widely credited as being a blueprint for the conduct of the Pacific War, 1941–45. This is, perhaps, a little facile, bearing in mind that US military plans for possible war with Japan had been initiated on the order of President Theodore Roosevelt.

ABOVE: **Plan Orange envisaged a trans-Pacific, island-hopping campaign, with Japan as the enemy. The US Marine Corps was virtually "re-invented" as the required assault force.** BELOW: **Boats now have engines but, over ten years after the Dardanelles disaster, landing techniques remain unimproved.**

LEFT: **Massed troops in unprotected wooden craft lacking ramps was not the ideal way to conduct an opposed landing. Fortunately, by August 1942 the US Navy had taken note and learned from British experience.**

Japanese–American relationships had deteriorated sharply in the first years of the 20th century. The Japanese annihilation of the Russian fleet at Tsushima (between Korea and Japan) in 1905 had been a sobering event, but also coincided with an unprecedented wave of Japanese emigration to the West Coast of the United States. At home, the US government was concerned at volatile interracial tensions; abroad it began to be worried at a newly confident Japan's expansionism. With the extensive Far Eastern interests of the United States under threat as he saw it, Roosevelt ordered military plans to be prepared against the possibility of hostilities. Thus began what would become Plan Orange, successively refined by generations of officers up until World War II.

The first full version of the plan appeared in 1911. The US Navy was then firmly Atlantic-centred. In those pre-Panama Canal days, it would take a full three months to get a battle-ready fleet to the Far East. The opening of the canal in 1914 shortened this somewhat. In the course of World War I, which was then commencing (and in which the United States remained uninvolved until April 1917), the US government learned that the British and Japanese, then bound by alliance, had agreed that German western Pacific island groups, notably the Marshalls and Carolines, would be mandated to the Japanese, while the southern groups would pass to the British. With the 1919 peace terms, these arrangements became official. Thus began the "Mandates question".

In 1921, the US government convened the Washington Conference, designed primarily to inhibit the ruinously expensive new naval arms race that had erupted between the late allied powers. In this it was successful in terms of capital ships and also in obliging Great Britain to revoke the Anglo-Japanese alliance through agreeing to its dilution, about which the Japanese were unforgiving.

Article XIX of the ratified agreement expressly forbade further fortification, or the establishment of naval bases in detached Pacific territories which the major powers "may hold or hereafter acquire". This was something of a mixed blessing for the USA for, where Japan had no territorial interests in the eastern Pacific, the war with Spain in 1896 had made the United States a colonial power in the western Pacific.

Guam, in particular, was strategically significant, while the

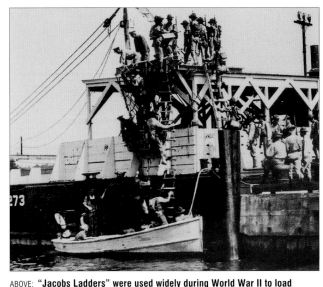

ABOVE: **"Jacobs Ladders" were used widely during World War II to load follow-up troops into LCVPs alongside transports. With considerable sea motion, this was hazardous for heavily laden troops.**

sprawling Philippines were more a social responsibility than an economic benefit. Neither could now be further fortified, nor could the United States afford to deploy a truly deterrent force. Owing to the proximity to Japan, early loss had, therefore, to be accepted in the event of war. This would leave the US government with two simple options – to accept the situation or to recover the territories. Of these, the first was not acceptable, leading inevitably to the second.

At this point the "Mandates" became significant, for any trans-Pacific expeditionary force would depend upon the US Navy for transport and support. During the late war the British had demonstrated the great potential of naval air power, and both the United States and Japan were working hard on naval aviation. The global aircraft carrier tonnage permitted to all three was now bound by Articles VII to IX of the Washington

ABOVE: **In the background, even the relatively lightweight launches are shown grounded well away from the shoreline. Any fully equipped infantrymen stumbling and falling were in danger of being drowned.**

Treaty but, in the myriad islands and atolls of the "Mandates", the Japanese had a deep natural barrier within which airfields could be constructed. Such land-based air cover would make US Navy fleet operations virtually impossible. The "non-fortification" clause of the Treaty was, of course, expressly designed to prevent the creation of such facilities and, to their credit, the Japanese observed the prohibition. Unfortunately, they regarded the "Mandates" as a military area, and made foreign access difficult. With opportunities for inspection being impeded or forbidden, the US government assumed the worst.

LEFT: **The 30ft Eureka boat (in the foreground) could carry 18 troops, had a draft of 1.2m/4ft and no ramp. The "Artillery Lighter" in the next berth had a ramp at the stern.**

ABOVE: **An amphibious tank on trials at Culebra, Puerto Rico, in 1924. The vehicle was based on a Christie-type tank chassis.**

This, then, was the background to Ellis's "Advanced Base Operations in Micronesia". As the treaty allowed the United States to develop facilities only in Hawaii (Pearl Harbor) and on the West Coast, Ellis highlighted the requirement to develop the means and the techniques for seizing islands as "advanced bases", allowing a steady westward advance across the Pacific.

Marines had been used traditionally by all major fleets for landing duties. During World War I, marine forces of both the United States and Great Britain had been expanded to the point where marine brigades had served ashore alongside regular Army infantry. Over the years, the US Marine Corps (USMC) was used extensively to maintain peace in the Caribbean and in Central America. Post-war reductions and economies, however, had seen the USMC reduced to the point where its future seemed limited to small-scale policing, ship-board detachments, ceremonial and guarding fleet bases. There were even those who advocated disbandment.

Ellis now eloquently justified the creation of an "Advanced Base Force". With Japan in mind as the most likely future enemy and the British failure at Gallipoli as a template from which to learn, the USMC began a transition to a fully self-contained expeditionary force, constituted as elements of both the US Navy Atlantic and Pacific fleets. In 1933, the arrangement was formalized as the "Fleet Marine Force" (FMF), with a strength of two independent 1,600-man battalions. These would be in addition to smaller detachments for minor commitments. Their purpose was to train and to develop equipment for amphibious warfare.

The USMC had its own, dedicated transport, the USS *Henderson* (AP-1), built to specific requirements during World War I. Interestingly, for future categorization, AP-1 was

ABOVE: **US Marines practising leaving a troopship during an exercise at Quantico, VA, in the 1920s. The scrambling nets shown are of the same pattern as cargo nets used on commercial shipping.**

designed to land troops as a fully contained combat unit, a distinction that saw the ship classed as an "expeditionary transport" (later AK "attack transport") as opposed to what were called by the British "troopships" and, by the US Navy, "convoy transport". Attack transports had to sacrifice some troop accommodation for extra equipment stowage.

Amphibious exercises, termed "Fleet Landing Exercises" (FLEX), were conducted regularly during the 1930s. Despite restricted budgets, accumulated experience resulted in the production of the "Tentative Landing Operations Manual" (TLOM), which, with updates, was adopted formally in 1938 as the US Navy's "Landing Operations Doctrine" (LOD). Many basic operational elements had, by now, been reasonably developed, including the value of a USMC aviation component for ground support, warship-based gunfire support, amphibious armour and the ramped small craft necessary for the delivery of artillery and vehicles over the beach. Boatbuilder Andrew Jackson Higgins had already begun his fruitful cooperation with the policy makers. By 1941, the FMF had a strength of some 23,000 men.

LEFT: **The Japanese occupation of Guam as seen by the artist Kohei Ezaki for a propoganda book. The preferred technique was to mount several simultaneous assaults over related, undefended beaches.**

# The Japanese Far East campaign

By far the world's most experienced power in amphibious warfare, the Japanese had perfected their techniques in over ten years of war with China. National pride had been slighted at the 1921–22 Washington Conference, where the major powers had not accorded the Japanese the status of a first rank naval power. Relegated to quantitative inferiority, Japan's forces henceforth strove for qualitative superiority and, by December 1941, had achieved this aim.

A central belief of the ruling elite, political as well as military, was that the nation must, at some stage, extend its frontiers to provide both the space and natural resources required. The most attractive option was to capture the Dutch East Indies and Malaya (now Indonesia and Malaysia), risking war with the region's colonial powers – the United States, Britain, the Netherlands and France. By December 1941, however, the last two were already out of the war and Britain appeared weakened. The time was right.

Since 1923, when the USA was declared the most likely future enemy, the Japanese Army had concentrated on developing techniques and plans for regional conquest, while the Japanese Navy had prepared for a Trafalgar-style battle with the US Navy spearheading the inevitable counter-attack.

In general, the army and navy did not enjoy good relations, with a degree of harmony continuously existing only in amphibious warfare. Realistic exercises developed rules for naval gunfire support, ship-to-shore procedures, the need for specialist craft and for air superiority.

Unhappy early experience in China led the Japanese to favour unopposed landings by night. In contrast to later US forces "wave" assaults, these were by columns of assault craft hitting several related beaches simultaneously. Defenders were rendered more confused by the use of rivers and creeks to land units to the rear. Infiltration, rather than confrontation, was widely practised.

Experience in China had led to the building of the first-ever large, multi-purpose assault ship in the *Shinshu Maru*. Also, the finest naval air arm in the world was developed.

To ensure air supremacy, the first target was air bases. Immense damage resulted at Pearl Harbor, in the Philippines and in Malaya. Following-up immediately were invasion forces, the first wave starting from Formosa (Taiwan) and a compliant French Indo-China (Vietnam) and Siam (Thailand).

ABOVE: **Japanese infantry going ashore from Daihatsu landing craft. These vessels looked primitive, but were inexpensive to build and highly versatile.**

LEFT: **Japanese infantry using one-man inflatables to cross a river on the Malayan peninsula during the invasion in 1942.**

Having lost command of the air, the Allied forces had difficulty in using their considerable sea power to counter enemy moves in what was a vast theatre of war.

Moving steadily down the Malayan peninsula toward Singapore, and with the Philippines captured, the Japanese launched the second-wave attack. Always moving under air cover launched from newly captured airfields, they initiated assaults at west and north Borneo from both Indo-China and the Philippines. This was followed by multi-targeted landings against south Borneo, Celebes (Sulawesi), Ambon, Sumatra and along the so-called "Malay Barrier".

Allied morale collapsed early and totally in the face of relentless Japanese progress. Landings were in limited strength but always unpredictable for either location or time.

With the Allied forces spread so thinly in such a vast area, little or no resistance was met, and the Japanese simply regrouped and advanced. The powerful carrier group that had ravaged Pearl Harbor, followed up with the Bay of Bengal, Ceylon (Sri Lanka) and Darwin, and became free to assist in the latter phases of the campaign.

By the end of February 1942 it was all over, a triumphant vindication of manoeuvre warfare. Japan controlled all that it had desired, the "Greater East Asia Co-Prosperity Sphere" stretching from Burma in the west, and to the Gilberts in the east.

In so great an area, Japanese lines of communication were stretched to the limit and, like those of the Allies before, were vulnerable to interdiction. As Allied forces regathered military strength, retribution was only a matter of time.

LEFT: **After landing infantry and establishing a beachhead, the Imperial Japanese Army swiftly landed armour, artillery and transport vehicles. Japanese light tanks were almost useless against Allied armour.**

# Operation "Jubilee", Dieppe

ABOVE: **Assault troops transfering from a Fairmile B-type Motor Launch (ML).**
LEFT: **The landing beach from a German defensive point located on a cliff. Beyond the relatively low sea wall is a wide, open space covered by a continuous line of reinforced, defended buildings.**

On August 19, 1942 the small French port of Dieppe was the focus of a major Allied raid. The intention was to hold the town for a few hours before withdrawing. Although the plan was driven by powerful political imperatives, the military objectives included:
• Testing planning, command and control procedures.
• Gauging likely German reaction to a surprise assault.
• Provoking a major air battle with the *Luftwaffe*.

Dieppe was within operational range of English south-coast airfields, on which the RAF had concentrated some 60 squadrons of fighter aircraft. Most of the 6,000 assault personnel were drawn from the 1st Canadian Army, which had yet to see action. The remainder comprised three British commandos, two of them Army, one Royal Marine.

The operation was started on July 7, but was aborted due to poor flying conditions over the Channel and Dieppe. This may well have compromised the second attempt.

Dieppe is situated in a dip in the continuous line of near-vertical chalk cliffs that form that part of the Normandy coast. It is thus dominated by high ground to either side and to the rear. Enemy gun batteries and emplacments on these heights commanded both town and seaward approaches. A planned proposal to seize these locations with paratroops was abandoned as being too weather-dependent.

The plan was to mount a frontal assault on the town, preceded by double assaults on either flank to neutralize the gun batteries. The town was fronted by a sea wall, backed by a promenade, wide ornamental gardens and a boulevard of substantial buildings, many reinforced as strongpoints. Plans to bomb the latter before the landing were vetoed in favour of on-demand naval support gunfire. Major warships could not be risked, so this was limited mainly to the 4in guns of eight Royal Navy Hunt-class destroyers.

An armada of 237 vessels, including 188 amphibious assault craft, carried 4,961 Canadian troops and 1,057 British commandos. The approach, early on August 19, was betrayed when vessels for the left-flank landings encountered an enemy convoy. The ensuing battle scattered the LCAs and alerted the garrison ashore. Despite a valiant effort the left-flank landings were a failure. In contrast, the right-flank landings were a total success.

At 05:20 the frontal assault went in on time, against defenders by now fully alert and untroubled by the pre-assault bombardment. The Germans laid a continuous hail of fire on the beach, cutting down the Canadian troops even as they left the LCAs. The Canadians should have been supported directly by medium tanks, but the LCTs carrying these were delayed by over 10 minutes. During this short space of time, the attack lost initial momentum, which was never recovered.

The troops remained pinned-down on the steep, shingle beach. Twenty-seven tanks were eventually landed, but only 19 succeeded in getting beyond the sea wall. These were

LEFT: **The first small British tank landing craft was originally called an MLC. The LCM (1) was superseded by the LCM (3). It was designed to be handled by davits, and could be hoisted part-loaded.** BELOW: **The raiders having withdrawn, the Germans are clearing the beach of casualties. Many of the Churchill tanks were immobilized by the soft shingle beach.**

then unable to progress into the town because of concrete obstacles. These, in turn, could not be destroyed by sappers owing to heavy enemy fire, which the tanks were unable to suppress. Gunfire from the tanks and the destroyers made little impression on the German defences.

An impasse resulted, but the military commander, offshore in a destroyer, misjudged the situation due to poor communications. He committed his floating reserve, which merely added to the numbers pinned down on the beach. By 09:00, however, the hopelessness of the situation had become apparent and, some two hours earlier than planned, a general

withdrawal was signalled. Naval craft took a terrible pounding as they beached, but succeeded in lifting nearly 1,000 survivors. By any standard, Dieppe was a disaster. Some 2,200 troops were taken prisoner. Of only 1,620 Canadians returning unwounded, approximately 1,000 had not landed. A quarter of the commandos had become casualties. Naval losses were a destroyer, 33 landing craft and 550 casualties.

The RAF had fought the air battle it had sought but, in destroying 48 of the *Luftwaffe*, it lost 106 aircraft. Having suffered under 600 casualties, the Germans were understandably jubilant at their considerable success.

# Operation "Watchtower", Guadalcanal

The devastating loss of four aircraft carriers at Midway meant that any further Japanese military advance would probably require the provision of land-based air cover. With New Guinea proving to be a difficult campaign, the Japanese were keen to hold the Solomons, to act as a defensive barrier against any planned US forces counter-strike. Japanese lines of communication were by now, however, stretched to the limit, and their presence in the Solomons was sparse, with the nearest major base being at Rabaul, some 966km/600 miles distant from the most southerly islands. Considerable risk thus attended the establishment of a reconnaissance flying boat base at Tulagi and an airfield at Lunga Point on Guadalcanal, 32km/20 miles away.

Despite equally meagre resources, US forces were keen to take the offensive in the Solomons. The news, on July 5, 1942, that the enemy was constructing an airfield, triggered firm action for, once complete, this base would give the Japanese local air superiority. The improvised nature of the resulting operation,

codenamed "Watchtower", resulted in the more popular name of "Shoestring". A total of 19,000 US Marines were drawn from regiments and battalions of different divisions and units, many without recent training. The force was embarked in 19 transports, with eight cruisers and 15 destroyers for escort and fire support. Bound for both Tulagi and Guadalcanal, all amphibious forces were commanded by Rear-Admiral Richmond K. Turner.

Direct air support was provided by three aircraft carriers, operating independently under Vice-Admiral Frank Fletcher.

Following an unopposed bombardment of the Lunga Point beaches, the first US forces amphibious operation since 1898 began early on August 7. Due to the forthcoming North African landings (Operation "Torch") taking precedence, no specialist landing ships could be allocated. Ship-to-shore movement was handled by a fleet of 36ft Higgins boats, 36ft Landing Craft, Personel, Ramped (LCP [R]), and 45 and 56ft Landing Craft, Mechanized (LCM). The Japanese forces, mainly being

ABOVE: **Although popularly known as Operation "Shoestring", 15 transports were deployed for the Guadalcanal landing, with a further eight for Tulagi. The powerful naval force was little used initially.**
RIGHT: **With very limited tidal range, this beach at Guadacanal allowed New Zealand troops to exit from the LCP (R)s almost at the jungle edge.**

LEFT: **A crowded transport, probably USS** *President Hayes* **(APA-20), ready to land US Marine Corps forces on Guadalcanal. Note the assault craft stowed on No. 2 hatch and the rigged scrambling nets. USS** *Quincy* **(CA-39), a San Francisco-class heavy cruiser, is in the background. USS** *Quincy* **was sunk at the Battle of Savo Island, off Guadalcanal, on August 9, 1942.**

construction and engineering personnel, offered negligible resistance. Beach congestion proved to be a major problem but, by dark, 11,000 US Marines were ashore and the airfield safely secured. Anticipated to be an easier target, Tulagi was allocated only three battalions of US Marines. Outnumbered,

ABOVE: **The characteristic rounded stern identifies this LCM as a 45ft Mark 2, and is from the the transport USS** *Aurelia* **(AKA-23). The light tank is an M3. The later M3A1 was very effective against Japanese armour.**

the 1,500 Japanese operating the flying boat facility were, however, well prepared. Less than 100 were to survive the ensuing vicious hand-to-hand combat.

Aircraft from Fletcher's carriers broke up several determined enemy air attacks and, by the evening of August 8, for the loss of one transport, both Tulagi and Guadalcanal appeared to be secure. Having given just 36 hours of air cover, Fletcher then moved his force away, anxious lest his irreplaceable carriers became targets for submarines. The Lunga Point airfield (soon to be renamed Henderson Field) was not yet operational, while most of the transport ships remained half unloaded.

Meanwhile, moving at speed down the Solomons chain from Rabaul was a powerful Japanese naval force under Vice-Admiral Gunichi Mikawa. Although sighted by US reconnaissance aircraft, this potent threat was misreported and misinterpreted.

In the early hours of August 9, in a powerful hit-and-run attack, Mikawa surprised and savaged the covering force, sinking four cruisers off Savo Island. Mikawa's force immediately withdrew, concerned that dawn would bring retribution in the shape of Fletcher's aircraft. He need not have worried, but his instinct to pull out prevented his force falling upon the now-defenceless amphibious transports. He thus failed to achieve his main objective, and "Watchtower" was saved.

To the US military, Guadalcanal became, like Verdun or El Alamein, a symbolic line in the sand. The Japanese were equally determined to recapture it and, for six months, both sides poured in reinforcements. It was the catalyst for six major and many lesser battles between the opposing fleets.

In an attritional campaign such as this, US forces would, inevitably, be the victors. Finally admitting defeat, and that the long advance had reached its limit, Japan suddenly withdrew its troops in February 1943. Overall losses had been two battleships, three carriers, 12 cruisers, 25 destroyers and at least 25,000 lives.

LEFT: **Five British assault convoys alone (this is KMF I) involved 156 merchant ships and 52 escorts. Sailing directly from the USA were another four convoys, comprising a further 200 vessels.**

# Operation "Torch", North Africa

Despite the trauma of the Japanese attack on Pearl Harbor, President Roosevelt adhered to a policy of "Germany first". For this he also overruled opposition from his Chiefs of Staff, who then, once recommitted to a major operation in the European theatre, pushed hard for an early cross-Channel assault. The experienced British, well aware that the US Army lacked battle experience, condemned this ambition as foolhardy. Roosevelt heeded their council, instructing General George C. Marshall and Admiral Ernest J. King to prepare plans for the invasion of North Africa by, at the latest, the end of October 1942. Just three months ahead.

Marshall appointed Lieutenant General Dwight D. Eisenhower as Commander-in-Chief (C-in-C), Expeditionary Force, North Africa. Admiral Andrew B. Cunningham, RN was sent to Washington to liaise at the highest level as Commander, Allied Naval Forces. Vice-Admiral Bertram Ramsay, RN headed the Anglo-American planning staff based in London.

Although the British 8th Army had been battling Italian forces and the German *Afrika Korps* since June 1940, their war had been confined to Libya and Egypt. Morocco, Algeria and Tunisia remained under the control of Vichy French authorities, in accordance with the terms of the armistice agreed with Germany in 1940. The coastline of these territories is some 2,414km/1,500 miles in length and there was considerable disagreement on where the Allied force should strike, assuming that the Germans would immediately use this as a pretext to occupy all Vichy territory.

The British wanted to land at Bizerta and Tunis, at the far eastern end, in order to thwart rapid German reinforcement from Sicily. Uncharacteristically, the US military vetoed this as too bold and simultaneous assaults were ordered at Casablanca, on the exposed Atlantic coast, and at Oran, the French naval base, also at Algiers. Forces landing at Algiers were charged with then progressing rapidly 644km/400 miles eastward to secure Tunis.

Up to 120,000 well-equipped French troops were known to be deployed in Morocco and Algeria but it was not known how hard they would resist in the name of Vichy. Allied forces numbers therefore reflected this strength – 19,500 troops for Casablanca,

LEFT: **Air-defence gun crews watching as assault craft move up for the Casablanca landing. Considerable opposition was encountered from warships of the Vichy French Navy.**

39,000 for Oran and 43,000 for Algiers. Very widely separated the three operations had to be autonomous. The Landing Ship, Tank (LST) was not yet available so, following ship-to-shore assault with LCAs and LCMs carried by the transports, port facilities would be quickly captured in order to land armour and heavy equipment. Aircraft carriers, ever in short supply, could give early air cover but would need to be quickly withdrawn, so the early capture of airfields was essential.

Under Rear-Admiral Henry Kent Hewitt, the Casablanca operation consisted of US forces and was staged directly from the eastern seaboard of the United States. It comprised three assaults, one at Fedhala, aimed at the capital, another at Safi around 241km/150 miles to the south and another at Port Lyautey, some 97km/60 miles to the north.

Landings were timed for the early hours of November 8, 1942. Darkness was preferred by the military, with no preliminary bombardment to either alert or antagonize the French. The beach landings were executed in conditions of heavy Atlantic surf and many LCPs were swamped and lost. Only the lightest of enemy resistance spared the struggling troops from suffering heavy losses.

At Casablanca port, shore batteries were troublesome and French naval units opened fire, only to be knocked out by heavy US Navy covering fire, assisted by aircraft from five small carriers. After three days of hostilities, and in the face of a large US build-up, the French, honour satisfied, cooperated fully in bringing Casablanca back to an operational port. Already delayed offshore, however, several loaded transports had been attacked and sunk by U-boats.

To the south, Safi had been selected as being a small port with a jetty suitable for unloading armour. Beach assaults here were accordingly preceded by the port being attacked by two old destroyers, carrying 400 assault troops. With just one casualty, the force seized the facilities and, by the afternoon, a converted train ferry was discharging tanks.

Port Lyautey had an all-weather airfield, which the French resolutely defended. The build-up, already hampered by heavy surf, was delayed further by air attacks and shore-battery fire, obliging the transports to be anchored further offshore. On November 10, therefore, another old destroyer was used to

ABOVE: **Although the AKA was an "attack cargo ship", the type also carried a large number of troops and equipment.**

crash the boom on the neighbouring river and navigate the shoal water to deposit another assault group at a point close to the airfield. Its capture followed quickly, and it was soon being used by US Army Air Force fighter aircraft.

The operations against Oran and Algiers were British-run and staged directly from Great Britain. Both enjoyed distant cover from the Gibraltar-based Force 'H' of the Royal Navy, deployed to meet any major counter-attack by the Italian Navy. Of this force, fortunately, there was to be no sign.

The Oran operation, too, involved three beaches, two being around 40km/25 miles on the flanks. Again with no preliminary bombardment, the assault force began to go ashore soon after 01:00 on November 8. Sand bars and strong currents made it difficult to steer the LCAs, but opposition was negligible and the landings proceeded in an almost textbook fashion. A noteworthy contribution was made by the three British "Maracaibos", a forerunner of the LST which were designed to land armour over the beach.

LEFT: **A Landing Craft, Mechanized (LCM 594) loaded with stores and light artillery heads toward the beach at Algiers. The Royal Navy played a major role in Operation "Torch".**

In Oran, however, there was disaster. To prevent the mass scuttling of ships and demolition in the French naval port of Mers-el-Kebir, and to seize the threatening shore batteries, a US assault force was embarked on two British ships. In an operation heavily criticized before the event, the ships were to break the defending boom before off-loading the assault forces at the far end of the harbour.

For some reason the ships were not ordered in until 03:00, by which time the French were on high alert. For nearly 3.2km/2 miles the ships were expected to run the gauntlet of point-blank fire from hostile French warships. Neither ship succeeded, both being destroyed with over 50 per cent casualties. Oran and the airfields were, nonetheless, in Allied hands within 48 hours.

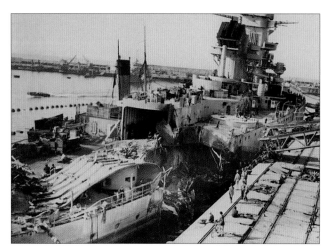

ABOVE: **US troops landing on the beach at Sureouf some 32km/20 miles from Algiers. Operation "Torch" signalled the entry of the USA into the war in the Mediterranean.**

The Algiers landings were notable in having senior officers embarked in specially equipped headquarters ships, notably HMS *Bulolo* which became the model for the design of subsequent US Navy AGC ships.

In this second British-controlled operation, two beaches were assaulted by US troops and one by a British unit. The landings, again in the small hours of November 8, attracted little opposition from shore batteries. British artillery observation officers had, however, been embedded in various units and these, in radio contact with fire support ships, were able to call down effective counter-fire. Again, inadequate training resulted in severe losses of assault craft. Unwieldy and under-powered at best, these required careful handling.

The harbour at Algiers was also to be attacked using two old destroyers carrying teams charged with securing the port. One, breaking the boom at the third attempt, succeeded in entering the port and landing the troops, only for all to be captured. Unable to assist, and now unsupported from ashore, the other destroyer was withdrawn but, severely damaged, sank the next day.

LEFT: **While in Casablanca port, the incomplete French battleship *Jean Bart* was heavily damaged by gunfire from USS *Massachusetts* (BB-59) and US Navy dive-bombers from USS *Ranger* (CV-4).**

French resistance in Algiers ceased on the evening of the landing and a general armistice with the Vichy Force was agreed on November 10. The four-month drive by Allied forces to Tunis had already commenced.

The generally light opposition encountered allowed many lessons to be learned cheaply. Use dedicated teams to move materiel as it was landed. Land materiel in the order in which it will be required. Designate beaches clearly, remembering that smoke screens that shielded the landing craft also blinded and disorientated coxswains. Check, and if possible, obtain up-to-date hydrographic data, offshore sandbars and inshore currents. Even the moderate Mediterranean tidal range, played havock with plans. The troops carried only essential equipment allowing the rapid turnaround of landing craft.

ABOVE: **Part of the massive convoy of 500 ships which transported troops and equipment from the USA laying at anchor off Algiers in November, 1943.**
LEFT: **Because the beach landings were virtually unopposed, many useful lessons were easily learned. Enemy air attacks on offshore shipping did, however, cause significant losses. A number of vessels at Casablanca were attacked and sunk by submarines.**

# Planning an amphibious operation

An early problem for planners is calculating the level of opposition that will need to be overcome. Superior headquarters will have defined the objective, but necessary knowledge of the enemy's strength, defensive positions and capability must be gauged through intelligence or covert operations by advance forces. It is important that this stage, while thorough, must be conducted without raising the least suspicion of an alert enemy.

Major maritime powers may then be able to allocate forces suitable for the task. Lesser powers may well have to decide at this point whether to proceed.

Unless, as in World War II, amphibious operations have become repetitive, considerable lead time is required. While the necessary shipping is procured and assembled, thorough training must be undertaken. Opposed landings offer a uniquely challenging experience, particularly for the initial

ABOVE: **USS *Missouri* (BB-63) bombarding Chongjin, Korea, October 1950. Plentiful naval gunfire was both effective and good for the morale of troops.**

TOP: **Cartographers and model makers produced accurate representations of targets.** ABOVE: **Note how the later waves of assault craft lacked the tight formation of the leaders, which were guided by a line of support craft. The effect of bombardment and the lack of heavy-calibre defensive fire are evident.**

waves of troops and the naval crews of the assault craft. All need to understand, through realistic rehearsal, what will be expected of them on the day.

By their very nature, amphibious operations tend to be complex but, as complexity and confusion go together, simplicity should be ruthlessly pursued in planning. It may, however, be necessary to complicate the timetable through the use of diversionary feints or flanking operations. Limited raids might be at night, but a major landing will probably commence at dawn, following a night approach.

Timetables have to be precise and controlled by "marshals", so that each element moves as required, coordinated, for instance, with incursions by spearhead forces or with a preliminary bombardment. Within this precision, however, there must be scope for a degree of flexibility for, as has so often been stated, "no plan survives the first contact with the enemy". Planners, therefore, should continually ask themselves "What if …?" and not be afraid to face the response robustly.

For operations targeted at specific objectives, the choice of landing site may be limited. A beach should, if possible, have a gentle slope. Too shallow an angle will cause landing craft to ground too far from the water's edge, resulting in the swamping of vehicles and perhaps the drowning of heavily laden troops. Too steep an angle will result in mobility problems for vehicles, with assault craft more easily being driven broadside on to the beach by breaking seas. Ideally, a landing will be timed for a rising tide, minimising the distance that first-wave troops have to cover before finding protection, yet allowing assault craft to quickly float clear to release space on the shoreline. An advantage is the provision of a safe withdrawal area for the essential repair of ships and other craft.

Routes inland from the landing site should be adequate to allow personnel and equipment to clear the danger of the beach zone without undue delay. Assault helicopters and air

LEFT: **President Roosevelt being briefed on proposed landing sites on the Japanese mainland by General MacArthur, Admiral Nimitz and Admiral Leahy in 1944.**
BELOW: **A US Navy Chance-Vought F4U-5 Corsair overflying Inchon, Korea. Note the Iowa-class battleship USS *Missouri* (BB-63) and chartered commercial vessels still in company colours.**

cushion vehicles facilitate rapid progress inland to avoid as far as possible further "Omaha"-type situations, where a beach foothold is won but held only at an inordinate cost in casualties.

Should follow-on equipment need to be discharged from ships, it is essential that these are "combat-loaded" to ensure that these supplies are delivered ashore in the order in which they will be required.

With overall responsibility until the moment of touchdown, the navy will require resources sufficient to prevent enemy naval attack. It will already have conducted covert surveys, and either swept or marked mine-free areas.

Local maritime superiority must be matched by at least a "favourable air situation". If this involves the commitment of invaluable aircraft carriers, the requirement for the early capture of an airfield is obvious.

A headquarters ship, with enhanced communication equipment, will accommodate the commander of the amphibious task force (usually naval), commander landing

force (army or marines) and the air-control officer. Calls for gunfire support will also need to be allocated to specific ships. Inter-service harmony is, at this point, of paramount importance.

LEFT: **If transport is the key to an army's fighting options, then fuel becomes as important as ammunition. More operations by LSTs were devoted to cargo and personnel than to carrying tanks.**

LEFT: **USS *Pocono* (ACG-16), an Andirondack-class amphibious force command ship. The vessel was launched on January 25, 1945, and was stricken from the Naval Vessel Register in December 1971.**

# Command and Control (C2)

Planning for an amphibious operation will have been structured around the means of achieving a clearly (it is to be hoped) designated objective. For a multinational organization such as NATO it is a prerequisite that the governments contributing elements to an Amphibious Task Force (ATF) will all have been working toward that common objective. This cannot be taken for granted for there may be, for instance, problems in inter-operability, logistics, and variations in doctrine, rules of engagement and, even, political bias. A further edge is added to this combination by the necessary involvement of naval, air, army and marine components.

The traditional starting point for amphibious force command was to view it as a naval operation leading to a military operation. Both parts being of equal importance in the realization of the objective, it appeared correct to appoint separate naval and military commanders usually, but not always, of equal rank. With cooperation, such arrangements could work well but, sometimes, inter-service friction became an issue (such as at Gallipoli and, disastrously, Norway in 1940) to the detriment of the operation.

Currently, it is more usual that the Commander, Amphibious Task Force (CATF) is naval, reflecting that service's prominent role. The Commander, Land Forces (CLF) will, by definition, enjoy equal status but, until his forces are ashore, coordination and final decision making are the responsibility of the CATF.

Ideally, in peacetime, the commanders and their staffs should work and train together within a common and permanent organization. This requires frequent exercises as, for instance, combat-equipped troops do not usually expect to embark and disembark in small craft, while armour and heavy equipment is hardly designed to be easily off-loaded over an open beach. For preference, a landing will be planned so as to be unopposed, but the location will probably be determined largely by the choice of objective. Exercises will expose the control limitations imposed by the range of communications and data processing equipment available on the designated command flagship.

Much will necessarily devolve upon subordinate commanders, as the force must travel and operate within the envelope of local superiority. The longer the passage,

RIGHT: **USS *Blue Ridge* (LCC-19) has been in US Navy service since 1970. The vessel is equipped with satellite communications equipment. The ship was the command flagship in Operation "Desert Shield" and "Desert Storm" from August 1990 to April 24, 1991.**

LEFT: **USS *Wright* (CC-2) was originally built as a Saipan-class aircraft carrier. In 1962, the vessel was converted to function as a mobile command post, for top-echelon commanders and staff, and equipped with facilities for worldwide communications.**

as in the Pacific during World War II, the larger the force becomes, as the support forces themselves require support in the form of fuel, stores and ammunition.

As a minimum, Anti-Submarine (AS) and Anti-Air (AA) forces, together with a Surface Action Group (SAG) require to be attached. These may need to be drawn from separate commands, and may give rise to problems if not placed under the control of the CATF (e.g. Fletcher's carrier force for "Watchtower" and Patton's command ship during "Torch").

For the CLF, the post-landing experience may be liberating, for he will assume overall responsibility and if, for instance, his force is in brigade strength, he is no longer answerable to divisional control. As with all competent commanders, the CLF must have the qualities of judgement and flexibility, for the reality of the situation once ashore will rarely meet with expectations, however good the planning

and the preliminary information gathered by intelligence. The enemy will adapt to circumstance, and the CLF must be ready to respond appropriately.

Judgement by both senior commanders is essential in deciding at which point centralized control is to be devolved downward. Tactical decisions are best made by commanders on the spot (note the disastrous dispersal of convoy PQ 17 in 1942 on orders from London). To quote the official manual, "effective command and control must comprise directions at the highest level necessary to achieve unity of purpose, combined with a delegation of responsibility to the lowest level commensurate with the most appropriate and effective use of resources". If effective Command and Control (C2) is vital to success, it follows that the new military science of Command and Control Warfare (C2W) is equally valuable by degrading the capability of the enemy.

ABOVE: **A view of the Joint Operations Room on board USS *Ancon* (AGC-4). Command personnel are at their stations surrounded by maps and status boards.**

ABOVE: **Another view of the Joint Operations Room on USS *Ancon* (AGC-4), from where the invasion of Sicily was controlled on July 3, 1943.**

# The amphibious force

World War II was the proving ground on which amphibious warfare came of age. Everything since has been a refinement of what then took place during the many seaborne operations undertaken during the conflict.

Isolated, and facing an occupied continental Europe, Great Britain began modestly with raids, but entertained the idea that Europe would eventually be invaded and liberated. Still under the threat of invasion, she developed concepts for specialist craft, the orders for which were placed in a still-neutral USA. These programmes were to take time to enter production. The British, meanwhile, used LSIs of sizes ranging from converted steam packets to modern cargo liners. The common specification was for troop accommodation and heavy davits under which were slung assault landing craft (LCA/LCVP).

Here were embodied the two major categories of amphibious warfare vessel – the Landing Ships (LSI, LST, LSD, etc.) intended to make a "shore-to-shore" open-sea transit, and the Landing Craft (LCT, LCU, LCVP, etc.) designed to function on arrival in the "ship-to-shore" mode.

Successive landings raised the requirement for further specialist craft, particularly rocket- or gun-armed support craft to accompany the first assault. Not capable of long ocean passages, smaller craft such as these would join the main assault force from intermediate locations, as with the landings in North Africa and on Sicily.

On the day, there were never sufficient assault landing craft, DUKW amphibious trucks or tracked landing vehicles (LVT). This gave rise to the design for the LPD, effectively a powered floating dock capable of accommodating many small vessels in a docking well for an ocean passage.

Such a ship could also stow a lesser number of larger craft, each pre-loaded with stores or transport. Should the LPD then be extended with storage for further vehicles and/or accommodation for a troop contingent, the type would become the more capable LSD. With the general introduction of helicopters for assault or

ABOVE: **The combined carrier/amphibious force is formidable as shown in this photo opportunity, but in practice any force would be more dispersed so as not to present such a concentrated target for underwater, surface or air attack.**

materiel transfer, a flight deck and hangar naturally followed, necessitating a radical rearrangement from which emerged the virtually self-contained LHD.

World War II amphibious operations were won with large numbers of basic vessels that were simple to the point of crudeness, leading to reasonable criticism of the current "all-eggs-in-one-basket" approach of the hugely expensive LHD and derivatives.

In today's major operation, an Amphibious Task Group (ATG) will be only one component of an Amphibious Task Force (ATF), which will include a carrier group, nuclear-powered attack submarine and a logistics group

ABOVE: **Naval air power has become a vital part of an amphibious assault. Here, an FJ-4 Fury is being launched as another is moving forward. An F2H-2 Banshee is being positioned on the starboard catapult, ready for launch.**

ABOVE: **A nuclear-powered attack submarine, such as the French *Amethyste*, is an essential component for the defence of an amphibious task force.**

RIGHT: **The helicopter has been proven to be a vital element of an amphibious operation, in the first instance to land troops, and then to deliver stores and reinforcements whilst also evacuating casualties.**

of "one-stop" tanker/ammunition/stores ships. A further development is the pre-positioning ship, usually with Roll-on, Roll-off (Ro-Ro) facilities and heavy lifting gear for cargo. This is loaded with heavy, follow-up equipment including armour, and may be held in forward areas for a considerable time.

Complete with various escort screens, an ATF becomes a very large formation which, in the satellite age, is impossible to conceal. It must, therefore, proceed within a protective "cocoon", with escorts providing anti-submarine, anti-air, anti-surface cover and even anti-space attack cover.

Denied concealment, the force must rely even more on deception or disruptive procedures to disguise the time and place of the planned strike. Ideally, it will not be placed within sight of the enemy's shore (except, perhaps as a show of strength in a time of tension) but use high-speed assault craft to operate from Over The Horizon (OTH).

The Landing Craft, Air Cushion (LCAC) is currently the US forces key asset, its size, rather than those of the earlier LCU, determining the docking well dimensions of the major amphibious warfare ship. With a loaded speed

of 40 knots (71kph), and limited over-land capability, it might permit a major shift in procedure whereby, using suitable topography, the LCAC would be used in combination with assault helicopters or tilt-wing aircraft to strike suddenly behind a defended shoreline. Analogous to earlier pre-emptive paratroop landings, such "hook" attacks would avoid the requirement for an initial "traditional" type of frontal assault.

ABOVE: **Part of the Falklands invasion force – hospital ships *Uganda* and *Hydra* refuelling from RFA *Olmeda*.** LEFT: **RFA *Fort Austin* (A386), a stores and ammunition carrier, with repair ship RFA *Diligence* (A132) alongside.**

# Pre-landing operations

In these days of satellite surveillance, it is difficult to envisage an operation against a technologically sophisticated opponent achieving surprise unless mounted over a short distance and supported by effective deception. Pre-landing operations must, therefore, be a fine balance between a beneficial contribution to the assault and maintenance of tactical surprise.

Diversionary and preparatory activities might considerably pre-date an assault and, as they may involve separate commands (even at higher command level) good personal relationships are helpful. Although technology has advanced since World War II, basic requirements here have remained the same.

Observation, intelligence or pure habit may indicate whether the defence will oppose the landing on the beach, or nullify a pre-assault bombardment by counter-attacking as the invaders move inland. In the first case, Naval Gunfire Support (NGS) and close-air support need to be closely coordinated up to and beyond the moment of touchdown. In the latter, preparations would be directed to making it difficult for the defence to move further reinforcements into the area. Historically, in an operation as large as that in Normandy, both approaches were found necessary.

World War II first saw the introduction of specialist teams of divers/combat swimmers to gather intelligence. Measurements of beach gradients and the disposition of obstructions gathered by them will be critical to the successful grounding of assault craft on the day; monitoring of tidal range may influence time and date; analysis of beach material is essential for the benefit of vehicles (at Dieppe in 1942, for instance, many tanks immediately shed tracks on landing due to the size of the shingle). Items of divers' equipment might be "lost" on alternative beaches in the interests of deception.

Mines laid in the surf zone are likely to have a short life, but detecting and countering is not easy. Removing by hand may be required, following a covert survey by a submarine-launched

ABOVE: **Royal Navy X-craft (midget submarines) landed divers to assess the load-bearing qualities of the Normandy beaches. Later, the vessels were used as fixed guidance beacons during the landings.**

ABOVE: **An air reconnaissance photograph of a Normandy beach at low tide. The obstructions were given names such as "Rommel's Asparagus" "Belgian Gate" or "Czech Hedgehogs".**

ABOVE: **Underwater Demolition Teams (UDT) remain invaluable in the clearance of paths through approaches with obstacles.**

ABOVE: **Forward observer teams are among the first ashore, with the task of supplying naval gunners with precise coordinates for close-support gunfire.**

LEFT: **Ports along the south coast of England were used as loading points for D-Day, June 6, 1944. Here at Weymouth, Dorset, troops can be seen loading stores and vehicles into a variety of vessels ready for landing on Omaha beach.**

Autonomous Underwater Vehicle (AUV). With the AUV recovered by the submarine, and the stored data downloaded and analysed, a specialist clearance team will be positioned by Swimmer Delivery Vehicle (SWD).

A World War II assault might be preceded by parachute and/or glider landings to secure vital bridgeheads to prevent enemy reinforcement and also to facilitate eventual breakout from the beachhead. Such procedures are still valid, although given further flexibility with the availability of assault helicopters and aircraft such as the tilt-rotor Bell Boeing MV-22B Osprey aircraft, now in service with the US Marine Corps.

The army prefers to attack at night but, in confined waters, the navy needs to see the target. Commonly, therefore, an approach will be in darkness, leading to an assault at first light.

Several World War II landings saw groups of assault craft hit the wrong beaches. In any but the simplest of approaches, therefore, a duty of the covert landing teams will be to lay dormant electronic beacons. By interrogating these ahead of the first wave, marshalling craft will be accurately positioned, providing a "gate" through which the assault wave will pass.

Pacific or "Torch"-sized amphibious groups relied, if necessary, on the massive firepower of the covering force to get to the objective in the face of major opposition. Particularly with the advent of ship-killing kamikaze aircraft, this tended to concentrate the formation. During the Cold War, however, this trend was firmly abandoned with the advent of tactical nuclear weapons. A single, nuclear-armed missile, launched at considerable range from an aircraft, submarine or surface ship, could now devastate a whole formation, making dispersion essential. Being used at sea, such low-yield weapons would not directly affect civilian populations and might not be considered as precipitating an all-out nuclear confrontation.

Future conflict may well be decided, not on the quality of fighting men, but on which side acquires superior technology.

ABOVE: **A platoon deploying from an assault craft, in single file to avoid bunching.**
LEFT: **A D-Day exercise by US Rangers, probably at Bude, Cornwall. A rocket grapnel has been fired while a medic attends to a "casualty".**

LEFT: **Reinforcements pouring on to Omaha beach after the D-Day landing. A Rhino ferry (RHF-19) loaded with troops and artillery is being manoeuvered into position by a bulldozer.**

# Securing the beachhead and breaking out

An amphibious assault is but one phase, the means of creating a beachhead ("lodgement") which can be enlarged and consolidated prior to breakout. While an unopposed landing is desirable, it may not be possible because it may place the invaders too far from their objective (the 1982 Falklands campaign provides an example of fine judgement). During the Pacific war, most island objectives were so small that every beach was defendable.

As the first waves go in, the operation is at its most vulnerable. Preferably, the defenders will be recovering from a preparatory bombardment that, having just lifted, has shifted to the flanks and rear. Hopefully, they will be preparing for an attack by airborne forces landing in the rear. Today, these

might well have been mounted from Over The Horizon (OTH), by troops in helicopters and LCACs.

Supported by light, amphibious armour the first waves will endeavour to push ahead over the cratered shoreline, creating a measure of space, albeit still under fire. At the direction of the landing force commander, larger landing craft carrying additional armour, artillery and engineer units will be ordered to land. It should be emphasized how important it is to establish a momentum, to create a balanced force ashore capable

BELOW: **A Beach, Armoured Recovery Vehicle (BARV), one of Hobart's "funnies", is being used to recover a Bedford OXC tractor unit and trailer from a beach in Normandy on June 14, 1944.**

LEFT: **After the Omaha beachhead was established on June 6, 1944, US Navy communication posts were set up, where radio, signal lamps and even flags (semaphore) were used to contact vessels at sea.**

of holding off an opponent who is already rushing in reinforcements. On the result of this action, the survival of the beachhead will hang, and the tactical commander will have sought to acquire space, or freedom of manoeuvre will be denied him. He should, by this stage, have been able to transfer his headquarters ashore.

During the expansion of the beachhead, supplies and reinforcements need to be put ashore at a rate compatible with the situation. Laden transports and cargo ships, having to loiter offshore, are vulnerable to attack (as at Guadalcanal and at Leyte) and their captains are obviously keen to offload and to move out. Early experience showed, however, that beaches receiving resources more quickly than could be distributed, rapidly became chaotic and vulnerable to air attack.

The tactical commander may need to redispose his forces in order to match them to the developing situation, but a rapid breakout ("exploitation") will normally be desirable to prevent the defence, which is blessed with the shorter lines of communication, sealing off the beachhead perimeter, neutralizing the "lodgement" until such time as a decisive counter-attack will drive it back into the sea.

Air superiority is highly desirable. There are fewer aircraft carriers in service today than during World War II. They might, as then, be used in the initial stages of the operation, but will certainly be withdrawn as quickly as possible. It is essential, therefore, that facilities for the operation of land-based air power are captured or constructed with some urgency.

An unpleasant possibility is that, while progress ashore has gone "according to plan", the enemy has been able to contest sea control, thereby hazarding, slowing and even preventing the necessary rate of build-up. The defence may then gain strength at a higher rate and the landing force commander,

anxious not be surrounded, may be moved to attempt break-out earlier than he would have wished. Already beyond the range of naval gunfire support, leading units may push ahead to the point where insufficiently secured lines of communication are in danger of being severed.

The terrain of the hinterland will have had considerable influence on the operation's logistics. The more mountainous or jungle-clad, the more that infantry will be preferable to heavy support. Reinforcement units may well be considerably larger than those of the initial assault force, and army rather than marines. They may, therefore, integrate the assault force and its command structure into their own, a situation that the original landing force commander might find difficult to accept. "His" assault, will, however, by then have developed successfully into a campaign.

BELOW: **The Landing Craft, Air Cushion (LCAC) is a fast and efficient vessel for beach landings, with the extra ability to carry vehicles beyond the beach.**

# Logistics

No amount of military genius can help a tactical commander whose logistics organization cannot deliver the men and materiel that he needs. Somewhat unexciting to many, logistics will depend upon the operational plan as much as the plan depends upon logistics.

The management of shipping is complex and, in an operation of any magnitude, is best undertaken by those who are experienced. Compared with their supplies, transport and stores, troops occupy little shipping space but, conversely, require passenger shipping which is always in short supply.

Until recent times, Britain had large mercantile and fishing fleets, together with a substantial reserve of skilled seamen. In war, shipping was government-controlled, the provision of tonnage for expeditionary warfare (or trawlers for minesweeping) being a matter of allocating suitable ships. By 1982, however, the Red Ensign fleet had diminished to the point that maintaining the 12,784km/8,000-mile sea line of communication to the Falklands depended considerably upon commercial shipping. This will always be expensive to charter at short notice, and there is no guarantee of availability.

Today, Britain has virtually abandoned the merchant marine. The few ships that remain sail mostly under flags of convenience, while the long tradition of seafaring has disappeared, it being cheaper to employ seamen from the Far East.

The experience of the USA was different in that their pre-war merchant marine was small in comparison to the volume of trade. Always having depended upon foreign flagged shipping, they replaced this during both World Wars with impressive programmes of vessels built to strictly standard designs.

The steady evolution of Plan Orange had identified that, in a Pacific war with Japan, the westward advance of US forces would require an enormous "fleet train" to support

ABOVE: **Pictured at Weymouth on England's south coast, US Rangers loaded in LCAs are waiting to be transferred out to the vessels that will carry the force to Omaha beach, Normandy, France.**

the battle fleet. Just how enormous was not apparent until it happened. When, in the latter stages of World War II, the British created a Royal Navy "Pacific Fleet" to assist the US Navy (USN), it arrived sadly deficient in support shipping and needed to depend upon the generosity of the USN for the replenishment necessary to keep the fleet continuously on station.

ABOVE: **Deck cargo being lifted by a mobile crane from the deck of an LST.**
LEFT: **A Multiple Gun Motor Carriage (MGMC) M16 from a mobile anti-aircaft battalion being reversed on to an LCT.**

ABOVE: **The bulldozer was cited by Admiral Halsey, USN, as being one of the three major elements crucial to success in the Pacific.** LEFT: **The pontoon bridge, here in Normandy, was a variation on the causeway (above). Note the "Gooseberry" breakwater in the distance.**

Beaching vessels, such as LSTs, speed up delivery by a reported factor of seven. The procedure, however, involves risk in a developing battle situation, where the need is for a small load to be delivered on a continuous basis.

Much modern commercial shipping carries no cargo-lifting gear, making it unsuitable until a deep-water port has been captured. Ship-to-shore movement will, in any case, require over-the-side transfer to LCVPs or LCUs, amphibious trucks and self-propelled modular pontoons, developed from the "Rhino" ferries of World War II.

Ships should be "combat-loaded", so as to discharge equipment in the correct order, with logistics specialists both aboard and in the handling parties ashore.

After 1945, the US merchant fleet again reduced rapidly, but the US Navy maintained sufficient tonnage in reserve for support. This, of course, has diminished and changed over the years but now, configured as the Military Sealift Command (MSC), has acquired considerable high-grade tonnage. Replenishment-At-Sea (RAS) has moved toward a "one-stop" operation, with a single ship supplying fuel, together with limited quantities of stores and ammunition. Transports tend to be specialized Roll-on, Roll-off (Ro-Ro) ships and container vessels. The concept of pre-loaded pre-positioning ships allows a core of essential equipment to be maintained in "hot-spots" without the need for expensive and politically sensitive foreign bases.

The Royal Fleet Auxiliary (RFA), in Britain, has received some modern purpose-built tonnage but still remains inadequate in terms of capacity. A major problem in the past was the habit of the military to retain supply ships in the operations area, using them as floating stores rather than creating large supply dumps ashore.

ABOVE: **Two British LCM (9) in distinctive Royal Marine camouflage. Note the roll-over canopy over the tank deck on the vessel in the centre. The "Mexeflote" in the distance is a self-propelled pontoon.**

LEFT: **A Norwegian fishing boat alongside a British Tribal-class destroyer during the first raid, March 1941. Two ex-Royal Dutch Mail fast motor ferries were used for the first time as LSI (M) on the raid. HMS** Queen Emma **(MV** Koningin Emma**) and HMS** Princess Beatrix **(MV** Prinses Beatrix**) would be used on many operations, including D-Day.**

# Operation "Claymore", Lofoten Islands

The concept of a "commando", as an elite unit trained to use unorthodox means to harass an enemy at perceived weak points, was resurrected by Prime Minister Churchill shortly after the debacle at Dunkirk. Raising and training these battalion-sized formations took time and it was March 1941 before a significant operation could be staged.

At the approaches to Narvik in occupied Norway (already the scene of major naval actions during the previous April) were the Lofoten Islands. Isolated and difficult to reinforce quickly, these supported large fish oil processing plants, the spectacular destruction of which would both affect the German war effort while providing a useful propaganda exercise for the British.

ABOVE: **The Lofoten Islands gave the newly formed British commando force one of its first experiences of action.**

ABOVE: **Fish oil from a ruptured storage tank burning on the surface of the sea in Stamsund Harbour. The commando force encountered no organized resistance.**

LEFT: **Packed into an LCA, some of the 500 men from Nos. 3 and 4 Commando are seen here evacuating from Stamsund Harbour. Five enemy vessels were destroyed in the harbour.**

Two newly converted fast LSI (M), both ex-Dutch North Sea ferries, were used to transport the two commandos involved. Each ship carried six LCAs and two LCMs under davits. Taking leave of their heavy passage escort early on the morning of March 3, the two ships moved in under destroyer cover, with each commando divided between two objectives.

Total surprise was achieved and opposition from the small German occupying force was light. Local citizens willingly assisted in the decision-making regarding the choice of material for demolition, there being no wish to hurt Norwegian interests more than necessary.

British military equipment and the preparation of the ships involved for the Arctic proved rather less than adequate, but all fish oil stocks and facilities were destroyed, along with several small German ships. Aboard the armed trawler *Krebs* captured by the destroyer HMS *Somali*, the invaluable Enigma settings for the current period were found.

Operation "Claymore" was an early example of a raid in force, with limited objectives. The raiders were ashore for less than ten hours, achieved their objectives and returned with over 200 prisoners, 60 collaborators and over 300 Norwegian volunteers, who wished to fight on with the British.

A useful, if unforeseen, consequence was the beginning of Adolf Hitler's irrational fear that the Allies planned eventually to invade Norway.

RIGHT: **The spectacular destruction of facilities in the March raid provided perfect cover for the operation's major objective, the capture of Enigma material from a German weather trawler.**

LEFT: **A fully loaded LCM from USS** *Leonard Wood* **(APA-12) departing for the landing area.**

# Operation "Husky", Sicily

On May 13, 1943, the last Axis forces surrendered in Tunisia. North Africa was clear and the next Allied attack would be against occupied Europe. A rapid move was vital in order to capitalize on the enemy's disarray, but the US military considered that any operation short of a cross-Channel thrust, aimed directly at the German heartland, would only prolong hostilities unnecessarily. The British argued the necessity of relieving pressure on the USSR and that, with over 40 divisions already in France, the Germans could deal with any cross-Channel invasion without weakening the eastern front. Italy, they reasoned, was weakened and war-weary. Strike there, and put Italy out of the war, thus creating a vacuum which the Germans would be obliged to fill with forces drawn from the east.

Reluctantly, the US military agreed on Sicily being the next objective, and an elaborate programme of deception was begun, aimed at encouraging the enemy's own ideas which favoured landings in Greece or Sardinia. Many high-ranking German officers still considered Sicily more likely, as it was within range of air cover based in North Africa.

RIGHT: **HMSub** *Unruffled* **returning to Malta after a patrol in the Mediterranean. The vessel was used in support of Allied victories in North Africa, Sicily and Italy. During these actions 12 cargo ships and three supply schooners were sunk. An Italian heavy cruiser was also disabled, and even a freight train attacked.**

ABOVE: **Bombed by *Luftwaffe* Ju-88 aircraft on the afternoon of July 11, the Liberty ship SS *Robert Rowan* caught fire. The crew were able to abandon ship without loss of life before the cargo of ammunition exploded.**

ABOVE: **Beaches on Sicily were often of shallow incline and consisted of sand that was too soft for wheeled vehicles. Before beach matting was laid, much equipment had to be manhandled off the beach.**

They appeared even more correct when, in the ten days preceding the landings, Allied air power attacked the island, seeking to reduce Axis strength and to destroy both airfields and communications. The main force of this action was applied at the western end of the island, to reinforce the notion of a likely landing site, as it is closer to North Africa.

Originally, in fact, the US forces were to have landed in the west, but the British, scheduled to assault the southern extremity around Capo Passero, objected that their left flank would,

thereby, be left vulnerable, and that the overall Allied strength should not be quite so divided. As adopted, therefore, Operation "Husky" would still need some 115,000 mainly British and Canadian troops going ashore in the south while, to the west, around the great coastal arc between Licata and Scoglitti, some 66,000 US troops would land. Over 2,500 ships and craft were required with convoys coordinated from the United States, Britain and around the Mediterranean. A powerful British naval force would cover against any attack by the Italian navy.

LEFT: **Gliders, particularly the US-built WACO CG-4A Hadrian, were used to considerable effect in the British sector. Difficult winds, poor navigation and inexperienced pilots unfortunately resulted in a high loss rate.**

LEFT: **British LCT (4) and those of US forces landed short of beaches which had parallel sand bars. Few pontoon causeways were available.**

As the invasion fleet approached during the small hours of July 10, 1943, the many unwieldy LSTs and LCTs were experiencing difficulties coping with a rough sea, raised by a brisk northwest wind, which also covered beaches with a heavy surf. The beaches had a shallow slope, with offshore sandbars, so that landing craft tended to ground far from the shoreline. The US Navy had brought new floating pontoons which linked to form ship-to-shore causeways but these, unfortunately, missed the initial landings. Another innovation, the DUKW amphibious vehicle was to prove invaluable in the operation.

Near Gela, US forces spearheaded their landing by dropping some 3,000 paratroops. Although considerably scatted by the strong breeze, they were able to disrupt a determined German response to the landings. Fortunately, the army and navy commanders, Major-General George Patton and Rear-Admiral Henry Kent Hewitt, cooperated harmoniously and naval support gunfire was frequently effective in breaking up counter-attacks by enemy armoured forces.

Still experiencing heavy resistance, the US military followed up, on the following night, with a division of paratroops. The news that it would be delayed was not received by most of the ships in the amphibious fleet offshore, and when the large formation of low-flying aircraft crossed the anchorage shortly after an enemy air raid, every gunner opened fire. Over 40 of these aircraft were shot down, with considerable loss of life. Opposition to the British landings was initially light, and these were preceded by an ambitious, brigade-strength gliderborne landing to secure a vital bridge. The strong wind again caused severe problems. Over half the 130 gliders crash-landed in the sea, just seven landing in the target area. The bridge, nonetheless, was taken and held.

British command relationships worked less smoothly than those of the US force. The British appeared content with their air support but the US Navy Rear-Admiral Hewitt complained that,

BELOW: **The DUKW amphibious vehicle was used for the first time on Operation "Husky", and proved to be a valuable asset.**

ABOVE: **Newly introduced, the DUKW, or "Duck", was a six-wheel drive amphibious vehicle.** LEFT: **Men of the 51st Highland Division wading ashore from a Landing Craft, Infantry (LC [I]).**

where British carrier-based aircraft were instantly available, the system for summoning RAF support was very slow. His actual words were somewhat stronger.

The British tactical army commander, General Bernard Montgomery, later strongly criticized the scattered locations of British senior commanders: "Cunningham (Royal Navy) is in Malta; Tedder (Royal Air Force) is in Tunis; Alexander (Army) is at Syracuse. It beats me how anyone thinks you can run a campaign in that way, with the three commanders of the three services about 966km/600 miles from each other". The planning staff of General Eisenhower, the Supreme Allied Commander were, meanwhile at Algiers.

Although the Germans bemoaned the fact that the Allies could deploy superior strength by land, sea or air at will, they deployed their own remaining air power effectively. The British sector, closest to an airfield on the Italian mainland, received the most attention, with sudden raids by single aircraft or small groups which were very difficult to detect and to intercept. By now, all vessels, particularly the large and valuable LSIs, were turned around rapidly. However, new ships were continually arriving, so the enemy never lacked targets. Losses were significant.

The large British fleet providing deep cover against the absent Italian Navy was taking some damage by Italian torpedoes from aircraft and submarines. Bored with these unfulfilling duties, its commander, Vice-Admiral Sir Algernon Willis, detached single ships or groups to supplement the busy bombardment groups. As in the US sector, naval gunfire had a very considerable effect.

The occupation of Sicily, which took under six weeks, became something of a race between US forces and the British to reach Messina. Just 3.2km/2 miles across the strait from the Italian mainland, it was the obvious centre for the inevitable evacuation of Axis forces. The northern and southern coasts of Sicily, each some 274km/170 miles in length, meet at the westernmost extremity around Marsala and Trapani. The eastern coast, runs northward from the British invasion beaches some

209km/130 miles to Messina. Where US forces had to break out and secure the island's vast heartland, British and Canadian forces appeared to have the simpler task of advancing along the coastal strip. Here, however, were the larger centres of population – Syracuse, Augusta, Catania and Taormina – while between the last two loomed the mass of Mount Etna. Crossed by a number of rivers, this coastal route could be, and was, resolutely defended. The crack SS-Hermann Göring and 1st Parachute (*Fallschirmjäger*) Divisions fought a steadfast retreat, buying time for evacuation plans to be completed at Messina.

With Patton's forces greatly dependent upon the northern coast road, and Montgomery's on the eastern, the Germans were puzzled why neither used their respective amphibious forces to bypass any opposition. The US military did just twice, and to good effect. When the more conventional General Montgomery finally overcame his misgivings, the incursion came too late to be of use.

The greatest surprise of the Sicilian campaign, the successful enemy evacuation, began on August 3 when Italian troops began to be ferried across the strait. They and the Germans were given ample time to set up numerous anti-aircraft and coastal gun batteries. Coastal craft, car ferries, Siebel ferries, MFPs – all were pressed into service. But this was no panic evacuation, the Germans not beginning to cross until August 10. Six routes were used and changed from day to day. The approach roads on the Sicilian side were blocked with men and transport, yet the overwhelming Allied air superiority appeared powerless to penetrate the defensive barrage. A bold naval stroke might well have stopped the exodus totally, but Cunningham, uncharacteristically, stated that there was "no effective method, either by sea or air". At some cost in men and boats only MTBs were used to challenge the enemy by night.

Around 130,000 Axis prisoners (7,000 German) were taken, but 100,000, including 40,000 Germans, escaped. Sicily was taken but, for the Allies, much remained for improvement, particularly in inter-service and inter-allied cooperation.

# Operation "Avalanche", Salerno

ABOVE: **The Sele river (centre) marked the boundary between the US beaches (left) and British (right). The choice of targets for a torpedo bomber is obvious.**

Following the Axis evacuation of Sicily the British Eighth Army waited 14 days before crossing the Strait of Messina on September 3, 1943. This move was followed, six days later, by the landing of the Allied Fifth Army, 322km/200 miles in the German rear at Salerno. It was intended thus to unbalance the enemy facing the Eighth Army by cutting lines of communication, while opening the way to the early capture of the major port, Naples.

Unusually, the Italian coastal area south of Salerno was a flat flood plain, fronted by 32km/20 miles of beaches that were very suitable for an amphibious landing. It also had considerable drawbacks, being bounded by high ground offering few exits but excellent defensive features. The location was beyond the range

of most Allied fighters operating from Sicily. Intelligence, also, indicated that the area German commander, Field Marshal Albert Kesselring, fully anticipated such an Allied attack.

From German experience in North Africa and Sicily, Kesselring knew that any Allied assault would be in irresistible force. Accordingly, he arranged only nominal resistance immediate to the shoreline. Artillery was well located in the mountainous hinterland, from which every detail of the Salerno operation could be observed and shelled. Kesselring kept back the main strength of the Tenth Army, including two armoured divisions, to respond as the battlefield situation developed.

With the Italian surrender just announced, Allied troops were in something of a holiday mood. It was not to last. Until the capture of nearby Montecorvino airfield, air cover would depend upon five British escort carriers (CVE). The combination of short flight decks and insufficient speed in near-windless conditions caused hard landings, which repeatedly broke the fragile undercarriages of the Supermarine Seafire fighters. The enemy, in any case, used fighter-bombers in damaging hit-and-run raids that were almost impossible to intercept.

The US Fifth Army under Lieutenant General Mark W. Clark comprised the British X Corps, attacking north of the Sele river, and the US VI Corps, attacking to the south. The landings early on September 9, went much as planned, with immediate resistance eliminated by bold, close-in naval gunfire. Due to an acute shortage of large landing craft, however, the build-up was slow, while Kesselring's reaction was resolute and immediate.

Every Allied movement attracted artillery fire while the few tanks already ashore were insufficient to deal with powerful German armour. The key to Allied survival quickly became the Bombardment Liaison Officers (BLO) attached to various units. At their request, cruisers and destroyers fired vast quantities of ammunition at targets that were clearly visible. The Germans frequently returned fire.

ABOVE: **USS *Philadelphia* (CL-41), part of the bombardment fleet. In the background, a YMS minesweeper is laying smoke.** LEFT: **The assault craft forming up and moving to the beach. On the horizon is the mountainous hinterland of southern Italy overlooking the Salerno plain.**

LEFT: **The value of the pontoon causeway is clearly evident here, the LST being grounded on a sand ridge. The Dodge WC-54 vehicles are considerably heavier than a Jeep. Metal matting has been laid, making vehicle movement easier.**

The *Luftwaffe* responded with specialist anti-ship formations equipped with the new, radio-controlled Fritz-X glider bomb. These were highly effective but used sparingly, so that they created more apprehension than damage. Meanwhile, the barrage of naval gunfire continued. By September 13, matters were critical. The operation had not only lost momentum but was bogged down. Allied infantry was continually pitted against German armour. There was no space for a mobile reserve but there existed insufficient strength to break out.

Thwarted, Clark considered (to the disgust of his fellow commanders) abandoning half of the beachhead to reinforce the other, but settled for reinforcement by two battalions of paratroops and 1,500 fresh soldiers landed from warships.

The crisis passed and, on September 16, Kesselring admitted defeat. He had insufficient resources to dislodge the beachhead and he had been refused reinforcement from further north. To the south, the Eighth Army under Montgomery had pushed up the coast and were poised to relieve Clark's predicament. To the latter's relief, the Germans began to pull out. Naples, which had been heavily damaged, was scheduled to have been taken by September 21, but was not

occupied until October 1. In these ten days, reinforcements and equipment had to come from the beaches, creating a logistics problems that led directly to the development of the "Mulberry" artificial harbour for the D-Day landings.

ABOVE: **A Sherman III (M4-A2) about to be driven ashore on to an Italian beach. It is a command vehicle well laden with combat accessories and with a wading trunk over the hull rear.** LEFT: **Before metal matting could be laid on the beach, a great deal of equipment had to be carried to the storage areas.**

USSR

MONGOLIA

MANCHURIA

• Peking

CHINA

JAPAN

• Tokyo

Okinawa
Apri 1– June 22 1945

Iwo Jima
Feb. 19–Mar. 16 1945

1945

MARIANAS

Wal
Dec. 23

BURMA

Hong
Kong

Leyte Gulf
Oct. 24–26 1944

Philippine Sea
June 19–21 1944

• Tinian
July 24 1944

1944

MARS
ISLA

THAILAND

FRENCH
INDOCHINA

Bataan/Corregidor
Dec. 1941–
May 1942

PHILIPPINES

• Guam
July 21 1944

Eniwetok
Jan. 31 1944

1944

• Ngufu
Oct. 16 1944

Kwajale
Jan. 31 1

1945

Palau
Sept. 15 1944

CAROLINE ISLANDS

MALAYA

• Singapore

BORNEO

SUMATRA

1944

Bismarck Sea
Mar. 2–4 1943

Guadalcanal
Aug. 7 1942–
Feb. 9 1943

Java Sea
Feb. 27–Mar. 1 1942

NEW GUINEA

Coral Sea
May 7–8 1942

SOLOMON
ISLANDS

JAVA

Port Moresby •

Lombok Strait
Feb. 18–19 1942

1943

1943

AUSTRALIA

RIGHT: **The first wave of attacking US Marines in LVTs heading to the beach at Iwo Jima as the first part of Operation "Detachment" on February 15, 1945. The smoke from naval support gunfire is lifting to reveal the objective. Mount Suribachi is clearly visible.**

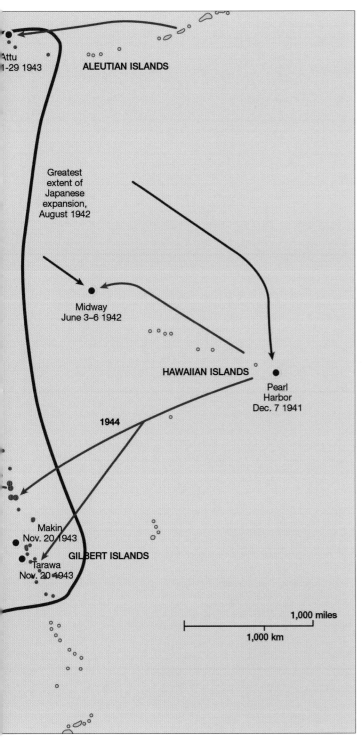

Attu
1-29 1943

**ALEUTIAN ISLANDS**

Greatest
extent of
Japanese
expansion,
August 1942

Midway
June 3–6 1942

**HAWAIIAN ISLANDS**

Pearl
Harbor
Dec. 7 1941

**1944**

Makin
Nov. 20 1943

**GILBERT ISLANDS**

Tarawa
Nov. 20 1943

1,000 miles

1,000 km

# The Pacific campaign

The surprise attack on the US Naval base at Pearl Harbor on December 7, 1941 was the beginning of Japan's rapid expansion into the Pacific. An invasion of the Philippines and Guam (December 10, 1941) and then the landings on the Burma mainland (December 11, 1941) were followed by actions to capture Borneo, Luzon, Hong Kong and Manila (January 2, 1942). By April 9, 1942, the last US troops had surrendered at Mindanao.

In May 1942, the Japanese Imperial Navy was again defeated at the Battle of the Coral Sea off New Guinea. What is said to have been the turning point of the war in the Pacific was the Battle of Midway (June 4/5, 1942), a decisive victory for US naval airpower. On August 7, 1942, the first amphibious landing of the war by US forces was launched against the Japanese on Guadacanal and Tulagi in the Solomons. The enemy ceased fire on February 9, 1943.

In 1943, the US military kept pressure on Japanese forces with amphibious assaults against targets, including the Aleutian Islands, Lae-Salamaua, Bougainville and Makin/Tarawa. The last actions of the year were the Allied (US, NZ and Australian) landings on New Britain.

The first landing of 1944 was against Kwajalein on January 31, which was captured by February 7. Further attacks were carried out during the year against other targets, which included the islands of Saipan (June 15), Guam (July 19) and Leyte (October 20). US forces landed on Mindoro (Philippines) on December 15, 1944.

On January 9, 1945, US forces attacked Luzon. By now, Japanese resistance had become resolute as enemy forces approached closer to the mainland. The assault on Iwo Jima (February 15, 1945) saw heavy fighting and many casualties on both sides. On April 1, 1945, the last amphibious landing of the war took place against Okinawa. After almost two months of bloody fighting, Japanese forces finally surrendered to the US Tenth Army on June 22, 1945.

The first atomic bomb (A-Bomb) "Little Boy" was dropped on Hiroshima on August 6, 1945, with devastating results. A second A-Bomb "Fat Man" was dropped on August 9, 1945, the target being Nagasaki.

On August 14, 1945, Japan accepted an unconditional surrender. The requirement for the planned amphibious assault on Japan was forgotten.

ABOVE LEFT: **This map shows Allied advances in the Pacific theatre from 1943–45. During this time, US military planners began the task of assembling a force to retake the island groups captured by the Japanese. The plan was to use a powerful amphibious force supported by warships to capture an island group, then use this as a base for the assault on the next group.**

LEFT: **The massive firepower of US Navy battleships was used to great effect for the pre-landing barrage. The ships also supplied support fire when requested by troops on the ground. This is USS *Nevada* (BB-36).**

# Operation "Toenails", New Georgia and Rendova

With the Japanese evacuation of Guadalcanal in February 1943, US forces sought to maintain momentum, moving in stages up the Solomons chain toward the enemy stronghold of Rabaul. The chosen method was to take only strategically significant islands, bypassing others, leaving the occupying Japanese garrisons to await their fate.

For both sides, airfields were vital, and governed the length of any advance. Less than 322km/200 miles from Henderson Field on Guadalcanal was the Japanese airstrip at Munda, on the island of New Georgia. This, with a small strip on neighbouring Kolombangara, was used as a staging post for Japanese air strikes on Guadalcanal. To the US military, the capture of Munda would be strategically vital.

Thinly spread over their vast conquests, the Japanese could not be everywhere. The native islanders detested them, in general remaining loyal to their, usually, Australian District Officers. Most of these had stayed on, leading a fugitive existence as "Coastwatchers" and provided an invaluable intelligence network as well as giving early warning of Japanese air raids coming down "The Slot", the channel running the length of the Solomons.

A division of Vice-Admiral William F. Halsey's US 3rd Fleet, the amphibious force of Rear-Admiral Richmond K. ("Terrible") Turner had been expanded considerably. He now controlled seven transport divisions, comprising Transports (APA), Cargo Ships (AK) and Fast Destroyer Transports (APD). Eighteen LSTs and 48 LCTs were also organized in divisions. Finally, there were the Coastal Transports (APC) and five Fast Destroyer Minesweepers (DMS).

ABOVE: **US troops clambering down landing nets to waiting landing craft at Empress Augusta Bay after the islands had been recaptured.**
LEFT: **The assault force was landed at the very edge of the jungle, which concealed Japanese troops in camouflaged positions.**

ABOVE: **US Marines using a bulldozer to haul a trailer loaded with supplies through the thick mud common to Bougainville Island.** LEFT: **The Japanese airfield of Munda on New Georgia under attack by US aircraft.**

Although on New Georgia the Japanese presence was concentrated around the Munda airfield, reports indicated small detachments at four other points. The US military reasoned that, if these were vital enough to interest the enemy, they were worth capturing.

As frontal assault on reef-fringed Munda would have been unnecessarily costly, the main landing was aimed at the northern end of the neighbouring island of Rendova. A natural harbour was here only 8km/5 miles across the strait from Munda and was backed by high ground reaching to over 914m/3,000ft, allowing Munda to be commanded both by observation and artillery. Five landings were conducted simultaneously on June 30, 1943. The four on New Georgia – at Viru Harbour, Segi Point, Wickham Anchorage and Onaiavisi – were minor actions, involving only APDs, LCTs and LCIs.

For Rendova, a first echelon of 6,300 troops was brought in by four APA and two AKs, with Turner flying his flag in USS *McCawley* (APA-4), known irreverently as the "Wacky Mac". Three further echelons made scheduled landings in APDs and LSTs. The initial ship-to-shore operation was "nearly perfect", all troops being ashore within 30 yards of the first wave. Within two hours, Munda was being shelled by US forces using 105mm howitzers.

Although the operations had been "soft", the Japanese reacted strongly with air attacks. Despite US fighter cover from Guadalcanal and the neighbouring Russells, the large ships were heavily attacked as they withdrew from Rendova. USS *McCawley* (APA-4) had off-loaded 1,100 troops, over 600 tons of equipment along with senior Army and Navy officers. The ship was, therefore, empty when torpedoed in the machinery space. Severely damaged and settling, the ship was taken in tow. After nightfall, almost unbelievably, USS *McCawley* was torpedoed and sunk in error by the US Navy PT boats.

The secondary landings had yielded no more than anchorages and inlets of use to minor warships. Although positions on Rendova rendered the Munda airstrip virtually unusable, this did not prevent the Japanese turning New Georgia into a latter-day Guadalcanal. Recent history was repeated as both sides built up their presence, the Japanese by a reinstatement of their "Tokyo Express". As vicious jungle fighting progressed ashore, fierce night skirmishes occurred offshore. These ranged from PT boats intercepting Japanese barge traffic to the fierce and damaging warship battles in Kula Gulf and Kolombangara. Only in August 1943 was New Georgia finally captured.

BELOW: **General MacArthur's policy of "hitting 'em where they ain't" resulted in many landings by US Marines being unopposed by Japanese forces.**

# Operation "Postern", Lae/Salamaua, New Guinea

Complementing Admiral Nimitz's drive across the Central Pacific was General Douglas MacArthur's southern campaign, aimed at threatening Japan via New Guinea, the Philippines, Formosa and China. Although this would always be the secondary threat, the Japanese could never afford to take it less than seriously.

Although conceited, MacArthur was nonetheless a master of manoeuvre warfare. Compared with Nimitz, he was always short of resources, always out-numbered. He compensated by outsmarting the enemy, encouraging them, via superior codebreaking, to believe that he would do what was expected, before doing something entirely different. He resisted being drawn into attritional jungle warfare but unbalanced the numerically superior enemy by seemingly opportunist moves, before quickly moving on. In a word, he maintained the tempo of an operation while, in the much-quoted phrase "hitting 'em where they ain't".

Japanese forces were concentrated on the north coast of New Guinea, among the main centres of population. This facilitated logistics and back-up by the Imperial Japanese Navy, but made them vulnerable to the amphibious, coast-hopping style of warfare practised by "MacArthur's Navy". No advance could safely be conducted beyond the maximum 321km/200 miles range of land-based air support. Just, however, as this influenced Japanese assessment of his next likely move, MacArthur would use Nimitz's fleet carriers to cover a more ambitious push forward, wrong-footing the enemy yet again. Airstrips would be rapidly constructed, releasing the carriers.

RIGHT: **US and Australian forces cooperated closely during the long New Guinea campaign. The US-built LCM(3) could accommodate a 30-ton tank. A Matilda medium tank of the Australian Army is being unloaded here.**

RIGHT: **For the most part, the Allies enjoyed air superiority, which permitted the under-strength "MacArthur's Navy" to take chances, as here, where seven LSTs are openly beached in line, an inviting target for attacking aircraft.**

ABOVE: **A Landing Ship, Tank (LST) loaded with Australian forces heads to the beachhead.** LEFT: **New Guinea was an infantryman's war, one of jungle-clad mountains and muddy tracks. The Japanese were dug in on the northern coastal strip.**

With US troops now across their lines of communication, the Japanese would either have to accept battle on MacArthur's terms, or as was often the case, embark on desperate jungle treks in order to rejoin the main force.

The huge island of Papua New Guinea is shaped like an ungainly bird, facing westward. Around 483km/300 miles from its "tail" lies the Huon Gulf, upon which is situated the settlement of Lae, with a useful, deep-water port and airfield. Strongly held by the Japanese, Lae had views across the gulf to Salamaua, some 40km/25 miles distant.

MacArthur wanted Lae, and his strategy was simple. During July 1943 his motor torpedo boats set up a blockade of the gulf, disrupting the endless convoy of supply craft upon which the Japanese garrison depended. He then moved a mainly Australian force from the interior in the direction of Salamaua in order to construct a dummy airstrip. A token US force was then moved up the coast.

To the Japanese, all the signs pointed to an imminent assault on Salamaua, and they moved 80 per cent of their strength from Lae as cover. The Allied force, having fooled the enemy,

thus avoided battle while remaining the focus of Japanese interest. Only 2,000 Japanese remained around Lae, and little opposition greeted the 9th Australian Division on September 4, as preceded by a destroyer bombardment, a landing was made 19km/12 miles to the east by the Amphibious Force ("VII Phib") of the 7th Fleet, under its capable commander, Rear-Admiral Daniel E. Barbey ("Uncle Dan the Amphibious Man").

Unable to retrace its steps quickly enough through the deep jungle mud, the greater Japanese force attacking Salamaua was helpless to intervene. This allowed Barbey's landing craft to speed to the landing site despite air attacks.

As the Australian troops closed on Lae from the east, 1,700 US paratroops were dropped to the west. The airstrip was quickly secured allowing further ground troops to be flown in. Declining battle with the now considerably larger Allied force, the Lae garrison withdrew, leaving the town by September 16.

The Japanese at Salamaua were now neatly contained and, with no hope of reinforcement or evacuation by sea they, also, escaped to the jungle on treks that resulted in the death of a very high proportion through disease, malnutrition or exhaustion.

LEFT: **Australian forces unloading fuel, vehicles and other supplies from LSTs of the US Navy.**

55

ABOVE: **Men of the 2nd Marine Division begin the break-out from the landing beach.** LEFT: **The deceptive calm of the transport anchorage while loaded LCVs prepare for the assault phase. Note the LVT being put afloat from the transport** *Doyen* **(AP-2) by cargo derrick.**

# Operation "Galvanic", Makin and Tarawa, Gilbert Islands

Around 2,253km/1,400 miles to the northeast of the still-disputed Solomons, and threatening their flank, lay the 16 scattered atolls of the Gilbert Islands, The Japanese occupied only two in force; Butaritari on Makin harboured a seaplane base and Betio on Tarawa an airfield. Admiral Nimitz wanted both islands as a staging point for an imminent advance on the neighbouring Marshall Islands.

As early as August 1942, a US forces raid on Makin had alerted the Japanese to US military interest, and both islands were systematically fortified, theoretically to allow the defenders to resist until relieved in three to seven days.

Planning for Operation "Galvanic" emphasized speed of execution, for the US Navy did not want to risk aircraft carriers a moment longer than necessary. The USMC had already witnessed this policy at Guadalcanal and had lost some trust in the commitment of the US Navy.

This would be the first strongly opposed assault. Both islands were ringed by shallow lagoons skirted by wide and barely submerged reefs. Tidal ranges were small and barely surveyed. Landing craft, LCMs and LCVPs, would be likely to ground due to the shallow water, so 125 LVTs were allocated to transport the initial three assault waves at Tarawa. Another 50 LVTs were to be on the assault at Makin.

Of the US 5th Fleet's Amphibious Corps, the 2nd Marine Division was allocated Tarawa. The less-experienced US Army 27th Infantry Division was sent to Makin. Total US strength was 27,600; enemy strength was an estimated 5,400, all being very well prepared.

For days before, aircraft from Vice-Admiral Spruance's 5th Fleet carriers had attacked a range of enemy-held islands, both to disguise the true objective and to reduce Japanese resources in aircraft and ammunition.

ABOVE: **Many of the 14 Japanese coast defence guns on Betio were of British manufacture and captured earlier at Singapore.** LEFT: **One of the many blockhouse-type defensive strongpoints built by the Japanese.**

ABOVE: **Firmly ashore but by no means yet secure, these US Marines are having to clear the mass of equipment blocking the narrow beach.** LEFT: **The hulks of abandoned LVTs bear silent witness to the ferocity of the defences at Betio.**

Both assaults were timed for early on November 20, 1943. That on Butaritari (Makin) initially met light opposition; fortunately, for with only 50 LVTs most of the 6,500 US troops had to wade 300 yards across the waist-deep lagoon. Less than 20 per cent of the planned backup LCM/LCVP supply journeys made it over the reef on the first day.

Fighting literally to the last man, the Japanese held out for four days. Far longer than scheduled, this delay vindicated the US Navy's caution when an escort carrier was torpedoed by a Japanese submarine and sank with only a few survivors.

Betio was "the real toughie". Just 3.2km/2 miles in length and of an area estimated at under 120 hectares/300 acres, it was a fortress. A solid barrier of coconut logs ringed the shoreline. There were 14 coastal gun and 25 field gun emplacements, dug-in tanks with 37mm guns, and innumerable covered and armoured machine-gun positions. There were also deep, fortified bunkers. Mined reefs and beach obstacles guided landing craft into the chosen field of artillery fire. Combined with carrier-borne air attacks, bombardment ships laid some 3,000 tons of ordnance on the defenders

over the two hours that preceded the first landing. It would prove to be "woefully inadequate". Inaccurate marking of the Line of Departure and unfavourable sea conditions saw the first waves of LVTs arrive 43 minutes late. As the support bombardment had ceased on schedule, this lapse gave the defenders adequate time to re-man their positions.

In negotiating the reef and lagoon, the lightly armoured LVTs and the troops thus took a terrible beating. With survivors trying to regroup under the cover of the log barrier, the follow-up troops were stranded on the reef as their assault craft grounded in the shallow water.

The assault stalled. Of the 125 LVTs launched 90 were disabled, the remainder being used to ferry the wounded to landing craft and returning with fresh troops, just 25 at a time.

Gradual reinforcement and raw courage saw the invaders slowly gain the initiative. Seventy-six hours later Betio was again silent. Over 1,000 US soldiers had died, and 4,700 Japanese were dead, just 19 were captured. Appalled at the carnage the USMC commander, Major General Holland M. ("Howlin' Mad") Smith was moved to write that "Tarawa was a mistake".

LEFT: **US forces were firmly established on Tarawa on December 31, 1943. The newly constructed airfield can be seen in the background, but off the beach there remain the hulks of LVTs and landing craft sunk during the landing.**

LEFT: **The twin island of Roi-Namur, the major objective on the Kwajalein Atoll, absorbed over 7,400 rounds of ordnance fired by ships of the US Navy in the 48 hours preceding the assault. Through unexpectedly rough conditions, the first two waves of LVTs are approaching the smoke-shrouded shore.**

# Operation "Flintlock", Kwajalien, Marshall Islands

Lying to the north of the Gilberts, the Marshall Islands were the first of the groups mandated to Japan following World War I to be attacked. Having been closed to foreigners, suspicions grew that, despite the conditions of the Washington Treaty, the islands had been well fortified. The bloody seizure of the Gilberts, besides giving valuable experience in opposed landings, provided the necessary base for reconnaissance and eventual occupation of the Marshalls.

Stung by the criticism of inadequate fire support at Tarawa, the US 5th Fleet would more than compensate at the Marshalls. That Tarawa had been a success at all had been due to the use of LVTs. However, such was the attrition rate that 300 were now considered the minimum for a division-strength landing. Deep bunkers and fortified emplacements on Tarawa showed the need for great numbers of flamethrowers, satchel charges and bazookas. Specialist underwater teams would be required to clear obstacles and mines.

A total of 26,500 Japanese troops were spread among the 34 atolls of the islands, where six airfields, four seaplane bases and three naval anchorages had been established. Resources permitted only one atoll to be hit at a time and Nitmitz decided on Kwajaleln. Here, major assaults would be staged on the two

ABOVE: **US troops and supplies being landed from an LST on Kwajalien Atoll on April 15, 1944, after the last Japanese had been defeated.**

islands, Kwajalein and Roi-Namur. The US Army 7th Infantry Division was allocated Kwajalein, where there was a 5,000-strong garrison. Roi-Namur, with 3,000 Japanese defenders, was allocated to the untried 4th Marine Division.

The strategy carried some risk (and attracted criticism) in that it would bypass several powerful enemy garrisons who, if unwilling to simply await their fate, would need to be neutralized later. For the moment, aircraft from Spruance's carriers swept the Marshall Islands clear of Japanese aircraft and completed essential photographic intelligence.

Prior to the assault on January 31, 1944, the island of Roi-Namur was subjected to a 48-hour naval bombardment which, later, was estimated to have killed or incapacitated over half of the defenders.

Overseen by senior officers on board USS *Appalachian* (AGC-1) the first, purpose-built Headquarters Ship, troops disembarked from transport ships to LCVPs. Those slated for the first wave then transferred to 244 LVTs, floated from new LSDs and LSTs. In rough conditions they were marshalled into approximately straight lines. Each wave was directly supported by rocket-firing LCIs (known as "Elsie Items") and some of the 75 available armoured LVTs, with 37mm guns, which could land and function as light tanks.

Small flanking islands had been seized earlier for the establishment of artillery. While they worked well, these subsidiary landings broke up the LVT and landing craft fleet, which never fully recovered formation.

Still shocked by the bombardment, the surviving Japanese fought courageously but within 48 hours, Roi-Namur, "a stinking mess of debris and dead Japanese" was subdued.

At Kwajalein, the landing was supported by three carriers, three battleships, a cruiser and nine destroyers. The bombardment used up approximately 1,000 x 16in,

ABOVE **On Einwetok, as ever, Japanese defenders fought to the end. Only 64 were taken prisoner, and some 2,700 died.**

1,340 x 14in, 400 x 8in and 5,000 x 5in rounds of ammunition. Neighbouring islets were again seized for the establishment of artillery batteries.

The first four waves of LVTs, supported by armoured LVTs and rocket-firing LCIs hit the beach within the space of 12 minutes. Follow-up landing craft experienced trouble, grounding on isolated coral reefs.

The island, which was 3.2km/2 miles in length, had been reduced to craters and tangled rubble in which small groups of Japanese troops were fought in vicious hand-to-hand combat. It took four days for US troops to fight their way from one end of the island to the other.

It would take until the April to clear pockets of enemy resistance throughout the Marshalls but, by then, the war had moved on. Boeing B-29 Superfortress aircraft were rapidly deployed to start bombing the Marianas, Nimitz's next objective.

LEFT: **An LCM from USS *Sumter* (APA-52), a war-built attack transport, being unloaded by SeeBees equipped with a bulldozer.**

# Operation "Overlord", Normandy

The Normandy landing was on a scale that made earlier operations appear to have been a rehearsal, and much depended on the success of the operation. Despite fighting on major fronts in the east and in Italy, Germany had gathered a massive military force in northern France. The Allied re-entry into "Fortress Europe" had long been anticipated. Mounted from England, the extent would be such that the only suitable locations were the beaches of either the Pas de Calais or Normandy. Deception was thus vital to the Allied cause, for any German guess had a 50 per cent chance of being correct.

Germany's best-qualified field officers commanded in France, Field Marshal Gerd von Rundstedt had overall regional control as C-in-C, while Field Marshal Erwin Rommel was responsible for Army Group B, whose 7th Army garrisoned the western Channel coast. The two agreed to differ over defensive strategy, the infantry divisions being entrenched within the extensive fortifications of the vaunted "Atlantic Wall", with the armoured divisions held back as the mobile reserve, to be rushed to whichever location the Allies committed to attack.

To move armour rapidly the *Wehrmacht* required road and rail links and, for months before, Allied tactical air forces had specifically targeted what appeared to be strategically significant bridges and junctions in random air-raiding patterns that indicated no particular preference.

Allied planners knew that success would hinge on a race for reinforcement. Once a beachhead was secured, resources would have to be poured in at a faster rate than the enemy could reinforce his defences. The Dieppe experience of 1942 had convinced planners that an assault on or near a major port would be doomed to failure. Thus, "Mulberry" was conceived: two complete port facilities made up of floatable concrete modules were to be towed across the Channel, positioned and sunk on site. These would allow large ships to discharge vehicles directly just 850 yards from the beach. Vehicle access would be via floating causeways.

Considerable pressure had been exerted by both the Soviet Union and United States to mount the assault even as early as 1942. The British had resisted strongly until the necessary resources and combat skills were available. Also, air and sea superiority had to be firmly established by Allied forces.

By 1944 the *Luftwaffe* was much reduced, with the best units withdrawn back to defend the "Fatherland" against the onslaught of the US and British heavy bomber forces.

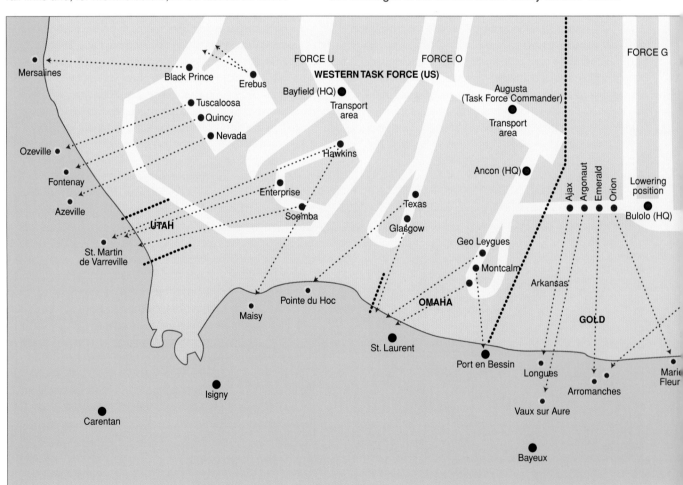

ABOVE: **No less than 33 LCIs were included in the V Corps assault convoy. The vessels are flying barrage balloons to discourage low-level air attack.**
RIGHT: **On D-Day a vast number of different types of vessel were used.**

A bonus of the now-established Allied air superiority over the English Channel was that *Luftwaffe* reconnaissance flights were rare. Unable to confirm any suspicions, the Germans were more susceptible to skilful deception. In south-east England, for instance, a wholly fictitious "American First Army Group" was created, with signal traffic so realistic that, for weeks following "Overlord", powerful elements of the German 15th Army were held back in readiness for a further landing in the Pas de Calais.

BELOW: **A schematic plan of the amphibious landings on D-Day, June 6, 1944. The beaches were codenamed "Utah" (US), "Omaha" (US), "Gold" (British), "Juno" (Canadian) and "Sword" (British).**

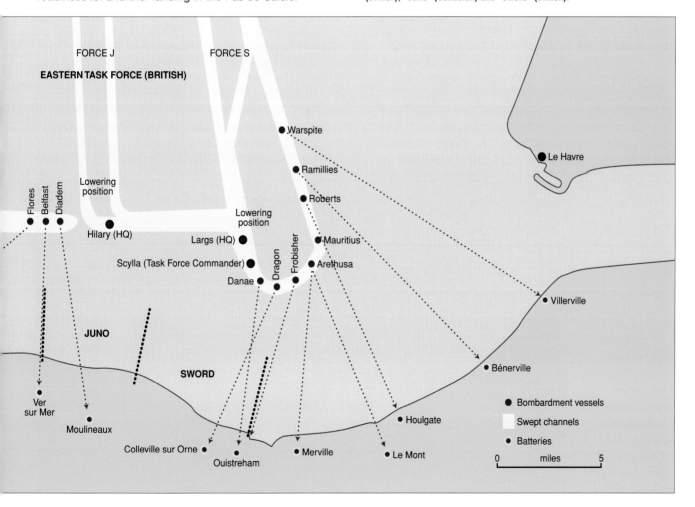

LEFT: **The view aboard an LCT prior to the Normandy landings. In the foreground is a Sherman M4A-1 tank fitted with deep water wading trunking, one for the exhaust the other for air to the engine.**

To create a beachhead of a size to base forces sufficient to contain known German strength, a five-division front was required. Five beach sectors were thus created, stretching some 96km/60 miles from the Orne estuary to a point on the Cotentin peninsula. In the east, the British beaches, "Gold" and "Sword", bracketed the Canadian "Juno". The long US forces "Omaha" beach then joined "Utah" in the far west.

Six hours ahead of the main assault, two airborne divisions would seize vital bridgeheads. The invading force was due to be built up at the rate of one and one-third divisions each day.

The maritime side of the operation was so large as to merit its own organization. Operation "Neptune" was headed by Admiral Sir Bertram Ramsay who, four years earlier, had overseen the Dunkirk evacuation. The two western (US) beaches, conduit for the US First Army, were the responsibility of the Western Task Force, under Rear-Admiral Alan G. Kirk. The British Second Army was to be passed through the three eastern beach sectors, controlled by Rear-Admiral Sir Philip Vian's Eastern Task Force. Until landed, all military forces were subordinate to the navy.

RIGHT: **A Dodge WC-54 ambulance being loaded on to an LST at Weymouth in Dorset prior to the D-Day landings. A damaged drive unit from a landing craft has been dumped on the quayside.**

By stripping every command of all possible vessels, the Royal Navy supplied the greater part of the 1,213 warships participating. As the average crossing was under 161km/ 100 miles, smaller assault craft could, weather permitting, make the passage. Complex vessels such as LSDs were thus little used. Among the craft assembled were 236 LSTs, 837 LCTs and 248 LCIs. British forces landed from LCAs, of which there were over 500. US troops landed from LCVPs, some 190 in total.

British ports and estuaries from Milford Haven, Wales to Great Yarmouth, Norfolk were full of shipping during the preparation phase. The coastal convoy system was heavily utilized. Experienced escort groups and Coastal Command squadrons were tasked with making the Channel inaccessible to U-boats. Air cover could be based on English airfields, greatly increasing aircraft utilization and pilot survival.

ABOVE: **Men of No. 47 (Royal Marine) Commando landing from LCAs on "Gold" beach, June 6, 1944. No. 47 Commando was tasked to capture Port-en-Bessin and then join US forces who had landed at "Omaha" beach.**

The Germans had confidence in the abilities of the "Oyster" pressure mine, familiar to the Allies and deemed unsweepable. Not for the first time in history, however, was a weapon thought so secret and important that it could not be used before the event. Again, the outcome was that huge stockpiles had been accumulated but, at the last minute, there was no opportunity to lay them. Subsequent night drops by the *Luftwaffe* and E-boats would demonstrate how large a nuisance these could have been. After some five years of war, the relatively shallow waters of the Channel were infested with mines of all types.

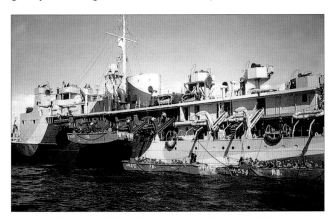

ABOVE: **US Rangers in British LCAs being loaded aboard HMS *Prince Baudouin*, a fast troop transport, prior to landing on "Omaha" beach.**

ABOVE: **British troops of the 50th (Northumbrian) Division move to "Gold" beach in LCVs. A transport ship burns after an air attack.**

LEFT: **Approaching touchdown, the troops in this LCV must have been relieved to see the personnel on the beach and apparent lack of opposition. Despite initial firece fighting, even on "Omaha" beach direct opposition was quelled relatively quickly.**

A cleared assembly area was thus created south of the Isle of Wight, served by four swept channels connecting with the coastal convoy route. From this area, eight parallel swept channels ran southward to the known German minefields, which ran parallel to the French coast. On D-Day, Fleet Minesweepers would work ahead of the armada to clear ten safe routes through the minefields before creating safe manoeuvring areas for fire support ships.

Because of the density of beach obstructions, landing had to be fixed for three to four hours before high water. To make it just before first light, the date was set for June 5, 1944, but poor weather enforced an anxious 24-hour delay. As it was, many beach obstacles were submerged.

Because of tidal differences along the length of the Normandy coast, "H-hour" on the two US beaches was at 06:30, one hour ahead of the remainder. More beach obstacles were exposed and could be avoided, but on "Omaha" the sheer width of beach was a drawback. The Germans had fortified the low bluffs that overlooked the sands, and exits were limited and well covered. Despite advice from his own senior US Marine Corps officers, Rear-Admiral Kirk limited the preliminary bombardment to only 40 minutes in order to maintain surprise for as long as possible. It proved to be painfully insufficient.

Tidal conditions enforced a delay on "Sword" but this was utilized for further heavy naval bombardment. Poor visibility caused by smoke and dust hampered air spotting. With the landings in progress, destroyers continually patroled close-in to attack requested targets and give visible support. During the critical opening phase these vessels gave a tremendous boost to the morale of those troops ashore.

Initial waves were supported by amphibious "DD" tanks. Once ashore, these were invaluable but, in the conditions, many were launched too far out and either came ashore in the wrong location or sank in the choppy seas. Following closely were the first LCTs, carrying tanks modified for beach clearance, which complemented explosive devices to establish safe paths through the minefields. Before D-Day was over, 132,000 Allied troops were ashore at the cost of just over 10,000 casualties. The race was on for reinforcement and resupply. It was won by the Allies thanks to meticulous planning and greater resources.

ABOVE: **"Omaha" beach two days after D-Day, in which US reinforcements, including heavy artillery, were moving inland. DUKW amphibious vehicles were being utilized to carry supplies from transport ships.** LEFT: **Deceptively peaceful, this view from Arromanches shows the "Mulberry" harbour, "Gooseberry", the floating causeways and the "Lobnitz" pierheads.**

65

# Operation "Infatuate II", Walcheren

By October 1944, the port of Antwerp, the facilities of which were desperately needed to support the Allied advance into Germany, was in British hands. Situated some 81km/50 miles up the Scheldt estuary, however, it remained unusable as the river was mined. In addition, the Germans, aware of the strategic importance of the port, still held the seaward end. The mainland, and the south bank around Breskens, was in Allied hands by October 31 but the north side, the island of Walcheren, remained heavily defended by the Germans.

Walcheren is some 13km/8 miles across. Only the coastal rim and the major towns lay above sea level. A first move, reluctantly, was to breach the sea dykes by bombing, flooding the interior and leaving the formidable German defences marooned on a narrow strip of land. Some 60 guns, of calibres from 2cm to 75cm, located in concrete emplacements around Westkapelle, were linked as a continuous line of defence.

Learning from the Dieppe experience, heavy support fire was supplied for the assault. In the event, the effect of the 15in shells fired from a battleship and two monitors from a range of 21km/13 miles was largely wasted as the weather was too cloudy to allow aerial spotting.

ABOVE: **As the smoke screen disperses, Royal Marine commandos are moving ashore in DUKWs. LCT 952 is positioned ready to land vehicles.**

ABOVE: **Commandos and equipment were transported in 35 LCTs. These personnel were embarked with "Buffalos", the British name for the LVT.**
LEFT: **On the left flank of the assault, the Westkapelle sea dyke was breached by RAF bombing, flooding the inland area.**

Fortunately, a 25-strong Support Squadron had been formed, comprising LCG (L), LCG (M), LCF and LCT (R), the approaches being too shallow for warships. A further innovation was US-supplied LVTs, known to the British as "Buffalos" and able to transport 24 equipped troops. There had, however, been no time to exercise with them.

Four hours after an assault was to be mounted across the river from Breskens, three Royal Marine Commando (Nos. 41, 47 and 48) were to be landed to straddle the gap in the sea dyke by Westkapelle.

A total of 181 craft of all types assembled off Ostend early on November 1. The weather at dawn was calm and heavily overcast as the force approached the Dutch coast. Landing was timed for 09:45, following naval gunfire and aerial bombardment, which was greatly reduced in effect by the overcast weather.

LEFT: **Indispensable on sand, perhaps even more so in the mud of Holland, tracked vehicles such as the "Weasel" and "Buffalo" were able to negotiate the foreshore and drive over the sea wall.**

LEFT: **A Sherman Crab flail tank landing from an LCT to clear mines. The type was one of those special vehicles developed by Major Percy Hobart of the 79th Armoured Division.**

It has been stated that this would be the most heavily opposed landing of World War II, and certainly the gun batteries and strongpoints, which had withheld fire down to approximately 3,000 yards, appeared to form a continuous line. Under a murderous barrage, the 25 craft of the Support Squadron engaged the enemy at near-suicidal ranges. All were damaged, some deliberately being beached to form unsinkable, stationary strongpoints. The battle, which lasted over three hours, drew the highest praise, but the price was considerable. Nine craft were sunk and eleven damaged, seven of them seriously. Personnel losses were 170 dead and 125 injured.

The dedication of the Support Squadron was not wasted. Many LVTs were floated from LCTs offshore and came ashore in company with the LCI (S). Once ashore, many were below trajectory of the large enemy guns, which could not be depressed sufficiently. Delayed by beach congestion, the LCTs of No. 47 Commando were shelled when ordered in, but were beached satisfactorily.

Established on either side of the gap, increasingly supported from the air, the commandos began to clear the enemy defences. German marines resisted resolutely, infantry less so, and prisoners began to be taken in embarrassingly large numbers. Despite great difficulties in resupply, progress was steady, Walcheren being cleared in eight days; the cost to the commandos

was 79 dead. Minesweepers quickly cleared the Scheldt, and massive quantities of supplies were passing through Antwerp by the end of November.

The assault on Walcheren, the last such in the European theatre during World War II, was successful largely because the German batteries fired on the Support Squadron rather than engaging the assault craft during the vulnerable approach phase. Although successful in the Pacific, the LVTs were difficult to handle in the river currents. Once ashore, the LVT was liable to sink in soft sand and mud, and it could not negotiate steep sand dunes. The "Buffalo" did, however, save many lives.

ABOVE: **Landing Craft, Gun (Medium) 101, sinking after being hit several times by shells from a German coastal battery.**

# Operation "Forager", Saipan, Marianas

ABOVE: **Submarines of the US Navy played a vital role in the Pacific theatre by attacking Japanese transport shipping and warships.**

The southern Mariana Islands were around 1,609km/ 1,000 miles from the US forces' forward base in the Marshalls, and any assault on them would need to be self-supporting, with carrier-based air support. Regarded by the Japanese as part of their home territory, the Marianas would be defended to the last. In US hands the Carolines to the south would cut off and provide flank cover for MacArthur's southern campaign. They would also provide the necessary air and naval bases for the staging of strikes directly at the enemy's home islands.

Staged in the same month as the Normandy landings, Operation "Forager" had to compete for resources, yet mustered 535 ships and craft and a total of 165,000 troops.

The southern Marianas, specifically Saipan, Tinian and Guam, lay in a 161km/100-mile straight line. Coral-fringed, all were rugged, relatively large and well-populated. Saipan, the most northerly, is just 2,092km/1,300 miles from Tokyo. Taken first, it would isolate Tinian and Guam from reinforcement.

Against Saipan and the smaller Tinian was ranged the Northern Attack Force, carrying General Holland M. Smith's "V Phib Corps". This comprised the reinforced 2nd and 4th

USMC divisions. A separate Southern Attack Force was allocated to Guam. Two further Army divisions were held in reserve. Saipan was to be attacked first, on June 15, 1944, with attacks on Tinian and Guam following at a date which depended on progress after the initial landing.

The invasion forces left from Hawaii and Guadalcanal, respectively 5,633km/3,500 miles and 3,862km/2,400 miles from the objectives. Shielding the force from a vengeful

LEFT: **Transport anchorages needed to be established at a distance from the shore, yet not so far as to hazard LCVPs and LVTs. This photograph shows USS** Sumter **(APA-52) (right) and USS** Almaack **(AKA-10) loaded with ammunition, attached to Transdiv 26, at anchor off Tinian.**

LEFT: **An LVT (4), loaded with US Marines, headed for Tinian. The "turret" mounted two 0.30in machine-guns. A single 0.50in heavy machine-gun is mounted in the rear of the cargo bay.**

LEFT: **The beachhead is now established, allowing a constant stream of LCVPs to bring ashore vehicles, stores and personnel. Note, a slipway has been built and covered with metal road matting.** BELOW: **US Marines were pinned down by Japanese forces who had pre-targeted the beach.**

Imperial Japanese Navy was Spruance's powerful 5th Fleet. Even as Saipan was attacked, Admiral Ozawa's battle fleet sailed for the Marianas. The resulting confrontation with Spruance, the Battle of the Philippine Sea, was one of the great aircraft carrier battles of World War II.

Saipan was defended in depth by nearly 32,000 Japanese Army and Navy personnel. There would have been more, but US submarines had intercepted most of the transports carrying reinforcements to the island.

Two hours of naval bombardment commenced at 04:30 on June 15. This was followed by 30 minutes of air strikes, then further bombardment until touchdown at 08:44. A large secondary landing was, meanwhile, in progress some 16km/10 miles to the north.

The two divisions were landed on a continuous 6,000-yard beachhead divided into eight equal sectors. In each sector, four assault waves would touch down within 21 minutes, putting the first 8,000 troops ashore. Each assault wave comprised 12 LVTs, covered by 18 armoured and gun-armed LVTs. Landing Craft, Control (LCC) flanked the lines of LVTs. Leading in each sector were three rocket-firing LCIs. Once the troops had landed, each LVT was driven through the incoming waves of LVTs to the transports and reloaded with fresh troops.

Fronted by a reef of up to 700 yards in width, the beaches fringed a flat and bare sandy plain nearly 1.6km/1 mile wide. Japanese artillery had pre-targeted every salient point and was too-well dispersed to have been neutralized by the pre-landing bombardment. As at Salerno, this destroyed anything that moved. US forces were pinned to the narrow beachheads, and objectives for Day 1 were not taken until Day 3.

LSTs followed-up the assault landing, unloading further LVTs and DUKWs on to the reef. Two LSDs off-loaded LCMs pre-loaded with 36 tanks. Despite this armour, destroyers still had to sail close to the reef in order to attack Japanese tank columns while under direct fire. Heavier fire support ships had been diverted to meet the urgent threat posed by the Japanese fleet, shortly to be engaged by Spruance.

By Day 3, the foothold was reasonably secure, with 50,000 troops and ample artillery ashore, but the whole island would require a further three weeks to conquer. It would be a tough assignment. Out of the 67,000 US troops eventually involved, over 16,500 were casualties, with more than 3,400 dead or missing. Over 24,000 Japanese died. The losses in US resources delayed the landings on Guam by a month.

ABOVE: **US Marines provide covering machine-gun fire as infantry supported by Sherman tanks advance on enemy positions.**

69

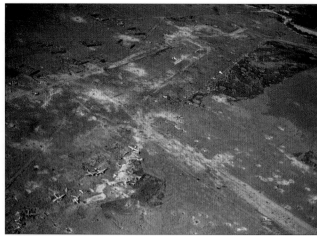

ABOVE: **The Japanese airfield, which was the main target on Hollandia, after attack by US Navy dive-bombers.** LEFT: **Australian troops waiting to load on board an LST as part of the second wave attack force for Lae.**

# New Guinea

The combination of General MacArthur's particular talents and the topography of New Guinea produced a mode of amphibious warfare entirely different to that imposed upon Admiral Nimitz for the Central Pacific Theatre.

The 2,253km/1,400 mile north coast of New Guinea is backed by vast tracts of mountain and virgin equatorial jungle. As with the previous colonial administrators, the Japanese "occupied" or "controlled" the island only by virtue of holding a string of coastal settlements. With no defence in depth, the region was quickly captured by the Japanese in 1942, but now this flaw exposed the Japanese occupiers to the same hazard of rapid defeat.

MacArthur did not have the resources, time nor inclination to give the enemy an advantage by advancing along the length of the coastline. He employed instead a series of amphibious bypassing operations, in which prior intelligence and deception were to play a major role.

By the end of 1943 the Japanese were thinking defensively, basing their defensive positions upon the appreciation of where US forces would strike next. As exemplified at Lae/Salamana in September 1943, General MacArthur, fully aware by code breaking and POW interrogation, effectively fooled the main Japanese force, by apparently doing what they expected him to do, before landing, nearly unopposed, in their rear.

In Rear-Admiral Daniel E. Barbey's "VII Phib", MacArthur had the (albeit ever-inadequate) mobility resource, but the key to his success lay in his establishment of joint-service headquarters, planning and command organization, promoting maximum flexibility through harmonious inter-service relationships at every level. This encouraged a tempo of operations that the

BELOW LEFT: **Landing craft and support vessels unloading supplies for the invasion force on Tanahmera Bay, Hollandia, in May 1944.** BELOW: **Sherman tanks of the US Marine Corps moving along the shoreline after landing.**

Japanese Army could never react with sufficient speed. There were 250,000 Japanese troops in positions along the coast. MacArthur successfully bypassed over half of them, leaving pockets which, cut off from resupply or any hope of rescue, were effectively neutralized.

Some 241km/150 miles along the coast from Lae, and within range of land-based air support, Madang was expected by the enemy to be MacArthur's next objective. His sights were, however, set on Hollandia, a major administrative and logistics hub a full 805km/500 miles distant.

ABOVE: **Bulldozers were vital on soft sand, but specialist US Marine Corps beach parties kept things moving.** BELOW: **Matilda tanks of the Australian Army passing through jungle in New Guinea on a training exercise.**

The land route to Hollandia was blocked by Japanese Army concentrations at Madang and Wewak, 161km/ 100 miles further east. Operation "Reckless" would bypass both, to simultaneously hit Hollandia (manned mainly by rear-echelon troops) and Tanahmerah Bay, around 32km/20 miles to the west. The two forces would advance toward each other to take a group of three, strategically important airfields, thus releasing aircraft carriers allocated by Nimitz to provide initial air cover. A third landing would be mounted at Aitape, 161km/100 miles east of Hollandia, to seize a secondary airstrip.

The landings were made on April 22, 1944 and, despite the difficulties of landing supplies over reef-fringed shores, then on to the boggy hinterland with almost impassable tracks, all major objectives were achieved within five days. As anticipated, the defenders offered little resistance, but a potentially dangerous Japanese counter-attack from Wakde, to the west, was neatly stopped by the rapid response of a further amphibious landing by US forces in Wakde.

Further rapid moves to Biak (May 27) and the western limits of New Guinea at Noemfoor (July 2) and Sansapor (July 3) took MacArthur's forces 805km/500 miles beyond Hollandia. Organised Japanese resistance on New Guinea had ended by late August 1944. MacArthur now looked to head north for the Philippines, some 1,127km/700 miles distant, a cause for considerable disquiet in Japan, where the Tojo administration had already stepped down following the taking of Saipan in June 1944.

The most versatile craft of "MacArthur's Navy" proved to be the LSTs, which moved almost everything but the tanks for which they were designed. Smaller LCTs penetrated where LSTs could not go, their crews living aboard for long periods in improvised accommodation. Follow-up LCIs were available in reasonable numbers but most "big ships" – APA, AKA, LPD – had to be allocated as the operation demanded.

LEFT: **Landings on this scale could not maintain a precise formation. Note the LSTs anchored at the rear, with LCVPs circling ready to move forward to the beach.**

# Leyte Gulf

When, on October 20, 1944, Lieutenant General Krueger's Sixth Army rolled ashore on Leyte, almost without opposition, General MacArthur had finally realized his driving ambition of returning to the Philippines. Encouraged by a perceived lack of Japanese aerial resistance, he had struck at a point halfway along the extensive Philippines archipelago. Their immediate seaward flank covered by Vice-Admiral Kinkaid's Seventh Fleet, Vice-Admiral Wilkinson and Rear-Admiral Barbey landed the US Army's II Corps on adjacent beaches at Leyte Gulf in an operation the near-perfection of which was born of hard-learned experience. Close air support was provided by Rear-Admiral Thomas Sprague's force of escort aircraft carriers (CVE) but deep cover, to prevent incursion by the Imperial Japanese Navy, was the responsibility of the powerful fleet carrier groups detached from Admiral Nimitz's 3rd Fleet. Admiral Halsey, the commander, answered to Nimitz; Kinkaid, on the other hand, was responsible to MacArthur. Although considerably reduced by nearly three years of operations, the Imperial Japanese Navy had not lost its appetite for a

"Trafalgar-like" battle that would decide, at a stroke, mastery of the Pacific. The Leyte landing triggered a pre-prepared naval battle plan of typical Japanese complexity.

The Japanese fleet would be divided into three main groups. A first group of carriers (virtually useless because of a lack of trained aircrew) would patrol north-east of the Philippines, providing a lure that the impulsive Halsey would be unable to resist. With the latter's force lured to the north, the way would be open for the other two groups to hit the 7th Fleet's amphibious force, laying at anchor in Leyte Gulf, from two directions simultaneously.

A major weakness of the Japanese plan was the reliance on land-based air support, now largely non-existent. Its creators, however, could not have forecast the divided command chains of Halsey and Kinkaid, who could communicate only with difficulty. They also could not have known that Nimitz

BELOW: **Japanese opposition near Dulag was sporadic but, taking no chances, this newly landed platoon was keeping under cover.**

LEFT: **The consummate showman and inspirational leader, General Douglas MacArthur, having made his carefully staged "I have returned" landing, was quick to return ashore to mingle with combat troops.**

had made a rare error in approving the wording of Halsey's functional directive. Certainly, the latter was ordered to destroy any enemy forces threatening the "Philippines Area", but this instruction carried a rider. "In case opportunity for destruction of major portions of the enemy fleet offers or can be created, such destruction becomes the primary task".

Halsey's carrier groups were already striking at Japanese ships approaching Leyte Gulf, but reports by his pilots of damage inflicted were over-optimistic to the point where Halsay believed that the enemy forces had been reduced to a level easily handled by Kinkaid's 7th Fleet. When a reconnaissance aircraft finally detected the decoy force, Halsey reacted exactly as the Japanese planners had anticipated and intended. Complying with Nimitz's directive, he headed northward with all four carrier groups and their battleship supporting force. Deeply involved with affairs at Leyte, Kinkaid rested comfortably in the belief that

the approaches to the gulf were controlled by the enormous power of the 3rd Fleet. Halsey omitted to appraise him of the fact his fleet was now heading away from Leyte at 30 knots.

Although the Japanese Navy's southern attack was eliminated in the night action of the Surigao Strait, the more powerful northern force left the unguarded San Bernadino Strait and headed southward toward the vulnerable (and still unaware) amphibious fleet in Leyte Gulf. By the greatest of good fortune, Sprague's escort carrier force lay in its path. A desperate and confused action ensued off Samar with US destroyers and escort carriers pitted against Japanese battleships and cruisers.

The Japanese commander, Admiral Kurita, had already been greatly uneasy at the lack of opposition to his progress and now, despite his overwhelming firepower, appeared unnerved by the ferocity of Sprague's defence. Thinking that he had actually encountered Halsey's carriers, Kurita withdrew his ships.

ABOVE: **USS *Princeton* (CVL-23) on fire, with USS *Birmingham* (CL-46) approaching to assist with firefighting.** RIGHT: **USS *Birmingham* went alongside when the bomb stowage on USS *Princeton* exploded and the vessel sank. The action took place during the Battle of Leyte Gulf, October 24, 1944.**

# Operation "Detachment", Iwo Jima

The Bonin Islands offered the most direct route to the Japanese home islands. Halfway between Saipan and Tokyo, Iwo Jima was the most attractive objective, having two completed airfields and a third under construction just 1,046km/650 miles from the Japanese capital. For the Japanese, its loss would be psychologically bad as it would be the first breach in their so-called "Inner Defence Zone". Recognizing now that a final campaign on the home islands was inevitable, the Japanese high command sought time to prepare. Strategically, Iwo Jima looked a certainty as the US military's next objective. Lieutenant General Kuribayashi was sent there at the time of the Saipan invasion (June 15, 1944) with orders to turn the island into an impregnable fortress.

Less than 8 x 5km/5 x 3 miles, the island lies on a north-east, south-west axis. At the southern extremity the dormant mass of the volcano Mount Suribachi dominates a triangular-shaped zone of flat, featureless sand that offers over 3.2km/2 miles of clear beaches on either coast. The northern half of Iwo Jima is almost flat, bordered by cliff-bound shores. Iwo Jima is made up of soft volcanic rock, not coral, and easily quarried. Kuribayashi had fully exploited this facility, creating numerous artillery positions, interconnected by tunnels with deep shelters for stores and ammunition magazines.

As of February 1945, the defenders numbered some 21,000, including many naval personnel and construction units. Their orders were to resist to the end, an attritional contest for which the prize would be time gained.

ABOVE: **The characteristic shape of Iwo Jima, with Mount Suribachi at the near end. Both Japanese airfields are visible. Beaches on either shore were assaulted.**
RIGHT: **Twelve rocket-firing LSMs advanced on the beach in line abreast, each releasing 120 projectiles aimed at positions just beyond the shoreline.**

The US military did not disguise their intentions. Every day for the two months preceding the d-day of February 19, 1945, the island was bombed. For the final three days the island received heavy naval bombardment. The Japanese simply retired to their deep bunkers and waited. Offshore, Vice-Admiral Richmond K. Turner controlled no less than 495 assorted vessels and, from his headquarters ship, USS *Eldorado* (AGC-11), he watched as some 500 LVTs manoeuvred into ten assault waves. Under a rolling naval barrage and preceded by 12 rocket-armed LCS (L) the first wave hit the beach unopposed and on schedule. Within 45 minutes, some 9,000 troops were ashore, closely followed by LSMs carrying medium tanks.

ABOVE: **Guided and protected by flanking destroyers, LVTs move in toward the dust and smoke-shrouded shore. The steep beach of volcanic ash and cinders proved difficult, offering little traction for vehicles.** LEFT: **The leading wave approaching the south-eastern beach. All were covered by fire from Mount Suribachi.**

ABOVE: **Trailing blazing fuel, a Nakajima Type 97 "Kate" disintegrating under close-range fire.** RIGHT: **The wooden deck on a US Navy carrier was vulnerable to kamikaze attack, unlike the armoured deck on a British carrier.**

The model operation now, however, hit problems. The beach was backed by a soft cinder terrace, up to 4m/13ft in height and with a 45-degree slope. Vehicles could not gain traction, walking was difficult, running impossible. A rising surf swung assault craft, stranding them broadside on to the beach. Into this the Japanese directed a heavy mortar bombardment which, unlike artillery shells exploding deep in the soft sand, caused the majority of the first day's 2,400 casualties. Growing stacks of stores added to the blazing equipment along the shoreline. By nightfall, leading elements of the USMC had advanced only 500 yards inland.

By now, 30,000 men were ashore but the expected Japanese counter-attack did not materialize. Kuribayashi was conserving his strength for a hard-fought defence. Mount Suribachi, the source of much of the defensive gunfire, was taken on the fourth day, enabling the main effort to be directed northward against two defensive lines that ran the width of the island. This advance involved the commitment of some of the floating reserve. This action was supported at every stage by naval gunfire.

BELOW: **The volcanic sand beaches on Iwo Jima gave some cover for infantrymen, but were almost impassable for vehicles.**

OPERATION "DETACHMENT", IWO JIMA

LEFT: **The commanding view from Mount Suribachi. The total absence of cover on the beach area gives an idea of the daunting task facing the assault force on Iwo Jima. Note that the steep beach gradient necessitated LSTs to maintain "ahead" power.**

In the amphibious assembly area, vessels suffered considerably from concealed Japanese artillery while, at sea, supporting 5th Fleet warships were being attacked by kamikaze aircraft. The carriers, providing all air support, were particularly favoured targets, USS *Bismarck Sea* (CVE-95) being sunk and the veteran USS *Saratoga* (CV-3)

crippled for three months by five hits within three minutes. The final outcome on Iwo Jima was never in doubt, US forces had attacked in overwhelming strength. Nonetheless, US forces suffered some 7,000 fatalities, 900 of them naval. The Japanese lost 21,000, and some 200 were captured alive.

LEFT: **A barren cinder-covered heap overlooked by the imposing spectre of Mount Suribachi. The objective of the assault was the command of two strategic airfields. This swamped LVT (A) (4) is lying alongside a Japanese wreck and the general debris at the end of an amphibious landing.**

ABOVE: **USS _Bunker Hill_ was struck by two kamikaze aircraft, which caused some 400 dead and missing.** LEFT: **Task Force 58 included 17 aircraft carriers. To counter this force, the Japanese were forced to use mass kamikaze attacks.**

# Operation "Iceberg", Okinawa

Okinawa is a large Pacific island, some 97km/60 miles in length and around 23km/14 miles wide. The southern half is rolling countryside, supporting the bulk of the then 450,000 indigenous population. The northern half is ruggedly mountainous. Only 563km/350 miles from the Japanese mainland, Okinawa was required for the operation of heavy bombers and as an assembly area and springboard for the planned invasion of Japan.

Operation "Iceberg" was never intended as a surprise attack, for several large airfields were within range. The task of aircraft from Mitscher's 5th Fleet carriers was to wear down enemy strength beforehand, even before it was known that massed kamikaze (suicide) attacks were planned. Several days of minesweeping preceded the first landing, where the offshore archipelago of the Kerama Retto had been captured as a forward emergency fleet base. The final six days before the main landing, on April 1, were devoted to heavy naval bombardment.

The amphibious operation followed a, by now, near-standard procedure that varied only to take into account local topographical differences. The assault, in the south-west, was on a 10km/6 mile front and adjacent to two major airfields.

ABOVE: **A medium-calibre coast defence gun spiked by the invaders. There were many such hidden bunkers built by the Japanese on Okinawa.** LEFT: **The deep and soft volcanic sand, which made up the steep beach on Okinawa, caused serious problems for the first wave of the attacking US Marines. Vehicles could not negotiate the beach until later in the operation, after metal matting had been laid.**

OPERATION "ICEBERG", OKINAWA

ABOVE: **The island of Okinawa was in the main very rocky. The landscape was totally unlike that of the coral atolls or the volcanic island of Iwo Jima.**

Against negligible opposition, the leading LCI (G) support craft moved through the anchored bombardment ships, approaching the beach in line abreast, followed by patrol craft marshalling the lines of following LVTs.

The leading line of the turreted and armoured LVT (A) was followed at strict six-minute intervals by five lines of standard ramp-equipped, troop-carrying LVTs. All cleared any obstructing reefs and landed the main assault waves within 30 minutes. Next were LSMs carrying Sherman tanks, then LCIs with follow-up infantry.

By the end of "L-Day", over 50,000 troops were ashore, virtually without loss. Occupying the island, however, would take until June 22, by which time 7,600 US troops would have been killed, together with 4,900 seamen lost in 368 ships sunk or damaged by air attack. No less than 131,000 Japanese troops died in the ferocious fighting.

ABOVE: **The great strength of the LVT was the ability to land troops beyond the vulnerable beach zone.** BELOW: **Initial waves hit the beach on time at 08:30, finding little direct opposition. By 16:00, some 50,000 troops were ashore, and the operation had proceeded with deceptive ease.**

# DUKW

ABOVE: **A supply depot on the Normandy beachhead a day after the landings on June 6, 1944. DUKW vehicles were also used to move troops and supplies inland. They were truly versatile amphibians, and remained in service after World War II.**

Although not a vessel, the DUKW was to become a vital element in any amphibious force, and one of the most useful vehicles in World War II.

The type was the brainchild of a civilian engineer Roger W. Hofheims, whose first project had been the Aqua-Cheetah. This was an amphibious vehicle powered by a mid-mounted Ford V8 engine driving all four wheels by chains. In later versions Dodge WC axles were used. Although improved, the vehicle was not accepted by the US Army.

The concept of an amphibious truck was taken up by the National Defense Research Committee (NDRC) and a prototype ordered from General Motors Corporation (GMC)

and boat designers Sparkman & Stephens. The vehicle was initially built on the AFKWX353 military truck chassis with the body designed by Roderick Stephens Jr.

In October 1942, an order was placed for 2,000 of the type to be built on the GMC CCKW353, with the amphibious version being coded as DUKW (D: 1942, U: amphibian, K: all-wheel drive, W: dual rear axles). Almost immediately it was named "Duck" by US troops.

The vehicle was first used at New Caledonia, March 1943, and again for Operation "Torch". Later in 1943, the British Eighth Army deployed 230 DUKWs for the landings

ABOVE: **First used in the Pacific at Kwajalein, New Caledonia, the DUKW, like the LVT, could negotiate offshore reefs. Here, as cargo carriers, the vehicles are coming ashore directly from transport ships. Capable of carrying 2 tons of cargo, the DUKW was described by US Admiral Turner as "the Army's most important contribution to the technique of amphibious warfare".**

ABOVE AND RIGHT: **Two DUKWs could be linked, providing the necessary buoyancy and platform to support a 10-ton vehicle. Vehicle wheels were guided in two narrow and shallow ramps.**

on Sicily. The type was used to ferry troops and supplies from transport ships to the beach. Once a beachhead had been established DUKWs were then used to move supplies inland.

Over 2,000 DUKWs were used for the Normandy landings on June 6, 1944. The vehicles were to transport 3,500,000 tons of supplies and equipment into France and Belgium between June 1944 and July 1945.

A total of 21,147 of the type were built and many were to remain in service with the armies of the USA, Canada, the UK and the USSR for many years after World War II. Further vehicles were supplied to the postwar armies of France, the Netherlands, Belgium and West Germany.

BELOW: **DUKWs shared the weakness of early assault craft for, lacking ramps, heavily equipped troops were required to leap 1.8m/6ft. Like an LCVP, a DUKW could be fitted within an LCM (3), or it could easily be carried under davits.**

LEFT: **The approach to Inchon was through poorly charted mudflats, subject to a 11m/36ft tidal range. Therefore, very large numbers of standard and armoured LVTs were used in addition to LCVPs and only eight LSTs.**

# Operation "Chromite", Inchon, Korea

Freed from 35 years of Japanese domination, Korea was divided post-war into a communist North and a democratic South. The latter, with only nominal defence forces, but allied to the United States, was suddenly invaded by North Korea in overwhelming strength on June 25, 1950.

Lately Supreme Commander, South West Pacific, General Douglas MacArthur was now effectively ruling Japan as C-in-C, US Army of Occupation. With the United National Security Council's condemnation of the North Korean action, MacArthur was created C-in-C of the newly reactivated US Eighth Army. Elements were quickly mobilized to assist South Korean forces but, no longer battle-hardened, they performed poorly. Within weeks, all were confined to a small pocket around the south-eastern port of Pusan. The US military moved urgently, meanwhile, to reactivate seasoned reservists, "mothballed" ships, aircraft and armour.

Despite vociferous doubters, MacArthur insisted once again that his policy should be to attack the enemy by surprise, rather than dissipate reinforcements in holding and developing the Pusan pocket. He impressed upon US Chiefs of Staff that the North Koreans, while fanatical to their cause, had no combat experience or any knowledge of manoeuvre warfare. Ninety per cent of their strength, he said, was concentrated around the Pusan perimeter, where their prime intention was devoted to pushing the defending forces into the sea.

While the Eighth Army was still able to hold the perimeter, MacArthur intended to make an amphibious landing over 161km/100 miles distant at Inchon on the west coast. From here the South Korean capital, Seoul, could quickly be recaptured, whereupon the two forces would break out and link up. With lines of communication already extended, the North Koreans would now find themselves cut off and, MacArthur stated, would panic.

Inchon, however, was a difficult objective, situated at the head of miles of river channels that wound tortuous routes through vast mudflats subject to tidal ranges of up to 11m/36ft and 5-knot currents. Approaching LSTs required 8.8m/29ft of water, which immediately determined both the date and time. The situation was urgent.

Commanding the immediate approaches to Inchon is the island of Wolmi. Following three days of air and naval bombardment, and a final attack from three, rocket-firing LSMs,

ABOVE: **Because Inchon was in occupied "friendly" territory, the 45-minute pre-landing naval bombardment had to be very precisely targeted on the docks area.**

LEFT: **Four LSTs beached at low water. Men and equipment were being loaded on to Red Beach one day after the initial landing.**

the 500-man garrison was overcome by a somewhat improvised force of three APDs, 17 LCVPs and three tank-carrying LCUs, launched from a single LSD. Just 20 US Marines were injured.

One tide, and a necessary six hours later, the main landing was staged at Inchon. The main landing depended upon eight ageing LSTs, lately operated by Japanese crews, the only vessels that could be deployed in the time available.

As Inchon was occupied "friendly" territory, the 45-minute preliminary bombardment had to be precisely targeted on the port area in order to minimize civilian casualties. The "beaches" were bounded by stone seawalls up to 4.6m/15 feet in height, major obstructions to the US Marine-laden LVTs and LCUs launched from LSDs. One LST hit the wall so hard that it was breached, allowing troops to disembark. Further breaches in the seawalls were made by using explosive charges.

Toward evening, mist, smoke and drizzle hastened the darkness. Fortunately, resistance was light, for all LSTs had to remain aground until the following tide. With the dawn, Allied air superiority was asserted and reinforcements came ashore. Within days, the UN main forces had linked up and, its spirit broken, the North Korean Army had begun a rapid withdrawal back to the security of the north.

MacArthur's gamble, his total faith in his own judgement and in the qualities of his remaining veterans of World War II, totally changed the course of the war, although, at this stage, it was very far from being decided. Following World War II, several senior military figures had predicted that amphibious warfare was outmoded. Inchon changed all that and a service that had come to be neglected gained a new recognition.

ABOVE: **The enormous tide range is clearly illustrated in this image of stranded landing craft.** RIGHT: **A McDonnell FH2-H Banshee flying over Korea, 1952. The type served with the US Navy and the US Marine Corps first as an escort fighter for US bombers, then for ground attack and photographic reconnaissance.**

# Operation "Musketeer", Suez

For the greater part of a century, the Suez Canal had functioned largely under Anglo-French control. In July 1956, however, the Egyptian president, General Gamal Nasser, unilaterally announced its nationalization, an action that brought the British and French governments to plan military action to effect not only the canal's recovery but also probable régime change in Egypt. In order to intervene in a manner that world opinion would accept as legitimate, a devious pact was agreed with Israel, whereby the latter would first attack Egypt. Pleading the "international importance" of the waterway, a joint Anglo-French ultimatum would then demand a ceasefire, to be followed immediately by forces of these nations moving in to "safeguard" the zone immediately bordering the canal.

An amphibious assault over the beaches fronting Port Said (at the canal's northern entrance) would coincide with British and French parachute drops to seize vital airfields

and key bridges. Reinforcements and heavy equipment would follow up immediately through captured Egyptian airfields and port facilities.

The British Parachute Brigade had not conducted recent drops, nor had the Royal Marine Commando Brigade practised amphibious landing. For the one there were insufficient transport aircraft, and the other a shortage of landing craft. Much of the equipment was from reserves "mothballed" at the end of World War II.

Recommissioning, assembly and specialized training took time (the French had to recall their only LSD from the Far East). This meant that the operation, following several revisions, could not be undertaken before November, 1956. The whole undertaking was politically driven. The physical scale and protracted time frame made both governments'

LEFT: **Blockships scuttled by the Egyptians to block the entrance to the Suez Canal at Port Said, photographed from a Royal Navy aircraft.**

ABOVE: **Not yet a well-practised exercise, troop and equipment movements on the flight deck on HMS *Ocean* appeared disorganized.** BELOW: **French troops in LVT (4), patrolling the deserted town of Port Fuad. All Allied vehicles were painted with a white "H" identifying letter.**

ABOVE: **Westland S-55 Whirlwind helicopters on the deck of HMS *Theseus*. A French Navy hospital ship can be seen in the background.**

intentions abundantly clear and world opinion became increasingly hostile, a situation skilfully exploited by government-controlled Radio Cairo.

The landing beaches had a very shallow slope so LSTs would need port facilities to discharge. The first wave, which went ashore at 04:50 on November 6 were embarked in 16 LVTs, dating from World War II, all that was available. Fortunately, opposition was limited for the second wave of LCAs (many of them ancient LCA [1]), grounded some distance out. This left the commandos to wade ashore before crossing a wide, open beach. The four LCTs that followed had to offload Centurion tanks into 1.5m/5ft of water. Quickly captured, however, the adjacent harbour basin permitted follow-up LCTs and LSTs to discharge at the quayside. Owing to the proximity of the civil population, only carefully controlled and very limited gunfire support from destroyers could be employed.

The US Marine Corps had been investigating the use of helicopters for the rapid insertion of spearhead forces, the technique being termed "Vertical Envelopment". Two British light fleet carriers thus joined the invasion fleet with a helicopter force embarked and with the intention of putting theory into practice. To the force commanders, however, the lift capacity did not match the anticipated opposition. The assault tasks were

allocated, successfully, to paratroops. A half-battalion-sized commando was, nonetheless, flown ashore within 90 minutes, with the carriers a distant 16km/10 miles offshore.

Although some Egyptian positions resisted, Allied forces were well supported by carrier aircraft. These along with aircraft operating from Cyprus, destroyed most of the Egyptians' Soviet-built aircraft in pre-emptive strikes against airfields.

Major crossings secured, armoured forces quickly headed out of Port Said and down the canal, already littered with blockships. International public opinion, led by the USA, had almost immediately called upon the British and French governments to desist. The British War Cabinet's resolve to continue was quickly broken, the French having to follow suit.

Committed to war by their politicians, and now disgusted to be let down by them, British and French forces ceased fire at 12:00 on November 7, barely 30 hours after the first landing. Operation "Musketeer" had been militarily successful, resulting in something of a renewal of Britain's run-down amphibious warfare capabilities.

ABOVE: **Peace observers from the United Nations Organization (UNO) arriving in Port Said on November 14, 1956, to supervise the front at El Cap.**

LEFT: **USS Cabildo (LSD-16) carried 5,500 troops of the 9th Marine Amphibious Brigade to An Thuang.**

# Operation "Starlite", Vietnam

Much of the amphibious warfare in Vietnam was carried out in its many muddy creeks. From time to time operations inland were integrated with over-the-beach landings staged by the Amphibious Ready Group (ARG) of the 7th Fleet, which transported units of the Marine Special Landing Force (SLF).

Although US Marine Corps (USMC) advisors had served with Vietnamese regular forces since 1955, it was only in March 1965 that USMC units were established ashore to counter growing Viet Cong (VC) influence.

The operation was launched on August 17, 1965 by 5,500 troops of the 9th Marine Amphibious Brigade (MAB) made up of the 2nd Battalion, 4th Marines; 3rd Battalion, 4th Marines; 3rd Battalion, 3rd Marines; and 3rd Battalion, 7th Marines.

Not yet fully appreciating that its strength lay in guerrilla warfare, the VC had formed the 1st Regiment, which, estimated at some 1,500, was located near Chu Lai. Intelligence indicated that its objective was 3rd MAB although, considering US military superiority in mobility and firepower, this was a risky strategy .

With Operation "Starlite", US forces suddenly took the initiative, exploiting the enemy's tendency to view a coastal peninsula as a position of strength. In this case, the enemy was based in an area of some 10 x 5km/6 x 3 miles. If the VC felt that the seaward flank was unassailable, however,

ABOVE: **USS Galveston (CL-93/CLG-3) was positioned offshore to provide any required supporting gunfire.**
RIGHT: **A Sampan of the US Navy's 15 Junk Division, which operated in South Vietnam waters, alongside a locally crewed Sampan. These vessels were intercepted to stop the supply of ammunition or other supplies to Viet Cong forces.**

LEFT: **The LVTE-1 version of the "Amtrac" was used for the first time on Operation "Starlite". The toothed-plough on the front of the vehicle was used to dig up mines and other explosives buried in the beach.**

they had overlooked the 7th Fleet which, on August 18, put a Battalion Landing Team (BLT) at regiment strength over the beach on the left flank of the VC positions.

A second BLT was landed by helicopter over three landing zones (LZ) to block the routes inland, while a third group used LVTs to cross the river that marked the right flank of VC positions. The light artillery fire from elements of 3rd Battalion, 12th Marines was augmented by naval support fire, available at any point along the coast, while carrier-based USMC air support flew unchallenged above. The VC forces were trapped and, over the next six days, would lose nearly 1,000 fighters, a fatality "exchange rate" of over 25:1.

In a bloody lesson, the Viet Cong learned to contain over-confidence and to avoid the sort of pitched battle that greatly favoured the US military tactics.

ABOVE: **Troops of the 9th Marine Amphibious Division landing on An Thuong beach from an LVT vehicle.** BELOW: **Viet Cong prisoners awaiting transport by USMC helicopter to the rear area for interrogation.**

BELOW: **Aircraft of the US Navy and US Marine Corps were used to attack the beach prior to the landing, and later for air support.**

# Operation "Corporate", Falklands

The Falklands was very much a tale of two landings: one amphibious operation secured the islands, another regained them. Beset by civil unrest, the military junta in control of the Argentine Government decided to refocus hostile opinion on to a universally popular cause, that of occupying the distant Falkland Islands, claimed (as the Malvinas) since 1833.

Some 402km/250 miles from mainland Argentina, the Falklands are nearly 322km/200 miles across. The group is formed from many islands, all rugged and with deep sea inlets. Most of their area is concentrated in the East and West Falklands, separated by the wide Falkland Sound. Population is sparse, settlements and roads almost non-existent. Incorporating Government House and the islands' main airfield, the capital, Port Stanley, is at the eastern extremity of East Falkland.

British military presence usually stood at the strength of one Royal Marine platoon. In April 1982, it was being relieved, so two platoons, totalling 69 men, were available.

With their national airline providing the islands' only air link, Argentine intelligence was well served. General Galtieri, president and Army C-in-C, decided wisely to act with minimum force but in overwhelming strength. For this the 700-strong 2nd Marine Infantry Battalion sufficed, embarked with their 19 US-supplied LVTs in the only available LST and two transports.

Port Stanley is located on the central inlet of three parallel sea inlets, and can be approached from any direction. During the night of April 1/2, 1982, a destroyer landed 50 Argentine Special Forces personnel some 3.2km/2 miles south of Port Stanley. These split, one group attacking the empty Royal Marine barracks to the west of the town, the other simultaneously surrounding Government House. Following a covert reconnaissance conducted by a submarine party, the main landing was made to the north of Port Stanley. Troops in the LVTs stopped only to secure the airfield before moving on to approach Port Stanley from the east.

ABOVE: **RAF Chinook helicopters were too heavy for the decks of the LPD, and usually remained at the hover when loading supplies to be moved ashore.**

ABOVE: **Following the well-proven US Marine Corps dictum of surprise, British forces landed at San Carlos Water without opposition.** LEFT: **To move the troops of the invasion force, the British government requisitioned a number of civilian ships. SS *Canberra*, a P&O liner, was used to transport No. 4 Commando, 3 Commando Brigade, Royal Marines to the Falkland Islands.**

LEFT: **HMS** *Plymouth*, **a Type 12 frigate, on fire and badly damaged after being hit by four bombs during an air attack by Argentine aircraft. A Type 21 frigate, HMS** *Avenger*, **is close by, and Royal Marines are moving in an LCM (9) to provide rescue for the crew of the damaged ship.**

Following reports of darkened vessels offshore, the Royal Marines had already concentrated around Government House and the town's eastern approaches. At each location a brisk exchange of fire saw the invaders take casualties. The Argentines, however, adhered closely to their "minimum force" orders, and warships available for gunfire support were not required. At 09:25, with the situation hopeless, Governor Rex Hunt ordered a ceasefire. Following the well-planned operation the Argentine flag was at last raised over the renamed *Islas Malvinas*. Transports were already off-loading heavy equipment

ABOVE: **Flying the traditional "Jolly Roger" flag to indicate a victory, HMSub** *Conqueror* **returning to Faslane, Scotland on July 3, 1982. The nuclear-powered vessel was used to sink the Argentine Navy cruiser** *General Belgrano* **(ex-USS** *Phoenix* **[CL-46]) on May 2, 1982.**

and, within two hours, Lockheed C-130 Hercules transports began to touch down with the first elements of the 25th Infantry Regiment, to become the garrison force.

For months previously, Argentina's increasingly bellicose behaviour in the region had provided numerous "clear warnings", but the British government appears not to have warned President Galtieri informally that any permanent territorial ambitions would be met with summary eviction. The British lack of firm action must be blamed, therefore, for Argentina's escalating boldness.

The government of Margaret Thatcher was riven by disloyalty and division. Whether, like Galtieri, the prime minister relied on the unifying potential of a decision to go to war, or whether she was simply being stubborn, remains a point of debate. Encouraged by support from the UN Security Council and assurances from the First Sea Lord that the Royal Navy could handle the situation, she made the commitment to remove Argentinian forces from the Falklands.

In truth, the Royal Navy had already been considerably weakened by many Defence Reviews, and was due to suffer further. Future cuts were to include the two LPDs, some if not all of the six LSLs and the recently completed carriers. The design of this type had resulted from the obvious shortcomings found at Suez in 1956.

For "measured response" there was no time and the "Task Force" that sailed southward on the longest-range amphibious operation in history (12,874km/8,000 miles) was largely a sequence of ships leaving as available. All were supported by the Royal Fleet Auxiliary (RFA) and a diverse range of Ships Taken Up From Trade (STUFT). The requirement for speed meant they were not combat loaded and the South Atlantic island of Ascension became the base for regrouping and loading.

The British were in two-brigade strength. The 3 Commando Brigade, amphibious-trained, left with the first part of the task force. It was followed by the 5th Infantry Brigade, which had not been trained in amphibious warfare.

The location for an amphibious assault, as fully expected by the Argentines, was to the south-west of Stanley. The actual choice was the unlikely San Carlos Water, 80km/50 miles distant and opening on to Falkland Sound. Beyond surprise, the location had the advantages of being undefended yet easily defensible. The excellent anchorage was surrounded by hills that made the enemy's use of missiles impossible. Inserted special forces had reported no evidence of the area being mined, and the route to Port Stanley was accessible by sea.

Argentina could deploy more, and superior aircraft, but, operating so far from their mainland bases, these could not loiter over the target. This allowed the two British aircraft carriers to establish a tentative local air superiority zone. Transport helicopters, crucial to manoeuvre warfare, were in desperately short supply following the sinking of the MV *Atlantic Conveyor* by two air-launched Exocet missiles.

A critical task for the Royal Navy was to prevent the Argentine fleet from intervening. This was achieved by the ruthless, but logical, sinking of the cruiser ARA *General Belgrano* by HMSub *Conqueror*. Thereafter, fear of nuclear-powered attack submarines kept the enemy's surface ships out of range.

The Argentines did not exploit the vulnerability of long British Sealines of Communication (SLOC) to submarine attack, but their fighter-bombers were a major threat, with

ABOVE: **Although having to follow a predictable flight path, pilots of McDonnell Douglas A4 Skyhawk aircraft of the Argentine Navy were able to stage fast and low bombing runs on British ships.**
LEFT: **In deceptively placid surroundings, close-in under high ground, a large commercial vessel is being unloaded by Westland Sea King helicopters.**

LEFT: **Troops unloading mortar ammunition from a Westland Wessex helicopter of the Royal Navy in preparation for the battle to retake enemy positions.**

frequent and skilful low-level attacks. Airborne Early Warning (AEW) aircraft of the Fleet Air Arm had been scrapped as a government cost-cutting measure. Advance warning of strikes utilized US-supplied intelligence, naval surveillance destroyers and special forces teams located in forward positions.

The combination of Harrier aircraft and Sidewinder air-to-air missiles (AAM) proved lethal to the raiding aircraft but, due to a shortage of war stocks, extra supplies of the missiles needed to be urgently procured from the USA.

On May 21, 3 Commando Brigade landed unopposed at San Carlos Water but had to await the arrival and reorganization of the 5th Brigade. With the British public learning daily of ships lost and damaged, London demanded rapid military success, leading directly to a decisive battle at Goose Green.

The direct thrust by 3 Commando Brigade across East Falkland was complemented by activity of 5th Infantry Brigade along the coastal route. To put the enemy off

balance, part of the latter was shipped up the coast, to Fitzroy in the two LSLs. The enemy had Bluff Cove under observation and air attack soon followed. Apparently unfamiliar with the lessons of history, senior officers had refused to order a rapid disembarkation as first priority. The ensuing air strike was devastating, resulting in the single greatest loss of life to the British in the Falklands campaign.

Under open skies 3 Commando Brigade was also vulnerable to air attack but the Argentines made poor use of the Pucara, an excellent ground-attack aircraft.

Naval gunfire support was widely used, not only in direct support but also to confuse, harass and distract the enemy. Several pinpoint actions were necessary to dislodge the Argentine forces from various hills overlooking Port Stanley and its approaches. This achieved, the outcome of the final battle was never in doubt. On June 14, the British forces took the surrender of over 10,000 Argentine troops.

ABOVE: **HMS *Invincible* off the Falkland Islands, June 12, 1982. On deck are Sea Harrier FRS-1 aircraft of No. 801 and No. 809 Squadron, Fleet Air Arm.**

ABOVE: **HMS *Hermes*, the flagship of the Falklands Fleet. On deck are Harrier GR3s of No. 1 Squadron, Royal Air Force and Sea Harriers of No. 800 Squadron, Fleet Air Arm.**

# The Middle East and current trends

Amphibious warfare came of age with the great operations of World War II which, by 1945, had defined the method to such an extent that doctrine changed little throughout the ensuing Cold War era. While this confrontation contained a real threat, this was outweighed in the West by the realities of restricted defence budgets. The British configured the Royal Navy primarily around a North Atlantic anti-submarine force. Starved of funds, the numbers of amphibious elements gradually shrank. Only the US military maintained an efficient amphibious force. Even the USA, as was evident in the 1950 landing at Inchon, Korea, had to draw on reserves to meet an emergency.

At Suez in 1956, the British used the small number of World War II surplus vessels that remained serviceable. Thanks to considerable ingenuity, and a lack of real opposition, the operation was successful, only to be let down by political pressures. Suez taught the sharp lesson that the world order had changed and that independent action was no longer possible without the approval of the United Nations and/or the USA.

Britain's commitment was to be tested in 1961 when Kuwait, in which Britain had enormous investment, was threatened with immediate invasion by the military dictatorship in neighbouring Iraq. Despite an agreement to underwrite Kuwait's defence, Britain could not move in a deterrent force for fear of appearing "aggressive". This was precisely what was required, as Iraq could mount an occupation of Kuwait in a matter of hours.

Warlike threats, however, had continued for so long that the British were able to make preparatory moves, although even the capacity to deploy a reinforced brigade group involved almost world-wide repositioning. When the Emir of Kuwait was finally persuaded to request assistance it was thus assembled quickly. Lack of suitable vessels saw troops needing to be flown in. Transport Command (RAF), immediately overstretched, had to charter commercial aircraft. It was also quickly discovered that otherwise friendly states, fearful of appearing partial, would vacillate over the question of rights to over-fly their territory.

ABOVE: **USS *San Antonio* (LPD-17) with USS *Carter Hall* (LSD-50) and guided missile destroyer USS *Roosevelt* (DDG-80) transiting the Atlantic Ocean on September 6, 2008.** LEFT: **A McDonnell Douglas AV-8B of the US Marine Corps approaching to land on USS *Essex* (LHD-2) during an exercise at Sasebo, Japan, on February 5, 2007.**

ABOVE: **Oil-funded states have no need for sophisticated weapons industries; military equipment and technology is purchased to meet a perceived level of threat.** LEFT: **An LVTP (7) launching from the docking well of a US Navy LPD.**

In 1990, Iraqi forces did overrun Kuwait, further threatening Saudi Arabia. This aggression triggered an immediate UN Security Council Resolution, allowing the USA to move significant strength into Saudi Arabia.

While leading command elements were flown in, using the by-now available Lockheed C-5 Galaxy and Lockheed C-141 Starlifter transport aircraft, the US Navy was able to quickly deploy the new Amphibious Ready Groups (ARG). Covered by a carrier strike group, an ARG was centred on a 30,000-ton helicopter assault ship (LHA) supported by an LSD, an LPD and two LSTs. Each ARG is capable of lifting a battalion-size Marine Expeditionary Unit (MEU). The rapid compilation of a full, multi-battalion Marine Expeditionary Force (MEF) was facilitated by the availability of fully loaded, pre-positioned ships, from bases in the Indian Ocean.

Such massive coalition military forces had been concentrated ashore, that the counter-attack became, essentially, a land campaign. The amphibious forces remained offshore as a floating reserve, but staged flanking strikes against the Iraqi forces. Such a continuous threat tied down considerable numbers of enemy troops. One reason for keeping these ships offshore was the heavy damage caused by mines to two valuable ships, an LPH and a CG. These incidents were a sobering reminder of how even such basic weaponry can threaten the most complex of sophisticated, multi-function ships.

ABOVE: **HMS *Albion* with HMS *Ocean* on manoeuvres. In 2020, *Albion* embarked on a unique deployment named Littoral Response Group eXperimental (LRG(X)) which included use of experimental unmanned aerial drones and autonomous vehicles for logistical and intelligence gathering purposes.**

With the collapse of the USSR and the end of the Cold War, fleets of the navies in the West had to reassess their amphibious capability and even fight government to maintain a force. The somewhat vague concept of the "international war on terror" filled the vacuum with navies moving from hi-tech ocean warfare to intervention strategy, with emphasis on home-waters warfare, while maintaining the ability to move complete military units at short notice. Joint expeditionary and carrier strike groups, carrying battalion, even brigade-sized forces, have thus replaced the earlier battle groups. This may yet change, with China and India seeking to be identified as regional military powers.

LEFT: **Major fleets have invested heavily in specialist amphibious vessels for intervention-type warfare. Two LCACs of the US Navy are shown here operating from a Wasp-class amphibious assault ship.**

# A Directory of Landing Ships

Where landing craft were, in general, smaller, open-topped vessels, designed to take the ground in the final phase of an amphibious operation, landing ships were essential to the preliminary moves of transporting troops and equipment to the actual location. Landings during World War II were often mounted from considerable distance, for instance from the US West Coast directly to the western Pacific, or the US East Coast to operations in the Mediterranean.

Stripped of pre-war luxury, passenger liners were converted to move previously unimaginable numbers of troops. Other ships, loaded with assault craft, moved troops to the exact point at which they were required. Dock ships were developed to transport sufficient numbers of assault craft.

Most landing ships were not intended to beach, but the LST was an exception. The vessel carried armour, vehicles and troops. Not only were small craft and amphibious vehicles carried but the type was used as a platform for their repair. The LST was converted for many other roles. The LST and the later LPD were to provide the means for a post-war revolution in the transport by sea of heavy military loads. Many of these vessels are detailed in this chapter.

LEFT: With the end of the Cold War, amphibious warfare has assumed a greater importance with the world's navies. This Royal Navy assault group led by HMS *Ocean* includes a tanker, store ship and anti-air/submarine escort.

# Landing Ship, Tank, Mark 2 (LST [2])

LST production in the USA began with a British requirement for 200 "Atlantic Tank Landing Craft", dated January 1942. Redesignated Landing Ship, Tank, Mark 2 (LST [2]) to differentiate the type from the British Maracaibo type (a converted oil tanker), the basic specification was progressed into a practical design by the renowned marine architect bureau of Gibbs & Cox. President Roosevelt considered specialist landing craft unnecessary but, just one month after the placement of the above order, the retired admiral overseeing the Lend-Lease Program advised the Chief of Naval Operations (CNO), Admiral Ernest J. King, of the

crucial requirement for the type in the future. With Japan just completing the conquest of the Far East, the LST order had, by June 1942, been increased to 390 vessels. By August 1945 it would have exceeded 1,150.

The general British requirement had been for a vessel of some 91.5m/300ft in length, able to carry 20 medium tanks and to cross the Atlantic. As designed, all were some 8.54m/28ft longer at 100m/327ft 9in. Box-shaped, with a long, rectangular-sectioned midbody and tightly rounded bilges, all had bluff bows with clamshell doors backed by a hinged ramp, lowered for cargo access. The tank deck was

located just above the load waterline and, as it was closed-off at the after end, vehicles were both loaded and unloaded through the bow doors.

The open upper deck was also used to carry wheeled transport. On the first 530 built, upper deck access was by a basic elevator. Later vessels had a rather steep, folding ramp, with the access opening covered by a hatch. Earlier LSTs had a vehicle deck ventilation system which required ten cylindrical trunks, protruding from and obstructing the upper deck. In later vessels these were removed, leaving space sufficient to carry an LCT (5) or (6) on skids or, alternatively, a wooden deck for the

ABOVE: **The prototype of the US Navy's LST. Very high sides to the hull combined with shallow draught, two small-diameter propellers and moderate-sized rudders made the vessel difficult to steer.** RIGHT: **Five of the 15 post-war LST-1156 class on exercise. Four maintain alignment with forward power, the nearest appearing to be reversing off. Controllable-pitch propellers removed the requirement for stern anchors.**

operation of light observation aircraft. Superstructure was minimal, and the diesel engines, housed in machinery spaces below the tank deck did not require a funnel. Twin propellers and rudders were located within the tunnel formed by protective skegs.

Steering, however, was rarely better than unpredictable. In ballast, this was worsened by the vessel's high sides which caught the wind, and the relatively low power of the locomotive-type diesel engines.

To be able to beach in the shallowest-possible water, draught was critical. Matching the natural slope of a beach, the draught aft was greater than that forward. For stability, sea-going draught was considerably increased with water ballast, pumped

out prior to beaching. With a considerable beam and (usually) low centre of gravity, the LST had a high degree of stability, but with a rapid, lurching roll, which made securing cargo difficult. To assist in refloating after beaching, a stern anchor and winch were fitted as standard. Along either side, suspended from the underside of the upper deck, were spaces used for troop accommodation. This proved to be a bonus, which allowed the carrying of two LCVPs, under davits, to be increased to four, then to six.

Many LSTs were fitted with heavy, often unauthorized, armament. On the stern was a single 3in gun, elsewhere up to seven 40mm and/or twelve 20mm cannon could be mounted.

ABOVE: **As with so many LSTs, 733 had a useful service life of barely two years, during which time the vessel had no real refit, being kept running by a combination of skill and ingenuity by the crew.**

LSTs were not used in action until early 1943, but quickly proved to be versatile. To enable the vessel to be beached further from the shoreline when required, modular pontoon units could be secured against the hull sides. These, once released, were either self-propelled or linked to form a causeway. In the Pacific campaign the tank deck could be loaded with LVTs, to be floated off over the bow ramp. LSTs carried every type of cargo, some being converted to forward-area hospital ships and others equipped with emergency repair facilities.

ABOVE: **"Drying out" could impose enormous strains on the hull of an LST if the beach was less than flat. While it solved the problem of a short ramp, the beach gradient could still be too steep.**

## Landing Ship, Tank (2)

**Displacement:** 1,625 tons (light); 2,365 tons (beaching); 4,080 tons (loaded)
**Length:** 96m/316ft (wl); 100m/327ft 9in
**Beam:** 15.3m/50ft 2in
**Draught (beaching):** 0.94m/3ft 1in (forward); 2.89m/9ft 6in (aft)
**Draught (loaded):** 2.4m/8ft (forward); 4.37m/14ft 4in (aft)
**Armament:** 1 x 3in gun, 7 x 40mm (2x2, 3x1), 12 x 20mm (12x1)
**Machinery:** 2 diesel engines, 2 shafts
**Power:** 1,343kW/1,800bhp for 10.8–12 knots
**Fuel:** 590 tons oil
**Endurance:** 16,560km/9,000nm at 9 knots
**Protection:** 13mm/0.5in splinter protection
**Complement:** 211–229
**Capacity:** Up to 1,900 tons distributed load on tank deck

# Landing Ship, Dock (LSD), Ashland class

ABOVE: **The width of the docking well of USS *Gunston Hall* is determined by the designed load capacity. To avoid excess stability, the hull narrows significantly at the waterline, resulting in a pronounced knuckle.**

Included in the British list of required ships of January 1942 (known to the US Government as the "1799 Program" from the number of hulls involved) were ten large vessels of an entirely new concept. The British were still thinking in terms of invading occupied Europe but, in order to use heavy armour in such action, the LST or LCT would be required. As the low speed of these types would put any attacking force in jeopardy a larger type of 17-knot vessel was specified, capable of carrying pre-loaded landing craft. The latter would be too large to be launched and recovered by davit or crane, so a "float-on, float-off" approach was proposed. In essence, the resulting ship would be a self-propelled floating dock.

The British draft specification was for a "TLC Carrier", reflecting both use and likely size, but the US Navy Bureau of Ships (BuShips), with a view to US military requirements, redrew the design around a docking well to accommodate 16 of the early type LCMs, then referred to as "tank lighters". With each LCM pre-loaded with a tank or support vehicle, an LSD would be able to lift 25 per cent of a full US Army tank battalion. Gibbs &

Cox again completed the final production design, now able to carry alternative loads of 16 LCMs, three US-pattern LCT (5), or two of the larger British LCT (3). A removable spar deck was added for stowage of "second-wave" vehicles.

ABOVE: **The relationship between an LSD and a floating dock is clearly shown in this picture of USS *Oak Hill* (LSD-7). The docking well extends to beneath the bridge structure.**

In these early LSDs, the docking well extended forward as far as width permitted. All accommodation, including that for crews of military vehicles, was placed above. Bordering the docking well, sided casings extended

from amidships to the square-shaped transom. An almost full transom wide, bottomed-hinged gate closed off the docking well. The gate was operated by two winches. Spanning the docking well was the removable spardeck, referred to as a "superdeck". A 35-ton crane was mounted on each side.

In the sea-going condition, the docking well, (i.e. dock bottom) was the freeboard deck and, thus, situated above the load waterline. To float cargo out, it was necessary to ballast the ship down to put sufficient water over the well deck. With levels equalized, the stern gate was lowered. In calm weather it was permissible to lower the gate while in the unballasted condition, allowing LVTs to drive straight off, using the gate as a ramp.

Although the LSD concept presented naval architects with some challenges, stability at all stages of flooding-down proved to be more than adequate.

Flooding-down took around 1¹/₂ hours and pumping-out around 2¹/₂ hours. To prevent a difficult motion, excess stability was reduced by adding pronounced flare to the lower hull. Ballasted the LSD had a slight stern-down trim, drawing nearly 9.46m/31ft aft, so propellers and rudders were partially recessed into the hull to reduce the danger of damage.

Steam turbine propulsion was originally specified but, because of a shortfall in manufacturing, the first group of eight LSDs were fitted with Skinner- patent "Uniflow" reciprocating steam engines. Other than in machinery, all 27 LSDs were essentially similar. Only four, numbered LSD 9 to 12, were eventually allocated to the British.

The LSD proved the ideal vessel for US military in Pacific operations, which relied on the use of large numbers of LVTs. The Casa Grande class (LSD-13 to

ABOVE: **USS** *Oak Hill* **(LSD-7). The large gate to the docking well is clearly visible.**

LSD-27) were equipped with double-level superdecks, permitting the carriage of LCMs on the well deck, with over 90 LVTs (or even DUKWs) above. First of class, USS *Ashland* (LSD-1) commissioned in June 1943, and with the USS *Belle Grove* (LSD-2) were fully worked-up for the forthcoming Operation "Galvanic", Gilbert Islands, in November 1943. At Makin, the USS *Belle Grove* (LSD-2) carried LCMs, each pre-loaded with a medium tank and it is recorded that all 26 craft were off-loaded in 12 minutes.

LEFT: **USS** *San Marcos* **(LSD-25), a Casa Grande-class vessel, carrying two utility LCVPs amidships. Lacking davits, the LCVPs are handled by the massive 35-ton capacity cranes. Note the spardeck ("superdeck") over the docking well.**

## Landing Ship, Dock (LSD), Ashland class

**Displacement:** 5,910 tons (light); 7,930 tons (loaded, seagoing); 15,530 tons (loaded, ballasted)
**Length:** 138.5m/454ft (wl); 139.6m/457ft 9in (oa)
**Beam:** 22m/72ft 2in
**Draught:** 4.8m/15ft 10in (mean, seagoing); 9.2m/30ft 3in (mean, ballasted)
**Armament:** 1 x 5in gun, 12 x 40mm (2x4, 2x2), 16 x 20mm (16x1)
**Machinery:** Steam turbines, 2 boilers, 2 shafts
**Power:** 5,222kW/7,000shp for 16.5 knots
**Fuel:** 1,500 tons oil
**Endurance:** 13,800km/7,500nm at 15 knots
**Protection:** Limited splinter protection
**Complement:** 326
**Capacity:** 3 loaded LCT (5) or (6), or 2 loaded LCT (3) or (4), or 14 LCMs, or 41 LVTs, or 47 DUKWs

LEFT: **Introduced in 1944, the LSM (R) was designed to saturate enemy beach defences immediately before craft with troops landed. Over 1,000 rockets could be fired within one minute at a fixed range of 4,572m/5,000yd.**

# Landing Ship, Medium (LSM) and Landing Ship, Medium (Rocket) (LSM [R])

With planning for amphibious warfare developing rapidly, requirements arose for more specific types of craft. Building programmes for these and, particularly, the demands for engines, competed with those for other urgently needed types of vessel. Firm production priorities were required.

The Landing Ship, Medium (LSM), of which no less than 350 were ordered between September and November 1943, was one priority. LSTs were proving very successful but, by prioritizing cargo capacity and simplicity, were slow. During a major operation this caused the type to be deployed in separate convoys. The smaller LCT was unsuitable for long sea passages. A speed of 12 knots

was demanded for the new craft, thus necessitating an improved hull shape. It was first designed as an LCT (7) but, in view of its unavoidably larger size, was redesignated as an LSM.

The existing LCT (6) could carry four 32-ton M4A-3 Sherman medium tanks. The dimensions were 36.72 x 9.76m/120ft 4in x 32ft , but range and speed was poor at 1,127km/700 miles and 7 knots.

The new LSM drew considerable uninformed criticism because the slender 62.07 x 10.37m/203ft 6in x 34ft hull, necessary to achieve 12 knots had room to accommodate just one extra Sherman. The vessel thus appeared too large for the task but, in naval ship design, speed is very much a defining

parameter. In addition, the LSM at cruising speed had a respectable range of 5,633km/3,500 miles, invaluable for a Pacific deployment.

Being so much longer, the LSM had to be deeper to keep hull stresses within acceptable limits. One disadvantage was the closed stern, dictating that vehicles loaded and disembarked over the bow ramp. The latter, once stowed, was protected by LST-type bow doors, the stowed height of which required a

BELOW: **The light construction of the type gave rise to some criticism but, during the final 18 months of World War II, more than 550 were delivered.The LSM was a faster vessel than the standard LST.**

high bow profile which was beneficial for seakeeping. The bows were bridged by a short foredeck upon which was a twin 40mm cannon mounting, useful for fire support over the beach. On the starboard side, amidships, the deck supported a narrow but high superstructure. This was two decks deep with an open compass platform at the top, the structure having a distinctive cylindrical shape.

Beneath the tank deck was crew accommodation for over 50 and up to 75 army personnel, mostly vehicle crews. The vessels twin propellers were powered by diesel engines similar to the type used in destroyer escorts and submarines. The LSM was seen as complementary to the rather smaller, troop-carrying LCI (L).

Like other amphibious vessels, the LSM had two significant displacements. One, around 1,100 tons, was a sea-going cargo carrier. To beach, however, the vessel could displace no more than about 740 tons. Thus, considerable water ballast capacity was required to guarantee adequate stability in all conditions. This ballast would be discharged to bring the vessel to beaching trim and displacement.

In September 1944, by which time some 80 LSMs had been delivered, a new role was defined as rocket-firing support craft, LSM (R). Heavy bombardment preceding an assault would be lifted as the first wave approached the beach. The defenders, however, could have survived and been able to rake the beach with

ABOVE: **In the LSM (R) 401 type, of which 36 were built, the design was greatly revised, with ten automatic-loading launchers. The vessels were also named, LSM (R) 527 being called USS St. Joseph River.**

gunfire. By December, the first of over 50 LSM (R) had been built. The vessels were to accompany the first assault wave and to saturate the landing area with a barrage of rocket projectiles to destroy mined areas and obstacles.

LSM (R) were decked over, the vehicle deck being divided into ammunition handling rooms and magazines. Armament varied considerably, with rapid development, culminating in 85 launchers, each mounting 12 projectiles. A 1,000-plus rocket salvo could be discharged in one minute, but a reload took 45 minutes. In addition to automatic weapons, a single 5in naval gun was mounted in the stern.

ABOVE: **On this standard LSM, note the characteristic starboard-side bridge structure and the ramp protruding above the bow doors. The rubbing strake was a necessary later addition.**

## Landing Ship, Medium (LSM)

**Displacement:** 520 tons (light); 1,095 tons (full load); 743 tons (beaching)
**Length:** 62.07m/203ft 6in
**Beam:** 10.52m/34ft 6in
**Draught (full load):** 1.95m/6ft 5in (forward); 2.55mm/8ft 4in (aft)
**Draught (beaching):** 1.07m/3ft 6in (forward); 2.16m/7ft 1in (aft)
**Armament:** 2 x 40mm (1x2), 4 x 20mm (4x1)
**Machinery:** 2 diesel engines, 2 shafts
**Power:** 2,148kW/2,880bhp for 13 knots
**Endurance:** 9,016km/4,900nm at 12 knots
**Protection:** Splinter protection to guns, bridge and pilot house
**Complement:** 58
**Capacity:** 5 medium tanks, or 3 heavy tanks, or 6 LVTs, or 9 DUKWs

# Landing Ship, Vehicle (LSV)

The US Navy used the designator AP for transports (*cf.* British "troopship"), for the movement of troops. More precisely, the APA was an "attack transport", intended to carry troops directly to a combat zone and to be self-contained when unloading. The common distinguishing feature of an AP was the large number of LCVPs, carried under davits and/or on deck.

Early in 1943 (just six months after Operation "Watchtower", the initial amphibious landing on Guadalcanal) two large minelayers and four very similar netlayers, almost complete, were identified as ideal for conversion to APA.

Displacing up to 8,000 tons fully loaded, these were large ships. The minelayers differed somewhat from the netlayers (not least in having a second funnel) but all featured long gallery decks, extending over half the length of the ship and flanking a narrow centreline casing. To facilitate the movement of vehicles from these spaces, a ramp gate was fitted into the wide flat stern.

ABOVE: **USS *Catskill* (LSV-1), originally classified as AP-106, was launched on May 19, 1942.**
LEFT: **The inclusion of a stern ramp made the class effective carriers of both tracked and wheeled amphibious vehicles.**

Because of the vehicle component, the type designator was changed from APA to LSV, although the ships were not designed to be beached. Vehicle capacity proved to be disappointingly small, the gallery decks being low and badly ventilated. Capacities were as follows:

|  | LVT | DUKW | Troops |
|---|---|---|---|
| LSV-1 and 2 | None | 44 | 800 |
| LSV-3 and 4 | 19 | 29 | 880 |
| LSV-5 and 6 | 21 | 31 | 800 |

Without vehicles, around a further 1,000 troops could be accommodated. The ships were valuable in being relatively fast but proved to have limited stability when damaged, resulting in planned defensive armament being considerably reduced.

Only the six were built and, having seen little combat use, survived to serve as support ships in the post-war US fleet.

LEFT: **USS *Montauk* (LSV-6) from the LSV-5 to LSV-6 group converted in October 1944. The vessel retains the original squared-off netlayer bow.**

## Landing Ship, Vehicle (LSV)

**Displacement:** 5,615 tons (light); 7,927 tons (full load)
**Length:** 137.56–138.47m/451–454ft (oa)
**Beam:** 18.3m/60ft
**Draught:** 5.19–5.49m/17–18ft
**Armament:** 3/4 x 5in guns (3/4 x1), 8 x 40mm (4x2), 18/20 x 20mm (18/20 x1)
**Machinery:** Steam turbines, 4 boilers, 2 shafts
**Power:** 8,206kW/11,000shp for 19.5 knots
**Fuel:** 2,020 tons oil
**Endurance:** Not known
**Protection:** Not known
**Complement:** 481

# Amphibious Force Flagship (AGC)

Even before US forces undertook the first amphibious operation in August 1942 the need for a headquarters ship, fitted specifically for overall control was appreciated. The US Navy had inspected HMS *Bulolo* upon completion in June 1942, a visit which highlighted the advantages of equipment space and accommodation when using a merchant ship hull as compared to the cramped conditions aboard even a large warship.

In October 1942, following the inspection, the US Navy allocated three standard C2 hulls, already under construction, for conversion to what were first called "Administrative Flagships",

BELOW: **The first vessel to be built as a Headquarters Ship was USS *Appalachian* (AGC-1). Under the command of Rear-Admiral Richard L. Conolly, the ship was first used during Operation "Flintlock", the assault on Kwajalien, January 31, 1944.**

then "Amphibious Force Flagships" (AGC). The "A" in the designator represented auxiliary status. Not being warships, fitted with no more than defensive armament and with relatively low speed, the vessel would not be used in the course of an operation to act as a regular warship.

The C2s were built over half the length with an extra deck to give more space for senior officers and staff of all forces deployed in the assault. Essential was the detailed plot in the command room and a comprehensive suite of communications with adequate backup equipment. All elements supporting the dynamics of the operation were in continuous two-way contact, so that any delay or complication could be quickly addressed by an appropriate decision direct from command staff. All requests for fire support or close air support were

ABOVE: **This vessel was a passenger liner until 1942, when it became US Army Transport USS *Ancon* (AP-66). On May 8, 1943, USS *Ancon* entered service, after conversion, as an amphibious command ship (AGC-4).**

also actioned through the flagship. Only when the battle situation stabilized were the military headquarters staff move ashore.

A total of 15 AGCs were commissioned during the war, with others still completing. Although most were C2 conversions and were generally known as the Appalachian class, they varied considerably. Indeed, a converted passenger liner USS *Ancon* (AGC-4) was the first of the type to be commissioned in August 1942. Some Attack Transports (APA) were fitted with basic command facilities.

## Amphibious Force Flagship, USS *Appalachian* (AGC-1)

**Displacement:** 7,430 tons (light); 12,800 tons (full load)
**Length:** 140.07m/459ft 3in (oa)
**Beam:** 19.22m/63ft
**Draught:** 7.32m/24ft (maximum)
**Armament:** 2 x 5in guns (2x1), 4/8 x 40mm (2/4x2), 18 x 20mm (18 x1)
**Machinery:** Steam turbines, 2 boilers, single shaft
**Power:** 4,476kW/6,000shp for 16.5 knots
**Fuel:** Oil
**Endurance:** 9,200km/5,000nm at 14 knots
**Protection:** Nominal
**Complement:** 520 (ship) plus 470 (staff)

LEFT: **Unusual features of USS *Henderson* (AP-1) included wide promenade decks to facilitate military drills. Note the foremast rigged much as in sailing ship practice.**

# USS Henderson and Doyen (AP-1 and AP-2)

The US Marine Corps (USMC) is the primary amphibious attack force in the US military, and AP-1 and 2 are significant because they were the first ships designed around integrated USMC formations. Marines operate in self-sufficient tactical units, which require to be transported to, and landed directly at, the point of attack. By definition, therefore, the ships would be the original attack transports.

Approved in 1912, USS *Henderson* (later AP-1) accommodated a USMC regiment of 75 officers and 1,600 other ranks with space for recreation and exercise. Four of the ship's 5in guns could be dismounted for transport ashore on special lighters. Fewer troops

would be carried in winter but stores and a water-distilling plant occupied a large space in the hull.

Hull design concentrated less on speed than on survivability, manoeuvrability and the moderate draught required to work close inshore. Commissioned shortly after the United States entry into World War I, USS *Henderson* was used during the war as a troop transport, and was not tried in the designed role under wartime conditions.

With further such construction denied by Congress, USS *Henderson* was used on various operations between the wars. Only during 1940, on reports of the successful British conversion of four fast Glen Line cargo liners to LSI (L), were

the first similar ships approved for the US Navy. USS *Doyen* (AP-2) (originally named USS *Heywood*) and USS *Feland* (AP-11) became the first purpose-designed attack transports, but did not enter service until 1943. However, numerous other mercantile hulls had already been converted to the role. The ships were unique in having a slipway incorporated in the stern, large enough to launch and recover a tank-carrying LCM (2). The ships were badly overweight, so the tank and LCM were not carried together as part of weight-saving measures. However, sixteen 30ft "landing boats" were carried for the USMC force of 60 officers and 670 other ranks.

ABOVE: **USS *Doyen* (AP-2) was launched in 1918 as SS *City of Baltimore*, and was originally named USS *Heywood* before adopting the name of a cancelled successor to Henderson. Note the unusual counter stern.**

## USS *Doyen* (AP-2)

**Displacement:** 4,500 tons (standard); 6,350 tons (full load)
**Length:** 122m/400ft (wl); 124.75m/409ft (oa)
**Beam:** 17.08m/56ft
**Draught:** 5.29m/17ft 4in (maximum)
**Armament:** 1 x 5in gun, 4 x 3in guns (4x1)
**Machinery:** Steam turbines, 2 boilers, 2 shafts
**Power:** 5,968kW/8,000shp for 19 knots
**Fuel:** Oil
**Endurance:** 18,400km/10,000nm at 16.5 knots
**Protection:** Nominal
**Complement:** 234

LEFT: **USS *Bower* (APD-40) was originally built as a Buckley-class destroyer escort (DE-637) and launched on October 31, 1943. The vessel was converted in 1945 and redesignated on June 25, 1945.**

# Destroyer Transports (APD)

By the late 1930s, the US Marine Corps (USMC) was preparing for the role of capturing forward bases in a Pacific campaign. Some operations would be on a small scale, for which a large transport ship would be unsuitable. The requirement was for a small vessel capable of a fast passage carrying a USMC unit, which could be landed and supported by the ship's guns. Many World War I flush-decked destroyers remained in low-grade reserve and were proposed as suitable for modification.

The prototype conversion was that on USS *Manley* (DD-74), later designated APD-1. The four banks of torpedo tubes were removed and replaced with four sets of davits for "Surf Boats". Also fitted were handling frames for two of the anticipated new landing craft. As passages of only 12 to 24 hours were envisaged, no special facilities were built in for the some 100 Marines to be conveyed.

Exercises showed that longer passages of several days, with troop contingents of 150, plus stores, were possible. Despite the forward boiler space being converted to troop accommodation, sufficient speed could still be developed. "Surf Boats" were replaced by Landing Craft, Ramped (LCP [R]) and the old 4in guns were replaced by the more versatile 3in weapon.

Twenty-six DD vessels were converted to APD before new destroyer escort (DE) hulls became available. No less than 100 Buckley and Rudderrow-class DEs were allocated but not all conversions were actually completed. These were built with a long amidships accommodation deckhouse for 162 Marines. Heavy double davits could each handle two LCVPs. Around 130 tons of cargo could be carried aft, handled by two derricks ("booms") stepped to a lattice-type mast. Typical armament included a 5in gun, three twin 40mm and six 20mm cannon.

Despite the role remaining viable, surviving APDs were scrapped without replacement during the 1960s.

## Destroyer Transport (DE) conversions

**Displacement:** 1,400 tons (standard); 2,130 tons (full load)
**Length:** 91.5m/300ft (wl); 93.33m/306ft (oa)
**Beam:** 11.29m/37ft
**Draught):** 3.86m/12ft 8in (maximum)
**Armament:** 1 x 5in gun, 6 x 40mm guns (3x2)
**Machinery:** Turbo-electric, 2 boilers, 2 shafts
**Power:** 8,952kW/12,000shp for 23.5 knots
**Fuel:** 350 tons oil
**Endurance:** 10,120km/5,500nm at 15 knots
**Protection:** Nominal
**Complement:** 214

ABOVE: **Early APDs were converted from World War I "flush-decked" destroyers. The forward boiler room has here been removed and funnels reduced from four to two. Note the four LCVPs in davits. USS *Barry* (APD-29) was converted from DD-248 in 1944.**

LEFT: **The war-built Andromeda class were completed as either AKA or APA. Both types carried troops, as seen on USS *Centaurus* (AKA-17). Note the heavy cargo mast aft, the LCVPs under davits and one of the two LCMs, just visible forward of the bridge. Also note the paravane cable at the bows.**

# Attack Cargo Ships (AKA)

Attack Transports (APA) and Attack Cargo Ships (AKA) were complementary, one type to accommodate combat troops, the other, equipment. In general, personnel require more space, so APAs were converted mainly from standard C3 hulls, and AKAs from the C2. US Maritime Commission (USMaC) codes defined a C2 as a cargo carrier of 122–137.25m/400–450ft waterline length. A C3 was larger, at 137.25–152.5m/450–500ft.

Urgency dictated the use of available shipping, but it was far from ideal. Designed for maximum capacity and ease of access, cargo spaces were large and open. By naval standards,

which emphasized survivability through watertight compartments, combat cargo ships were considered vulnerable.

To support the Pacific campaign of 1944, the US military joint staff planners requested a massive total of 133 APAs, 53 AKAs and 13 AGCs. Of these, the AKAs fell into five classes of which four – the Arcturus, Andromeda, Tolland and Charleston – had similar overall dimensions. The smaller S4s of the Artemis class were faster and accommodated over 250 troops.

Hold spaces were divided horizontally by two or three decks. By standardizing headroom, problems were created as military equipment became larger.

Across the hatches were stowed the craft by which the cargo was landed. A typical complement was made up of six LCM (6), two LCM (3), 13 LCVPs and one LCPL. To handle these, two tetrapod-type masts were constructed with at least four derricks ("cargo booms") of 30- to 40-ton safe working load. By the end of the war, 55-ton derricks were being trialed.

Although considerably reduced in post-war reserve, the above classes remained in the US Navy's cargo inventory until the mid-1960s.

ABOVE: **USS *Medea* (AKA-31), an Artemis-class vessel, with her decks crowded with troops, probably upon arrival in San Francisco Bay, California, circa late 1945 or early 1946.**

## Attack Cargo Ship (AKA), Andromeda class

**Displacement:** 6,990 tons (light); 13,355 tons (full load)
**Length:** 132.68m/435ft (wl); 140.07m/459ft 3in (oa)
**Beam:** 19.22m/63ft
**Draught:** 7.93m/26ft (mean, full load)
**Armament:** 1 x 5in gun, 8 x 40mm (4x2), 18 x 20mm (18x1)
**Machinery:** Steam turbines, 2 boilers, single screw
**Power:** 4.476kW/6,000shp for 16 knots
**Fuel:** 2,000 tons oil
**Endurance:** 29,450km/16,000nm at 12 knots
**Protection:** Nominal
**Complement:** 368 (war), or 247 (peace)

# Motor Minesweeper (AMS)

As it was general policy to assume that waters within the 183m/100-fathom line would be mined, it is obvious that clearance was a necessary prelude to any amphibious operation.

The Japanese military had not developed sophisticated magnetic mines – but it could never be assumed that they had not. A potential landing beach was as obvious to the defenders as to the attackers. Extended shallow approaches, unswept, could see the valuable transports in the assault fleet anchored miles offshore, increasing the vulnerability of the assault forces, and slowing the follow-up resupply.

Despite the risk of alerting the enemy, therefore, a necessary preliminary was a high-speed sweep of the proposed Transport Area(s) by Destroyer-Minesweepers (DMS). Closer inshore, the very shallow approaches (such as those at Leyte) were swept by Auxiliary Motor Minesweepers (YMS), later called Motor Minesweepers (AMS). These, the Albatross class, were 41.48m/136ft in length. The Pacific Ocean was often found to be of greater hazard than the enemy to the small ships. Sweeping the 18.3m/10-fathom line, a DMS could counter fire from shore batteries with a 5in gun and 40mm cannon. Inshore the AMS mounted a single 3in gun and two Oerlikon 20mm cannon. A destroyer support was always required.

From 1942 the AMSs were built by a wide variety of small shipyards with workers skilled in wooden ship construction. As a result there was a considerable variation in detail. Common to all was the short raised forecastle and heavy, full-length rubbing strake. Some, however, had two funnels, some one and others none. Mainmasts, sometimes with derricks fitted, were optional. All were equipped to sweep magnetic or contact mines.

Following the Korean War, the improved Bluebird class was built to the same basic design.

ABOVE: **Motor Minesweeper USS *Firecrest* (AMS-5), when in service as YMS-192.**

## Motor Minesweeper (AMS), Albatross class

**Displacement:** 270 tons (standard); 350 tons (full load)
**Length:** 41.48m/136ft (oa)
**Beam:** 7.47m/24ft 6in
**Draught:** 2.44m/8ft (maximum)
**Armament:** 1 x 3in gun, 2 x 20mm (2x1)
**Machinery:** 2 diesel engines, 2 shafts
**Power:** 746kW/1,000bhp for 15 knots
**Fuel:** 16 tons oil
**Endurance:** 10,120km/5,500nm at 12 knots
**Protection:** Nominal
**Complement:** 50

LEFT: **USS *Tallahatchie County*, ex-LST-1154, was, with her only steam-powered sister, USS *Talbot County* (LST-1153), converted to an Advanced Aviation Base Ship (AVB) in 1962. Here, the vessel appears to be being used as a landing ship.**

# Landing Ship, Tank (LST), LST-1153 type

After World War II, rapid evolution of new weapons systems made the LST look especially vulnerable. Studies to develop a 20-knot version, however, resulted in a vessel that would be expensive, over-large and no longer expendable.

Two prototype steam turbine-powered variants of the LST-1153 (later Talbot County) type were completed in 1947. The modest increase in speed proved expensive. The new ships were not liked. The steam plant was unreliable due to over complexity, and required more skilled personnel. Endurance was inferior to that of the earlier, diesel-powered LST, and the hull still pounded heavily in a head sea.

Gibbs & Cox were charged with refining the LST-1153 design further, producing in 1951 the LST-1156 (Terrebonne Parish) type. Fifteen of these were built between 1952 and 1954. All had four diesel engines, driving two propeller shafts and, for the first time, controllable-pitch propellers for easier reversing off a beach. Displacement and forward beaching draught again inevitably increased, necessitating a longer ramp. This needed to be strong enough to load a 60- to 75-ton tank (the M60A1 Patton main battle tank weighed 52.6 tons). An internal turntable for moving vehicles was also provided. An additional requirement was

accommodation and facilities for 380 troops to support the embarked vehicles. The increase in length, however, made it possible for 14 knots to be achieved on the same 6,000 bhp engine power.

The Korean War raised a demand for a 17-knot LST. The resulting LST-1171 (De Soto County) type was 15 per cent longer and of nearly 40 per cent greater beaching displacement. No longer cheap or expendable, the LST could be refined no further.

## Landing Ship, Tank, LST-1153 type

**Displacement:** 2,585 tons (light); 3,330 tons (beaching); 5,780 tons (full load)
**Length:** 112.24m/368ft (wl); 117.12m/384ft (oa)
**Beam:** 16.93m/55ft 6in
**Draught (beaching):** 1.09m/3ft 7in (forward); 3.36m/11ft (aft)
**Draught (loaded):** 2.49m/8ft 2in (forward); 4.9m/16ft 1in (aft)
**Armament:** 6 x 3in guns (3x2)
**Machinery:** 4 diesel engines, 2 shafts
**Power:** 4.476kW/6,000bhp for 14 knots
**Fuel:** Oil
**Endurance:** 18,400km/10,000nm at 10 knots
**Protection:** Nominal
**Complement:** 157
**Capacity:** Maximum 1,395 tons distributed load

ABOVE: **Speed and refinement proved to be expensive. Here, USS *Washtenaw County* (LST-1166) is at anchor, loaded and ready to sail from Subic Bay, October 1969. Note also the stacked LCVPs.**

LEFT: **USS *Plymouth Rock* (LSD-29)**, a Thomaston-class LSD, may easily be identified from earlier classes by the staggered funnel arrangement.

# Landing Ship, Dock (LSD), Thomaston class

Vessels deployed for a World War II amphibious operation needed to be organized into fast (15–16 knots) convoys for larger ships and slow (11-knot) convoys for LSTs. Until 1945 this was a necessary inconvenience but the Cold War greatly enhanced threats which resulted in such formations looking highly vulnerable. From 1947, therefore, all new ships had to be designed as an all-20-knot amphibious force.

The design for a replacement LSD was a predictable balance between cost and capability. The vessel was required to transport 21 LCM (6), each of around 17 x 4.3m/56 x 14ft. The welldeck was covered with a light spardeck ("superdeck") and, forward, a temporary mezzanine deck, on which to carry 48 LVTs. This was 13 more than in war-built ships. Alternatively, the spardeck could be used as a helicopter landing deck.

Much sleeker in looks than the utilitarian, war-built predecessor, the eight new ships had three times the engine power, and easily exceeded 23 knots. The engine room was located below the docking well and laid out on the unit principle. The need to exhaust the steam turbines on each side resulted in the characteristic staggered positioning of the funnels.

The area between the funnels was not bridged by the spardeck, allowing the well to be served by the two large cranes. A 7.5-ton capacity gantry crane which spanned the full width also ran the length of the well.

A secondary role for the LSD was in the long-distance transport of smaller warships such as minesweepers or PT boats. The LSD was also used as a temporary dry dock, although facilities for heavy repair were limited.

ABOVE: **USS *Thomaston* (LSD-28).** Most of the 3in gun armament fitted to this class was quickly removed, as it was ineffective against attack by modern aircraft.

## Landing Ship, Dock (LSD), Thomaston class

**Displacement:** 6,880 tons (light); 11,270 tons (full load)
**Length:** 155.55m/510ft (oa); waterline length variable
**Beam:** 25.62m/84ft
**Draught:** 5.8m/19ft (mean, loaded)
**Armament:** 16 x 3in guns (8x2), 16 x 20mm (8x2)
**Machinery:** Steam turbines, 2 boilers, 2 shafts
**Power:** 17,904kW/24,000shp for 23 knots
**Fuel:** Oil
**Endurance:** 23,290km/13,000nm at 10 knots
**Protection:** Nominal
**Complement:** 405
**Capacity:** 21 LCM (6), 48 LVTs, or 2,400 tons cargo load

LEFT: **Simply a modified version of an LSM (R), USS Carronade (IFS-1), launched on May 26, 1953, and commissioned into US Navy service on May 25, 1955, remained the only one built. Rapid series production could be started in an emergency.**

# Inshore Fire Support Ship (IFS)

Although highly valued for close-in fire support, the war-built LSM (R) had limitations, not least in that it took a considerable time to reload between salvoes. Nor was it equipped to pinpoint and neutralize mortar fire, which caused considerable disruption and casualties on the beach.

The US Marine Corps wanted a suitably armed, shallow-draught, manoeuvrable vessel with sufficient protection to attack from a short range. For the designer, this created a clash of priorities in matching shallow draught and limited size with the new overall 20-knot requirement in amphibious warfare vesels. Possible future series

production demanded a simple design, while the cost constrictions imposed saw the concept considerably reduced.

The one-off USS Carronade (IFS-1) was the post-Korean War compromise to the above specification. Although looking superficially like a landing craft, the new classification emphasised a considerable difference. The laws of hydrodynamics conspire against light displacement hulls being driven at high speed and, by accepting a 15-knot maximum for the vessel USS Carronade could be 15 per cent shorter and required only 50 per cent the engine power of a 20-knot equivalent. Hoping for a new, high-

velocity, flat-trajectory gun, the US Marine Corps was probably disappointed in the ship mounting a standard, forward-firing 5in Type 38 gun and two mountings of twin 40mm cannon. The long foredeck, however, carried eight of the new Mk 105 twin rocket launchers each capable of launching six rounds per minute. To support such massive firepower, a 6,000-round magazine was provided, although the lack of depth in the hull did not allow this to be located entirely below normal load waterline.

USS Carronade was stricken from the US Naval Register on May 1, 1973 and sold for scrap September 1, 1974.

LEFT: **USS Carronade (IFS-1) was placed on US Navy reserve on May 31, 1960, after just five years in service. The ship was recommisioned as LFR-1 on January 1, 1969, and served during the Vietnam War as the flagship for Inshore Fire Division 93.**

## Inshore Fire Support Ship, USS *Carronade* (IFS-1)

**Displacement:** 1,040 tons (light); 1,500 tons (full load)
**Length:** 72.59m/238ft (wl); 74.73m/245ft (oa)
**Beam:** 11.9m/39ft
**Draught:** 3.05m/10ft
**Armament:** 8 x launchers, 1 x 5in gun, 4 x 40mm guns (2x2)
**Machinery:** 2 diesel engines, 2 shafts
**Power:** 2,313kW/3,100bhp for 15 knots
**Fuel:** Oil
**Endurance:** Not known
**Protection:** 19mm/0.75in splinter deck over magazine **Complement:** 162

LEFT: **USS *Vancouver* (LPD-2) was launched on September 15, 1962, and served with the US 7th Fleet. During the Vietnam War, the ship was awarded 11 battle stars.**

# Landing Ship, Personnel, Dock (LPD), Raleigh class

By the late 1950s, it was apparent that the helicopter would become a potent complement to the landing craft, and studies began for the specification for a ship to accommodate both. Helicopter development was in its infancy, however, and to build such a large and expensive vessel would be a considerable gamble. As an interim measure, therefore, the functions were divided between two new classes of ship, Landing Ship, Personnel, Helicopter (LPH) and Landing Ship, Personnel, Dock (LPD).

It was hoped that the LPD would carry a "balanced load" of assault troops, equipment and transport together with the assault craft and helicopters for a landing. If successful, this might lead to the phasing-out of the APA and AKA ships.

Superficially similar to the Thomaston class, USS *Raleigh* (LPD-1) was recognizable by the permanent helicopter deck in place of the "superdeck". The square transom and stern gate were retained but the docking well was reduced to 51.24 x 15.25m/168 x 50ft, large enough for nine LCM (6). Forward of the well, and linked via ramps, was vehicle garaging and cargo spaces on several levels.

The standard assault helicopter was the Sikorsky CH-46A Sea Knight, the size of which dictated space for only two landing spots and no hangar facilities. A small foldable hanger was added but this could accommodate only one Bell UH-1 "Huey", the ubiquitous combat helicopter. Although capable of carrying over 900 troops, a Raleigh-class LPD was considered suitable to support only a company-level operation. It became necessary to view an LPD and the more expensive LPH as a working combination.

Obviously in need of further refinement, building of the LPD-1 design was limited to just three ships. The last, USS *La Salle* (LPD-3) had better accommodation and was equipped with improved communications for the role of flagship.

ABOVE: **LPDs were built with a permanent helicopter deck in place of the temporary "superdeck" on the LSD. USS *La Salle* (LPD-3) was the third and last of the class to be built.**

| Landing Ship, Personnel, Dock, Raleigh class (LPD-1 and 2) | |
| --- | --- |
| **Displacement:** 8,040 tons (light); 13,900 tons (full load) | |
| **Length:** 152.5m/500ft (wl); 159.15m/521ft 10in (oa) | |
| **Beam:** 25.62m/84ft | |
| **Draught:** 6.41m/21ft | |
| **Armament:** 8 x 3in guns (4x2) | |
| **Machinery:** Steam turbines, 2 boilers, 2 shafts | |
| **Power:** 17,904kW/24,000shp for 21 knots | |
| **Fuel:** Oil | |
| **Endurance:** 17.664km/9,600nm at 16 knots | |
| **Protection:** Nominal | |
| **Complement:** 490 | |
| **Capacity:** 9 LCM (6), or 3 LCM (6) plus 1 LCU, or 4 LCM (8), or 20 LVTs | |

# Landing Ship, Personnel, Dock (LPD), Austin class

ABOVE: **The LPD was designed to be a complement to the more expensive LPH. Its layout was based on that of existing LSDs, but with a shorter well deck. This is the USS *Ponce* (LPD-15).**

Continuing the programme initiated with the Raleigh class, the 12 Austin class were very similar, but with an extra 14.64m/48ft in hull length to rectify the shortcomings of the earlier class. Cargo capacity was increased by over 50 per cent and the docking well dimensions to 120 x 15.24m/393ft 6in x 50ft  This allowed two LCM (6) and four LCM (8) to be transported. As the LCM (8) had almost twice the displacement of an LCM (6) , it was capable of carrying a M60 Patton main battle tank which weighed 53.6 tons. All landing craft were loaded by gantry cranes running the length of both well and other decks.

Although the helicopter deck was also enlarged, the hangar facilities for a flight of four CH-46A Sea Knight helicopters still proved impracticable on a ship of this size. The lack of full maintenance facilities for helicopters were to limit the ship operating as an independent unit.

During the time in service of the class, the LCAC and the LCU were introduced. As these were designed to fit the docking well in existing amphibious warfare ships, the Austin class could transport an LCAC, or one LCU plus four LCM (8) or 28 LVT. It is worth noting that, as LVTs became considerably larger since World War II, fewer could be accommodated.

By design, six of the LPDs were built as flagships for either an amphibious squadron or transport division. These ships could be distinguished by an extra deck on the superstructure.

So spacious were these facilities that USS *Coronado* (LPD-11), like the Raleigh-class USS La Salle (LPD-3), saw long service as a fleet flagship.

Phased retirement for the class would probably have commenced in the late 1990s but for repeated delays to the replacement LPD-17 (San Antonio-class) programme. They were gradually phased out of US Navy service between 2005 and 2017, but after withdrawal from US Navy service, in 2007 USS *Trenton* (LPD-14) was sold to the Indian Navy and renamed INS *Jalashwa*.

## Landing Ship, Personnel, Dock (LPD), Austin class

**Displacement:** 10,000 tons (light); 16,900 (full load)
**Length:** 173.85m/570ft (oa)
**Beam:** 25.62m/84ft
**Draught:** 7m/23ft 3in (mean)
**Armament:** 8 x 3in guns (4x2)
**Machinery:** Steam turbines, 2 boilers, 2 shafts
**Power:** 17,904kW/24,000shp for 23 knots
**Fuel:** Oil
**Endurance:** 14,168km/7,700nm at 20 knots
**Protection:** Nominal
**Complement:** 490 (plus 90 in flagship)
**Capacity:** 2 LCM (6) plus 4 LCM (8)

RIGHT: **Twelve Austin-class vessels were built and numbered LPD-4 to LPD-16, with the first being launched on June 27, 1964. Note the carrier-style side galleries at the helicopter deck on the USS *Ponce* (LPD-15).**

LEFT: **The Anchorage class was built after the introduction into service of the high-speed Type 1610 LCU, and designed to carry three of the type. USS** *Portland* **(LSD-37) was the second to enter service.**

# Landing Ship, Dock (LSD), Anchorage class

By the late 1960s the war-built LSDs were becoming obsolete and, to maintain the force, five replacements had to be built. Although the starting point for the design was that of the preceding Thomaston class, the hull was lengthened considerably in order to accommodate three LCU-1610. These craft had become the replacement for earlier LCTs. Each was capable of lifting three 55-ton M103 heavy tanks. The resulting docking well was 131.15m/430ft long which, even in a hull lengthened by some 12.2m/40ft, extended into the bow section.

Externally, the new vessel resembled the earlier class but had a longer superstructure and a braced tripod mast to provide a vibration-free platform for the SPS-40 air-defence radar antenna.

Accommodation was provided for 376 troops. For landing, two LCM (6) were carried topside, together with two LCPLs. All of these were handled by the two 50-ton cranes.

As with the Thomaston class, the helicopter deck did not extend fully to the stern, ending some 15.25m/50ft forward of the stern gate. Again similarly, this deck was removable, with no permanent hangar facilities. However some 90 tons of aviation fuel was carried for the aircraft. Only one Sikorsky CH-53 Sea Stallion aircraft could be handled at a time.

As built, the class had the usual eight 3in DP guns in twin mountings spaced around the superstructure. Later the forward port and aft starboard mountings were removed. US Atlantic Fleet units were then fitted with a single Close-in Weapons System (CIWS) mounting.

None of the class remained in US Navy service beyond 2003.

ABOVE: **The stern of the Anchorage-class vessel has the short helicopter deck and one-piece loading gate. A total of five Anchorage-class vessels were built: USS** *Anchorage* **(LSD-36), USS** *Portland* **(LSD-37), USS** *Pensacola* **(LSD-38), USS** *Mount Vernon* **(LSD-39), and USS** *Fort Fischer* **(LSD-40).**

## Landing Ship, Dock (LSD), Anchorage class

**Displacement:** 8,200 tons (light); 13,700 tons (full load)
**Length:** 162.87m/534ft (wl); 171.41m/562ft (oa)
**Beam:** 25.62m/84ft
**Draught:** 6.1m/20ft (mean)
**Armament:** 8 x 3in guns (4x2)
**Machinery:** Steam turbines, 2 boilers, 2 shafts
**Power:** 17,904kW/24,000shp for 22 knots
**Fuel:** Oil
**Endurance:** 25,760km/14,000nm at 12 knots
**Protection:** Nominal
**Complement:** 322
**Capacity:** 3 LCUs, or 15 LCM (6), or 8 LCM (8), or 50 LVTs

LEFT: **This excellent overhead of USS *Guadalcanal* (LPH-7) clearly shows the rounded bow and the lack of catapults and arrestor gear that defined the ship as a helicopter carrier.**

# Landing Ship, Personnel, Helicopter (LPH), Iwo Jima class

In essence, the Landing Ship, Personnel, Helicopter (LPH) and the Landing Ship, Personnel, Dock (LPD) were complementary. As the designators indicate, both carried personnel (the LPH around twice as many as the LPD) but, for landing operations, one carried helicopters, the other, assault craft. The LPH force would thus establish the beachhead and the LPD force would land with heavy equipment. Together the craft could land a fully equipped US Marine Corps combat formation.

US Marine Corps interest in an initial assault by helicopter ("Vertical Envelopment") dated back to 1947, it having been appreciated that a World War II style of amphibious landing was no longer possible. The vast assemblies of shipping could now be virtually destroyed by a single nuclear strike.

Post-war funding, for what would be an entirely new type of warfare, was limited and initial trials were made with modified war-built escort carriers (CVE). These culminated in the successful conversion of the USS *Thetis Bay* (CVE-90, redesignated CVHA-1 (Carrier, Helicopter, Assault) which, in 1956, could carry some 950 troops and 20 helicopters.

A second escort carrier, USS *Block Island* (CVE-106), was also listed for

ABOVE: **USS *Inchon* (LPH-12) was fitted with the later addition of SPN-35 radar, housed in a conspicuous dome.** RIGHT: **Even with rotors and tail units folded, Sikorsky CH-46 and CH-53 helicopters take up a lot of space on the flightdeck of USS *Tripoli* (LPH-10). The deck-edge elevators are great spacesavers.**

LEFT: **Boeing Vertol CH-46 Sea Knight** helicopters are here visible forward with larger Sikorsky H-53 Sea Stallions aft. Up to 25 helicopters can be carried. This is the converted Essex-class carrier *Boxer*, renumbered (LPH-4).

conversion. This was cancelled, but the ship was significant in being designated the first Landing Personnel Helicopter (LPH-1) ship.

Rendered obsolescent by the new "super carriers", several war-built Essex-class carriers were made available for limited conversion. These large ships could accommodate 2,000 troops and a considerable quantity of cargo. Designed for the steady motion required for flightdeck operations, all were popular with troops unaccustomed to sea travel. Still capable of 27 knots, the ships were usefully fast but, because of heavy usage, all were becoming expensive and difficult to maintain. The type proved the LPH principle, but clearly needed to be superseded by purpose-built ships.

A continued restricted funding resulted in considerable debate over the specification for the new ship. The US Marine Corps' preference was for vessels flexible enough to carry either two-thirds helicopter/one-third assault craft, depending upon circumstances.

The LPH design adopted, therefore, was based on that of a proposed but abandoned 21-knot, single-screw escort carrier. Carrying only the smallest of assault craft under davits, the vessel would be effectively an all-helicopter ship designed to work with LPDs. Without angled deck, catapult or arrestor gear, the LPH could operate only specialized fixed-wing aircraft.

In order to maximize deck space for eight helicopter spots (and, rapid troop loading) both elevators were positioned on the side of the ship. This necessitated large access doors in the hull plating.

A Sikorsky CH-53 Sea Stallion weighs 10,200kg/22,444lb empty and up to 19,090kg/42,000lb on take-off. With larger aircraft in mind, the LPH was fitted with 18,181kg/40,000lb capacity elevators and a flight deck stressed to 27,273kg/60,000lb. The hangar deck headroom of 6.09m/20ft gave the relatively small ship a high profile and generous freeboard. Conversely, it put the hangar deck and, thus the lowered elevators, close to the waterline, limiting permissible ship movement.

The ship could transport as many troops as a converted Essex class, with around half the crew. An LPH could, however, carry less cargo.

The type was also expected to work as anti-submarine escort carriers (a role which was never seriously practised) or as a base ship for minesweeping variants of the CH-53.

Less than a year after the launch of the last LPH (USS *Inchon* (LPH-12)), the first LHA (USS *Tarawa* (LHA-1)), which combined the roles of LPH and LPD, was launched in 1973.

The last of the class to be decommissioned, in June 2002, was USS *Inchon* (LPH/MCS-12).

## Landing Ship, Personnel, Helicopter (LPH), Iwo Jima class

**Displacement:** 10,990 tons (light); 18,300 tons (full load)
**Length:** 169.58m/556ft (wl); 180.56m/592ft (oa)
**Beam:** 25.52m/83ft 8in (wl)
**Draught:** 8.08m/26ft 6in (maximum)
**Armament:** 8 x 3in guns (4x2)
**Machinery:** Steam turbines, 2 boilers, single shaft
**Power:** 16,785kW/22,500shp for 21 knots
**Fuel:** Oil
**Endurance:** 18,400 km/10,000nm at 20 knots
**Protection:** Nominal
**Complement:** 594
**Capacity:** Up to 25 helicopters

ABOVE: **USS *Guadalcanal* (LPH-7)** was fitted with a Sea Sparrow Point Defence Missile System (PDMS) forward of the island and on the port quarter. Note the deck-edge elevator.

# Landing Ship, Tank (LST), Newport class

LSTs were valued particularly highly as, due to being the largest vessel routinely capable of beaching, the type could deliver the greatest quantity of cargo ashore during the earliest and most critical phase of a landing.

This class had a 34m/111ft bow ramp, stowed at sea on the long foredeck and positioned over the bows using a projecting gantry. To facilitate this, the doors in the rounded bow section above the knuckle line opened outward. The ramp could be supplemented by four rectangular pontoon sections which were stowed against the sides of the after hull. Deploying the main ramp uncovered a second vehicle exit from the covered tank deck. The decks were stressed for 75-ton vehicles, in excess of the current M1A2 Abrams tank at 63 tons. LVTs and other heavier vehicles were loaded and discharged through a gate and ramp set into the stern. Lighter vehicles could be carried on the upper deck, the fore and aft ends linked by a tunnel passing through the amidships structure. To satisfy the general endurance requirement for 16,093km/10,000 miles at 20 knots, diesel propulsion was specified, the six engines being exhausted through two side funnels, conspicuously unequal in size. Reversing was achieved through the use of controllable-pitch (CP) propellers. Alignment for beaching was assisted by a bow thruster. In the restricted-draught beaching condition, around 400 troops and some 500 tons of cargo could be transported.

Twenty ships were completed of the 27 planned but the arrival of air-cushioned landing craft that enabled over-the-horizon attacks made the class effectively obsolete. Twelve of the class were sold to other navies while the rest were decommissioned, the last of them in 2002.

ABOVE: **USS *Frederick* (LST-1184), showing the arrangement of projecting horns to operate a sliding ramp. Note the vehicle access through the superstructure.**

LEFT: **The stern door on USS *Cayuga* (LST-1186) has been lowered to provide the entry ramp for an LVT. Note the side shelves to carry pontoons, and the frame for the stern anchor.**

## Landing Ship, Tank Newport class, LST-1199–1205

**Displacement:** 4,950 tons (light); 8,525 tons (full load)
**Length:** 159.26m/522ft 2in (wl); 171.15m/561ft 2in (oa)
**Beam:** 21.2m/69ft 6in
**Draught:** 1.8m/5ft 11in (forward); 530m/17ft 4in (aft)
**Armament:** 4 x 3in guns (2x2)
**Machinery:** 6 diesel engines, 2 shafts
**Power:** 12,309kW/16,500bhp for 22 knots
**Fuel:** 1,750 tons oil
**Endurance:** 26,220km/14,250nm at 14 knots
**Protection:** Nominal
**Complement:** 262

# Amphibious Force Flagship (AGC), Mount McKinley class

During World War II, the US Navy commissioned 15 AGCs, and three more shortly afterwards. Numbers were driven by the fact that no single ship was equipped to handle the mass of incoming and outgoing communications and intelligence traffic. Besides the precaution of a back-up vessel, additional AGCs could share the operation rather than simply "double up". As an interim measure, some APAs were fitted to function as basic "relief flagships".

The enemy was quick to appreciate the significance of the AGC, which needed to be anchored inconspicuously in the transport area, worsening the general problem of electronic interference. Electronic Support Measures (ESM) and Electronic Countermeasures (ECM) were fitted to counter the extra complication of enemy jamming

activities. The main function of the AGC still included the joint embarked staffs' maintenance of the master plot of the operation as it developed, and providing a base for the military headquarters staff until developments enabled it to be landed ashore.

By the late 1960s, with the amphibious force much reduced, only five AGCs remained in service and these, headed by USS *Mount McKinley* (AGC-7), were beginning to deteriorate. Badly cramped for the large crew required, the AGC lacked sufficient generating capacity and were unable to accommodate the large automated combat information systems now becoming universal.

The type appeared ever more overloaded. Extra accommodation was added on the superstructure, the after 5in gun being removed

ABOVE: **Equipped with a late-1944 electronics suite, USS *Teton* (AGC-14) is seen here in company, unusually, with an LSV, probably USS *Ozark* (LSV-2). Note how the forward cargo derricks are used to handle small craft.**

and replaced with a helicopter pad. Kingposts, masts and derricks were retained both to handle a wide range of small craft and to support (at the required separation) a carrier-scale electronics outfit, including pencil-beam height finder, air search radar and Tactical Air Navigation (TACAN).

No longer capable of exceeding 15 knots, and beyond effective modernization, the ACGs were replaced in the early 1970s by Blue Ridge-class command ships.

ABOVE: **USS *Mount McKinley* (AGC-7) was originally built in 1943 as a transport ship USS *Cyclone*. The vessel was renamed on December 27, 1943, and commissioned on May 1, 1944.**

## Amphibious Force Flagship (AGC), Mount McKinley class, 1960s C2 conversion

**Displacement:** 7,200 tons (light); 15,300 tons (full load)
**Length:** 132.68m/435ft (wl); 140m/459ft (oa)
**Beam:** 19.22m/63ft
**Draught:** 8.62m/28ft 3in
**Armament:** 1 x 5in gun, 8 x 40mm (4x2)
**Machinery:** Steam turbines, 2 boilers, single screw
**Power:** 4,476kW/6,000shp for 15 knots
**Fuel:** 3,875 tons oil
**Endurance:** 61,180km/33,250nm at 12 knots
**Protection:** Nominal
**Complement:** 520

# Attack Transport/Cargo Ship (APA/AKA), Mariner class

ABOVE: **USS *Tulare* (AKA-112) with a full complement of nine LCM (6) carried on the hatch covers. LCVPs are nested in some LCMs, with three more LCVPs on No. 2 hatch. Others are carried under davits.**

The C2 and C3 standard ships that were widely converted to APAs and AKAs during World War II were designed as merchant ships by the US Maritime Commission. With the post-war requirement for an all-20-knot amphibious force, the commission was again tasked with designing a commercial carrier suitable for conversion to military use.

The US Marine Corps wished to lift the same cargo weight (i.e. deadweight, or dwt) as a C3. But, with finer lines, the 20-knot ship would have to be over 30.5m/100ft longer, thus falling into the C4 (Mariner) category. Few commercial operators had trading patterns that suited so large or fast ship, and they could be used only with the assistance of a government subsidy.

The huge hull included seven holds, each with two between deck levels. Commercially, these were served by seven pairs of kingposts but, for the two APAs, USS *Paul Revere* (APA-248) and USS *Francis Marion* (APA-249), and one AKA, USS *Tulare* (AKA-112), (the only three converted from the 35 completed C4-S-1A/B) this standard cargo gear was removed in favour of the already familiar quadripod-type masts, one forward and one aft of the superstructure.

The two completed APAs retained only the earlier Nos. 3 and 6 holds, with Nos. 2, 4, and 5 retained as access trunks. The superstructure was extended aft to provide further accommodation for a 1,650-strong

US Marine Corps battalion and facilities for the ships to operate as flagships. Six LCM (6), 12 LCVPs and two LCPLs were carried. In both types of conversion the area aft, above the No. 7 hold, was built as a helicopter pad, without a hangar.

The AKA retained holds Nos. 2 to 6 inclusive, together with the trunk of the earlier No. 1. The original short superstructure was retained but on the raised forecastle there was a gun platform for a twin 3in mounting with fire director. The AKA carried nine LCM (6) and 14 LVCPs.

---

### Attack Transport/ Cargo Ship (APA/AKA), Mariner class

**Displacement:** 10,700 tons (light);
16,850 tons (full load)
**Length:** 161.04m/518ft (wl);
172.02m/564ft (oa)
**Beam:** 23.18m/76ft
**Draught:** 8.24m/27ft (maximum)
**Armament:** 8 x 3in guns (4x2)
**Machinery:** 2 steam turbines, 2 boilers, single shaft
**Power:** 16,412kW/22,000shp for 21 knots
**Fuel:** Oil
**Endurance:** 18,400km/10,000nm at 20 knots
**Protection:** Nominal
**Complement:** 529

ABOVE: **Both USS *Paul Revere* (APA-248) and USS *Francis Marion* (APA-249) ex-SS *Prairie Mariner* were sold to Spain in 1980. The latter, seen here, was later transferred to Spain, undergoing little change.**

# Attack Cargo Ship (AKA), Charleston class

ABOVE: **The hull form was a refined development of the Mariner class. The Charleston class (this is USS *St Louis* [AKA-116]) featured a wide transom stern, permitting the fitting of a helicopter landing pad. Note the German-designed Stülcken masts.**

The Mariner class conversions proved expensive and, being vessels with commercial features, not ideal. US Navy planning was also moving in the direction of ships with docking wells, not least because handling an LCM (6) by derrick hoist while in an open sea or rolling in an exposed anchorage, could be dangerous. The conversions were limited to just three ships as it appeared that LPDs and LSDs, working jointly, incorporated the functions of both the APA and AKA type. As far as cargo was concerned, however, the assumed demise of the AKA proved premature, with five Charleston-class vessels added to the force in the late 1960s.

The design was purely that of a military cargo carrier, with no concessions to alternative commercial service. The hull form was developed from that of the already-efficient Mariner class and showed a one-knot improvement in speed with the same power plant. The deep-load displacement was increased by nearly 17 per cent. A bulb-type bow assisted efficiency at service speed while more cutaway underwater stern sections reduced radiated propeller noise, and also improved rudder response and manoeuvrability, important for Replenishment At Sea (RAS).

A transom stern increased afterdeck width, enabling the provision of a helicopter pad capable of accepting the largest transport machines. The pad was connected to all four cargo levels by one of seven elevators on the ship. There were just four holds, served by derricks stepped on two heavy goalpost-type and two Stülcken-type masts. The latter, then popular commercially, permitted the 70-ton heavy-lift derricks to serve adjacent hatches. Their precise control allowed the number of landing craft carried and type to be up-rated safely to four LCM (8), five LCM (6), seven LCVPs and two LCPLs.

The last of the classic lift-on/lift-off AKAs, the Charleston class were decommissioned between 1992 and 1994.

## Attack Cargo Ship (AKA), Charleston class

**Displacement:** 13,725 tons (light); 18,650 tons (full load)
**Length:** 167.75m/550ft (wl); 175.53m/575ft 6in (oa)
**Beam:** 25.01m/82ft
**Draught:** 7.76m/25ft 5in (maximum)
**Armament:** 8 x 3in guns (4x2)
**Machinery:** 2 steam turbines, 2 boilers, single shaft
**Power:** 16,421kW/22,000shp for 22 knots
**Fuel:** Oil
**Endurance:** 18,400km/10,000nm at 20 knots
**Protection:** Nominal
**Complement:** 336

ABOVE: **Decommissioned for over a decade but still a valuable reserve, USS *Mobile* (AKA-115), USS *El Paso* (AKA-117) and USS *Charleston* (AKA-113) are standing idle, stripped of electronics and running rigging.**

LEFT: **USS *Tarawa* (LHA-1)** was the first of the new class of amphibious assault ships. The vessel was launched on December 1, 1973 and commissioned on May 26, 1976. The ship was decommissioned on March 31, 2009 and may still become a museum ship.

# Landing Ship, Helicopter, Assault (LHA), Tarawa class

The US Navy's amphibious force of the mid-1960s comprised a large number of ships, crewed by highly trained personnel. Tight budgets demanded that crew numbers be reduced, and it was this, rather than requests from the US Marine Corps, that encouraged the "all-in-one" approach to the design of the LHA. A Marine battalion would be embarked on the vessel along with armour, transport and general equipment, together with helicopters and landing craft. However arranged, a 20-knot ship combining the functions of existing LPH, LSD and AKA was going to be large and expensive, but a significant overall reduction in crew numbers allowed improved in-service costs. Fewer and larger ships would also reduce building and maintenance costs.

The US Marine Corps was somewhat critical of a ship offering a target as large and as distinctive as a World War II strike carrier (CVA) and capable of being rendered inoperative by a single major mechanical failure.

The new LHA, was subject to lengthy design studies which indicated that a fleet of four, with supporting LSD and LST, could replace a force of over twice the number of existing vessels. This

argument was sufficiently strong for the procurement of further LPH and LPD to be cancelled from mid-1966.

For a battalion-sized lift, a force of six Sikorsky CH-53A Sea Stallion transport helicopters (each lifting around 55 troops), 18 Boeing CH-46A Sea Knight twin-rotor assault helicopters (17 troops each) and two Bell UH-1E Iriquois was required, with tankage for 1,200 tons of aviation fuel.

To achieve lift-rate, nine deck landing spots were necessary. Flight deck and hangar space were maximized by locating one elevator on the centreline at the stern and a second close by on the port deck edge. The latter is folded against the hull when not in use, to keep overall width to within the limitations of the Panama Canal.

Above water, the hull was essentially parallel and rectangular in section.

ABOVE: **USS *Peleliu* (LHA-5)** listing majestically in a tight turn. The empty pockets at the bow were originally for fire-support 5in guns. Both elevators are located aft, and the hangar area covers only half the length of the ship.

ABOVE: **USS Saipan (LHA-2) flooding down to exercise LCUs, of which she can accommodate four.**

LEFT: **A later image of USS Saipan (LHA-2), now fitted with two CIWS. Proven to be difficult to modernize, USS Saipan was stricken in 2007.**

A massive stern gate enclosed an 80 x 23.4m/262 x 77ft docking well, large enough to carry four LCU-1610, but also able to carry the LCAC that entered service later. A crane behind the island structure was used to handle two LCM (6) and two LCPL.

As if to emphasize that the ship was not an aircraft carrier, the island was large and located inboard, to allow vehicles to pass outboard. No aircraft catapults or arrestor gear were fitted but vertical/short take-off and land (V/STOL) aircraft worked aboard satisfactorily. Indeed, in "strike" configuration an

LHA could carry up to 20 McDonnell Douglas AV-8A Harriers and six helicopters.

Despite the size of the ships, the overall design was very compact, with the 1,900 troops and vehicles being accommodated on several deck levels.

Original armament included three 5in guns, considered necessary for fire support and a Raytheon/General Dynamics Sea Sparrow Point Defense Missile System (PDMS) launcher. These were located in boxes set into each "corner" of the flight deck. All 5in guns were

later removed, the forward mountings being plated-over to improve flight deck layout. The Sea Sparrow was superseded by two 21-round Rolling Airframe Missile System (RAM) launchers and two 30mm Close-In Weapon System (CIWS).

Although fitted with a comprehensive electronics suite, the LHA were not expected to function as amphibious flagships. Perhaps not surprisingly with so ambitious a concept, the ships, while impressive, had proved to be something of a disappointment in service. Planned Service Life Extension Programs (SLEP) appeared to be too complex to be cost effective. All new ships were, therefore, cancelled and the remaining ships had all been decommissioned by March 2015 – USS Belleau Wood (LHA-3) was in such poor condition that the vessel was used as a target in 2006. They were replaced by the America-class amphibious assault ships from 2014 onwards.

LEFT: **The side opening and elevators allow access to the hangar deck. The docking well is now entered through the stern gate. USS Belleau Wood (LHA-3) is armed with two CIWS and two RAM launchers. One of each is visible on the after quarters.**

### Landing Ship, Helicopter, Assault (LHA), Tarawa class

**Displacement:** 25,120 tons (light); 39,400 tons (full load)
**Length:** 237.14m/777ft 6in (bp); 254.2m/833ft 5in (oa)
**Beam:** 32.31m/105ft 11in (wl); 40.23m/131ft 10in (overall width)
**Draught:** 7.91m/26ft (mean)
**Armament:** 3 x 5in guns (3x1), 1 x 8-cell Sea Sparrow BPDMS
**Machinery:** Steam turbines, 2 boilers, 2 shafts
**Power:** 57,442kW/77,000shp for 24 knots
**Fuel:** Oil
**Endurance:** 18,400km/10,000nm at 20 knots
**Protection:** Not known
**Complement:** 940

# Landing Ship, Dock (LSD), Whidbey Island/Harpers Ferry class

By the late 1970s, the question of whether to modernize or replace the Thomaston class was raised. Built for a nominal 30-year life, the class might have given further service through a Service Life Extension Program (SLEP), but some showed material deterioration, and none could meet modern accommodation standards without major work. Most importantly, however, the size of the ships was not compatible with the transportation of the new Landing Craft Air Cushion (LCAC), due to enter service in 1984.

Amphibious vessels laying offshore were, by now, vulnerable to attack by shore-based Surface-to-Surface Missiles

(SSM). The LCAC was seen as the means by which the LSD could operate from safely Over The Horizon (OTH).

A force of 66 amphibious warfare ships was required to lift US Marine Corps troops in combat ready units. The SLEP would have allowed a delay, but at very considerable cost, while the question of eventual replacement would remain. A new type, designated the LSD-41 (Whidbey Island class) was, therefore, adopted as a ship-for-ship replacement programme for the Thomaston class. Confusingly, many of the new ships had the same names as used on earlier LSDs.

The design parameters for the class were a docking well large enough for four LCACs, together with accommodation for 400 troops and ever-bulkier equipment. A new factor was the high noise levels of the LCAC, which required all berthing to be removed from the wing walls of the well deck and moved forward, another factor which seriously increased vessel size and cost. At 130 x 15.24m/440 x 50ft, the docking well could accommodate three LCUs, ten LCM (8), or 64 amphibious assault vehicles (AAV).

Facilities for the LCAC dominated the design, with a requirement for extensive maintenance facilities and accommodation

LEFT: **USS Tortuga (LSD-46)**, one of the class built to replace earlier Thomaston-class vessels. BELOW: **USS Fort McHenry (LSD-43)** anchored off the coast of North Carolina, with the amphibious assault ship USS **Bataan (LHD-5)** in the distance, while embarking personnel and equipment from the 22nd Marine Expeditionary Unit.

for 64 specialist personnel. Free ventilation of the docking well was important as were the guidance systems to allow the LCAC to dock and undock with the ship stationary or moving. A barrier across the docking well closes off forward areas.

As is customary, no hangar facilities are provided for the helicopters, but the elevated flight deck is large enough to provide landing spots for two Sikorsky CH-53Es or similar types. The port and starboard cranes are each rated at 60 tons to enable a main battle tank to be lifted over the side and on to an LCAC.

No medium-calibre guns were specified as the class is designed to operate beyond the range of enemy fire. The defensive armament of two Raytheon Phalanx (CIWS) has, however, been supplemented by two 21-round RIM-116 RAM launchers.

A new innovation was the adoption of medium-speed diesel engines, two driving each shaft. The superior fuel economy allowed fuel storage to be reduced by almost 33 per cent. The planned 12-ship Whidbey Island-class programme saw ships being delivered at around one-year intervals but, within this timeframe, US Marine Corps strategy had evolved to meet changing threats. It became apparent that the increasing amount of equipment could not be accommodated in the class, as completed. A new class was developed in the externally, almost-identical LSD-41 Cargo Variant, or LSD-49 (Harpers Ferry class).

The primary difference between the classes is the docking well of the LSD-49 being large enough for only two LCACs. Simply reprioritizing the various spaces aboard a standard LSD-41 was not possible as the revised weight distribution would reduce the stability range of the ship

ABOVE: **Compared with earlier docking ships, LSD-41 vessels have minimal radar signature reduction features incorporated in their design. USS *Tortuga* (LSD-46) is carrying a Sikorsky SH-60 Seahawk helicopter aft.**

to below an acceptable minimum. Alternatively the docking well load is reduced to one LCU or four LCM (8). Two LCPLs and a utility craft are carried on deck, where a 30-ton crane mounted on the starboard side replaces two 60-ton cranes on the LSD-41. For cargo, the LSD-49s can offer over 1,200m²/12,917sq ft of vehicle parking and around 1,330m³/ 46,996cu ft of cargo stowage.

Regular updates kept the class in front-line service until their decommissioning began in 2021, at least a decade before it was at one time envisaged.

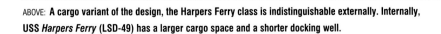

ABOVE: **A cargo variant of the design, the Harpers Ferry class is indistinguishable externally. Internally, USS *Harpers Ferry* (LSD-49) has a larger cargo space and a shorter docking well.**

## Landing Ship, Dock, LSD-41 class

**Displacement:** 11,350 tons (light); 16,220 tons (full load)
**Length:** 176.8m/579ft 8in (wl); 185.8m/609ft 2in (oa)
**Beam:** 25.6m/83ft 11in
**Draught:** 6.25m/20ft 6in (full load)
**Armament:** 2 x 21-cell RAM PDMS, 2 x CIWS
**Machinery:** 4 diesel engines, 3 shafts
**Power:** 31,034kW/41,600bhp for 22 knots
**Fuel:** Oil
**Endurance:** 14,720km/8,000nm at 18 knots
**Protection:** Kevlar patches over limited vital areas
**Complement:** 315

# Landing Ship, Helicopter, Dock (LHD), Wasp class

The LHD is best considered as an LCAC-capable version of the Tarawa class (LHA), the change of designation being political rather than implying any significant change of function. Hull form and size are similar, the major difference being in the provision of a longer, narrower docking well, 98 x 15.2m/322 x 50ft. This was capable of accommodating three LCACs, compared with only one in an LHA. Alternatively, an LHD can load two LCUs or six LCM (8). The stern gate on an LHA lifted in two sections, horizontally divided, but on the LHD this has reverted to the older LSD type, where the bottom section lowers. This provides a ramp to facilitate launching an LCAC from a dry well.

Larger-area bilge keels have been fitted, presumably to reduce the roll of the ship at lower speeds. A bow-bulb has also been added, probably for greatest efficiency at service speed.

ABOVE: **USS *Makin Island* (LHD-8) is powered by two General Electric LM-1500 gas turbine engines.**

Accommodation for 1,900 troops is on the same scale as in an LHA. The steam power plant is also similar. USS *Makin Island* (LHD-8) is an exception, however, and was commissioned in 2008, some eight years after USS *Bonhomme Richard* (LHD-6). As no further steam-powered ships will be built for the US Navy, LHD-8 is powered by two General Electric LM-1500 gas turbines.

Changing political conditions show in the aviation arrangements. To underline the fact that an LHA was not an aircraft carrier, the efficiency of the flight deck was reduced by mountings for medium-calibre guns (since removed) and a large intrusive island structure. From the outset, armament on the LHD was totally defensive, allowing the flight deck to be squared-off both forward and aft. Flight deck and hangar areas are increased by the adoption of two deck-edge elevators, one aft of amidships, port side, the other on the starboard quarter. The latter replaces the aft centreline elevator on the LHA. Greater usable flight deck width is enabled by the narrower island, reflecting a more flexible attitude to what are essentially specialized aviation requirements.

LEFT: **Despite the width of the superstructure, USS *Wasp* (LHD-1) can easily accommodate the Bell Boeing MV-22 Osprey flown by the USMC.**

LEFT: **A Sikorsky CH-53 Sea Stallion about to land on USS *Kearsarge* (LHD-3). The docking well on the vessel is large enough to accommodate three LCACs. Note the CIWS on either quarter and the centreline Sea Sparrow launcher.**

The LHD can be a multi-purpose vessel, albeit an expensive alternative to a small conventional aircraft carrier. Operations in the "Harrier Carrier" mode have been a little restricted by the requirement to maintain nine landing spots for helicopters.

A new factor was the certification of the long-awaited Bell Boeing V-22A Osprey VTOL aircraft. These are operated from an LHD's flight deck but are very large for existing elevators. In vertical take-off mode, the Osprey weighs up to 23.4 tons as opposed to a CH-53 Super Stallion at almost 19 tons, but is well within the 34-ton lift capacity of the elevator. The Osprey carries less than half the troops, but at twice the speed, thus doubling flight deck activity for operations at the same range. It does, however, have over twice the range of a CH-53E, and the US sees it as a possible replacement for helicopters in spearhead operations.

LEFT: **Flagship of an Amphibious Ready Group (ARG), the USS *Essex* (LHD-2) is shown leading an Austin-class LPD and a Harpers Ferry-class LSD. The vessel would normally be used in conjunction with a carrier group.**

## Landing Ship, Helicopter, Dock, LHD-1 to LHD-7

**Displacement:** 27,900 tons (light);
40,750 tons (full load)
**Length:** 237.14m/777ft 6in (wl);
257.3m/843ft 8in (oa)
**Beam:** 32.31m/105ft 11in (wl)
**Draught:** 8.53m/28ft (full load)
**Armament:** 2 x 8-cell Sea Sparrow BPDMS,
2 x 21-cell RAM launchers
**Machinery:** Steam turbines, 2 boilers, 2 shafts
**Power:** 57,442kW/77,000shp for 24 knots
**Fuel:** 6,200 tons oil
**Endurance:** 18,400km/10,000nm at 20 knots
**Protection:** Not known
**Complement:** 1,082

# Landing Ship, Personnel, Dock (LPD), San Antonio class

L PD construction appeared to have ended in 1971, with the commissioning of the last of the LPD-4 (Austin class). LPD-16 was never built, and a new type of well deck ship was being developed. The Austin class vessels were planned to last 45 years, but the expensive SLEP modernization was cancelled, and the class began to be phased out in 2005. Their characteristics nonetheless having proved useful, they were given replacements in the LPD-17 (San Antonio class) built from 2000 onward. As is the way of these things, however, the new ships were also expected to replace the LSD-36 (Anchorage class), Charleston amphibious cargo ships as well as Newport class tank landing ships. The LPD-17 programme coincided with post-Cold War western fleets being reorganized with a new emphasis on expeditionary and "littoral" warfare.

Not surprisingly, therefore, they are larger (at 25,000 tons fully loaded displacing around 50 per cent more than the average LPD-4) and are very expensive with the cost having risen from $1.6 billion for the first ship to over $2billion for the last of the class. A total of 14 ships were planned to be in service but in 2018 the US Navy decided to procure an additional 13 improved versions.

ABOVE AND BELOW: **The total enclosure of all electronic antennas within low radar-signature towers gives USS *San Antonio* (LPD-17) a very angular appearance. The class follows the new trend for diesel propulsion.**

In appearance, the ships in the class are dominated by radar signature reduction measures which, with suppression of exposed detail and sharply sculpted oblique surfaces, makes the ship appear to radar smaller than true size. Masts have evolved into 28.3m/93ft octagonal-section Advanced Enclosed Mast/Sensors (AEM/S) System "towers" 10.7m/35ft in diameter. This mast is constructed of multi-layer frequency-selective composite material designed to allow friendly frequencies whilst reflecting potentially hostile frequencies. The tapered octagonal shape was developed to reduce radar cross section and

RIGHT: **The docking well on USS *San Antonio* (LPD-17) extends forward to a point just short of the hangar doors. Forward, there are three levels of vehicle decks which extend to beyond the forward funnel.**

enclosing vital electronic systems has also improved equipment performance whilst significantly reducing maintenance costs.

Unlike earlier LPDs, the LPD-17s incorporate covered facilities for the aviation element. The permanent flight deck initially had landing spots for two Sikorsky CH-53Es or four Sikorsky CH-46Es, but the standard aircraft now are a brace of MV-22 Osprey tilt-rotor aircraft which can be operated simultaneously. Room is available to place four MV-22s on the flight deck and one in the hangar deck

The docking well is sized to carry two LCACs, or one LCU and fourteen amphibious assault vehicles. Up to 700 troops can be accommodated, in addition to the standard complement of around 360.

Following a period when highly valuable amphibious warfare ships appeared to carry minimal defensive armament, the LPD-17s have two Rolling Airframe Missile launchers, two eight cell Vertical Launch System (VLS) for Evolved Sea Sparrow Missiles (ESSM),

two Bushmaster II 30mm close-in guns, plus a number of turrets mounting pairs of machine guns. A full air-defence sensor and weapon integration system is also fitted. USS *Portland* (LPD-27) has been used to successfully test a next-generation solid-state laser weapon system

The ships are fitted with the AN/SPQ-9A multi-purpose surface search and fire control radar used with the Mk-86 gun fire-control system. This two-dimensional surface-search radar provides target range and bearing but not elevation for engagement as it is intended primarily

to detect and track targets at sea level. It can also detect and track low altitude (sub-610m/2000ft) aerial targets.

Accounting for some of the high cost, the LPD-17 has three-dimensional air search radar (SPS-48), contributing to a fully integrated air defence system which permits data to be shared between ships in a fighting formation.

Reminiscent of NASA spacecraft recovery operations from the 1960s and early 1970s, in December 2022 USS Portland was tasked with the recovery of the Artemis 1 uncrewed moon-orbiting mission Orion capsule. After landing safely in the ocean on its parachutes, the capsule was taken into the ship's flooded stern well deck.

ABOVE: **Viewed from above, it is apparent that minor radar-reflective detail is screened by high bulwarks. For so bulky a vessel, USS *Green Bay* (LPD-20) has a commendably clean wave system.**

## Landing Ship, Personnel, Dock (LPD), San Antonio class

**Displacement:** 25,300 tons (full load)
**Length:** 200m/655ft 9in (wl); 208.48m/683ft (oa)
**Beam:** 29.5m/96ft 9in (wl)
**Draught:** 7m/23ft (full load)
**Armament (as fitted):** 2 x 21-round RAM, VLS, CIWS and 2 x 30mm cannon
**Machinery:** 4 diesel engines, 2 shafts
**Power:** 31,037kW/41,600bhp for 22 knots
**Fuel:** Oil
**Endurance:** 18,400km/10,000nm at 20 knots
**Protection:** Not known
**Complement:** 361

# Landing Craft, Control (LCC), Blue Ridge class

ABOVE: **Over time in service, the deck area has been greatly simplified as radio communications have been superseded by satellite links. USS** *Blue Ridge* **(LCC-19) is 40 years old.**

The merchant ship-type hulls of wartime-built AGCs could not be expected to survive beyond the 25-year "special survey" milestone, making early 1970s replacement urgent. Considerable debate was given to the specification for the new ships – a cruiser conversion could retain much valued support firepower, a modified light carrier would provide the necessary internal volume, while a Mariner or P4 conversion would be cheaper.

The first two, however, would be built on 25-year-old hulls, while the latter would only just meet the 20-knot requirement. The Iwo Jima-class LPH programme was nearing completion and, offering both space and the necessary speed, two further hulls were added for conversion.

To emphasize the amphibious status, the designator was changed from AGC (where "A" denoted "Auxiliary", not "Amphibious") to LCC, or Landing Craft, Control (rather misleading, and not to be confused with the British LCC of World War II). The AGC numbering sequence held, however, the ships becoming LCC-19 and 20.

The building of only two reflected the fact that computerization and, soon after, satellite communications, made it possible to distribute control of the amphibious group and task force commanders between other, increasingly better equipped ships. Although intended for amphibious warfare, both USS *Blue Ridge* (LCC-19) and USS *Mount Whitney* (LCC-20) have been deployed in the role of 6th and 7th US Fleet flagship. Only

the hull form and machinery from the Iwo Jima class vessel was retained. A prominent sponson runs along each side of the ship, mainly to incorporate a larger boat complement. The overall length, particularly in earlier days was required to give necessary separation between a wide variety of communications antennas, for which the upper deck acted as ground plane. There is a helicopter pad but no hangar facilities and self defence takes the form of two 20mm Phalanx CIWS systems and Bushmaster 25mm cannons.

After over half a century in service, the class retain the distinction of being the only amphibious command and control ships purpose-designed from the keel up.

LEFT: **Wide side sponsons accommodating boats make for a spacious, unencumbered weather deck on USS** *Mount Whitney* **(LCC-20). Despite being steam-powered, the ship lacks a true funnel. Note the CIWS mounting at the bow.**

## Landing Craft, Control (LCC), Blue Ridge class

**Displacement:** 12,750 tons (light), 19,300 tons (full load)
**Length:** 176.8m/579ft 8in (wl); 188.5m/618ft (oa)
**Beam:** 25.3m/82ft 11in (wl)
**Draught:** 8.2m/26ft 10in (full load)
**Armament:** 4 x 3in guns (2x2), 2 x 8 round Sea Sparrow BPDMS launchers (all since removed)
**Machinery:** Steam turbine, 2 boilers, single shaft
**Power:** 16,412kW/22,000shp for 21.5 knots
**Fuel:** Oil
**Endurance:** 23,920km/13,000nm at 16 knots
**Protection:** Kevlar plastic armour added later; extent unknown
**Complement:** 690

# Maritime and Prepositioning Force (MPF), Bob Hope class

ABOVE LEFT AND ABOVE: The eight Watson- and seven Bob Hope-class vessels (USS *Bob Hope* [T-AKR 300] shown) are direct derivatives of the three Shughart class, acquired in 1994 from the Maersk company.

Today's much-changed strategic policy requires that essential heavy equipment is stored semi-permanently at a forward location, to be moved by sea to any trouble spot in the world while troops are flown in by transport aircraft.

Much of this material is loaded aboard ships of the Maritime Prepositioning Force (MPF). The force is maintained by specialist teams, the ships sailing regularly on exercise, not least to prevent them becoming an easy, high-value target for pre-emptive attack. Having discharged the vital first-wave support task, the MPF

ships revert to "sealift", the general transport duties associated earlier with large numbers of AKAs.

World War II-built AKAs were standard cargo ships, relying upon cargo derricks to load and discharge over the side. Methods have since been revolutionized by the introduction of vessels such as Roll-on, Roll-off (Ro-Ro) ships and the use of cargo containers. Foreign merchant ship design being ahead of that of the USA caused the latter to purchase large ships mainly from European operators in order to expand the Rapid Reaction Force (RRF) during the 1980s. The ships were modified with the

addition of cranes and larger side openings to service the existing loading ramps.

Stemming from these conversions were the US-designed and built Watson and Bob Hope classes. All displaced a massive 62,000 tons, and were classified T-AKR (i.e. Ro-Ro cargo ships operated by Military Sealift Command (MSC). All had a small (by naval standards) crew of around 26 civilians. The vessels can carry 100 tracked and 900 wheeled vehicles. All have modularized pontoon sections, some self-powered, which can be used as a floating jetty, a temporary causeway or to transport vehicles. Non-trailerized heavy gear and containers are unloaded by the four 55-ton deck cranes. Three of the Bob Hope class ships remain in service in the mid-2020s.

ABOVE: The Bob Hope-class USS *William S. Seay* (T-AKR 302). Note the cranes in paired lift mode and the use of the side door. The loading ramp is carried as deck cargo.

## Maritime and Prepositioning Force (MPF), Bob Hope class

**Displacement:** 34,410 tons (light); 62,100 tons (full load)
**Length:** 271.28m/889ft 5in (bp); 289.56m/949ft 4in (oa)
**Beam:** 32.3m/105ft 10in
**Draught:** 11.25m/36ft 10in (full load)
**Armament:** None in peacetime
**Machinery:** 4 diesel engines, 2 shafts
**Power:** 48,639kW/65,200bhp for 24.5 knots
**Fuel:** Oil
**Endurance:** Not known
**Protection:** Nominal
**Complement:** 27 (peace); up to 95 (war)

129

# America class

USS *America* (LHA-6) is the lead ship of the amphibious assault ship class named for it, designed to replace the Tarawa-class amphibious assault ships and provide an upgraded amphibious warfare capability to the US Navy. The *America* was built by Huntington Ingalls Industries in Pascagoula, Mississippi, laid down in 2009, launched in 2012, and commissioned into US Navy service in 2014. The *America*'s primary role is to transport and support a Marine Expeditionary Unit (MEU) comprised of ground troops and their equipment, and then deliver them into battle using helicopters and MV-22B tilt-rotor transports, supported by helicopter gunships and F-35B multi-role combat aircraft. Other aircraft, including AV-8B Harriers, can also operate from the ship.

Although based on the design of the USS *Makin Island*, the 45,693-ton *America* differs by having much greater space to support enhanced aviation activities but at the cost of not having a well deck. This decision, which has caused considerable controversy, was a significant shift in design approach. This lead ship in the class does not have the capability nor multi-role flexibility of more traditional amphibious ships in that it cannot launch landing craft and amphibious assault vehicles. The well deck is, not unreasonably, considered to be a defining feature of such a large amphibious warfare vessel and it enables the USMC to conduct amphibious

ABOVE: **The *America* returns to Huntington Ingalls Shipyard, Pascagoula, Mississippi, after completing sea trials, November 2013. The maximum beam of America-class ships was set at 32m/106ft because of the need for the ships to pass through the Panama Canal.** LEFT: **USS *Tripoli* (LHA-7) is launched at Huntington Ingalls Industries in Pascagoula, Mississippi, USA, May 2017. *Tripoli* was successfully launched after the dry-dock was flooded to allow it to float off for the first time.**

ABOVE: **USS America with F-35Bs, MV-22 Ospreys and helicopters on deck. The class LHA prefix stands for 'Landing Helicopter Assault'.** ABOVE RIGHT: **USS America's Phalanx CIWS (close-in weapon system) undergoing maintenance. It was designed to defend against incoming threats such as aircraft, missiles, and small boats. It can hold between around 1,000 to 1,500 20mm rounds, fires at a rate of 3,000 rounds per minute and at a speed of 1,100m /3,600ft per second.** BELOW: **MV-22 Osprey takes off from the USS Tripoli (LHA 7), Philippine Sea, 2022.**

operations. Senior USMC and USN officers lobbied hard to ensure the well deck was restored in later ships of the class – these ships have a smaller island to allow for flight-deck maintenance of MV-22s in the absence of a larger hangar deck. This led directly to the 2015 initiative launched by the USMC Commandant to ensure that aviation did not dominate the capabilities of the

USMC and that this was reflected in the platforms developed to enable the Marines to conduct operations.

The America uses the same hybrid-electric drive system (gas turbine propulsion plant and electric auxiliary systems) designed and built for the Makin Island, replacing the maintenance-heavy steam turbines of earlier US Navy ships. The unique auxiliary propulsion system (APS) uses auxiliary propulsion motors powered by the ship's electrical grid rather than main engines to power the carrier's shaft, greatly improving the ship's fuel efficiency. The system allows the ship to operate on a single gas turbine at low speeds, which can significantly reduce fuel consumption. The electric motors can however provide a boost of power when needed, allowing the ship to reach its top speed of over 22 knots. The hybrid-electric drive

system also offers improved reliability and flexibility as use of the electric motors reduces the load on the ship's gas turbines and extends their lifespan. This can also improve the ship's ability to operate in a variety of conditions and speeds, making it more versatile in different operational scenarios.

The ship's crew is typically 1,204 officers and enlisted personnel and it can transport over 1,870 Marines.

In terms of self-defence, the USS America is equipped with a variety of weapons including two Rolling Airframe Missile (RAM) launchers, two Phalanx close-in weapons systems (CIWS), and several .50mm calibre machine guns. It also has an advanced radar system for detecting incoming threats.

At the time of writing the class includes America, Tripoli, Bougainville (first in the class to have a well deck) and Fallujah.

### America (LHA-6) class

**Displacement:** 45,693 tons (full load)
**Length:** 257m/844ft (overall)
**Beam:** 32m/106ft
**Draught:** 7.9/26ft
**Armament:** 2 x Rolling Airframe Missile launchers, 2 x Evolved Sea Sparrow Missile launchers, M242 Bushmaster Machine Gun System, 7 x twin .50 BMG machine guns
**Machinery:** Two marine gas turbines, two shafts
**Power:** 52,000 kW/70,000 bhp for 22+ knots
**Endurance:** unknown
**Complement:** 1,204 officers and enlisted personnel

# Gunboats, Fly and Insect class

The drawn-out campaign in Mesopotamia (Iraq) began simply enough when a flotilla of Royal Navy and Royal Indian Marine vessels landed a brigade of troops to safeguard the Anglo-Persian Oil Company's installations on the Shatt-al-Arab. Reinforced, the military then advanced some 113km/70 miles up the waterway to Basra to create defence in depth against the expected Turkish offensive.

Supported by naval sloops and armed auxiliaries, infantry moved along either bank, with deceptive ease, advancing a further 80km/50 miles to Kurnah, at the confluence of the Tigris and Euphrates rivers, whereon lay the main centres of population.

For "combined operations" the situation in Mesopotamia was virtually unique in that the annual wet season saw the great marshes flooded with

waist-deep water, the elevated river banks remaining as the main "highway". It was said that there was "too much water for the Army, not enough for the Navy" and the campaign was confined largely to the river corridors.

The major Royal Navy vessels initially involved were of the 1,070-ton Cadmus class of colonial sloop. As the dry season approached, and the rivers narrowed and became shallow, the ships' size and draught restricted mobility. The danger was to be stranded within range of enemy artillery.

The Royal Navy was greatly assisted by the flat-bottomed stern-wheel vessels of Messrs. Lynch and facilities at the Anglo-Persian shipyard in Abadan.

In Great Britain, Yarrow & Company, Scotstoun, Glasgow, were building a series of 12 (later increased to 16) river gunboats in sections for transport.

ABOVE: **HMS** *Gnat* **on the China Station in the summer of 1922. Commercial interests on the great Chinese rivers were endlessly disrupted by the actions of local warlords.**

Designed specifically for this campaign, the sections were assembled at Abadan, where an Admiralty Overseer employed by Yarrow supervised a multinational workforce at the rapidly expanded shipyard.

Known as the Fly class, the small vessels were called "China Gunboats" at Yarrow's in order to conceal their true role. At working displacement, the type drew no more than 0.6m/2ft, but could carry a 4in gun, together with a 12pdr, 6pdr and 2pdr "Pom-Pom" and two Maxim machine-guns. The vessels were useful but, because of weight reduction lacked adequate armour protection. The single screw worked

LEFT: **HMS** *Ladybird*, **an Insect-class gunboat at Port Said, Egypt, November 1917. The very shallow hull meant that machinery and boilers extended into the superstructure. The high spotting position was required in order to observe over river banks.**

in a tunnel in the after hull. The single boiler was vulnerable to the constant attack by snipers.

First of the class was HMS *Firefly*, commissioned in November 1915. An enthusiastic First Sea Lord, Admiral Sir John "Jacky" Fisher, wrote to Lord Jellicoe; "I went specially to Glasgow to hustle these gunboats and see them packed in pieces and sent off. They were a wonder! And I do hope old Yarrow will receive commendation and a GCMG (medal) or something".

In parallel with the Fly class, a larger type of river gunboat was being built. The Insect class was termed the "Large China Gunboat" class, and although the vessels were really intended for operations on the River Danube, they were not used. Twelve vessels were built by five shipyards and commissioned from March 1916. Capable of limited open-sea passages, several were deployed in the Mesopotamia campaign.

With two screws and two boilers, the Insect class was faster, more manoeuvrable and less vulnerable. The type was also far more heavily armed but with light protection. The inevitable result was larger ships with deeper draught that became too large for operations during the dry season.

In order to view over high river banks, both types of gunboat were fitted with high masts with spotting platforms. The Insect class could also mount 6in howitzers which became useful for indirect support fire, using forward spotters with telephone communication.

Owing to what Fisher described as the "pestilential climate", the Insect class was fitted with hand-operated ice-making machines. According to one commanding officer, these resulted in only "perspiration and profanity. No ice."

Baghdad was occupied in March 1918, the gunboats having been used as amphibious warfare vessels before the term had been invented.

ABOVE: **Still useful during World War II, surviving Insect-class vessels served with the Inshore Flotilla, North Africa. Modifications on HMS *Aphis* included a built-up bow for open-sea use, light automatic weapons, rafts and a larger bridge.**

## Gunboat, Insect class

**Displacement:** 625 tons (normal); 645 tons (full load)
**Length:** 70.15m/230ft (bp); 72.44m/237ft 6in (oa)
**Beam:** 10.98m/36ft
**Draught:** 1.37m/4ft 6in (maximum)
**Armament:** 2 x 6in guns (2x1), 2 x 12pdr guns (2x1), 6 Maxim
**Machinery:** Vertical triple-expansion, steam reciprocating engines, 2 boilers, 2 shafts
**Power:** 1,492kW/2,000ihp for 14 knots
**Fuel:** Oil
**Endurance:** Not known
**Protection:** Splinter-proof
**Complement:** 55

# Landing Ship, Tank (LST), Maracaibo type

Early British amphibious operations showed that raids against defended locations were unlikely to succeed without armoured support. An urgent requirement developed for a seagoing tank carrier, to land 25- to 40-ton vehicles directly on to a beach, rather than using slow over-the-side loading into smaller craft. It was 1940 and, with no earlier experience of such a vessel, it was decided to convert three small oil tankers.

The ships had been designed for the Shell Oil Company to negotiate the shallow bar at Maracaibo, Venezuela, when carrying crude to the company's Aruba refinery. The hull was consequently very wide and shallow.

To reduce wasted space and free surface area (the latter affected stability) the design incorporated a raised centreline trunk deck some two levels 5m/16ft in height. The bridge block was forward of amidships and the heavy steam machinery located aft.

In conversion, the trunk was extended to the sides of the ship creating two long vehicle spaces, the trunk provided further garaging, maintenance and accommodation area. Much of the original forward oil tankage was allocated for water ballast. Flooded at sea for stability and trim, the tanks were pumped out before grounding to reduce the forward draught to around 1.2m/4ft.

ABOVE: **Although improvised, the Maracaibo type was significant in that it proved the case for the LST. The vessels were selected for their shallow draught.**

Even so, this still required the design and incorporation into the modified bow of a two-part ramp, extendable to around 30.5m/100ft to allow tanks to be landed. Ten- and 25-ton cargo derricks were also provided. The original oil-cargo tanks were also utilized to extend fuel space.

All three ships proved invaluable at the Oran sector of the North African (Operation "Torch") landings. In practice, however, the vessels were too large for the task. The three Maracaibo-type vessels gave excellent experience for designing of what would soon become the Landing Ship Tank LST (1).

ABOVE: **HMS *Bachaquero*, one of the oil tankers converted to an LST, being unloaded at Bone harbour, Sicily, on March 16, 1943. Over 100 Bren Gun Carriers and crews were carried on the vessel.**

## Landing Ship, Tank (LST), Maracaibo type

**Tonnage:** 4,890 tons (gross);
   5,710 tons (displacement)
**Length:** 19.52m/64ft
**Beam:** 10.98m/36ft
**Draught (seagoing):** 3.28m/10ft (mean)
**Draught (beaching):** 1.29m/4ft 3in (forward);
   4.58m/15ft (aft)
**Armament:** 4 x 2pdr "Pom-Pom" (4x1),
   6 x 20mm (6x1) smoke mortars
**Machinery:** 2 vertical triple expansion steam
   engines, twin shafts
**Power:** 2,238kW/3,000ihp for 10 knots
**Endurance:** 11,408km/6,200m at 10 knots
**Complement:** 98
**Capacity:** 18–22 tanks, 2 LCMs on deck,
   210 troops

ABOVE: **HMS** *Bruiser*, one of the three vessels built. A sister ship, HMS *Boxer*, was converted to a navigational training ship after World War II and was later used for experimental radar trials.
LEFT: **HMS** *Thruster*, the third vessel in the class, at sea. The 40-ton crane is in the raised position.

# Landing Ship, Tank (LST), LST (1) class

Even as the experimental Maracaibo-type tankers were being converted, specialist ships were also being designed and built. Prime Minister Churchill's demand for an ocean-going tank-carrier capable of lifting the full 60-tank establishment of an armoured division proved impractical because of size and draught. In place of this a class of three 20-tank capacity ships was built. As the original project had, unofficially, been referred to as a "Winston", the smaller type became known as "Winettes". Classified as "Tank Assault Carriers", all were later recategorized as Landing Ships, Tank, Mk 1 (LST [1]) to differentiate from other LST types then in series production. Uniquely, all were named from the outset; HMS *Boxer*, HMS *Bruiser* and HMS *Thruster*.

Without earlier experience for guidance, designers had to make some presumptions. One was that

a 17-knot speed was critical, a full six knots faster than later, mass-produced LSTs. This required a hull with a finer entry and a deeper draught. Thus able to beach but only on slopes of 1 in 37 or steeper (*cf.* 1 in 50 for later LSTs) a two-part, 36.25m/119ft forward ramp was still required. This could be lengthened with an 26m/85ft causeway extension. Clamshell-type bow doors maintained the external shape, protecting a vertically hinged watertight door.

The engine and boiler room were located (inconveniently) amidships, necessitating loading being offset to starboard to allow through access for vehicles. Although capacity was less than that of later LSTs, the class introduced an open upper deck, accessible by elevator from the enclosed tank deck. A 40-ton crane was supplied to handle the small landing craft carried on deck. Elaborate

by later standards, these relatively fast ships proved valuable for special operations.

**Landing Ship, Tank, LST (1) class**

**Displacement:** 3,616 tons (beaching); 5,410 tons (full load, seagoing)
**Length:** 118.95m/390ft (bp); 122m/400ft (oa)
**Beam:** 17.15m/49ft
**Draught (beaching):** 1.6m/5ft 6in (forward); 4.54m/14ft 10in (aft)
**Armament:** 4 x 2pdr "Pom-Pom" (4x1), 8 x 20mm (8x1), smoke mortars
**Machinery:** Steam turbines, 2 shafts
**Power:** 5,222kW/7,000shp for 17 knots
**Fuel:** 2,100 tons oil
**Endurance:** 14,270km/8,000nm at 14 knots
**Protection:** Nominal
**Complement:** 165
**Capacity:** 13 x 40-ton or 20 x 25-ton tanks, or 28 loaded trucks, plus 193 troops

LEFT: **The British LST (3) was larger and more powerful than the diesel-driven US-built LST (2). After the war all were retained in service. British-built L3044 was modified to carry one LCT and five LCAs on deck.**

# Landing Ship, Tank, Mark 3 (LST [3])

With completions beginning at the end of 1942, the LST (2) programme in the US eventually ran to over 1,000 hulls. Of these, 114 were transferred to the British under the Lend-Lease Program and required for mainly Allied joint operations. But the British needed more to assist in the recovery of territories seized by the Japanese. The refusal by the US government was partly political, so the British built their own LSTs.

The resulting LST (3) makes an interesting comparison with the more familiar LST (2). Against an April 1945 delivery target, 45 were ordered from British yards and 35 (later 74) from Canadian. Off these, 35 and 26 respectively were completed before hostilities ended in August 1945.

US-built diesel engines were offered, but not auxiliaries, necessitating the installation of frigate-type steam reciprocating engines, one to each shaft.

Because of the distances involved in Pacific operations, a British Staff Requirement specified 15 knots (LST [2] was 10.8 knots). The penalties on hull design were such, however, that 13 knots was agreed. The result was a deeper beaching draught, caused by finer lines made heavier by a riveted hull. Riveting was necessary because neither British nor Canadian yards had yet adopted welding for ship building.

ABOVE: **HMS *Reggio* (L3511) was one of 16 further steam-driven LSTs modified to carry assault craft under davits. The vessel is entering Grand Harbour, Malta.**

Externally the LST (3) differed from the smaller LST (2) in having a larger funnel and two substantial kingposts mounted against the front of the bridge for handling LCAs.

The open upper deck was connected to the tank deck by a ramp. As an alternative to motor transport, the upper deck could accommodate five LCM (6) or causeway pontoon units, resting on skids and launched over the side. Further causeway units could be carried against the sides of the hull.

All US-supplied LST (2) were returned in 1945, the LST (3) remaining as the standard post-war British tank landing ships. British-built vessels were numbered LST 3001–3045 and those Canadian-built were numbered LST 3501–3574.

## Landing Ship, Tank, LST (3)

**Displacement:** 4,980 tons (full load, seagoing); 3,065 tons (beaching)
**Length:** 100.53m/330ft (bp); 106m/347ft 6in
**Beam:** 16.83m/55ft 3in
**Draught (beaching):** 1.4m/4ft 7in (forward); 3.51m/11ft 6in (aft)
**Armament:** 10 x 20mm guns (4x2, 2x1)
**Machinery:** 2 vertical steam reciprocating engines, 2 shafts
**Power:** 4,103kW/5,500ihp for 13 knots
**Fuel:** Not known
**Endurance:** 14,720km/8,000nm at 11 knots at seagoing displacement
**Protection:** Some splinter protection
**Complement:** 104
**Capacity:** 15 x 40-ton or 27 x 25-ton tanks, plus 14 loaded trucks and 168 troops

# Landing Ship, Emergency Repair (LSE)

The Operation "Torch" landings of November 1942 were staged at several differing locations. As the largest such operations to date, valuable lessons were learned, none more so than that the attrition rate in small assault craft was far higher than planners had anticipated. Landing Ships, Tank (LST) were not yet available, so the assaults were dependent on smaller craft off-loaded from attack transports (APA) and cargo ships (AKA). On the Atlantic coast of Morocco heavy surf was a problem. Inexperienced coxswains had to cope with darkness, unexpected sea currents, falling tides and, often,

strafing by aircraft or being targeted by artillery. Not surprisingly, craft collided when ranged together on landing. Others broached in the surf, stranded and became swamped through poor load distribution. Many salvageable craft were simply abandoned and left to break up. Total loss rates varied widely from around 20 per cent to an unsustainable 94.2 per cent.

In the same way that the US Marine Corps soon identified the need for dedicated teams to move stores quickly away from a beach, the US Navy moved to establish an organization for the salvage and repair of assault craft. Larger craft, such

ABOVE: **The function of the LSE was primarily to reduce the high attrition rate among small landing craft. Many were recoverable, but were often abandoned.**

as LCTs, were often docked in LSDs, for which the latter had been neither designed nor intended. For smaller craft, some 40 US-built LST (2) were earmarked for conversion to Auxiliary Repair Ships (ARL). Two vessels, ARL-5 and 6, were transferred to the Royal Navy, being referred to as Landing Ships, Emergency Repair, or LSE (1) and (2).

Conversions varied but on most the ramps were removed and bow doors permanently sealed. The elevator was removed, the opening becoming an access hatch. An A-frame could be stepped to the port-side deck edge to support a 50- (later 60-) ton derrick.

ABOVE: **Landing Ship, Emergency Repair (LSE) quickly became non-standard with the addition of more workshop and accommodation space. The heavily braced kingpost supports a 60-ton derrick.**

| Landing Ship, Emergency Repair, LST (2) as ARL |  |
| --- | --- |

**Displacement:** 1,490 tons (light)
**Length:** 96.4m/316ft (wl); 100m/327ft 9in (oa)
**Beam:** 15.3m/50ft 2in
**Draught:** 3.35m/11ft (normal operating condition)
**Armament:** 1 x 3in gun, 8 x 40mm (2x4), 8 x 20mm (8x1)
**Machinery:** 2 diesel engines, 2 shafts
**Power:** 1,343kW/1,800shp for 10.8 knots
**Fuel:** Not known
**Endurance:** 34,518km/18,760nm at 10 knots
**Protection:** 9.5mm/$^3$/8in plate for splinter protection
**Complement:** 108

# Fighter Direction Tender (FDT)

The British Landing Ships, Headquarters (LSH) and the US Navy equivalent (AGC) were equipped to undertake the control of the airspace over an operational area as part of the headquarters function. Again, however, it took only the first real test, the North African (Operation "Torch") landings, to highlight shortcomings. Maintaining a running plot of friendly and enemy aircraft entailed the use of radars, high-frequency direction finding, beacons and considerable specialist manpower.

The British solution was to convert three LST (2) into what were first called Fighter Direction Tenders (FDT). Several masts and the large, rotating search radar antenna made the type conspicuous. For the conversion, bow doors were permanently sealed, and the tank deck was divided into generator spaces, offices and accommodation for an extra 170 highly trained RAF personnel.

The nature of the conversion left the vessels lightly loaded, with a low centre of gravity (CG). The resulting large height gave a rapid roll that did not suit

the use of unstabilized antennas. A solution was to lay some 700 tons of pig-iron slabs on the weather deck, giving extra protection and raising the CG. Even this measure proved inadequate, designers resorting to what, usually, was the necessity for fuel and fresh water tanks being given large free surface areas. This would allow a pronounced transverse shift of CG on rolling.

Several small commercial vessels were also converted for Fighter Direction, most combining the function with a high-angle, heavy anti-aircraft armament. The definitive conversions were, however, to have been to the three Boxer-class LST (1) (HMS *Boxer*, *Thruster* and *Bruiser*), but only the named ship appears to have been fully modified. HMS *Boxer* became a familiar sight at post-war Portsmouth in service as a navigation training ship.

ABOVE: **Landing Ship, Tank (LST-216) was one of three LST (2) to be converted to a Fighter Direction Tender (FDT). All three vessels were positioned for the D-Day landings on June 6, 1944.** BELOW: **HMS *Boxer* after conversion to a Fighter Direction Ship in preparation for the Normandy operation.**

**Fighter Direction Ship, HMS *Boxer*, as modified**

**Displacement:** 5,970 tons
**Length:** 118.81m/390ft (bp); 121.86m/400ft (oa)
**Beam:** 14.93m/49ft
**Draught:** Not known
**Armament:** Unarmed
**Machinery:** Steam turbines, 2 shafts
**Power:** 5,222kW/7,000shp for 16 knots
**Fuel:** Not known
**Endurance:** Not known
**Protection:** Nominal
**Complement:** approximately 500

LEFT: **Built in Australia as a coastal passenger liner, HMS** *Bulolo* **was converted to be the first combined-services headquarters ship, capable of coordinating a full-scale amphibious operation.**

# Landing Ship, Headquarters (LSH)

The unsuccessful attempt by Free French forces (Operation "Menace") to capture Dakar in September 1940 resulted in two innovations of major importance to the development of amphibious warfare. A requirement for an ocean-going tank carrier produced the LST, while the need for a dedicated command platform resulted in the LSH.

Aboard the cruiser HMS *Devonshire* during the attack, military and naval staffs worked around the clock "in an infernal sweating twilight", and communications and procedures conflicted. The force commander was at the mercy of any naval emergency and was later to write: "Seldom have I felt so impotent as

during this operation…[I was] heading northwards at 25 knots while my forces were proceeding south at 12 knots."

An earlier proposal for a purpose-built Headquarters Ship, about which nothing had been done, was confirmed in January 1942 for completion within six months. The Australian-built coastal liner SS *Bulolo* was converted to accommodate an all-service staff, some 500 in total and including nine senior officers, sufficient to control a division-scale landing.

A war command room was provided, together with separate Army and Navy operation rooms. Two modern radar systems, not least to support the Fighter Direction (FD) function (which was

to prove inadequate) were carried. A mass of communications equipment necessary to link the various elements of the operation, until such time as a headquarters could be established ashore, was also carried.

Completed mid-1942, HMS *Bulolo* was involved in the Algiers sector of the North African landings. Before this, however, the ship had impressed the US Navy sufficiently to place an order for three of the type, which became the first AGCs.

A further three larger LSH (L) – the HMS *Hilary*, *Largs* and *Lothian* – were to follow. Also around 12 small LSH (S), based mainly on frigate hulls, were used on minor operations.

ABOVE: **To conceal her significance, the external appearance of HMS** *Hilary* **has been modified to the minimum. The A-frame at the bows was used when streaming minesweeping paravanes.**

## Landing Ship, Headquarters (LSH), HMS *Bulolo*, on conversion

**Displacement:** 9,330 tons (full load)
**Length:** 121.7m/339ft (bp);
   125.82m/412ft 6in (oa)
**Beam:** 17.77m/58ft 3in
**Draught:** 6.56m/21ft 6in (full load)
**Armament (designed):** 4 x 4in guns (2x2),
   5 x 40mm (5x1), 14 x 20mm (14x1)
**Machinery:** 2 diesel engines, 2 shafts
**Power:** 4,588kW/6,150bhp for 15 knots
**Fuel:** Not known
**Endurance:** 14,720km/8,000nm at 12 knots
**Protection:** Nominal
**Complement:** 264 + embarked ships

# Landing Ship, Infantry (LSI)

I n British terminology, the function of a troopship was simply to transport a large number of troops from one point to another. The Landing Ship, Infantry (LSI), on the other hand, carried a military formation direct to the point of attack, to be embarked in assault craft for the landing. To suit the scale of various operations, the LSI was built in sizes classified as Large, LSI (L), Medium, LSI (M), or Small, LSI (S).

The concept of ships carrying both troops and assault craft had been considered pre-war. But a purpose-built vessel was rejected as being little superior to a converted merchant ship and too expensive. With the German capture of Norway in April 1940, the case for the LSI was made and three new Glen Line

cargo liners (SS *Glenearn*, *Glengoyle* and *Glenroy*) were identified as suitable vessels for the transport of 1,000 troops and twelve LCAs. Weighing up to 14 tons loaded, the LCAs were designed to be carried under davits. The British were fortunate to have a company, Welin Maclachlan Davits Limited, with considerable design ingenuity, whose products were later fitted to all US-built APAs. Later in the war, the Glen-class ships were fitted with revised davits and stowage, enabling the transportation of 24 LCAs. Three LCMs were carried on deck, and handled by the ship's cargo gear.

In size and capacity a Glen class compared directly with the C3 conversions that became the US standard – slightly longer, a little narrower and with around

ABOVE: **More powerfully armed than the US-built APAs, the Glen class had six 4in HA guns in three twin mountings, together with full director control. HMS** *Glenearn* **is shown here at anchor during an exercise.**

10 per cent less troop capacity (US troop formations differing in size from British equivalents). In general, designated cargo spaces were easily converted into compartments for messes and military stores other than vehicles. Not so obvious, perhaps, was that space needed to be created for the fuel tanks and the evaporators necessary for the production and storage of considerable quantities of fresh water. Space was also required for increased generator capacity and for fuel tanks to supply the LCAs. In addition, extra space (some refrigerated) was required for

LEFT: **SS** *Empire Javelin*, **originally named SS** *Cape Lobos*, **was launched in 1944 for service with the US War Shipping Administration. The vessel was a bareboat chartered by the Transport Department of the British Ministry of War, and managed by the Blue Star Line.**

galleys, bakeries, ammunition magazines and a sick bay. Although built to the same high standards as commercial cargo vessels, the Glen class were now intended to be used in war, so subdivision and stability range had to be improved. Paradoxically, following all this work, the ships were still very much in the "light" condition, much valuable space being used to accommodate permanent solid ballast.

The Glen class were considered a valuable asset and used only for special operations. With the planning for the eventual invasion of Europe proceeding apace, however, further LSI (L) were obviously going to be required. With no further tonnage suitable for conversion, the British sought US assistance, acquiring 13 C1s during 1943. These smaller, single-shaft ships were slower

and more vulnerable than the Glen class, but were intended to carry 1,000 troops over only short distances. The vessels carried 18 LCAs under davits.

Operated by the Ministry of War Transport with civilian crews, the class was identified by the lead ship, HMS *Empire Broadsword*. Following the successful Normandy landings, planning attention was switched to the Far East. The surviving 11 ships were transferred to the White Ensign and renamed after famous racehorses. Nine were "tropicalized" and sent to the Pacific, but operated mainly in casualty evacuation.

Further down the scale, the difference between the LSI (M) and LSI (S) was mainly a matter of degree. Being converted from passenger ferries all were valuable as, despite limited range, being

ABOVE: **Following service as Armed Merchant Cruisers, the Royal Canadian Navy's HMCS** *Prince Henry* **and HMCS** *Prince David* **were reconverted to LSI (M). Both were used for the Normandy landings on June 6, 1944.**

capable of around 24 knots. Best were the two Ex-Canadian National Steamships (CNS) ferries, HMCS *Prince David* and HMCS *Prince Henry*, and the Dutch HMS *Princess Beatrix* and HMS *Queen Emma*. Carrying some 450 and 375 troops respectively, each carried two LCMs in addition to six LCAs. Similar in size and speed, but accommodating only 200–250 troops, were the nine mainly ex-Belgian State Railways LSI (S).

ABOVE: **Dutch-flagged, HMS** *Princess Beatrix* **(shown here) and HMS** *Queen Emma* **were built for the Harwich-Hook service. Much modified as LSI (M), they retained their distinctively shaped funnels.**

---

### Landing Ship, Infantry, LSI (L), Glen class

**Tonnage:** 9,840 tons (gross);
　　15,500 tons (displacement, full load)
**Length:** 146.1m/479ft (bp);
　　155.86m/511ft (oa)
**Beam:** 20.28m/66ft 6in
**Draught:** 9.3m/30ft 6in (loaded)
**Armament:** 6 x 4in guns (3x2),
　　4 x 2pdr "Pom-Pom" (4x1), 8 x 20mm (8x1)
**Machinery:** 2 diesel engines, 2 shafts
**Power:** 8,952kW/12,000shp for 18 knots
**Fuel:** Not known
**Endurance:** 22,080km/12,000nm at 14.5 knots
**Protection:** Nominal
**Complement:** 523
**Capacity:** 3 LCMs, 24 LCAs, 1,098 troops

# Landing Ship, Carrier, Derrick Hoisting/ Gantry/Stern-chute (LSC/LSG/LSS)

Landing Ships, Infantry (LSI) carried mainly LCAs, (i.e. troop-carrying craft); the ability to transport heavy equipment, and the LCMs with which to land it, was limited to what could be stowed on deck. For any landing larger than a raid, therefore, LSIs would require support by vessels dedicated to carrying cargo and LCMs. The latter were required in numbers sufficient to facilitate rapid ship-to-shore movement. To carry both heavy equipment and LCMs on the same ship appeared advantageous, but this was difficult in practice as a 35-ton loaded LCM (I) needed specialized means of launch and recovery.

A dedicated LCM carrier was the obvious answer but this, in 1940, was beyond Britain's resources to produce. Until such a vessel, ultimately the LSD, could be obtained from the USA (the first four not being delivered until September 1943), suitable examples would need to be modified from ships already in service.

ABOVE: **Three Dale-class tankers were equipped with gantries to handle 15 LCMs, stowed on deck and moved on rollers. The ships transported small craft, but were not used as assault ships. RFA** Derwentdale **lies at anchor in 1942.**

RIGHT: **Two railway-owned train ferries were requisitioned to carry 13 LCMs apiece. This is the stern ramp of HMS** Princess Iris.

The simplest means of shipping LCMs in numbers was to carry them as deck cargo, using heavy-lift derricks for launch and recovery. Sir W. G. Armstrong Whitworth & Company Limited had recently built a suitable vessel for Belship, a specialist Norwegian shipping company, and ten were ordered by the Ministry of War Transport (MoWT). Only the first two, HMS *Empire Charmian* and *Empire Elaine*, were designated Landing Ship, Carrier, Derrick Hoisting (LSC).The ships were built with machinery aft and the bridge forward of amidships. Three 120-ton lifting derricks were stepped against substantial posts. The large hatch covers were reinforced to support the distributed load of 21 pre-loaded LCM (I). Substantial ballasting and pumping capacity permitted the ships to maintain stability, while working heavily loaded.

Three tankers (RFA *Derwentdale*, *Dewdale* and *Ennerdale*) were modified to Landing Ship, Carrier, Gantry (LSG). Carrying liquid cargoes, the deck-piping was retained, which limited the LCM capacity to 15, six stowed forward of the bridge, nine behind. These were handled by massive lifting gantries on each side. Pre-loaded with a maximum of 9 tons, the LCMs were slid to the gantries.

Because the LSGs could at the same time carry some 7,000 tons of hazardous cargo (or, in the Far East, fresh water) the type were used to deliver LCMs to a front rather than to a specific operational location.

A third variety of interim LCM carrier came from the modification of two of London & North-Eastern Railway's (LNER) three train ferries to Landing Ships, Carrier, Stern-chute (LSS). These were old vessels dating from World War I. Beamy and slow (11 knots), the vessels had a low freeboard deck fronted by a bluff bow and flanked by narrow side decks. Over 80 per cent of the length was laid to four parallel tracks for railway rolling stock, which was loaded and discharged over the stern. When converted, the stern was reconfigured as a ramped slipway and, mainly on the existing rails, 13 LCM (I) were stowed on trolleys. At the forward end of the vehicle deck a traversing system was installed to align LCMs from the side tracks to the centre, from where the boats were launched.

The conversions were made during 1940 but age, lack of endurance and speed made the two ships unsuitable for front-line service, and they were used

ABOVE: **One of two of railway-owned ferries, HMS *Daffodil* had a train deck running almost her complete length. Thirteen loaded LCMs could be carried and trolley-launched over the stern ramp.**

only to transport LCMs. During 1943 both were converted back to transport railway rolling stock to the shattered European network, after the D-Day landings. From early 1942, LSDs built in the USA used the most simple and versatile means of launching small craft in numbers, that of float-on, float-off.

## Landing Ship, Carrier (LSC), HMS *Empire Charmian*

**Tonnage:** 7,510 tons (gross); 14,500 tons (displacement, full load)
**Length:** 126.88m/416ft (bp); 132.22m/433ft 6in (oa)
**Beam:** 20.36m/66ft 9in
**Draught:** 8.08m/26ft 6in (mean)
**Armament:** 1 x 4in gun, 1 x 12pdr, 6 x 20mm (6x1)
**Machinery:** Diesel engine, single shaft
**Power:** 1,865kW/2,500bhp for 11 knots
**Fuel:** Not known
**Endurance:** 4,232km/2,300nm at 10 knots
**Protection:** Nominal
**Complement:** 40
**Capacity:** 21 LCM (I), 295 troops

# Commando Carriers

To rapidly increase the number of available flight decks during World War II, the Admiralty embarked on the extensive series of "no-frills" Colossus/Majestic-class carriers, collectively termed the "Light Fleets". Rapid increase in aircraft size and weight, however, demanded a larger version. These, and the opportunities to improve speed by a full five knots, increased standard displacement from the "Light Fleets" 13,190 tons to 18,310. By completion of the first of what became known as the Centaur class, this had increased to 20,260 tons.

As the war progressed, so did the Royal Navy's priorities; carrier construction was being reduced. Few "Light Fleets" were completed by the end of the war and only four of a planned eight of the class had been laid down. Post-war, the hulls were slowly completed to launching condition, mainly to clear the shipyards. HMS *Albion*, HMS *Bulwark* and HMS *Centaur* were launched between 1947 and 1948, but HMS *Hermes* was not launched until 1953. On completion, the

first three were already obsolete, and HMS *Hermes* was completed in 1959 to a considerably updated specification.

British amphibious warfare specialists had been following with interest US Marine Corps trials in using carrier-borne helicopters to land spearhead troops. In 1955 they requested suitable aircraft and ships to develop the method in the Royal Navy. The Suez crisis occured shortly afterward. Here, with minimal rehearsal, two "Light Fleets" were able to validate the concept ("Vertical Envelopment") for the first time in combat.

The US Navy ordered the first dedicated Landing Ship, Personnel, Helicopter (LPH), USS *Iwo Jima*, in February 1959. The Royal Navy's three Centaur-class ships, only marginally effective in the strike role, were relatively new and available for conversion. Government funding permitted only two, HMS *Albion* and *Bulwark*, to be modified into what were designated as "Commando Carriers". Both ships were selected because, as yet, neither had received any modernization.

ABOVE: **Although stripped of aircraft handling equipment, HMS *Bulwark* (R08) here retains the original aircraft carrier configuration. The vessel is at US Naval Station, Mayport, Florida.**

Portsmouth Dockyard converted HMS *Bulwark* (1959–60), then HMS *Albion* (1961–62). The major alteration lay in the removal of equipment associated with "fixed-wing" operations – catapults and arrestor gear. Maintenance facilities were installed for each carrier's 16 helicopters, initially Westland S-55 Whirlwind but replaced by Westland Wessex HAS-1 on their introduction in 1961. Developed from the US-built Sikorsky S-58 Choctaw, the Wessex could lift 16 equipped Royal Marines. HMS *Albion* could accommodate 800 troops, HMS *Bulwark* around 730. Both ships were fitted to carry four LCVPs under davits, to allow the troops to be landed during non-flying weather conditions.

From early in 1966, government policy was to run down the Royal Navy carrier force, for which there would be no replacement. HMS *Hermes*, last of the class to be completed, was kept in front-line service until 1971, escaping disposal

by a two-year conversion to join the Commando Carriers. On her completion to this role in 1973, HMS *Albion* was, in fact, decommissioned.

Benefiting from the experience gained with earlier refits, that carried out on HMS *Hermes* was more effective. To maximize hangar and flight deck area, the forward elevator had been located on the port deck edge, US Navy-style. This formed, in the raised position, part of the overhang of the fully angled flight deck. This extra capacity allowed some 73 Royal Marines to be accommodated. A total of 16 Westland Wessex helicopters and four LCVPs, together with a flight of four Westland S-61 Sea King ASW helicopters were carried. A second full Commando could be accommodated in an emergency.

Conversion again involved the removal of "fixed-wing carrier" equipment, the large Type 984 three-dimensional radar being replaced by a "single bedstead" Type 965 air search unit.

With the introduction of V/STOL, HMS *Hermes* regained front-line status, operating both Hawker-Siddeley Sea Harrier FRS-1 and Sea King ASW/ AEW while still retaining Commando capabilities. The ship was to demonstrate during the 1982 Falklands War the continuing relevance of the aircraft carrier. After the war the ship was sold to India. HMS *Albion* was scrapped in 1973 and HMS *Bulwark* in 1984.

ABOVE: **HMS *Albion* (R07) was built as a Centaur-class aircraft carrier in 1947 and converted into a "Commando Carrier" in 1962. The Westland Wessex HU-5 entered operational service in 1964. The type could carry up to 16 troops or, underslung, artillery or a light vehicle. Sixteen were carried by each "Commando Carrier", although, as can be seen, only eight could be spotted simultaneously. A complement of 800 Royal Marines was accommodated onboard.**

LEFT: **Although operating helicopters only, HMS *Hermes* (R12) retained the angled deck and "ski jump". Note the side elevator, set into the overhang.**

## Commando Carrier, HMS *Hermes*

**Displacement:** 23,900 tons (standard);
  28,700 tons (full load)
**Length:** 198.25m/650ft (bp);
  227.02m/744ft 4in (oa)
**Beam:** 27.45m/90ft (wl)
**Draught:** 8.85m/29ft (mean)
**Armament:** 2 x quadruple Sea Cat PDMS
**Machinery:** Steam turbines, 4 boilers,
  2 shafts
**Power:** 56,696kW/76,000shp for 28 knots
**Fuel:** 3,380 tons oil
**Endurance:** 8,832kW/4,800nm at 20 knots
**Protection:** Not known
**Complement:** 1,830 plus 733 troops
**Capacity:** 20 helicopters

LEFT: **HMS *Manxman*, launched on September 5, 1940, was the last of six Abdiel-class fast minelayers built for the Royal Navy in World War II. In 1960 the vessel was converted to a Support Ship for minelayers. Two 4in gun mountings and two boiler rooms were removed to create space for workshops and accommodation.**

# Minesweeper Support Ship

ABOVE: **Designed as a minesweeper support ship, the layout of HMS *Abdiel* was similar to that of HMS *Manxman*.** LEFT: **HMS *Abdiel* also functioned as an Exercise Minelayer, but in wartime could be used to lay mines.**

Amphibious operations always need to be preceded by mine clearance. Minehunters/sweepers are small ships and are not intended to work alone. Submarines and destroyers have, in the past, been supported by large, purpose-designed tenders or depot ships.

Of only 360 tons, the Ton-class Coastal Minesweepers (CMS) for instance, were deployed in the Far East during the so-called "Indonesia-Malay Dispute" of 1963–66, often as patrol craft and only supported by HMS *Manxman*, a Fast Minelayer. Laid down in 1939, the ship was the last of six in the class. When new the vessel could make 36 knots (although invariably credited with over 40 knots). Later two of the four boilers were removed to create new space for extra generator and evaporator capacity. The design featured two long mining decks,

terminating in doors set into an almost flat transom. These galleries ( a weak point from the survivability aspect) were ideal for storage of spare equipment to support CMS. This experience probably influenced the decision to build the 1,375-ton HMS *Abdiel*. Launched in 1967, the vessel was diesel-driven and functioned as an Exercise Minelayer, with minesweeper support duties. For this the ship was built with unusually spacious facilities for a small warship. As an Exercise Minelayer, the task was to lay all types of modern mine for Minehunters/sweepers to find, classify and neutralize (or recover). The capacity of 44 mines was also useful offensively, but in this context the lack of speed was a limiting factor.

HMS *Abdiel* was used between 1974 and 1975 in support of CMS deployed to clear mines and unexploded

ordnance from the Suez Canal, which had been closed following the Yom Kippur War (also the October/Ramadan War), October 6–25, 1973.

| Minesweeper Support Ship, HMS *Abdiel* |  |
|---|---|

**Displacement:** 1,375 tons (standard); 1,500 tons (full load)
**Length:** 74,57m/244ft 6in (bp); 80.83m/265ft (oa)
**Beam:** 11.74m/38ft 6in
**Draught:** 3.05m/10ft (mean)
**Armament:** Light automatic weapons, normally unarmed
**Machinery:** 2 diesel engines, 2 shafts
**Power:** 2,014kW/2,700bhp for 16 knots
**Fuel:** Not known
**Endurance:** Not known
**Protection:** Not known
**Complement:** 123

LEFT: **The replacement RFA *Sir Galahad* was of an uprated design that was nearly 13m/42ft 8in greater in length. She and the modernized *Sir Bedivere* were recognizable by their distinctive mast and funnel.**

# Landing Ship, Logistic (LSL), Sir Lancelot class

Suez highlighted the parlous condition of the Royal Navy's amphibious capability. Commencing in 1960, new vessels began to replace the older vessels from World War II. Launched early in 1964, RFA *Sir Lancelot* was the first of six versatile 17-knot landing ships. All were built to commercial standards and, until transfer to the Royal Fleet Auxillary (RFA) in 1970, were operated under charter.

All had a raised forecastle and afterdeck, designed for "drive-through" operation with doors and ramps at either end. The tank deck, accommodating 16 main battle tanks, was connected

by ramp to the open upper deck amidships, where there was stowage for 34 large vehicles. Cranes served the upper deck and, via a hatch, the tank deck. Aft was a helicopter landing platform, but no hangar. Accommodation was for over 400 troops.

Not designed to beach, except in an emergency, the ships carried powered "Mexeflote" pontoons against each side of the hull in place of small landing craft. Designed to have considerable range, the type could operate worldwide. The original RFA *Sir Galahad* was lost in the Falklands, being replaced by a

new ship of the same name in 1987. At 145m/480ft and displacing over 8,500 tons, the ship was considerably larger than other LSLs. The ship had arranged two interconnected internal decks, linked to the upper deck by both ramps and a scissor-type lift. While having much the same vehicle capacity, alternatively, it was possible to stow up to six large helicopters on the vehicle deck. These were lifted to the two landing spots on the upper deck by elevator. Both types of LSL were used very effectively as mine forces support ships in the Arabian Gulf. For these duties a fully containerized Forward Support Unit, completely fitted-out for rapid deployment, was carried. The last of the class in Royal Navy service, *Sir Bedivere*, was retired in 2008.

ABOVE: **RFA *Sir Bedivere*, as built. The half-lowered stern ramp was for the use of vehicles only; there was no stern docking well.**
LEFT: **RFA *Sir Geraint* shows the class appearance as built in the 1960s. Note how the helicopter deck was one level higher than that of the later design.**

## Landing Ship, Logistic (LSL), Sir Lancelot class

**Tonnage:** 4,475 tons (gross); 3,270 tons (displacement, light); 5,675 tons (displacement, full load)
**Length:** 111.72m/366ft 4in (bp) 125.66m/412ft (oa)
**Beam:** 18.24m/59ft 10in
**Draught:** 4m/13ft (mean, seagoing)
**Armament:** Light automatic weapons only
**Machinery:** 2 diesel engines, 2 shafts
**Power:** 6,956kW/9,400bhp for 17 knots
**Fuel:** 816 tons oil
**Endurance:** 14,270km/8,000nm at 15 knots
**Protection:** Nominal
**Complement:** 68

# Landing Platform, Dock (LPD), Fearless class

Having returned the four Lend-Lease, Casa Grande class LSDs at the end of World War II, the Royal Navy operated none of the type for the next 20 years. The US Navy continued development and, between 1962 and 1963, commissioned two Raleigh-class LPDs, a more versatile type that exchanged some docking well space for extra garaging and stowage. When, following Suez, the British replaced the outdated Amphibious Warfare

Squadron, the Raleigh-class design was acquired as the basis for two LPDs of almost-identical dimensions. The ships were not designed to beach.

Fitted to act as Headquarters Ships for brigade-size operations, HMS *Fearless* and HMS *Intrepid* could each accommodate 400 troops on a long passage, and up to 700 on a short passage. Four LCA (later LCVP), each carrying 30-plus platoon, were stowed

under davits. Above the docking well the helicopter deck was large enough to handle four to six assault helicopters. No hangar was provided. The original ship was designed around the then main battle tank, the Centurion (52 tons), two of which could be carried by each of the six LCMs. With the larger Chieftain (54 tons) and later, the Challenger (62 tons), however, the capacity of both ship and embarked LCM was reduced. Only four LCM (9) were carried in later days. Never armed with anything heavier than point-defence weapons, the two ships were in service for 40 years and were superseded by the Ocean and Albion class.

ABOVE: **Despite having a layout similar to the US-built Raleigh-class LPD, HMS** *Fearless* **(shown here) and HMS** *Intrepid* **were instantly recognizable by the tall mainmast.**
LEFT: **The ship's LCM (9) preparing to form up prior to moving to the beach. Two Westland Sea King helicopters are stowed on the flight deck, as no hangar space was provided.**

## Landing Platform, Dock (LPD), Fearless class

**Displacement:** 11,060 tons (standard); 12,120 tons (full load); 16,950 tons (ballasted)
**Length:** 152.5m/500ft (wl); 158.6m/520ft (oa)
**Beam:** 24.4m/80ft
**Draught (seagoing):** 6.25m/29ft 6in (mean)
**Draught (ballasted down):** 7.02m/23ft (forward); 9.76m/32ft (aft)
**Armament:** 4 x quadruple Sea Cat PDMS, 2 x 40mm (2x1)
**Machinery:** Steam turbines, 2 boilers, 2 shafts
**Power:** 16,412kW/32,000shp for 21 knots
**Fuel:** 2,040 tons oil
**Endurance:** 9,200km/5,000nm at 20 knots
**Protection:** Not known
**Complement:** 556

# Landing Ship, Medium (LSM), Ardennes class

Further to military-manned (RN) and civilian-manned (RFA) amphibious warfare ships, there was also the "navy" operated by the Royal Logistics Corps (RLC). Not intended for offensive use except in an emergency, the vessels were used for training and in the supply of various garrisons.

The two "flagships" were the *Ardennes* and *Arakan* which, although classed as LSMs, had little in common with LSMs of World War II, not least in being appreciably larger. Speed was sacrificed for a wider beam and shallow draught, deck dimensions being tailored to carry five 54-ton Chieftain main battle tanks and for 24 TEU containers. As the latter were stacked, two 3-ton derricks were fitted for cargo handling.

For offensive use, the design looked vulnerable. The clamshell bows and the folded internal ramp dictated a very high forecastle making for dry seakeeping but necessitating a wheelhouse at an even higher level. Both wheelhouse and accommodation (34 troops in addition to 35 crew) were thus raised one level, allowing the deck below to be extended.

ABOVE: **On the Ardennes class, the vehicle deck extends to the after end of the bridge structure. Although head-on to the beach, the stern anchor has not been dropped.**

A surprisingly large afterdeck suggested that the whole superstructure could, with advantage, have been located further aft.

The RLC adopted the practice of naming craft after campaigns and battles commencing with the letter "A" (Army). No distinction, however, was made between class or size, so that the nine 290-ton Landing Craft, Utility (LCU) (also known as Ramped Powered Lighters – RPL), although far smaller than the Ardennes class, were named similarly from *Arromanches* to *Arezzo*.

ABOVE: **The considerably high bow is required to accommodate a usefully sized rigid loading ramp. The height also improves dryness but makes for poor visibility forward from the bridge. The large spaces under the side decks are kept empty or used to ballast the ship.**

## Landing Ship, Medium (LSM), Ardennes class

**Displacement:** 870 tons (light); 1,660 tons (full load)
**Length:** 70.15m/230ft (wl);
73.2m/240ft (oa)
**Beam:** 14m/45ft 10in
**Draught:** 17.7m/5ft 9in (maximum)
**Armament:** None
**Machinery:** 2 diesel engines, 2 shafts
**Power:** 1,492kW/2,000bhp for 10 knots
**Fuel:** 150 tons oil
**Endurance:** 5,980km/3,250nm at 10 knots
**Protection:** Nominal
**Complement:** 35 plus 34 troops

LEFT: **Like most modern merchant vessels – car carriers, container or cruise ships – the design of HMS *Ocean* was volume critical, resulting in an efficient underwater form and angular topsides. Note the Vulcan Phalanx CIWS mounting at the bow.**

# Landing Ship, Personnel, Helicopter (LPH), HMS Ocean

Design parameters for large amphibious warfare vessels are virtually limitless, balancing the conflicting demands of troop-carrying with both the heavy equipment and means of delivery. The simple approach is to include everything, but this results in ships the same size as the LHD in US Navy service. Such vessels can be unaffordable or unjustified by smaller navies, hence the requirement to make compromises. For the British this was to return to the original "Commando Carrier" concept as central to a battalion-sized operation and dependent on dock landing ships to provide heavy cargo capacity, the necessary landing craft and further troop accommodation.

Britain's capability to design and build large ships had contracted dramatically over recent decades. Savings were clearly apparent in adopting the existing hull design of HMS *Invincible* as a starting point. The resulting HMS *Ocean* was an impressive ship but made no concessions to elegance. The ship incorporated commercial standards wherever appropriate. The bold union between the volume-maximized upper hull and the finer hull about the waterline was much like those of container ships or Pure Car Carriers (PCC). Both types set similar design problems. Some account was also taken of the need to reduce radar signature. The extreme flare beneath the ship's quarter overhangs required subsequent modification as being hazardous to the lowering of the LCVP(5) slung under the davits. These were then recessed into very large rectangular apertures in the side of the hull.

Up to 500 troops could be carried on

ABOVE: **HMS *Ocean* was not designed with a docking well. The ramp mounted on the stern was to allow light vehicles to be transferred to and from the four LCVP (5) carried on the ship.**

ABOVE: **In British service, the extending stern ramp on the ship was used to link with a "Mexeflote" pontoon to off-load light vehicles. The unobstructed flight deck was long enough (130m/427ft) for the operation of Harrier V/STOL aircraft.**

an extended passage, plus 300 more in an emergency. Light vehicles and 105mm artillery would be off-loaded into landing craft via an off-centre ramp set into the wide stern. Each LCVP could accommodate a platoon, together with two light vehicles. A second ramp accessing the vehicle deck was located on the starboard side, below the bridge.

HMS Ocean was built with a full-length flight deck with a large, starboard-side island. There were, of course, no catapults or arrestor gear, the non-carrier status being further emphasized by the lack of a "ski jump" for V/STOL aircraft. The hangar space was believed to be the largest ever incorporated into a Royal Navy ship, with headroom and area sufficient to accommodate 12 Merlin helicopters which were too large for the elevators on HMS Invincible. As an

alternative, 12 Sea King and six Lynx could be stowed below. The flight deck was stressed for occasional use by Chinook helicopters or Harrier V/STOL aircraft, for which a 130m/427ft take-off run was possible. HMS Ocean also operated Apache attack helicopters at times.

Main propulsion came from two commercial-type, medium-speed diesel engines, located in separate compartments. Both engines were fitted with a gearbox for reversing due to the relatively high output speed. Considerable criticism was made over the choice of comparatively low-power units which limited the ship's sustained speed to a modest 18 knots. For quiet operation, the ship could be propelled by shaft-mounted electric motors.

Over the course of its 20-year Royal Navy service, Ocean saw action on several occasions including the 2003 invasion of Iraq, when the ship supported British ground forces and air strikes against enemy targets. Ocean was decommissioned in March 2018 but

the Brazilian Navy acquired it for £84.6 million as a replacement for the aircraft carrier São Paulo. It was renamed Atlântico (A140) and became the flagship of the Brazilian Navy with the capability to operate fixed-wing medium-altitude long-endurance unmanned drones, as well as crewed tiltrotor VTOL aircraft.

## Landing Ship, Personnel, Helicopter (LPH), HMS *Ocean*

**Displacement:** 21,580 tons (full load)
**Length:** 193m/633ft 6in (bp);
    203.4m/667ft 8in (oa)
**Beam:** 28.5m/93ft 6in (wl);
    36.1m/118ft 6in (extreme width)
**Draught:** 6.65m/21ft 10in (mean)
**Armament:** 3 x Vulcan Phalanx CIWS, some
    smaller
**Machinery:** 2 diesel engines, 2 shafts
**Power:** 13,726kW/18,400bhp for 19 knots
    (maximum)
**Fuel:** 1,500 tons oil
**Endurance:** 14,720km/8,000nm at 15 knots
**Protection:** Not known
**Complement:** 497 including aircrew,
    plus 12 Merlins

# Landing Platform, Dock (LPD), Albion class

As early as 1985 the Royal Navy began preparations for the replacement of the two Fearless-class LPDs, after some 20 years service. Problems arose because the British shipbuilding industry had been reduced to the size where only one company could build ships of the required size. The perfectly competent Admiralty design organization was passed over in favour of a commercially produced design. Nine years and five design studies eventually produced the basis of a proposal which was then modified until an acceptable contract figure could be met. By the time that the two Albion-class ships entered service, HMS *Fearless* and HMS *Intrepid* had not been combat-capable for a considerable period.

That said, the Albion class has proved to be useful. Somewhat smaller than HMS *Ocean*, and accommodating fewer troops (305 against 500 or in emergency 710 against 803) both ships in the class have superior command and control facilities. The ships carry both the naval task group and the army/marine landing force commanders (CATG and CLF) and staffs. Real-time information on the battle situation is enhanced by radar-equipped and unmanned drones.

The Albion class each carries four LCUs in a docking well accessed by a large stern gate. In the lowered position, but with the ship not flooded down, the gate is used as a loading ramp for the LCUs. Garaging is provided for six tanks and up to 16 large or 36 smaller vehicles. The vehicle decks are interconnected by ramps which also link with the flight deck

LEFT: **HMS** *Bulwark* **(L15) on exercise with 4 Assault Squadron Royal Marines (ASRM). The ship is flooded down and has 3m/9.8ft of water in the docking well, permitting the use of fully loaded LCUs.**

and docking well. Note, the dimensions of four LCU (10), are the same as those of two US-pattern LCACs stowed in tandem. In addition, four LCVP (5) are carried topside under davits.

Construction and fittings greatly reflect current commercial practice. The vehicle decks are also accessible via a starboard-side door and ramp. The cargo spaces are accessed by doors in the hull on each side. The latter are fitted for rapid stores transfer by the use of pallets.

Flooded down, there is an average 3m/9.8ft water depth in the docking well which equates to some 2,500 tons of water. The influence of this on stability is monitored by a dedicated

computer system but ship movement in an anchorage can, nonetheless, create "sloshing", which can cause damage to closely berthed landing craft.

Diesel-electric propulsion has great advantages in being very responsive to demand and requiring few skilled personnel for operation and maintenance. The diesel-generator sets can be located with consideration to both quieteness and convenience, while the electric propulsion motors are located aft, shortening propeller shafts and reducing vulnerability.

With a full-width superstructure of considerable length, the Albion class has a helicopter landing deck at the

aft end. Space is provided for two Westland Merlin or Sea King helicopters and space for a further, parked aircraft. One CH-47 Chinook may be operated as an alternative. Refuelling facilities are available, but there is no hangar.

The 2010 Strategic Defence and Security Review concluded that, to cut Royal Navy running costs, one of its two Albion-class LPDs would be placed into extended readiness (uncrewed reserve) while the other ship is held at high readiness for operations. The vessels would then alternate between extended readiness and high readiness for their remaining service lives.

*Albion* was the first to be placed at extended readiness, then their status was swapped as *Bulwark* entered extended readiness.

ABOVE: **HMS** *Bulwark* **(L15) shows how modern warships, with dimensions driven by volume requirements, increasingly follow the design of current merchant vessels.**

## Landing Platform, Dock, HMS *Albion* (L14) and HMS *Bulwark* (L15)

**Displacement:** 14,600 tons (standard); 16,980 tons (loaded); 18,500 tons (flooded)
**Length:** 162m/531ft 9in (bp); 178m/584ft 3in (oa)
**Beam:** 28.9m/94ft 10in
**Draught:** 6.1m/20ft (mean, seagoing)
**Armament:** 2 x Goalkeeper CIWS, some smaller
**Machinery:** Diesel-electric, 2 shafts
**Power:** 12,000kW/16,100bhp for 18 knots (maximum)
**Fuel:** Not known
**Endurance:** 14,720 km/8,000nm at 15 knots
**Protection:** Not known
**Complement:** 325 plus 305 Marines

LEFT: **The Dutch and Spanish influence on the design of the Bay class extended even to the first use in Royal Fleet Auxiliary service of the very high holding capacity Pool TW anchor. RFA Lyme Bay (L3007) was the last in the series to be built.**

# Landing Ship, Dock (LSD), Bay class

Built to support HMS *Ocean* and the two Albion class ships were the, originally, four Bay-class vessels in RFA service. The ships were replacements for the Sir Lancelot class, but there the comparison ends for all are built to an entirely different concept, greatly influenced by the Dutch Rotterdam and Spanish Galicia designs which entered service 1998–2000.

The British types are larger and, indeed, almost the same displacement as the Albion class. Visually, the type is unmistakable with a large seven-deck accommodation and bridge superstructure located forward. A funnel is not required as the propulsion

and auxiliary diesel engines exhaust below the waterline. Not designed to be beached, the class are equipped with "Mexeflote" powered pontoons, stowed on the sides of the hull. Internally there is a docking well, large enough to accommodate a single LCU (10) or two LCVPs. No LCVPs are carried. The ships have facilities to transport some 350 troops or 700 on short voyages.

The clear afterdeck was designed to operate two Westland Merlin or Sea King helicopters, or a single Chinook. There is no hangar. Two 30-ton cranes are mounted at the forward end of the helicopter landing deck. A permanent gantry with a capacity of 200 tons is used

for transferring cargo and stores from the deck. The class have over twice the vehicle capacity of an LSL, reportedly with room for up to 32 Challenger 2 battle tanks or 150 light trucks.

The class is the first in RFA service propelled by podded propulsors. Known as "Azipod" thrusters, these combine propeller and electric propulsion motor in a unit which may be rotated through 360 degrees, removing the requirement for rudders or propeller and shafts.

RFA *Largs Bay* (L3006) was sold to the Royal Australian Navy in 2011 where it now serves as HMAS *Choules* (L100).

LEFT: **RFA *Cardigan Bay* (L3009) can maintain a precise alignment and position using two "Azipod" azimuth propulsion units in combination with bow thrusters.**

| Landing Ship, Dock (LSD), Bay class |  |
|---|---|

**Displacement:** 16,150 tons (loaded)
**Length:** 176.6m/579ft (oa)
**Beam:** 26.4m/86ft 7in
**Draught:** 5.8m/19ft
**Armament:** For, but not with, 2 x Vulcan Phalanx CIWS
**Machinery:** Diesel electrics, 2 podded propulsors
**Power:** Not known
**Fuel:** Not known
**Endurance:** 14,720km/8,000nm at 15 knots
**Protection:** Not known
**Complement:** 60 plus 356 marines

# Sealift Ship, Point class

ABOVE: **MW** *Anvil Point* **is one of six ships in the Point class. All were initially owned, operated and crewed by Foreland Shipping, a British company.**

The final component of the UK's Joint Rapid Deployment Force (JRDF) were the Hartland Point class vehicle carriers. Like T-AKRs, all are built to current commercial standards, with full Roll-on, Roll-off (Ro-Ro) access. The ships are not drive-through, but the full-width stern door (which also acts as a loading ramp) and unobstructed vehicle decks permit on-board turning space. There are three interconnected internal vehicle decks, with further stowage on the upper deck and beneath the bridge block. This space is protected by deep bulwarks and a distinctive apron over the forward end. A 40-ton pedestal-type crane is located on the starboard side, facilitating the handling of containerized cargo.

Further to the usual armoured vehicles, transport and artillery the ships (as with any commercial Ro-Ro) carry considerable freight pre-loaded on trailers. The need for such adaptability was amply demonstrated during the 1982 Falklands campaign, when the MV *Atlantic Conveyor* was lost.

Building of what is a commercial design was contracted to a German shipyard who built four. The other two ships were built by Harland & Wolff, Belfast. One addition is a passive, flume-type stablization system which, unlike an active fin system, can be effective with the ship at anchor.

The ships are twin-screw, with the diesel engines exhausting through a

funnel offset to port. Propulsive power was considerably increased in the last three built, with a corresponding improvement in speed. The UK Ministry of Defence (MoD) purchased a 22-year charter from Forland Shipping, which owned, operated and crewed all six ships in the class.

Two of the ships (MV *Longstone* and *Beachy Head*) were released from the contract with Forland Shipping, leaving four now available for service with the UK military.

LEFT: **MV** *Longstone* **was under commercial charter to Transfennica who operated a Ro-Ro cargo ferry service in the Baltic. The four remaining ships are available to the MoD at short notice.**

## Sealift Ship, Point class

**Displacement:** 22,000 tons (loaded)
**Length:** 182.39m/598ft (bp); 193m/632ft 9in (oa)
**Beam:** 26m/85ft 3in (wl)
**Draught:** 7.4m/24ft 3in (full load)
**Armament:** Unarmed
**Machinery:** 2 diesel engines, 2 shafts
**Power:** 13,055kW/17,500bhp for 18 knots (first three); 16,188kW/21,700bhp for 21.5 knots (last three)
**Fuel:** 1,100 tons oil
**Endurance:** 22,080km/12,000nm at 17 knots
**Protection:** Not known
**Complement:** 18

# Future Littoral Strike Ship (FLSS)

The Future Littoral Strike Ship (FLSS) is a new class of amphibious assault ship currently being developed for the Royal Navy. It will form an important element in the UK's future defence strategy and FLSS is a key component of the Royal Navy's Future Commando Force, which is the initiative to modernize the Royal Marines to make them more agile and flexible, taking them away from operating like infantry units and returning them to their original specialist commando and amphibious roles.

The FLSS will be designed to support a range of operations including disaster relief and humanitarian (HADR) missions. For offensive operations, such as amphibious assault and special forces missions, it will deliver troops and equipment to shore, while also providing fire support and command and control capabilities. The ship will be capable of carrying a mix of helicopters, boats, and vehicles, and will be equipped with the

ABOVE: **The FLSS ships will play a key role in Britain's future defence strategy, enabling the Royal Marines to become more agile and flexible.**
BELOW: **FLSS ships will deliver troops and equipment to shore, while also providing fire support and command and control capabilities. The ships will carry troops, helicopters, boats and vehicles.**

RIGHT AND BELOW: **The new forward-located FLSS ships would provide the Royal Marines with a base from which to launch assaults from RIBs (below) or helicopters, including the Merlin (right).**

very latest communications, intelligence, and surveillance systems.

The FLSS concept was first proposed in the UK's 2015 Strategic Defence and Security Review, which called for a new class of vessel that could operate in littoral waters – the shallow coastal regions where traditional naval vessels cannot operate. The plan would be to have these ships permanently based in forward locations nearer to potential areas of interest than UK bases. In 2019, the UK Government stated that two new "globally deployable, multi-role" ships would be procured for "... exerting British influence through greater forward presence."

The Royal Navy has set out a number of requirements for potential designs for the FLSS including a minimum speed of 18 knots, a range of at least 5,000 nautical miles, and the ability to operate in Sea State 5 conditions (waves of up to 6m/19ft in height). The FLSS must be capable of launching and recovering a range of helicopters, including the Apache attack helicopter and the Merlin transport helicopter. The ship must also be able to launch and recover boats, including landing craft and rigid inflatable boats.

The Royal Navy has also stated that the FLSS must have a modular design to allow it to be rapidly reconfigured for different missions while having the ability to add and remove mission-specific equipment and systems, such as medical facilities and command and control suites as required. The ship will operate autonomously, or as part of a naval task group, for which the UAVs it will carry could provide additional airborne protection.

Several designs for the FLSS have already been proposed by UK shipbuilders.

# Landing Ship, Dock (LSD), Ouragan class

With a view to operations in the Indian Ocean, South-east Asia and the Pacific, France created a small but effective amphibious force as soon as post-war circumstances permitted. The LSD, capable of ocean voyages yet able to land a force directly "over the beach", was well proven during World War II. The French Navy designed and built two ships which were somewhat smaller than the other LSDs.

The bridge structure is set to starboard on the elevated helicopter deck that occupies the amidships area. Enclosed by a stern gate, the docking well is 120m/394ft in length, accommodating either two EDIC-type LCTs or eight LCM (8). All may be pre-loaded.

Flooded-down, the docking well has a depth of 3m/9ft 10in, sufficient to prevent large landing craft fouling the sill when undocking. Floating off, the larger landing craft requires the raising of the movable deck over the docking well. This deck, in whole or in part, may be used for an extra helicopter landing spot or for the stowage of vehicles or stores. For the latter, two 35-ton cranes are provided. There is no helicopter hangar. Up to 470 troops may be accommodated and, as an alternative to landing craft, up to 1,500 tons of general cargo can be carried.

Intended for worldwide independent operation, the two ships in the class are equipped with comprehensive repair facilities and a command centre equppied to control a complete amphibious operation. Both ships have also proved to be valuable when used for disaster relief.

Following 40 years in service, the ships were sold to Argentina.

ABOVE: **Only two of the class were built: FS *Ouragan* (L9021) and FS *Orage* (L9022). Both were withdrawn from service in 2007.**

LEFT: **The design of the ship is interesting in that by locating the island to the side and by using diesel propulsion, thus eliminating the requirement for a funnel, a large flight deck area has been created.**

## Landing Ship, Dock (LSD), Ouragan class

**Displacement:** 5,965 tons (light); 8,500 tons (loaded); 15,000 tons (flooded)
**Length:** 144.5m/473ft 9in (bp); 149m/488ft 6in (oa)
**Beam:** 21.5m/70ft 6in (wl)
**Draught:** 5.4m/17ft 9in (mean, seagoing); 8.7m/28ft 5in (mean, flooded)
**Armament:** 2 x twin Simbad PDMS, 2 x 40mm guns (2x1), 2 x 30mm guns (2x1)
**Machinery:** 2 diesel engines, 2 shafts
**Power:** 6,714km/9,000bhp at 15 knots
**Fuel:** Not known
**Endurance:** 16,560km/9,000nm at 15 knots
**Protection:** Not known
**Complement:** 205 plus 470 troops

# Landing Ship, Medium (LSM), Champlain class

ABOVE: Utility took second place to style in this class, which looked expensive for amphibious operations. Named after French explorers, all were originally designed for the transport of one company of troops and their vehicles.

In service with the French Navy for over four decades, the Champlain class were known as Batiment de Transport Léger (BATRAL) light ferry ships. The elegantly shaped hull was not designed to assist with quantity nor inexpensive production, but did result in a respectable vessel speed of 16 knots.

The class was built over a 12-year period, and individual ships showed variations as the design developed. All have a box-shaped superstructure block topped by a small funnel. In the last three ships, the superstructure was one deck higher, with troop accommodation increased from 138 to 180. Capacity below was large enough to carry up to 12 vehicles and 330 tons of stores. The bow ramp could support 40 tons, more than sufficient for light tanks or armoured personnel carriers.

The last three built also carried an LCVP and an LCP on deck, ahead of the bridge. To handle these, a 35-ton hydraulic crane was carried. On the first two ships there was a cargo derrick supported by a substantial frame on the bridge.

All were completed with an elevated helicopter deck, capable of handling an Aérospatiale Alouette (Lark) light helicopter, but there was no hangar. The last in the series, FS *La Grandière*, was built speculatively and only later acquired by the French Navy. The ship had differences in detail, notably an enlarged helicopter deck.

The design attracted export orders from friendly states – Gabon, Ivory Coast and Morocco – while Chile built two under licence. The vessels proved to be effective station ships, serving from New Caledonia to French Guiana and were withdrawn from French service in 2017.

ABOVE: **One of the two earlier ships, FS *Francis Garnier* (L9031) had a superstructure one level fewer than that of the greater-capacity FS *Dumont d'Urville* (L9032) shown in the photograph at the top of the page.**

## Landing Ship, Medium (LSM), Champlain class

**Displacement:** 820 tons (standard); 1,385 tons (loaded)
**Length:** 68m/223ft (bp); 80m/262ft 3in (oa)
**Beam:** 13m/42ft 8in
**Draught:** 3m/9ft 10in (maximum, seagoing)
**Armament:** 2 x 81mm mortars, 2 x 20mm guns (2x1)
**Machinery:** 2 diesel engines, 2 shafts
**Power:** 2,686kW/3,600bhp for 16 knots
**Fuel:** Not known
**Endurance:** 6,440km/3,500nm at 13 knots
**Protection:** Nominal
**Complement:** 52 plus 180 troops

# Landing Ship, Dock (LSD), Foudre class

A class of two ships, FS *Foudre* (L9011) and FS *Siroco* (L9012), commissioned in 1990 and 1998 respectively, were designed to transport and deploy troops, vehicles, and equipment, primarily for amphibious assault operations.

Designed by the same bureau of DCN, Brest, a Foudre class vessel may be mistaken in profile for a smaller Ouragan class vessel. Neither has an obvious funnel but, in proportion, the bigger ship has a larger bridge structure and longer flight deck amidships. From any other angle, it will be apparent that, where an Ouragan's bridge block is offset to starboard, that of a Foudre class is full width. Although larger, the class was designed similarly around a force of some 380 troops. The class was designed to embark a mechanized regiment of the French Rapid Action Force whilst also acting as the force's logistical support vessel once in the area of operation. The 168m-/550ft-long ships were designed with a large well deck that could accommodate 10 French-designed CTM landing craft to allow for the rapid loading and unloading of troops and equipment directly from the ship to the shore.

The class was developed from the outset for operating helicopters to provide critical aerial support, troop transport, and reconnaissance capabilities in support of amphibious

operations. Four Super Pumas or two Super Frelon helicopters could be accommodated and operated from a flight deck amidships. At 1,740 sq m/ 18,700 sq ft, *Siroco* had a larger flight deck from the outset, extended aft compared to that of the *Foudre*. Both ships could add an additional landing spot aft if required.

Extending operational options are two LCVPs and side access doors in the hull. A neat arrangement lies in the moveable deck comprising five buoyant pontoon sections which can function similarly to the British "Mexeflote". The sections, together with any cargo carried on them, are handled by two side-mounted 37-ton capacity cranes.

The ships can transport a variety of vehicles, depending on the mission – tanks, armoured vehicles, trucks, engineering equipment, and other

ABOVE: **FS *Siroco* (L9012) at the French naval base of Toulon. The second of the class, built four years after FS *Foudre* (L9011), it differs only in minor details but has a larger flight deck.**

military vehicles to support amphibious operations. The Foudre class have a very large vehicle/cargo capacity, with a cumulative load of 1,880 tons. A 52-ton capacity elevating platform has the power to lift an AMX-10RC heavy armoured car (15 tons) and Leclerc main battle tank (40 tons), although light tanks

ABOVE: **An LCU approaches the stern gate to the flooded docking well on FS *Siroco* during operations in the Lebanon.** LEFT: **FS *Foudre* (L9011) at Toulon naval base. Note how the *Siroco* (above) has fewer permanent apertures in the upper hull than *Foudre*.**

RIGHT: *Siroco* was acquired by the Brazilian Navy in 2015 and was renamed *Bahia* (G40). BELOW: **Rear view of the *Foudre* well deck during a 2011 refit.**

were more usually carried in French service.

Due to procurement delays, FS *Foudre* had been in service for over four years before her sister ship was even laid down. As the FS *Siroco* was thus built to an improved specification with a slightly different layout, FS *Foudre* was subsequently updated in French service.

They were key components of France's naval expeditionary forces and were deployed in numerous international operations and exercises. In 2003, *Foudre* was involved in the UN peacekeeping mission in Côte d'Ivoire. The ship provided critical assistance by transporting troops, equipment, and supplies to support peacekeeping efforts in the region. FS *Siroco* played a significant role in Operation *Barkhane*, a French military operation in the Sahel region of Africa, where it provided logistical support and contributed to regional stability efforts.

During the Lebanon War in 2006, *Siroco* served during Opération *Baliste*, then as part of Opération *Séisme Haiti* in 2010 as part of the Haiti earthquake relief effort. In late 2013, the ship served as the flagship of the European Union Naval Force Somalia. *Siroco* was acquired by the Brazilian Navy in 2015, became the *Bahia* (G40), and was formally commissioned into Brazilian service in 2016, operating EC725 and SH-60 helicopters. FS *Foudre* was sold to the Chilean Navy in 2011 and was renamed *Sargento Aldea*. The Foudre class ships have been succeeded by the Mistral class amphibious assault ships in the French Navy.

### Landing Ship, Dock (LSD), *Foudre/Bahia*

**Displacement:** 11,330 tons (standard); 12,000 tons (full load); 17,200 tons (flooded)
**Length:** 168m/550ft 10in (oa)
**Beam:** 23.5m/77ft
**Draught:** 5.2m/17ft
**Armament:** 3 x twin Simbad PDMS, 3 x 30mm guns, 4 x 12.7mm machine guns
**Machinery:** 2 diesel engines, 2 shafts, bow thrusters
**Power:** 15,500kW/20,800 bhp for 21 knots
**Endurance:** 20,300km/11,000nm at 15 knots
**Protection:** Splinter-proof
**Complement:** 160 crew plus 450 to 900 troops

# Landing Ship, Helicopter (LH), Mistral class

The Mistral class, which eventually ran to five ships, were originally ordered as Foudre class, but the specification was considerably uprated to multi-purpose landing and command ship, similar to but smaller than the US Navy's LHAs. The class, which actually replaced the French Navy's Foudre and Ouragan class amphibious assault ships, includes *Mistral*, *Tonnerre* and *Dixmude* in French Navy service, as well as the *Gamal Abdel Nasser* (ex-*Vladivostok*) and *Anwar El Sadat* (ex-*Sevastopol*), originally built for the Russian Navy but sold instead to Egypt

when the Russian deal was cancelled after Russia's annexation of Crimea.

All have a full-length 6,400 sq m/ 7,097sq yd flight deck with six deck spots available for aircraft up to the size of Sikorsky CH-53E Super Stallion or Bell-Boeing MV-22 Osprey. Two elevators, each capable of lifting up to 13 tons, provide access to the hangar space below where up to 20 Super Puma, Super Frelon or Eurocopter NH-90 helicopters can be stowed, armed or undergo maintenance. This is above a 57.5m/189ft docking well with a stern

ABOVE: **The design presents a compact appearance, without the heavily sculpted changes in the hull plating. The somewhat over elaborate funnel would appear to present an unnecessary and undesirable infra-red hot spot.**

gate. The docking well is only half the length of that in the smaller Foudre class but is wider and can accommodate up to four amphibious landing craft. Each ship can accommodate up to 450 troops, or twice that many for short term operations. The ships' 2,650 sq m/ 2,898sq yd vehicle hangar can carry a battalion of 40 Leclerc Main Battle Tanks, or a tank company of 13 Leclercs along with up to 46 other vehicles.

On a moderate displacement, these volume demands translate to ships with an unusually high freeboard. The resulting advantage of a dry flight deck is offset by increased transverse accelerations countered by active fin stabilizers. In profile, the counter and stern gate are vertical, while the bow

LEFT AND ABOVE: **FS *Mistral* is seen here both complete (left) and in an advanced state of fitting out but lacking electronic systems (above). Note the centreline helicopter lift, on the stern.**

form is very similar to that of a maritime car carrier, or PCC. The angled funnel casing has exposed smoke pipes, currently the style in the commercial maritime world but, on a warship, likely to provide hot spots, detectable by enemy infra-red equipment.

*Mistral* was laid down in 2003, launched in 2004, and commissioned in 2006. The *Tonnerre* was laid down in 2003, launched in 2005, and commissioned in 2007, while the *Dixmude* was laid down in 2009, launched in 2010 and commissioned in

2012. The *Gamal Abdel Nasser* and the *Anwar El Sadat* were both commissioned into Egyptian Navy service in 2016.

The French Navy ships have evacuated French nationals from dangerous locations, supported UN peacekeeping operations, anti-piracy and humanitarian missions. They are equipped with a hospital that can accommodate up to 69 patients at a time and the entire vessel can be converted into a hospital ship in times of crisis. They have a modular design that allows for the installation of additional medical

facilities and equipment as needed.

These ships are the first major French warships to be fitted with "Azipod" azimuth propulsors, eliminating shafts and rudders. Both ships are equipped with extensive command and medical facilities. FS *Mistral* will also act as a replacement for the cadet training ship FS *Jeanne d'Arc*.

---

### Landing Ship, Helicopter (LH), Mistral class

**Displacement:** 16,500 tons (standard); 21,500 tons (loaded)
**Length:** 199m/625ft 6in (wl); 210m/688ft 6in (oa)
**Beam:** 28m/91ft 10in (wl); 32m/104ft 11in (extreme)
**Draught:** 6.2m/20ft 4in (mean, seagoing)
**Armament:** 2 x Simbad missile systems, 3 x 30mm auto-cannons, 2 x 7.62mm miniguns, 4 x 12.7mm maching guns, 2 x NARWHAL20 (RWS), each with 20mm cannons
**Machinery:** Diesel-electric, 2 Rolls-Royce Mermaid azimuth thrusters driving five-bladed propellers
**Power:** 14,174kW/19,000shp for 19 knots
**Endurance:** 19,800km/10,700nm at 15 knots
**Protection:** Not known
**Complement:** 160 plus 450 troops

---

ABOVE: *Dixmude* (L9015) in Jounieh bay, Lebanon, 2012. The Mistral class have a unique bow shape that helps reduce their radar signature and increase their stability in rough seas. The ships also have a bow thruster for improved manoeuvrability in port.
RIGHT: A USMC M1A1 Abrams embarks on the *Tonnerre*, 2009. The ship's vehicle hangar can accommodate up to 40 Main Battle Tanks.

# Landing Craft Carrier, Shinshu Maru

In modern amphibious warfare, the *Shinshu Maru* is deserving of recognition in that the vessel was the first-ever ship to be designed for the purpose of transporting loaded landing craft. Japanese landing craft of the time were the various types of Daihatsu, the largest, when loaded with a light tank, displacing around 37 tons.

The concept of the ship, and funding, stemmed from the Imperial Army, which explains the over-ambitious design. Built with a false identity and operating under a mercantile name, *Shinshu Maru* was surrounded by such secrecy that even today much detail is unclear.

Twenty landing craft of unknown size were accommodated in two long side galleries, being launched down a slip through large doors set in the wide stern. The craft appear to have been lifted aboard by the large crane stepped from the massive tripod at the forward end. This served as a hatch in the foredeck and permitted craft to be placed directly on launching rails. Access to the galleries was provided by side doors amidships, which probably facilitated the loading of armour via ramps or the handling of more general cargo, as an alternative to landing craft. An open afterdeck was served by a single heavy cargo derrick, rigged from a second substantial tripod mast. The superstructure was bulky, as it enclosed a large floatplane hangar, with aircraft catapults on the foredeck.

The hull was low, and the gallery deck was almost certainly the freeboard deck. With completion overseen by the Imperial Navy, it was recognized that the ship's stability range was very limited. A "torpedo bulkhead" was therefore added.

ABOVE: **An artist's impression of *Shinshu Maru*. There are only two photographs in existence.**

LEFT AND BELOW: **Daihatsu craft are visible aft and forward, adjacent to doors accessing the superstructure. Smaller craft are operated via the many davits.**

## Landing Craft Carrier, *Shinshu Maru*

**Displacement:** 9,000 tons (standard); 11,780 tons (full load)
**Length:** 150m/492ft 2in
**Beam:** 22m/72ft 2in
**Draught:** 8.2m/26ft 9in
**Armament:** 5–8 x 75mm guns (5/8 x 1)
**Machinery:** Steam turbines, 2 shafts
**Power:** 5,968kW/8,000shp for 19 knots
**Fuel:** Not known
**Endurance:** Not known
**Protection:** Not known
**Complement:** Not known

LEFT: **Japan began the war with a large number of fine cargo ships. Reckless use in action was a contributory cause of the nation's defeat. Discharge of cargo and troops by Daihatsu craft, as seen here, was laborious and possible only through the initial lack of Allied air power.**

# Attack Cargo Ship, Kibitsu Maru

During the 1930s, when Japanese forces faced the technically backward Chinese, the Imperial Navy was presented with few problems. War with the USA, however, was a different matter. The widespread area of Japanese occupation would make this a maritime-based war against an opponent who, with time, could only become stronger.

The Pacific Ocean became a theatre of manoeuvre warfare on a grand scale, where the side with superior amphibious capabilities had the initiative and the greater number of options of where to strike next. Like US forces at the outset, the Japanese were lacking specialized ships and

drew on an extensive merchant fleet for vessels which could be rapidly converted. In the Japanese military organization, the Army was the dominant authority and it was the Army that requisitioned merchant ships used as attack transport and cargo ships.

The success of the *Shinshu Maru* against almost non-existent Chinese opposition encouraged the Army to convert more merchant ships to landing craft carriers. These could carry up to 20 Daihatsu craft on rails for launching through stern doors. The conversions were complex and redefined the internal layout, greatly reducing access and capacity for cargo or accommodation.

Ships such as the *Kibitsu Maru*, typical of those requisitioned, compared poorly with equivalent US Navy ships. The conversions did not impinge on troop space below, although it should be appreciated that Japanese troops were more accustomed to enduring long sea passages on the open decks.

Although loading facilities were sometimes split to accommodate a Daihatsu trackway, the ships retained cargo-lifting gear. Increasingly the ships were used for cargo carrying as the attrition of the merchant fleet from submarines, aircraft and surface vessels of the US 7th Fleet increased.

ABOVE: **Japanese troops were resilient and undemanding, and were prepared to travel on open, crowded upper decks with a minimum of facilities. In the East Indian archipelago, however, the distances travelled were usually relatively short.**

## Attack Cargo Ship, *Kibitsu Maru*

**Tonnage:** 8,000 tons (gross);
9,650 tons (deadweight);
12,000 tons (displacement, loaded)
**Length:** 142m/466ft (wl)
152.5m/500ft (oa)
**Beam:** 20m/64ft 3in
**Draught:** 7m/23ft (mean, loaded)
**Armament:** 8 x 75mm guns (8x1), 2 x 81mm mortars, up to 60 x 25mm guns
**Machinery:** Steam turbines, 2 boilers, 2 shafts
**Power:** 7,460kW/10,000shp for 19 knots
**Fuel:** Not known
**Endurance:** Not known
**Protection:** Nominal
**Complement:** Not known

# Landing Ship, Tank (LST), Type 1

ABOVE: **The distinguishing feature of the Type 1 was the long, sloping after end for the carriage and launching of various landing. The barriers across the rails may be to prevent the afterdeck from being swamped by a following sea.**

As 1943 progressed, Japan's requirements were not so much for amphibious warships designed for further conquest but for specialized vessels built to support and supply garrisons in the Solomon Islands. US air power was dominant by day, so the Japanese needed ships fast enough to operate overnight, taking minimum time to turn around. The solution was typically innovative, relying in no way on outside influence. Known generally as a Type 1, or Class 1, the vessel was of under 2,000 tons (loaded) displacement, although it appeared much larger. Designed to be built rapidly, the Type 1 incorporated plating that was either flat or had no more than simple curvature. The hull lacked sheer or camber and, although flush-decked, had freeboard that diminished forward to aft. Indeed, freeboard aft was

zero, the clear afterdeck acting as a slipway for four pre-loaded and trolley mounted Daihatsu craft.

Amidships were cargo holds of some 250 tons capacity, served by conventional cargo-lifting gear. The ships were capable of 22 knots and, in an emergency, could launch the landing craft at speeds up to 16 knots.

By late 1943, orders are believed to have been for 46 but, despite build simplicity, only 21 were actually completed. The type was used to transport alternative launchable deck loads, such as midget submarines, human torpedoes or amphibious tanks, but was equally used to transport troops and equipment.

By May 1944, when the Type 1 entered service, US forces dominated the area and, despite a reasonable armament for their size, progressively boosted by

radar, sonar and even depth charges, the class suffered greatly, with only five ships surviving to serve as repatriation transports after the surrender of Japan.

---

### Landing Ship, Tank (LST), Type 1

**Displacement:** 1,500 tons (standard);
   1,750 tons (loaded)
**Length:** 89.06m/292ft bp; 96.08m/315ft (oa)
**Beam:** 10.22m/33ft 6in
**Draught:** 3.58m/11ft 9in
**Armament:** 2 x 5in DP guns (2x1),
   15 x 25mm guns (3x3, 1x2, 4x1)
**Machinery:** Steam turbine, 2 boilers,
   single screw
**Power:** 7,087kW/9,500shp for 22 knots
   (maximum)
**Fuel:** Not known
**Endurance:** 6,810km/3,700nm at 18 knots
**Protection:** Nominal
**Complement:** Not known

ABOVE: **The Daihatsu Type A was the largest built. Unlike other Daihatsu types, this vessel was relatively heavily armed.**
LEFT: **Two Daihatsu Type B landing craft abandoned on a beach in the Pacific.**

# Daihatsu Landing Craft

Unique among small landing craft, the Daihatsu design dated from the late 1920s and, serving Japanese requirements very well, the type continued in production for almost two decades. Daihatsu was the adopted Allied term embracing different Japanese sub-types, measuring between 10 and 17m/33 and 56ft overall. Of these, the 14m/46ft type was the most common.

Although displacing anything between 6 and 37 tons, the general design features were similar. Based on a traditional fishing boat, the craft were of a "sampan-shaped" in appearance, with a continuous sheer line. The stern was either rounded or had a curved transom. Strength and longitudinal stability was by two built-on, parallel and protruding keels, terminating forward as two pronounced skegs. The bow was fitted with a ramp.

Designed for loading and discharge while laying alongside a larger ship in open anchorages, the Daihatsu had heavy, braced rubbing strakes, incorporated into the structure of the craft to improve overall stiffness on what was an open and shallow hull.

The type was built in the thousands, options including an open vehicle deck, protected helmsman's position or light steel canopy and protective, hinged side plates. The type does not appear to have been adapted for lifting by davits.

## Daihatsu Landing Craft (Type B)

**Displacement:** 21 tons
**Length:** 14.57m/47ft 10in
**Beam:** 3.35m/11ft
**Draught:** 0.76m/2ft 6in (mean)
**Armament:** 2/3 x 25mm guns,
    2 x machine-guns
**Machinery:** 1/2 petrol or diesel engines,
    single shaft
**Power:** 44.8–111.9kW/60–150hp for
    7.5–8.5 knots
**Endurance:** 80–160km/50–100nm at 7.5 knots
**Protection:** None
**Complement:** Up to 12, depending on duty

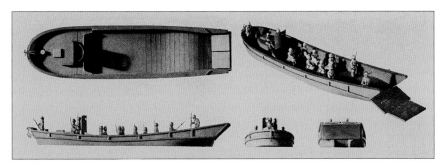

ABOVE: **The Daihatsu Type B was mainly used to transport troops or supplies. The full-width loading ramp was adopted by the US Navy for use on the Higgins boat.**

# Coastal Minesweeper (CMS), Kasado/ Takami class and Support Ship, Hayase

The Korean War of the early 1950s alerted the world to the dangers of Communism and re-awakened the menace of seaways being mined. Japan was still very much under US military protection and, despite a firm non-aggressive stance, the country was strategically important due to the geographical location between China and the USSR.

Japan still possessed a minimal naval capability but the rapid expansion in mine warfare craft being primarily defensive followed the programmes undertaken, post-Korean War by her allies. Historically, these programmes were the last to use wood for the building of warships.

The 21 Kasado-class minesweepers, commissioned between 1958 and 1967, closely paralleled the design of US-built MSC and MS that were already

in service. Size and displacement were much the same but, in appearance, the Japanese craft did not have a funnel, while the heavy rubbing strake terminated below the bridge.

The 19 Takami class built between 1969 and 1978 retained the same hull but now had a funnel and lower bridge, more closely resembling the many "NATO-standard" CMS, such as the British-built Ton class. The Takami class was effectively an updated version of the Kasado class, designed for minehunting, with new sonars and facilities for clearance divers.

Japan's first post-war-built minelayer, *Souya*, was commissioned in 1971. The 2,150-ton ship was used not only as an Exercise Minelayer but also as a command ship for a mine countermeasures group. The *Hayase* was built to act as a general support and repair ship, replacing the ageing US-built LST *Hayatomo*, which had been used in that role. In parallel with the Takami class, the Japanese built inshore

ABOVE: **The shape of the *Hayase* is very similar to JMSDF frigates of the period. The after hull is deep, with two flush doors in the square transom, which may have been used for a secondary minelaying role. Note the crane, mounted on a pedestal, and the large drums of heavy minesweeping cable. A second ship, *Souya*, had a considerably wider beam.**

minesweepers. These, at just 53 tons displacement, were smaller than Western equivalents and were classed as Minesweeping Boats (MSB). Older units of the Kasado class were modified for support in harbour clearance.

LEFT: **Although only 46m/150ft in length, the 20 Yakami-class vessels (*Awaji* shown here) were classed by the Japanese as "coastal" rather than "inshore".**

## Coastal Minesweeper (CMS), Takami class

**Displacement:** 380 tons (standard); 450 tons (full load)
**Length:** 52.34m/171ft 7in (oa)
**Beam:** 8.81m/28ft 10in
**Draught:** 2.41m/7ft 10in
**Armament:** 1 x 20mm gun
**Machinery:** 2 diesel engines, 2 shafts
**Power:** 1,074kW/1,440bhp for 14 knots
**Fuel:** Not known
**Endurance:** Not known
**Protection:** None
**Complement:** 47

# Landing Ship, Tank (LST), Miura class

Japan's post-war amphibious capability began simply with the transfer of smaller craft such as LSMs and LCUs. Only in 1960–61 were four LST (2) acquired. These World War II vessels gave a decade of service before the Japanese Maritime Self-Defence Force (JMSDF) built replacements. The three Atsumi class were commissioned between 1972 and 1977 and the three Miura class between 1975 and 1977.

Post-war, US-built LSTs became larger, mainly to achieve higher speeds. With different priorities, the JMSDF did not follow this trend. The Japan archipelago is made up of many islands, and the frequency and severity of volcanic activity emphasized the suitability of amphibious warfare ships for use in disaster relief. Built with this role in mind, the Atsumi class were actually smaller than the US-built LST (2), measuring only 89m/292ft against

100m/328ft overall. Despite the smaller size, superior peacetime building methods allowed a top speed of over 13 knots. Except for a low funnel, the vessel closely resembled an LST (2). An LCVP was carried under davits on each side aft, with a third on deck, forward of the bridge. This was handled by crane or derrick. Twenty vehicles could be accommodated, along with 120 troops. A useful 400 tons of cargo could be carried as an alternative.

The three Miura-class ships, built in a parallel programme, were more military. Of much the same length as the LST (2), the type was more slender and had more than twice the engine power to sustain 14 knots. In addition to the LCVPs, two LCM (6) were carried on deck, handled by a transverse gantry crane. Ten heavy battle tanks plus 200 troops or, alternatively, 1,800 tons of cargo could be carried.

ABOVE: Unusually fast at 14 knots, the Miura-class ships had a transverse gantry crane to handle the two LCM (6) carried on deck. Two LCVPs are carried abaft the funnel on davits. Number 4152, shown here, is *Ojika*.

---

### Landing Ship, Tank (LST), Miura class

**Displacement:** 2,000 tons (standard); 3,800 tons (loaded)
**Length:** 98m/321ft 4in (oa)
**Beam:** 14m/45ft 10in
**Draught:** 3m/9ft 9in (mean, seagoing)
**Armament:** 2 x 3in guns (1x2), 2 x 40mm guns (1x2)
**Machinery:** 2 diesel engines, 2 shafts
**Power:** 3,282kW/4,400bhp for 14 knots
**Fuel:** Not known
**Endurance:** Not known
**Protection:** Nominal
**Complement:** 116

LEFT: **Although much smaller, an Osumi class vessel resembles a US Navy LHA. The afterdeck has landing spots for Boeing CH-47 Chinook helicopters. The docking well can accommodate two US-built LCACs.**

# Landing Ship, Tank (LST), Osumi class

The exact rationale behind the *Osumi* design is not easy to define. With flat and unobstructed upper deck areas, island superstructure, enclosed vehicle storage and accommodation, together with a docking well closed by a wide stern gate, an Osumi class vessel is, in all but type, an LSD.

In the Japanese Maritime Self-Defense Force (JMSDF), however, the Osumi class is a Landing Ship, Tank (LST) and they are thus numbered. This is despite LSTs, as generally understood, being designed to load and discharge over the beach. Even as designed, however, the class

of three ships is scarcely conventional, except in that the docking well is sized to carry two US-built LCACs. The island superstructure to starboard is relatively wide, leaving only vehicle access between the forward and aft areas of the upper deck.

Both areas of the upper deck have an elevator, linking to a common garage space below. Neither elevator is large enough to carry a helicopter. At the after end there are landing spots for two Boeing CH-47 Chinook-sized aircraft. There is no dedicated hangar accommodation so helicopters are

lashed to the deck. Fourteen main battle tanks (or 1,400 tons of cargo) may be stowed below, with access to the docking well deck. The forward part of the upper deck is another designated area for vehicles, which are exposed to the weather despite the high freeboard. The extreme bow section is reduced one level, similar to a British Invincible class vessel as built.

On the port side is a large 70-ton capacity hydraulically operated crane. Unusually, minor landing craft other than the LCACs do not appear to be carried, except as deckloads.

Accommodation is provided for 330 troops, or 1,000 in an emergency.

ABOVE: **As on the British-built Invincible class, the short forecastle deck appears to be poorly-utilized space. The deck area forward of the bridge is not used by helicopters.**

| Landing Ship, Tank (LST), Osumi class |  |
| --- | --- |

**Displacement:** 8,900 tons (standard); 12,000 tons (full load)
**Length:** 170m/557ft 4in (wl); 178m/583ft 7in (oa)
**Beam:** 25.8m/84ft 7in
**Draught:** 6m/19ft 8in
**Armament:** 2 x Vulcan Phalanx CIWS
**Machinery:** 2 diesel engines, 2 shafts
**Power:** 19,396kW/26,000bhp for 22 knots
**Fuel:** Not known
**Endurance:** Not known
**Complement:** 135 plus 330 troops

LEFT: *Aishima*, a Sugashima-class minesweeper, is built of wood rather than glass-reinforced plastic (GRP). Note the 20mm Sea Vulcan Gatling-type cannon mounted on the forward deck.

# Coastal Minesweeper (CMS), Sugashima class

At 58m/190ft overall, Sugashima-class vessels of the JMSDF are shorter than the Hunt class in Royal Navy service. During the Normandy landings on June 6, 1944, such vessels were vital for the clearance of the approaches to the beaches. The shallow waters were cleared of mines by a total of 98 fleet and 149 coastal minesweepers. A further 40 were held in reserve.

The hull design of the type follows that of most European-built coastal minesweepers, with a long, full-height forecastle and a short afterdeck. The continuous flare of the lower hull acts to increase the waterplane, improving stability with increasing angles of heel. A major departure is the use of wood for construction, and this is common to all current Japanese mine-warfare craft. Apparently it is considered that the perceived advantages of GRP do not warrant the expense of creating a purpose-built production facility.

The forward end of the afterdeck forms a covered stowage for ROV/AUVs and extends between the two large funnel casings, which is a major recognition feature.

A comprehensive range of both positional and plotting electronics is carried, mainly of licence-built European origin. Up to eight clearance divers may be accommodated.

ABOVE: **Two of the fleet of Sugashima-class vessels in Japanese naval service. Note the distinctively large funnel casings.** LEFT: **The PAP-104 Mk 5 Remote Operating Vehicle (ROV) is standard equipment on all Sugashima-class vessels.**

## Coastal Minesweeper (CMS), Sugashima class

**Displacement:** 510 tons (standard); 620 tons (loaded)
**Length:** 58m/190ft 4in (oa)
**Beam:** 9.5m/31ft 2in
**Draught:** 2.5m/8ft 3in
**Armament:** 1 x 20mm Sea Vulcan cannon
**Machinery:** 2 diesel engines, 2 shafts with CP propellers, 2 electric creep motors
**Power:** 1343kW/1800bhp (diesels), 261kW/350hp (electric)
**Endurance:** 4600km/2500nm at 10 knots
**Protection:** None
**Complement:** 37+8

# Landing Ship, Tank (LST), Alligator class

This series of 14 ships was built at Kaliningrad, on the Baltic coast, over a period of some 14 years. While representing a considerable increase in size over the standard World War II-built LST (2), all were far smaller than the contemporary US-built equivalent. The more modest size limited speed to an extent (an Alligator class could still make 18 knots), but improved versatility by widening accessibility to landing beaches.

The drive-through design included bow and stern ramps, the former being enclosed by clamshell doors. The class could carry an estimated 24 heavy tanks, together with vehicles on the open upper deck. For beaching, payload was limited

to around 600 tons, but this could be increased to 1,500 tons for freighting. The cargo-handling equipment varied from a single 5-ton crane forward to a 5-ton crane both forward and aft. An additional larger 15-ton crane could be mounted forward.

The superstructure was typical of a 1960s merchant ship – curved bridgefront, combined mast and funnel, and sweeping curves to the curtain plating. The size resulted from the need to carry 300 troops accommodated above the tank deck. Defensive fire was by an automatic reloading 40-tube 140mm rocket launcher mounted in a small deckhouse. All were fitted with 57mm cannon

ABOVE: **Although first appearing in the early 1970s, the Alligator class has not yet been entirely withdrawn from service.**

in a dual-purpose twin mounting forward of the bridge. Up to four 25mm cannon were mounted aft. Quadruple mountings for light point-defence SAMs, either the SA-N-5 (NATO name: *Grail*) or SA-N-8 (NATO name: *Gremlin*) could also be mounted. By the end of a long period in servce, the Alligator class was superseded from 1975 by the Ropucha class.

## Landing Ship, Tank (LST), Alligator class

**Displacement:** 3,400 tons (standard); 4,500 tons (loaded)
**Length:** 114.07m/374ft (oa)
**Beam:** 15.5m/50ft 10in
**Draught:** 4.5m/14ft 9in
**Armament:** 2 x 57mm guns (1x2), 1 x 140mm multiple rocket launcher, 4 x 25mm guns (2x2), PDMS on occasion
**Machinery:** 2 diesel engines, 2 shafts
**Power:** 6,714kW/9,000bhp for 18 knots
**Fuel:** Not known
**Endurance:** 20,240km/11,000nm at 15 knots
**Protection:** Nominal
**Complement:** 92 plus 300 troops

ABOVE: **The well-designed hull shape of the Alligator class permits a speed of 18 knots. The bow doors and stern ramp allow a drive-through configuration for the tank deck.**

# Landing Ship, Medium (LSM), Polnochny class

Between 80-100 Polnochny class vessels were built in Poland between the 1960s and reportedly the 1980s. Although many were retained under both the Polish and Soviet flags, there were frequent transfers to friendly states and they could consequently serve anywhere from Algeria to Vietnam.

In profile, a Polnochny class vessel resembled a large LCT, but had the upper deck and interconnecting ramp of an LST. The tank deck was accessible only through the bow doors, and could accommodate six heavy tanks. As usual, vehicles and cargo could be stowed on the upper deck, accessed by the ramp.

In order to realize the much-demanded 18-knot speed, designers had to compromise with the hull shape. The bow is "ship-shaped", with earlier vessels having a fuller, convex flare. Later vessels had a more seakindly concave flare. The finer-hulled craft could be loaded with 180 tons of cargo; the earlier version carried 250 tons. Again,

for a vessel required to be at the forefront of an amphibious attack, the large superstructure appeared vulnerable, with a long, fullwidth deckhouse. This feature is longer again in the later, wider beam type. Accommodation was for 180 troops, compared to 100 in the earlier vessel.

Early ships were distinctive in having recesses along either deck edge for the stowage of live charges. These were towed by two remotely controlled motor boats to the beach area for mine clearance. Many of the later vessels were modified as anti-aircraft support craft, with the addition of improved electronics equipment and up to four quadruple launchers for SA-N-5 or SA-N-8 point defence missiles. Some of the class mounted a 30mm Gatling-type cannon at the stern. Gradually phased out in favour of large hovercraft, a few remain active in the Russian Navy with a number also remaining in service with export customers.

ABOVE LEFT: **Probably anchored in a shallow area of the Mediterranean Sea, these two Polnochny vessels are of the early A type with short superstructure and straight stern.**

ABOVE: **A later Polnochny C type with extended superstructure. What appears to be a ramp is in fact a hatch to facilitate crane-loading of vehicles down to the tank deck.**

## Landing Ship, Medium (LSM), Polnochny C type

**Displacement:** 720 tons (standard); 1,150 tons (loaded)
**Length:** 81.6m/267ft 6in (oa)
**Beam:** 10.1m/33ft 2in
**Draught:** 1.9m/6ft 3in
**Armament:** 2–4 x 30mm guns (1/2 x 2), 1 x 140mm multiple rail rocket launcher (in some), 2–4 x PDMS
**Machinery:** 2 diesel engines, 2 shafts
**Power:** 5,000bhp for 18 knots
**Fuel:** Not known
**Endurance:** 5,520km/3,000nm at 14 knots
**Protection:** Nominal
**Complement:** 40 plus 180 troops

# Landing Ship, Tank (LST), Ropucha class

To replace the Alligator-class LSTs, around 24 Ropucha class LSTs were built in Poland. This resulted in a close resemblance to the smaller Polnochny class. From a quarter-bow view, the transition from the constant-freeboard after end to the severe, straight-line sheer of the bow section is very marked. What appears to be a ramp, located on the forward end, is, in fact, a hatch. Vehicles are not carried on the foredeck, and hatch loading is by crane where ramp facilities are not available.

The tank deck is "drive-through", with doors and ramps fitted at each end. Accommodation for up to 225 troops is located topside, in a long, full-width

deckhouse comprising most of the lowest level of the four-deck superstructure. The bows are extremely raked and flared, the extreme forward end being squared off and overhanging the bow doors.

For a diesel-powered ship, the funnel casing is a massive angular structure.

Forward and aft of the main superstructure are twin-mounted 57mm cannon with dedicated fire control radar mounted on a pedestal immediately abaft the funnel. As with the Polnochny class, a number were converted, in some cases temporarily, as anti-aircraft support craft and fitted with up to four Landing Ship, Tank (LST), Ropucha class small point-defence missile launchers. Some

ABOVE: **Around 12 Ropucha-type vessels were built. The tank deck is drive-through but, when the ship is used for cargo, freight is loaded by crane through the large hatch in the foredeck.**

have also carried a later type of the 40-barrelled 122mm barrage rocket launcher. An apparent innovation was to fit temporary mine-launching rails on the tank deck. As an alternative to ten medium tanks or a variety of smaller vehicles, a total of 92 mines could reportedly be carried and laid presumably via the stern door. A number of the class has been decommissioned and some were put out of action during the Russian invasion of Ukraine in 2022.

ABOVE: **Only three Ropucha vessels are known to have been converted for anti-aircraft support. Note the air/surface search radar dome and the single 76mm gun which replaced the earlier twin 57mm cannon.**

## Landing Ship, Tank (LST), Ropucha class

**Displacement:** 2,770 tons (standard); 4,100 tons (full load)
**Length:** 105m/344ft 3in (wl); 112.5m/368ft 10in (oa)
**Beam:** 15m/49ft 2in
**Draught:** 3.7m/12ft 2in (maximum, loaded)
**Armament:** 4 x 57mm guns (2x2), 1/2 x 122mm multiple rail rocket launchers (in some), 2/4 x PDMS (in some)
**Machinery:** 2 diesel engines, 2 shafts
**Power:** 14,323kW/19,200bhp for 17+ knots
**Fuel:** Not known
**Endurance:** 6,440km/3,500nm at 16 knots
**Protection:** Nominal
**Complement:** 95 plus 225 troops

# Landing Ship, Dock (LSD), Ivan Rogov class

Four of these massive ships were planned, but only three were ever built. Despite costs and complexity, the lead ship was scrapped following only 20 years in service (the Alligator class was still in use after 50 years, and the Ropucha class over 30 years). The second vessel, *Aleksandr Nikolayev*, was unsuccessfully offered for sale after 17 years in service. A planned fourth ship was cancelled. The whole programme gives the impression of being undertaken primarily to gain experience in what is a difficult area of ship design.

The specification was driven by the requirement to accommodate, transport and land a 500-plus battalion of naval infantry, together with vehicles and

equipment. The solution contrasts interestingly with US-built equivalents, of approximately the same size.

In the latter, the superstructure is positioned forward and all helicopter operations are conducted aft, the flight deck covering the docking well. The Ivan Rogov class, in contrast, has the superstructure three-quarters aft and over the docking well. Helicopter operations are, therefore, split between the fore and aft decks. Unlike US vessels, the Ivan Rogov class is designed to carry four helicopters with hangars on each deck.

The foredeck, one level lower than the aft deck, can also be used to carry vehicles. These can directly access, via a hoistable ramp, the bow doors

ABOVE: **The open foredeck is connected by a shallow ramp and doors with a vehicle garaging area inside the superstructure.**

and ramp. The doors are level with the tank deck, which can accommodate up to 25 heavy tanks,

The docking well can house six Ondatra-class landing craft, similar in size to an LCM (8). This would suggest a size of approximately 75 x 11.5m/ 246 x 37ft 9in, which would allow three Lebed-type LCAC craft to be carried. Being enclosed, the Lebed-type can transport up to 120 troops – a considerable advantage over the US-built LCAC. Unusually for such large ships, vessels in the Rogov class are gas turbine-powered.

LEFT: **Folding doors enclose the main helicopter hangar. The vehicles and helicopters area is located in the central area of the superstructure, with accommodation on each side. Note the 30mm Gatling-type guns in twin mountings, with directors.**

## Landing Ship, Dock (LSD), Ivan Rogov class

**Displacement:** 11,600 tons (standard); 14,100 tons (loaded)
**Length:** 149.9m/491ft 6in (wl); 157.5m/516ft 4in (oa)
**Beam:** 22m/72ft 2in (wl)
**Draught:** 4.2m/13ft 9in
**Armament:** 2 x 6mm guns (1x2), 4 x 30mm Gatling-type guns (4x1), 1 x SA-N-4 (Gecko) SAM system, 2 x SA-N-8 (Gremlin) PDMS, 1 x multi-rail 122mm barrage rocket projector
**Machinery:** Gas turbines (COGAG configuration), 2 shafts
**Power:** 26,856kW/36,000shp for 21 knots
**Fuel:** Not known
**Endurance:** 7,360km/4,000nm at 18 knots
**Protection:** Not known
**Complement:** 239 plus 565 troops

LEFT: **Featuring one of the largest areas of flat superstructure plating at sea today, the MV *Johan de Witt* differs from MV *Rotterdam* in having smaller masts. The funnel casing is reduced to a minimum. Note the side access doors and hull openings for stowing LCVPs.**

# Amphibious Transport Ship (LPD), MV Rotterdam and MV Johan de Witt

International cooperation to develop common ship designs has an unfortunate tendency to become unravelled, but an exception was the Spanish-Dutch project for a large amphibious transport. Results so far include the Dutch ships MV *Rotterdam* (1998) and MV *Johan de Witt* (2007), the Spanish ships MV *Galicia* (1998) and MV *Castilla* (2000), and the four British Bay class. The MV *Rotterdam*'s sister ship was to have been identical, but the design was lengthened by 10.35m/40ft and the ship was named MV *Amsterdam*.

Except for topside detail, the Dutch and Spanish ships are effectively identical. The high freeboard of the hull and the large block superstructure are relieved only by subtle changes of plane to reduce their radar cross section, and openings for a considerable number of encapsulated life rafts. Unlike the British variant, all have a short but large funnel casing.

Three doors per side serve storage and transport areas while facilitating disembarkation to small craft alongside. Thirty main battle tanks can be carried, while the docking well is large enough to accept Dutch, US or British LCUs, and LCMs. There are two large helicopter landing spots and two cranes. Six NH-90 or four Chinook helicopters may be hangared. Motor transport is transferred to the helicopter deck by elevator. Over 600 marines can be accommodated, with 150 more carried in an emergency.

The MV *Johan de Witt* is 10m/33ft longer than MV *Rotterdam*, with an even larger superstructure block to house a complete marine battalion. Externally, she differs in having masts and funnel significantly reduced in size. The addition of side stowage aft to accommodate landing craft under davits aids identification. The docking well is shorter but wider, and able to accommodate a standard 29.8m/98ft British LCU (10).

Self-defence takes the form of two CIWS guns and up to ten 12.7mm machine guns.

ABOVE: **The two-tone paint scheme on the MV *Johan de Witt* is proficient in reducing the effect of the vessel's large bulk. Note the access doors to the large helicopter hangar.**

## Amphibious Transport Ship (LPD), MV *Rotterdam*

**Displacement:** 10,800 tons (standard); 12,750 tons (loaded)
**Length:** 142.4m/466ft 10in (wl); 166.2m/544ft 11in (oa)
**Beam:** 23.3m/76ft 3in
**Draught:** 5.23m/17ft 2in
**Armament:** 2 x 30mm Goalkeeper CIWS
**Machinery:** 4 diesel-generators powering 2 electric propulsion motors, 2 shafts
**Power:** 12,384kW/16,600shp for 19 knots
**Fuel:** 830 tons
**Endurance:** 11,040km/6,000nm at 12 knots
**Protection:** Not known
**Complement:** 113 plus around 600 marines

ABOVE: **A company of troops leaves a Yudao-class vessel. Note that the ramp is made up of two folding sections.** LEFT: **Two Yudao-class vessels are here berthed alongside a frigate.**

# Landing Ship, Medium (LSM), Yudao class

China has historical claims to offshore land from the size of Taiwan to reefs once considered insignificant. The amphibious means to enforce such claims was by little more than war-built ships. By the 1960s, the vessels were in urgent need of replacement. With no previous experience upon which to draw, the Chinese began modestly, producing perfectly serviceable, updated versions of the LCU and LCM.

More ambitious designs were built in the 1980s including eight Yudao-class 1,500-ton LSMs that appeared to combine the main features of the LSM (1) and LST (2). Earlier ships had been modified over the years, with the superstructure extended from only the starboard side to full width, spanning the vehicle deck. Side spaces aft had also been adapted for minelaying. The Yudao class combined such features with larger size and

ramped forward and after ends. The tank deck was covered with an upper deck and not intended for wheeled transport. All accommodation was above, built over the through tank deck and, as a result, very bulky for the size of craft.

Having the weak feature of an exposed bow ramp, not protected by doors, and the blunt entry, the class, despite its size, was both slow and incapable of safely being used for an extended sea passage. Better described as a large LCU, the Yudao class was not a success in service.

An apparent derivative was the one-off *Yudeng* of 1994, also rated an LSM. The ship resembled a slightly enlarged French-built Champlain class. With an improved forward entry, and bow doors enclosing the ramp, it had a speed of 17 knots.

LEFT: **Only one Yudeng-class vessel was built in 1994. Categorized as an LSM, the substantial build quality contrasts with the general utility of amphibious ships.**

## Landing Ship, Medium (LSM), Yudao class

**Displacement:** 1,460 tons (loaded)
**Length:** 78m/255ft 9in (bp)
**Beam:** 12.6m/41ft 4in
**Draught:** 3.1m/10ft 2in (maximum, seagoing)
**Armament:** 8 x 25mm guns (4x2)
**Machinery:** 2 diesel engines, 2 shafts
**Power:** Not known
**Fuel:** Not known
**Endurance:** Not known
**Protection:** Nominal
**Complement:** About 65

# Landing Ship, Tank (LST), Yukan/Yuting class

ABOVE: **The Type 072-II (Yuting II class) can discharge up to 12 tanks directly through the bow doors, or float an LCU from a floodable docking well. Note the LCAs carried in davits.**

Built as a replacement for China's remaining war-built LSTs, the Yukan class differed in having a drive-through configuration. To achieve this, all accommodation was moved topside, resulting in a bulkier superstructure. The term "drive-through" also needs to be qualified, as only the forward ramp had a 50-ton rating. With the after ramp reportedly being able to support only 20 tons, heavy armour thus needed to be both loaded and disembarked through the bows. The beaching payload of 500 tons also limited the number of heavy vehicles carried. The Yukan class was fitted with the SEMT-Pielstick medium-speed diesel engine. This lightweight unit was compact enough to fit in the space below the tank deck.

Following the building of seven Yukan-class vessels, an improved version, designated Yuting, was introduced. Both types were relatively small, some 20m/66ft longer than an LST (2). As the ships can carry two LCA/LCVPs, the small docking well would appear to be an expensive complication. Two deck cranes were added and the under-utilized space aft remodelled as a helicopter pad, although without a hangar. Hull dimensions remained unchanged. Some 12 Yuting-class vessels were built between 1991 and 2001.

Reported capacity for both the Yukan and Yuting classes was 250 troops and 10 tanks. This was increased to 300 and 12 when a Yuting II was introduced in 2002. This was 10m/33ft longer but retained the same beam measurement. To compensate for reduced stability, the helicopter deck was lowered one level. Space for the extra accommodation saw the superstructure block extended to the full width of the ship.

The extra length enabled the dimensions of the docking well to be extended to hold two small air-cushion vehicles (ACV) but these, each with a troop capacity of only ten, are of limited use.

ABOVE: **The Yuting II class is thought to be capable of 18 knots, the hull being nicely faired. Note the access tunnel connecting the foredeck with the helicopter deck, and twin 37mm cannon on the forecastle.**

## Landing Ship, Tank (LST), Yuting I class

**Displacement:** 3,430 tons (loaded)
**Length:** 119.5m/391ft 10in (oa)
**Beam:** 164m/53ft 9in
**Draught:** 2.8m/9ft 2in
**Armament:** 6 x 37mm guns (3x2)
**Machinery:** 2 diesel engines, 2 shafts
**Power:** 7,087kW/9,500bhp for 18 knots
**Fuel:** Not known
**Endurance:** 5,520km/3,000nm at 14 knots
**Protection:** Not known
**Complement:** 104 plus 250 troops

# Landing Ship, Personnel, Dock (LPD), Yuzhao class

China's astonishing progress, from being a client state for ex-Soviet era vessels to a builder of large, sophisticated warships, brings to mind the similar route taken by Japan in the early 20th century.

At around 18,000 tons standard, and 210m/689ft in length, the first of the Yuzhao class, named *Kunlun Shan*, is around the same size as USS *San Antonio* (LPD-17), but more closely resembles the much smaller Dutch-built Rotterdam type.

LEFT: **The vast well deck of the Yuzhao class. On board are Payi-class air cushion vehicles (ACV), each capable of carrying a maximum of 10 troops.**

Commissioned at the end of 2007, the vessel has a relatively longer superstructure, with accommodation for a marine battalion of 800 men. Two Z-8 heavy helicopters are also hangared in a space extending forward between the large funnel casings. A wide, clear landing deck extends to the stern.

A full-width, single-piece stern gate serves the docking well, which is probably large enough to accommodate four LCAC-type craft, or up to six LCUs. These can load and discharge directly on to ramps connecting the forward end of the docking well with two vehicle decks. A starboard-sided deck crane facilitates over-the-side loading of landing craft.

The ship is powered by four, licence-built SEMT-Pielstick diesel engines, driving to two shafts. The ship is relatively lightly armed, with a single 76mm gun forward and four 30mm Gatling-type cannon on the upper superstructure, allowing a wide arc of defensive fire.

An estimated eight examples are in PLAN service and the type is also offered for export – the Royal Thai Navy took delivery of HTMS *Chang (III)* in April 2023.

## Landing Ship, Personnel, Dock (LPD), Yuzhao class

**Displacement:** 18,000 tons (standard); 21,000 tons (loaded)
**Length:** 689ft/210m (oa)
**Beam:** 28m/91ft 10in
**Draught:** 7m/23ft
**Armament:** 1 x 76mm gun, 4 x 30mm Gatling
**Machinery:** 4 diesel engines, 2 shafts
**Power:** 35,210kW/47,200bhp for 21 knots
**Endurance:** 10,000km/6,250nm at 18 knots
**Protection:** Nominal
**Complement:** 175 plus 600–800 Marines

# Amphibious Warfare Vessels

China is famously and understandably secretive about many of its military assets, and this extends to its amphibious warfare vessels. This is therefore an overview and summary of the vessels known to be in service for these types of operations.

Until the end of the 1970s, China relied on US-built Second World War-vintage tank landing ships (LSTs).

ABOVE AND BELOW: **PLAN 072A Landing Ship Tank** *Wuhan*, **commissioned in 2005.**

These were replaced by the Chinese-designed Type 072 (known by NATO as the Yukan), seven of which entered the People's Liberation Army Navy (PLAN) service between the early 1980s and the 1990s.

These were succeeded by the large 120m-/394ft-long Type 072II landing ships (NATO – Yuting class), the first PLAN amphibious warfare ship to have a flight deck for helicopter operations. The ships can carry 250 troops, 10 tanks or 500 tons of cargo and of the four built, three remain

active with the PLAN East Sea Fleet.

The eleven examples of the Type 072 III or Yuting I class that entered PLAN service are an improved variant of the Type 072II and feature a stern helicopter platform.

The next development of the Type 072 line was the Type 072A class, with forward and rear decks connected by a tunnel through the superstructure. With an estimated full load displacement of 4,800 tons, fifteen have been built and remain in service. Up to 10 armoured vehicles can be carried along with 250 troops and the ships' helipad can operate two medium helicopters.

The Type 074 (NATO – Yuhai class), is a series of medium landing ships (LSM) with a displacement of around 800 tons. These ships are something of a composite design and are enlarged versions of the 1960s-designed Type 271 landing ship crossed with the best elements of the 1960s Type 079 landing ship. Type 074s can carry up to 100 tons of cargo made up of six light amphibious tanks or two main battle tanks, or 350 fully equipped troops. Although this is a blend of two old

designs, the resultant vessels feature a great deal of automation meaning this relatively large ship has a complement of just 56.

The Type 074A, or Yubei class, with a standard displacement of 650 tons, is an upgraded, more advanced medium landing ship with a catamaran hull design. It has a 200-ton capacity and can carry 250 fully-equipped troops. It is the first PLAN LSM to incorporate the infrared stealth feature of locating engine exhausts near the waterline. Three to six tanks can be carried with 70 fully equipped troops or, instead, just 250 fully equipped troops.

The Landing Helicopter Dock (LHD) Type 075 (with the NATO reporting name Yushen class landing helicopter assault) is a class of currently three amphibious assault ships designed for the PLAN, capable of carrying and deploying helicopters, armoured vehicles, and landing craft. They have an estimated displacement of around 30,000 to 40,000 tons and can accommodate up to 30 helicopters, operating them from a seven landing spot flight deck that runs for most of the whole 237m/778ft of the ship's length. The ship's well deck and vehicle deck are one homogenous space allowing for greater flexibility and easier deployment of the amphibious vehicles carried, including three Type 726 LCAC air-cushioned landing craft.

This deck area is large enough to accommodate a fully-equipped mechanized infantry company of PLAN marines, together with tanks and artillery. The first of the class, *Hainan*, was commissioned in April 2021 and was, along with the second ship *Guangxi*, declared operational in late 2022.

# Landing Ship, Dock (LPD), San Giorgio class

These two interesting ships of the Italian Navy could only be fully funded by configuring the second, MM *San Marco* (L9893), for disaster relief. As built, however, too much was attempted on a limited displacement. The full-length flightdeck was divided by the starboard side island. The forward end terminated in a forecastle deck one level lower. A 20.5 x 7m/62 x 23ft docking well was large enough for one of a new class of 18.5 x 5.1m/61 x 17ft LCM. Three LCVP were carried on deck and handled by crane. Surprisingly, in

view of the large, merchant ship-type bow bulb, the class was expected to beach, being equipped with a ramp, enclosed by faired-in clamshell doors.

Below the flight deck, and connected to it by an elevator, was a 100 x 20.5m/ 328 x 67ft vehicle stowage area. Due to the lack of height, helicopters were carried on deck. Design limitations quickly became apparent, both ships being substantially altered between 1999 and 2001. A very deep sponson was added on the port side. This was 5m/16ft wide, and provided landing

ABOVE: MM *San Giorgio* (L9892). Too much was designed into a limited displacement, so the two ships have undergone considerable modification.

spots for two helicopters. Three AW-101, five Agusta Bell AB 212 or SH90 helicopters can be carried. The forward flight area was enlarged and improved by extending the upper deck over the forecastle area and squared off, carrier-style. The bow doors were permanently sealed, all transport now being put ashore by landing craft. Some 350 troops could be accommodated. Unusually, the ships have a water-transfer, passive stabilization system fitted.

ABOVE: Both LCVPs have to be accommodated on the outside of the hull of the San Giorgio class. A very large sponson to accommodate these vessels was constructed on the port side of the ship, prone to slamming.

## Landing Ship, Dock (LPD), San Giorgio class

**Displacement:** 7,665 tons (loaded)
**Length:** 118m/386ft 11in (bp); 133.3m/437ft 1in (oa)
**Beam:** 20.5m/67ft 3in
**Draught:** 5.25m/17ft 3in 6.5m/21ft 4in (flooded down)
**Armament:** 2 x 20mm guns (2x1), PDMS to be fitted
**Machinery:** 2 diesel engines, 2 shafts
**Power:** 12,533kW/16,800bhp for 20+ knots
**Fuel:** Not known
**Endurance:** 13,800km/7,500nm at 16 knots
**Protection:** Not known
**Complement:** 163 plus 350 troops

# Landing Ship, Dock (LPD), MM San Giusto

ABOVE: **A first derivative of the San Giorgio class, MM *San Giusto* (L9894) presents a pleasing compact appearance from the starboard side, marred somewhat by the incongruously sited launching davits opposite the island.**

Effectively the third unit of the San Giorgio class, MM *San Giusto* (L9894) was not commenced until the other ships had been in service for several years. The ship therefore incorporates some improvements, based on experience with the earlier ships in the class.

The hull is almost identical except that the vessel was never designed to take the ground and was not fitted with bow doors or a ramp. MM *San Giusto* was slightly longer as built and the foredeck carried the same low structure as earlier

ships, for mounting a later type of 76mm OTO-Melara cannon.

From the port side, the vessel appears very similar, carrying three LCVPs under heavy gantry davits on a long sponson running just one level below the upper deck. The starboard side island superstructure is even wider than that on the earlier ships, the "taxiway" connecting forward and after flight decks is both narrow and restricted by the upper parts of the LCVP davits.

Two light helicopters can be operated

simultaneously amidships. All three ships are equipped for night operations. Although not fitted with sonar equipment, any of the class will be able to support a specialist anti-submarine group by providing a base for five helicopters.

*San Giusto* may be immediately identified by the square tower base to the mast. The role of the vessel in peacetime is as a training ship for cadets of the Italian Naval Academy.

The *San Giusto*, along with the other two ships of the San Giorgio class, is expected to be replaced in the early 2030s by three new 16,500 ton landing ships.

ABOVE: **Three LCPs are stowed under gantries on the port-side platform to be replaced by a San Giorgio-type sponson. Note the "bumper" protection on each side of the open stern gate.**

### Landing Ship, Dock (LPD), MM *San Giusto* (pre-modernization)

**Displacement:** 5,600 tons (standard); 7,950 tons (loaded)
**Length:** 118m/386ft 11in (bp); 137m/449ft 2in (oa)
**Beam:** 20.5m/67ft 3in (wl)
**Draught:** 6m/19ft 8in (mean, seagoing)
**Armament:** 2 x 76mm gun, 2 x 20mm guns (2x1)
**Machinery:** 2 diesel engines, 2 shafts
**Power:** 12,533kW/16,800bhp for 20 knots
**Fuel:** Not known
**Endurance:** 13,800km/7,500nm at 16 knots
**Protection:** Not known
**Complement:** 198 plus 266 training or 350 troops

# LHD Trieste

Launched in 2019, Italy's *Trieste* (L9890) is a multipurpose amphibious warfare ship and a landing helicopter dock (LHD) with impressive aircraft carrier capabilities. Designed from its inception as a flexible, multipurpose, modular vessel, the ship began sea trials in 2021 and, at 245m/803ft long and 36m/ 118ft wide, is the largest Italian military ship built since World War II – it will also be the largest vessel in the Marina Militare fleet. The ship's mixed air wing of AW101 and NH90 helicopters, and Lockheed Martin F-35B Lightning II jets, enables it to undertake a wide range of missions from its 230m-/755ft-long flight deck.

Constructed by the Fincantieri shipyard in Naples at a cost of 1.17 billion euros, below the hangar level the ship has a floodable stern well deck suitable for the operation of a range of amphibious warfare vessels directly from the ship on to the surface of the ocean.

These include four of the 23.8m-/78ft-long Italian-designed Cantieri Navali Vittoria LCM23 landing craft. These large but versatile LCMs can travel at up to 22 knots and can carry up to two amphibious assault vehicles, two self-propelled artillery units or a 60-ton Ariete

ABOVE: **Designed from the outset as a flexible, multi-purpose vessel, the *Trieste* launched in 2019.** BELOW: ***Trieste* under construction at Fincantieri's shipyard, Castellammare di Stabia, Italy.**

RIGHT: *Trieste* is the largest Italian military ship built since World War II. BELOW: Built in Naples at a cost of 1.17 billion euros, the ship's floodable stern well deck enables operation of a range of amphibious warfare vessels directly onto the surface of the ocean.

main battle tank (MBT). The *Trieste* can also accommodate Landing Craft Air Cushion (LCAC) vessels, or L-CAT roll-on/roll-off catamaran landing craft and RHIB (Rigid Hull Inflatable Boat) high-speed craft. The *Trieste* is configured to carry up to 1,200 linear metres of wheeled and tracked vehicles which can also include B1 Centauro tank destroyers and other armoured fighting vehicles, and up to 600 soldiers. In short it is designed to carry the most technically

advanced amphibious equipment and vehicles of European and NATO navies. A fully equipped hospital will be available onboard, complete with operating rooms.

The vessel has also been conceived to carry out command and control functions in case of emergencies at sea, evacuation of nationals and humanitarian assistance operations.

Power comes from two Rolls-Royce MT30 gas turbines delivering up to 40 MW of power giving a maximum speed

of 25 knots and range of around 7,000 nautical miles. The turbines form part of a COmbined Diesel eLectric Or Gas (CODLOG) propulsion system, and an additional electric propulsion system is to be used for low speed sailing, in line with the Italian Navy's Green Fleet environmental policy.

Self-defence is in the form of short/medium range air defence missiles, three Oto Melara 76mm Super Rapid gun systems, three Oto Melara KBA 25/80mm cannons, and smaller-calibre machine guns. A towed sonar array provides protection against torpedo attack.

## LHD *Trieste*

**Displacement:** 21,500 tons (loaded)
**Length:** 245m/803ft 10in (overall)
**Beam:** 47m/154ft 2in
**Draught:** 7.2m/23ft 7in
**Armament:** 3 x Oto Melara 76mm/62 Strales anti-aircraft guns, 3 x OTO Melara 25/80 RCWS with Oerlikon KBA 25mm, 2 x Oto Melara ODLS-20 (decoys launchers), Vertically launched Aster 15 and 30 missiles or CAMM ER anti-aircraft missiles
**Machinery:** CODOG system featuring 2 x Rolls-Royce MT30 gas turbines and 2 x MAN 20V32/44CR diesel engines
**Speed:** Up to 25 knots
**Endurance:** 30 days
**Complement:** 460 crew plus up to 600 soldiers

# Minesweeping Drones

Modern mines are sophisticated in design, and this requires suspicious areas to be investigated by remotely controlled craft. Shallow coastal waters have required German naval planners to develop a high level of expertise in mine countermeasures.

An innovation of the late 1970s was Troika, groups of three drone craft remotely controlled from a specially equipped minehunter, designated a Type 351. Six sets of three drones, known as *Seehunde* (Seals), were built, configured primarily to counter magnetic mines, although conventional sweep gear could also be used. This, however, was essentially area minesweeping (equivalent to the use of helicopter-towed sleds used by the US Navy), while investigation of

a beach approach demands special minehunting techniques.

Over the years the Seehunde, which are designed to be explosion-resistant, have been continuously updated and are now able to deploy Remotely Operated Vehicles (ROV). Bottom coverage by the average vehicle is limited, and requires input guidance to where the mines are located. Towed sidescan sonar is invaluable, identifying "minelike objects", even if barely buried in the sand.

Such sonars are built into "towfish" which are required to be towed by an ROV where the data is stored or transmitted in real time to the control ship. Classification and evaluation of objects located is possibly followed by close visual examination by remote TV. The mine can be exploded by an expendable "one-shot" device which has to be precisely targeted. This level of capability demanded a new generation of craft and ROVs. A SWATH-hulled catamaran control vessel, for example, provides a

ABOVE: **Three of the 18 Troika vessels built for the German Navy moored alongside a quay. The *Seehunde* (Seals) are operated in "threes" under remote control from a Type 351 minehunter.**

more stable command platform.

Seehunde is complemented by "intelligent" sacrificial one-shot devices such as Seefuchs (Seafox). This fibre-optic guided, one-shot mine disposal vehicle is used for semi-autonomous disposal of naval mines and other ordnance found at sea.

LEFT: **A Seafox C being launched from its handling cradle. The type is described as a One-Shot Mine Identification and Disposal (OSMID) vehicle, and is guided to the target by signals through a fibre-optic cable linked to a controller on a minesweeper.**

---

### Minesweeping Drone, *Seehund*

**Displacement:** 91 tons (light); 96.5 tons (loaded)
**Length:** 24.92m/81ft 9in (oa)
**Beam:** 4.46m/14ft 7in
**Draught:** 1.8m/5ft 11in
**Armament:** None
**Machinery:** 1 diesel driving a Schottel directional propulsor
**Power:** 332kW/445bhp for 9.5 knots
**Fuel:** Not known
**Endurance (for transit):** 957km/520nm at 8.8 knots
**Protection:** Explosion-resistant mountings for machinery
**Complement:** 3 for transit; none while operational

# Landing Ship, Tank (LST), Frosch class

Built for the navy of the German Democratic Republic (East Germany) the 12 Frosch-class vessels were based on the Soviet-built Ropucha class but were smaller for operations in the Baltic Sea.

Few, if any, appear to have been fitted with stern doors for access to the tank deck, all movement thus being through the bows. As with the Ropucha class, the forecastle was not raised, but had a prominent sheer to increase forward freeboard. Much of the ramp was exposed, only the lower half being enclosed within the bow doors. The doors were not watertight, acting both to protect the ramp from impact with the sea and to present a less bluff entry. The forward run had a prominent knuckle at the junction of the wide upper hull and the relatively fine lines of the underwater hull. As the class had a speed of 18 knots, the correct compromise appears to have been reached.

The Ropucha class featured a long superstructure based on a single-level deckhouse. In contrast, the Frosch superstructure had a two-level house over most of the length. As was customary, the foredeck was largely unobstructed for stowage of motor vehicles. Around 12 heavy battle tanks could be accommodated.

As a cargo carrier, a Frosch could lift some 600 tons. Indeed, a further two were built around 1980 with cargo hatches and an 8-ton capacity crane. Designated as Amphibious Warfare Support Ships (AWSS), these were known as the Frosch II. The earlier vessels now became Frosch I.

As with the Ropucha class, twin 57mm cannon were mounted ahead and aft of the bridge structure. Forward of the bridge were two 40-tube, 122mm barrage rocket launchers. Mines could be laid over either quarter. The class was quickly disposed of following German reunification.

ABOVE: **A Frosch II, the cargo-carrying variant of the basic design. The bows have a unique design in that the ramp is largely exposed, protected by only two small bow doors.**

## Landing Ship, Tank (LST), Frosch I class

**Displacement:** 1,745 tons (standard); 2,150 tons (loaded)
**Length:** 90.7m/297ft 4in (bp); 98m/321ft 4in (oa)
**Beam:** 11.2m/36ft 9in
**Draught:** 2.8m/9ft 2in
**Armament:** 4 x 57mm guns (2x2), 4 x 30mm guns (2x2), 2 x 40-tube 122mm barrage rocket launchers
**Machinery:** 2 diesel engines, 2 shafts
**Power:** 8,952kW/12,000bhp for 18 knots
**Fuel:** Not known
**Endurance:** Not known
**Protection:** Nominal
**Complement:** Not known, plus one company of troops

# Juan Carlos I

Commissioned in 2010, Spain's *Juan Carlos I* aircraft carrier, also known as the L61, is a multi-purpose amphibious assault ship aircraft carrier that exemplifies Spain's commitment to maritime defence and power projection.

Designed and built by Spanish shipbuilding company Navantia, the ship was named after Juan Carlos I, the former King of Spain who abdicated in 2014. It is the Spanish Navy's flagship.

Spain had been planning to build an aircraft carrier since the early 2000s, as part of its efforts to modernize its military and increase its capabilities for expeditionary operations. The country had previously operated the *Principe de Asturias*, a smaller carrier, but it was decommissioned in 2013. Initially known as the Strategic Project Vessel, ordered in 2003, construction on the *Juan Carlos I* began in 2005

at Navantia's shipyard in Ferrol, northwestern Spain, and it was launched in 2009. The ship was then commissioned into the Spanish Navy at a final cost of €462 million, more than 30 percent over the original budget.

*Juan Carlos I* is a versatile and flexible vessel that can transport and deploy troops, equipment, and aircraft in support of combat operations. Equipped with a well-dock and spacious flight deck, the ship offers unparalleled flexibility in executing amphibious warfare missions. The 231m/758ft long, 27,000-ton ship has a large flight deck and hangar facilities that can accommodate up to 30 helicopters, or up to 12 Harriers, or F-35s along with up to 12 helicopters.

ABOVE: **The ship pictured in Las Palmas, May 2011. It can carry 913 soldiers and up to 46 Leopard 2E tanks in its capacious hangars below the flight deck.** LEFT: **The *Juan Carlos I* can carry up to four of the Spanish-designed and built LCM-1E landing craft, each of which in turn can carry 6 light tactical vehicles, or up to 170 personnel with equipment.**

RIGHT: The fully-floodable well deck is large enough to accommodate a 26.8m-/88ft-long Landing Craft Air Cushion (LCAC).

BELOW: HMAS *Canberra*, built in Italy, was commissioned in 2014. Note the MH-60 Black Hawk preparing to take flight from *Canberra's* deck.

Below decks, the vessel has 6,000sq m/65,000 sq ft of hangar and garage space and a fully-floodable stern well deck that can accommodate, embark and disembark four Spanish-designed and built LCM-1E landing craft or one large Landing Craft Air Cushion.

The ship can accommodate up to 900 sailors and 1,200 marines, making it one of the largest ships in the Spanish Navy.

The ship features advanced command and control systems, facilitating seamless coordination among naval, air, and land forces involved in amphibious operations. The ship's integrated communication and information systems provide real-time situational awareness, enhancing decision-making capabilities and operational effectiveness during complex combat scenarios.

While the ship had not seen combat at the time of writing, it has been involved in a number of international missions and exercises, including anti-piracy operations off the coast of Somalia, disaster relief operations in Haiti, and joint military exercises with other NATO countries.

The design for *Juan Carlos I* was also selected by Australia for two new ships in its navy's fleet. These were to be known as Canberra-class landing helicopter dock ships. Navantia built the ships from the keel to the flight deck level in Spain, then the ships were taken to Australia for completion by BAE Systems Australia. The first, HMAS *Canberra,* was commissioned in 2014, and a sister ship, HMAS *Adelaide*, the following year.

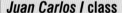

## Juan Carlos I class

**Built by:** Navantia
**Commissioned:** September 30, 2010
**Displacement:** 26,000 tons
**Length:** 231m/757ft
**Beam:** 32m/105ft
**Draught:** 6.9m/23ft
**Flight deck length:** 202m/663ft
**Aircraft:** AV-8B Harrier II and Chinook, Sea King and NH90 helicopters
**Armament:** 4 x 20mm guns, 4 x 12.7mm machine guns, 2 x Basic Point Defense Missile System (BPDMS), 1 x Vertical Launching System (VLS)
**Machinery:** 2 x diesel/gas turbine powerplants
**Power:** 2 x 11 MW
**Speed:** 21 knots (39kmh/24mph)
**Range:** 9000 nautical miles
**Complement:** 260 plus Air Wing of 172

LEFT: **HS *Chios* (L173)** at Piraeus, pictured alongside the Hellenic Navy frigate HS *Themistokles* (F465). Note the stern helipad and hangar over the well deck entrance, for the operation of medium helicopters. BELOW: **HS *Chios*** at Phaleron Bay. The Jason class was the result of a concerted effort to increase Greece's military shipbuilding experience and capacity, thereby reducing reliance on foreign suppliers. When they entered service, the class replaced World War II-vintage LSTs.

# Jason class

The Jason class ships of Greece's Hellenic Navy are tank landing ships (LSTs) developed to replace US-built LSTs of World War II vintage. The Greek-designed and -built class represent Greece's ambition to develop its own military shipbuilding capacity and experience, as well as ensuring the availability of a credible amphibious force to project Greek power in the Mediterranean and Aegean. The class was developed in the 1980s through the cooperative efforts of the shipbuilders

Elefsis Shipyards, the National Technical University of Athens, and end users the Hellenic Navy. The first examples were laid down in 1987 but the completion of the class was delayed due to financial issues.

Along with Zubr class Landing Craft Air Cushion (LCAC), the five ships making up the Jason class are the Hellenic Navy's primary amphibious warfare ships. HS *Samos* (L174) was commissioned in 1994; HS *Chios* (L173) in 1996; HS *Ikaria* (L175) and HS *Lesvos*

(L176) in 1999, and HS *Rodos* (L177) in 2000 – all were built by Elefsis Shipyard.

Although an impressive 1,200 infantry can be transported for short voyages, a typical force carried would be 350 troops. The craft can also carry up to 22 main battle tanks, or armoured personnel carriers, artillery, truck or other equipment weighing up to 250 tons, all of which can be loaded/unloaded through bow and stern ramps. Four LCVP 36-F Fast Landing Craft can also be carried.

A helipad flight deck and hangar maintenance facilities are included over the well deck entrance. This facilitates the operation of medium helicopters such as the NH-90 or Super Puma.

The Jason class are equipped with the advanced Thomson-CSF TRS-3030 Triton G radar system to detect and track incoming threats. This is complemented by the Thomson-CSF Vega II command and control system, including a Pollux TRS3220 fast-scanning radar as a fire control radar system. Although each ship is armed

ABOVE: **HS** *Chios* **(L173), which was commissioned in 1996, unloads tanks at Kos, 2013.** BELOW: **HS** *Ikaria* **(L175), commissioned into the Hellenic Navy in 1999, in the gulf of Corinth, waiting to pass the Corinth Channel, 2013. With a 230m-/755ft-flight deck, the class can operate a mixed air wing of AW101 and NH90 helicopters, as well as Lockheed Martin F-35B Lightning II jets. Although the class were commmissioned from the end of the 20th century, it took another twenty years for the decision to pair the ships with modern and credible amphibious assault vehicles.**

with an Oto Melara 76mm/62 compact naval gun, two Breda 40mm/70 guns and two Rheinmetall 20mm guns in twin mounts, the ships do lack a modern CIWS (close-in weapon system) to detect and destroy short-range incoming missiles and enemy aircraft.

The Greek ambition to not be reliant on foreign shipyards was commendable but, perhaps for budgetary reasons, the Jason class were not paired with modern amphibious warfare vehicles to embark,

such as the Soviet/Russian BMP-3F. Consequently, Greek marine forces had for well over two decades to continue to employ landing tactics taken from World War II. That was, however, until 2022 when it was announced that Greece was to receive a large number of refurbished ex-USMC AAVP-7A1 Amphibious Assault Vehicles to equip its marine force. This pairing will make the five Jasons and their modern, offensive cargo a formidable force in the region.

## Jason class

**Displacement:** 4470 tons (fully loaded)
**Length:** 116m/380ft 7in
**Beam:** 6m/19ft 8in
**Draught:** 15.3m/50ft 2in
**Armament:** 1 x Oto Melara 76mm/62 compact gun, 2 x 40mm/L 70 Breda-Bofors guns, 2 x twin Rheinmetall Rh202 20mm
**Machinery:** 2 Wärtsilä Nohab 16V25 diesels driving 2 shafts
**Power:** 9,200 hp/6.76 MW
**Endurance:** 8,700km/4,700nmi at 16 knots
**Complement:** 120 plus 350 troops carried
**Capacity:** 250 tons of vehicles or equipment

# A Directory of Landing Craft

It would be very simple if amphibious vessels could be divided into landing ships, for shore-to-shore passages, and landing craft, designed for ship-to-shore movement. In general, such definitions work well but, as ever, there are exceptions, not least because "shore-to-shore" might mean an ocean passage or a short-sea crossing. Larger types, such as the LCT and LCI (L), were often used on limited open-sea crossings.

Developed to meet evolving needs, landing craft came in many forms, from the large Landing Craft, Tank (LCT) to the smaller Landing Craft, Personnel (LCP). Austere wartime conditions concealed a vast amount of skilled and innovative design. Craft, for instance, needed to be trimmed in order to be grounded in the shallowest waters, then be refloated. Vehicle/cargo decks needed to be spacious and accessible, yet the craft had to remain stable despite carrying all types of military equipment and personnel.

Modern-day amphibious landings require a different mode of operation, hence the entry into service of the Landing Craft, Air Cushion (LCAC). This type allows Over The Horizon (OTH) operations away from the danger of shore-based artillery and missile batteries.

This chapter documents the development of the landing craft from 1921 to the present day.

LEFT: **A Zubr-class LCAC approaching the landing zone during *Zapad* 2009 (West 2009) military exercises held by Russian and Belarusian forces at the training centre for the Baltic Fleet near Baltiysk, Kaliningrad.**

LEFT: **Early craft built to the requirements of the US Marine Corps were based heavily on the design of the British "X-lighters" used at Gallipoli. When the removable bullet-proof canopy was fitted, the type were known as "Beetles".**

# Early Landing Craft, 1921-41

Before 1934 the US Navy lacked a commitment to amphibious warfare, and early developments must be credited to the US Marine Corps (USMC). This force was in the process of transformation from something akin to a static police force to a seaborne assault force resolved on defining and developing the techniques of amphibious assault. With Japan identified as the most likely future enemy, the US war plan (Plan Orange) detailed the requirement to seize islands in the Pacific for advanced bases. This would involve opposed landings, for which the USMC was largely remodelled.

From the outset, funding was desperately short, but the early 1920s saw the first innovations. For landing personnel, a standard ships' boat proved unsuitable. Underpowered, they handled poorly in surf. The V-shaped bottoms dug into sand, causing the craft to broach and tip. Refloating was difficult. Above all, the type provided little protection for the marines.

Known officially as a barge, but popularly as a "Beetle", the first personnel landing craft appeared in 1924. Designed to carry a full 110-man USMC company, it was fitted with a rounded, bullet-proof steel canopy. Alternatively, a 75mm field gun or, with canopy removed, an artillery tractor could be carried. At 15m/50ft long and weighing 24 tons, it could be handled only by heavy ships' cranes. It proved to handle poorly in surf and had too great a draught. Efforts to improve it were finally abandoned around 1930.

The 1920s also saw USMC experiments with amphibious tanks, able to support personnel landing on an open beach. Prototypes were developed by the influential designer J. Walter Christie. At this stage, the technology lacked the maturity to be successful, but the concept remained dormant, eventually to resurface as the Landing Vehicle, Tracked (LVT), which was used in a significant a role in the Pacific War.

Also in service was the 45ft Artillery Lighter, with a shallow draught but unpowered. It had to be towed to a point just beyond the surf line before being turned and winched to the beach stern-first. Wheeled equipment was rolled ashore over short folding ramps. The weight of the lighter proved to be too heavy for standard cargo lifting gear.

Only in 1934 could sufficient funds to be allocated to reconsider specialist landing craft for personnel. Amphibious assault thinking at this stage dictated two sizes of craft. The "X-Boat" would carry a 12-man USMC "squad", together with a crew of six. This included two gunners to lay down covering fire. The speed was to be a high 15 knots and the type would comprise the first wave. The "X-Boats" would be followed by "Y-Boats" of the second wave, each carrying a two-squad "section" of marines.

ABOVE: **The LCP (R), or Landing Craft, Personnel (Ramp), was similar to the LCP (L), but was fitted with a bow ramp for more rapid disembarkation.**

ABOVE: **The LCP (L), or Landing Craft, Personnel (Large), was built in both the UK and the USA. It could accommodate a platoon, but did not have bow doors.**

LEFT: **Carried under davits, the LCP (R) could be set afloat fully loaded. It was carried widely by APA, AKA and APL, and was powered by either diesel or petrol engines. The gun tubs allowed covering fire but formed a bottleneck short of the ramp.**

bow, and heavy skegs to protect propellers and rudders. The type had a useful top speed of 20 knots.

The US Navy acquired a Eureka in May 1937, in addition to other types, including some of its own design. Some were built of wood, some were of steel and the specification was changed continuously. A basic requirement emerged for an 18-troop capacity, a length not exceeding 9m/30ft (to be accommodated under davits) and a maximum loaded launch weight not exceeding 15,000lb.

A final decision was made when, in July 1940, the British military identified the 36ft Eureka as a 15-knot improvement over the existing 10-knot ALCs, and ordered 50.

With a war also looming for the USA, the US Marine Corps was authorized to acquire 335. With modifications, the design eventually became the ubiquitous LCP (L).

This programme, if it ever began, was quickly outdated by the approach of Andrew J. Higgins to the relevant authorities. Higgins ran a towage and construction company in New Orleans, and hoped to interest the US Navy in his Eureka craft. Designed to cope with the snags and shallows of Louisiana swamp country, the vessel had a continuously curved spoon-shaped

ABOVE: **Two Canadian coastal passenger ships, HMCS *Prince David* and *Prince Henry*, were modified to Landing Ships, Infantry (LSI), carrying LCAs under davits.**

ABOVE: **LCAs are guided to shore by a converted Vosper 70ft launch. Note the loud-hailer and the chemical smoke generator.**

ABOVE: **US Rangers in LCAs manned by Royal Navy personnel leaving harbour to join HMS *Prince Charles* (the letters PC on the side of the vessel denoting this) in preparation for the D-Day landings.**

## Early Landing Craft, Eureka

**Displacement:** 12,500lb (light); payload about 5,000lb
**Length:** 9.3m/30ft 6in (oa)
**Beam:** 3.31m/10ft 10.5in
**Draught:** 0.61m/2ft (forward); 0.9m/3ft (aft, light)
**Armament:** 1 x 0.30in machine-gun
**Machinery:** Petrol engine, single shaft
**Power:** 38kW/50hp for 9 knots
**Fuel:** 454 litres/120 gallons (US)
**Endurance:** 239km/130nm at 8 knots
**Protection:** None
**Complement:** 3 crew plus 18 troops

# Landing Craft, Tank, LCT (5) and (6)

Early British planning for the invasion and conquest of occupied Europe required huge numbers of craft to land armoured vehicles. The programme was so large that the still-neutral USA was approached for assistance. A drawback was that, in order to be able to cross the Atlantic safely, the resulting craft would be of too great a size and draught to beach satisfactorily.

The British had already developed a tank landing craft, known as a TLC. This would be modified frequently and become known as LCT (1) to (4). In talks with the US military, the British proposed an "Atlantic TLC" (which later became the LST) and a "Tank Ferry", small enough to be carried as deck cargo on an LST delivery passage. Having ordered 200 LST

and 400 "Tank Ferries", the British left the US Navy Bureau of Ships (BuShip) to prepare the detailed design.

Once agreed, the specification for the LST governed the size of the LCT. It was decided that the latter would be craned aboard, chocked and secured to the deck of an LST. On arrival, the smaller craft would be launched sideways by the simple expedient of tilting the LST, using the vessel's considerable built-in water ballast capacity.

Initially classed as a Yard Tank Lighter (YTL), the craft was recognized as a new type of LCT from July 1942 and recategorized as LCT (5). The vessel was built in three sections which could be shipped over separately and bolted together while afloat.

Where earlier British LCTs were intended for extended passages, the LCT (5), limited by size, usually needed to be towed over similar distances. Governed by beaching draught, the hull was broad and shallow. A loaded speed of 7 knots reduced to 3.5 knots when operating in a short head sea. The hull would flex alarmingly in these conditions.

The LCT (5) had neither rise of floor nor turn of bilge. The bottom of the hull aft curved upward to meet the base of the counter near the load waterline. This allowed the three small-diameter propellers (each with a rudder) to be raised above the keel line. The loading ramp had a distinctively curved front face. On a beach of shallow slope, the ramp could prove to be too short.

ABOVE: **A line of LCT (5) discharging on a beach of ideal slope, enabling transport to land without causeways. Vulnerability to air attack is obvious.**
LEFT: **Superseding the LCT (5), the LCT (6) had a sided superstructure to facilitate a drive-through capability. The beach is steep, so the vessels' engines are being used to maintain position.**

LEFT: **USS LST-228, wrecked in the vicinity of Bahia Angra Island, off Tercina, Azores. The vessel went ashore on January 19, 1944. Note that LCT (6) 582 is about to be washed off the deck of the vessel. Both were lost in this incident.**

A short, raised afterdeck housed basic accommodation for the crew of 13. Outboard of the deep comings that flanked the tank deck were narrow side decks, which allowed rapid fore-and-aft access for personnel. At loaded draught, the tank deck was above the waterline, but scuppers were provided to discharge water. If water accumulated the stability of the vessel could be affected.

From April 1943, some were completed as a drive-through design. These were termed LCT (6) and were intended to dock with a ramp on an LST to speed up the transfer of vehicles. In this mode, the LST (6) could even act as a bridge, connecting a deeper-draught LST to the beach. This type of craft had the accommodation divided along each side of the after end of the tank deck. The small pilot house was mounted on the starboard side. Details and capacity were, otherwise, very similar.

First deployed in the Pacific toward the end of 1942, in time for the climax of the Gudalcanal campaign, LCTs would go on to make a huge contribution to US forces' success. In total, 1,435 were built and usually operated as very large flotillas. The senior officer of a flotilla was a lieutenant commander who, typically, controlled three "groups" of 12 LCTs. Commissioned officers were in short supply so a group, organized in two "divisions", became the responsibility of a lieutenant, often a reserve officer. LCTs were not commissioned ships in the US Navy, the commander being called Officer in Charge.

ABOVE: **USS LCT (6) 1362, a 143-ton Landing Craft Tank, underway, probably soon after completion in October 1944. Note the sprayed-on pattern camouflage.**

## Landing Craft, Tank, LCT (5)

**Displacement:** 134 tons (light); 285 tons (beaching)
**Length:** 32.03m/105ft (wl); 35.38m/116ft (oa)
**Beam:** 9.76m/32ft
**Draught (light):** 0.47m/1ft 6in (forward); 1.14m/3ft 9in (aft)
**Draught (beaching):** 0.86m/2ft 10in (forward); 1.27m/4ft 2in (aft)
**Armament:** 2 x 20mm guns (2x1)
**Machinery:** 3 diesel engines, 3 shafts
**Power:** 504kW/675bhp for 8 knots
**Fuel:** 11.1 tons oil
**Endurance:** 1,288km/700nm (loaded) or 2,2208km/1,200nm (light) at 7 knots
**Protection:** 63.5mm/2.5in plastic armour to pilot house, 7.50mm/2in to gun tubs
**Complement:** 13–15
**Capacity:** 5 x 30-ton, 4 x 40-ton or 3 x 50-ton tanks, or alternatively 9 lorries or 150 tons (maximum) cargo; no troop accommodation

# Landing Craft, Mechanized, LCM (2), (3) and (6)

The unpowered Artillery Lighter proposed for the USMC during the late 1920s was hopelessly impractical, even though artillery was not required during the assault phase. What was wanted, however, was light armour to be put ashore rapidly to support the first attack. Early amphibious tanks had failed so, in 1930, the USMC requested a specialized craft, capable of putting a light tank ashore or, alternatively and with minimum modification, artillery or personnel.

Funding, as ever, was limited, and time was lost in the USMC having difficulty in defining an ideal small

tank. Finally, in 1935, a requirement was made for BuShips to design a 13-knot craft that could transport a 12,000lb vehicle.

The British Army had been experimenting with what was termed an MLC (Mechanized Landing Craft, or sometimes Motor Landing Craft) for over a decade and, by 1938, had produced the prototype for what would later become the LCM (1). A first US-designed craft appeared in the same year and was of a different design concept. Where the British craft retained buoyancy within a very deep, pontoon-type double bottom, with side

ABOVE: **Two LCM (3) from the attack cargo ship USS *Almaack* (AKA-10) unloading armoured bulldozers after the initial landing. Note the pedestal-mounted heavy machine-gun on KA10-7.**

bulwarks, the US craft had a shallow double bottom with added buoyancy dependent upon wide side walls. This difference was significant for, where the British design had far more usable space, the load was carried very high and could become unstable if carelessly loaded. The US craft carried the cargo lower and had greater in-built stability. The side walls were intrusive, making the cargo deck narrow, and

RIGHT: **The sharply raked coamings on the LCM gave full support for the ramp in the housed position, while allowing improved seakeeping in a head sea. The helmsman could steer from a lower, protected position.**

hazardous to load at sea. Opinion was that the craft was unnecessarily large to carry only a 5-ton tank.

Then, in 1940, the USMC was ordered to use standard US Army tanks of which the then-smallest was the M5A1 Stuart of around 18 tons. Being designed at the time, however, was the M4 Sherman, starting at 30 tons. Fortunately, the creative mind of Andrew J. Higgins had already been applied in this direction, somewhat in competition with BuShips. The Higgins' "Tank Lighter" was a 13.7m/45ft vessel weighing 18.75 tons, allowing it to be handled by cargo derricks. It could accommodate a 27-ton M3A1 Grant but would prove to be too narrow for a Sherman. With the design available and the requirement urgent, two orders for 50 each were placed in mid-1941.

The alternative BuShip design, also 13.7m/45ft, was officially favoured and 147 were built as LCM (2). The craft was unusual in having a rounded stern but could safely load only 30,000lb. With a M3A1 Grant aboard, the Higgins boat was felt to be at the safe limit, so work began to find a suitable 15.25m/50ft craft for new and larger vehicles.

Inadvertently, the British now influenced events in favouring existing Higgins' craft, ordering 250 of what was designated Mark 2 MLC. This craft was duly lenghtened by Higgins and, in May 1942, was used in comparative landing tests against a 15.25m/50ft BuShips design. In conditions of heavy surf the type proved to be far superior and was adopted for production (from July 1942) as the LCM (3).

First used in Operation "Torch", November 1942, the LCM (3) appeared everywhere, more often ferrying 60 troops rather than tanks. The type was too large to be carried under davits, and had to be handled by a cargo derrick. It could not be pre-loaded and had to be lifted empty. The relatively shallow bottom meant that engines had to be located in a stern compartment, further reducing cargo space.

Nevertheless, LCM (3) production eventually ran to over 8,600. Still officially limited to a 30-ton tank or 60,000lb of distributed cargo, however, it was dangerous to carry heavier vehicles. This was remedied by adding an extra 1.8m/6ft of length in the mid-body, creating the LCM (6). A total of some 2,700 were delivered.

ABOVE LEFT: **Ugly and slow, the LCM (1), originally known as an MLC, was nonetheless a well-designed craft.** ABOVE: **The LCM remained in British military service after World War II. Note the raised helmsman position at the stern.**

---

### Landing Craft, Mechanized, LCM (3)

**Displacement:** 23.21 tons (light); 52 tons (loaded)
**Length:** 15.25m/50ft (oa)
**Beam:** 4.3m/14ft 1in
**Draught (light):** 0.76m/2ft 6in (forward); 1m/3ft 3in (aft)
**Draught (loaded):** 1.37m/4ft 6in (forward); 1.68m/5ft 5in (aft)
**Armament:** 2 x 50in heavy machine-guns
**Machinery:** 2 diesel engines, 2 shafts
**Power:** 164–336kW/220–450bhp for 8 to 11 knots
**Fuel:** Not known
**Endurance:** 1,012km/550nm at 7 knots
**Protection:** 6.4mm/¼in plating around helm position
**Complement:** 4
**Capacity:** 1 medium (30-ton) tank, or 60,000lb cargo, or 60 troops

# Landing Craft, Infantry (Large), LCI (L)

One of the key types of landing craft in World War II, the LCI (L) was designed purely for the transport and rapid disembarkation of infantry.

Again this began as a British requirement, early in 1942, for a "giant raiding craft". The specification was for a vessel to carry a 200-man company at over 17 knots with an endurance of up to 48 hours. Preliminary calculations indicated that the craft would be of at least 45.7m/150ft overall length.

With British war production at maximum capacity the USA was requested to finalize a design and then build 300 craft. Such numbers went well beyond raiding requirements and indicate early planning for the eventual invasion of Europe in 1944.

The outcome definition required a forward beaching draught of only 0.61m/2ft, which had to be reconciled with hull characteristics seaworthy enough to make an Atlantic crossing. With raiding still in mind, quiet machinery, good manoeuvrability and a low silhouette were specified. Troops would disembark rapidly via two gangways, which extended from either side. At this point in landing, troops were perceived to be most vulnerable.

Politically astute, the British interested the US Army in the proposed craft, thus elevating priority in a country already busy with emergency war programmes. A suggestion to give Higgins a free hand in the craft's production was, however,

vetoed as his manufacturing facilities were already fully occupied with essential work for the US Navy.

BuShips thus translated the requirements into a practical design. This was not easy, the difficult dimensions/ draught combination having a detrimental effect on speed, with only around 15 knots being predicted. Despite this, power and propellers were specified for at least 17 knots. Three diesel engines and three shafts were proposed, but shortages dictated two shafts driving larger-diameter propellers.

Four automotive diesel engines powered each shaft, coupled ingeniously by means of an inflatable collar that

removed the requirement for gearing. As the engines were not reversible, the craft were fitted with variable-pitch and reversible propellers.

The short, high forecastle was extended toward the bridge by high protective bulwarks, flanked by narrow and partly sponsoned side decks upon which were mounted the 8.5m/28ft (later 11m/36ft) gangways. These were slid forward and lowered by means of a transverse beam termed a "cathead". Troops leaving their accommodation, immediately below, were screened by the high bulwarks until the gangways were lowered. A low centreline superstructure was provided for

ABOVE: **LCI (L) 351 was the lead craft of a revised design which featured a higher, round-sectioned bridge structure. The side gangway ramps were retained. Note the high protective bulwarks.**
LEFT: **Crude but effective, although vulnerable to damage, the side gangways were later superseded – in LCI (L) 641 onward – by bow doors and ramp.**

ABOVE: **The poor design of the gangway is evident here. It was difficult to access at the inboard end, and too steep for fully equipped infantry.**

ABOVE: **Infantry reinforcements being delivered to "Gold" beach by LSIs of the Royal Navy on D-Day "Plus One", June 7, 1944.**

British-designated craft. US craft were to be built with a higher bridge.

LCI (L) were built in non-shipbuilding facilities that simply assembled and fitted out steel modules trucked-in from subcontractors. As much complex curvature as possible was designed out. Craft delivered to Britain travelled in convoys accompanied by larger craft or tugs. In general, they were good vessels at sea but required careful ballasting for ocean voyages as well as an alert helmsman prepared for the vessels' tendency to yaw heavily prior to broaching.

From LCI (L) 351 (mid-1943), the superstructure was widened to the sides of the hull to allow rapid exit by troops from below. Accommodation facilities

were upgraded as it had been found that the craft were capable of longer sea passages than those originally envisaged.

A year later, and commencing with LCI (L) 691, the somewhat vulnerable and exposed gangways were removed in favour of bow doors and an extendable landing ramp.

US-operated LCIs were better protected than British vessels, carrying heavier defence. The extra weight came at the cost of significantly increasing beaching draught and a knot of speed when loaded. Externally, the US type differed in having a rounded pilot house/compass platform. A total of some 940 LCI (L) were completed as personnel carriers.

Over 330 more became Landing Craft, Support (Large), rocket craft or small headquarters ships.

ABOVE RIGHT: **Later craft mounted five 20mm cannon in single mountings, one at each corner of the superstructure and one on the forecastle. The tubular guard is to limit the firing arc.**

LEFT: **Troops here are embarking via the side gangways and passing through the protective bulwark to the access to the accommodation deck.**

## Landing Craft, Infantry, LCI (L), 351 type

**Displacement:** 246 tons (light); 250 tons (beaching); 390 tons (loaded)
**Length:** 46.67m/153ft (wl); 48.34m/158ft 6in (oa)
**Beam:** 7.09m/23ft 3in
**Draught (beaching):** 0.91m/3ft (forward); 1.52 m/5ft (aft)
**Draught (loaded):** 1.73m/5ft 8in (forward and aft)
**Armament:** 4/5 x 20mm guns (4/5 x 1)
**Machinery:** 8 diesel engines, 2 shafts
**Power:** 1,194kW/1,600bhp for 14 knots (sustained), or 16 knots (maximum)
**Fuel:** 110 tons oil
**Endurance:** 14,720 km/8,000nm at 12 knots
**Protection:** 70mm plastic armour to pilot houses and gun tubs
**Complement:** 28 plus 205 troops

ABOVE: **Built in vast numbers, the LCVP was the most basic and widely used assault craft. Aboard a transport, an LCVP would fit inside an LCM.** RIGHT: **LCVPs being used as liberty boats for the crew of USS *Hyde* (APA 173). The designation "21" gives some indication of the number of craft carried.**

# Landing Craft, Vehicle, Personnel (LCVP)

The LCVP was a combination of the LCV (Landing Craft, Vehicle), and the LCP (Landing Craft, Personnel).

From late 1940, the 36ft Eureka or Higgins boat was adopted as the standard US assault craft, although not being officially labelled an LCP (l) until July 1942. Although seaworthy, troops on the Eureka had to leap from the side on landing, risking injury, even drowning.

During the late 1930s, the Japanese had been observed using ramped Daihatsu craft in landing. BuShips refused a similar arrangement for the Eureka, but this was changed when Higgins built speculative prototypes. From May 1941 the BuShips experimented with the layout for a craft

that, with a ramp, had the versatility to carry a small vehicle or artillery just as easily as personnel. As a second-echelon craft, it was not armoured. Later termed an LCV, the type had an open cargo deck 5.87m/19ft 3in in length.

In parallel, otherwise unaltered LCP (L) equipped with ramps became known as LCP (R). The ramp was flanked by two forward-firing positions for 0.30in Browning machine-guns.

Both types began to be used together and, of the two, the versatile LCV proved by far the more useful. The open design lacked stiffness, which did not allow the boat to be loaded before launching. The raised helmsman's position also made it

impossible to be stacked under davits, fewer thus being carried. Over 2,600 LCP (R) had been built by the end of 1942, when it was superseded by the LCVP, essentially an improved LCV. With positions for the helmsman and gunners recessed into a stiffened hull, the vessel could be stacked and lowered fully loaded. The LCVP had a wider ramp and could accommodate 36 troops. By 1945, a staggering 23,350 had been produced.

ABOVE: **In an LCV, forerunner of the LCVP, the elevated steering position in the stern made the helmsman vulnerable to enemy fire, or even being swept overboard.**

---

### Landing Craft, Vehicle, Personnel (LCVP)

**Displacement:** 8 tons (light); 12 tons (maximum, loaded)
**Length:** 11.25m/36ft 10in (oa)
**Beam:** 31.7m/10ft 5in
**Draught:** 0.66m/2ft 2in (forward); 0.91m/3ft (aft, loaded)
**Armament:** 2 x 0.30in machine-guns
**Machinery:** 1 diesel or petrol engine, single shaft
**Power:** 168kW/225bhp diesel or 187kW/250hp petrol engine for 9 knots
**Fuel:** Not known
**Endurance:** 188km/102nm at 8 knots
**Protection:** 6.35mm/0.25in plate to ramp and sides
**Complement:** 3
**Capacity:** 36 troops, or 1 x 6,000lb vehicle, or 8,100lb distributed cargo

# Landing Craft, Support (Small)/(Large), LCS (S)/(L)

ABOVE: **The LCS (L) (3) was well-armed. Note the 3in gun forward, below a twin 40mm mounting. There is a second twin 40mm mounting aft and four single 20mm cannon.**

Although naval fire support was effective in the pre-assault phase, it had been recognized, even before the war, that the early waves of assault craft would require close support to suppress any surviving beach defences. The Higgins boat carried two forward-firing machine-guns for this purpose. Further similar hulls, compatible with davit stowage on APAs, were completed for the support role. Later designated LCS (S), they differed in being decked, except for a rectangular cockpit area. On some this was open, on others covered by a steel canopy, open at the rear.

Davit capacity limited weight to 9 tons, so the open cockpit version was preferred, with an armament of a 0.30in and 0.50in machine-guns

and 4.5in rocket launchers. A useful addition was chemical smoke generator equipment. The petrol engines made the type unpopular with APA captains.

While valuable, the LCS (S) lacked the firepower necessary to silence Japanese strongpoints. Destroyers were too valuable to be risked inshore, leading to conversion of the 48m/158ft LCI to "LCI Gunboats", later LCS (L). A local Pacific Fleet initiative saw 48 LCIs undergo conversion with added protection and a variety of 40mm and 20mm cannon plus 0.50in heavy machine-guns.

The "official" version, the Mark 3 – LCS (L) (3) – appeared late in 1944. Completely rearranged internally, it had a 3in general-purpose gun firing over protective bulwarks forward. Twin 40mm

cannon were carried on a high mounting. A second twin 40mm cannon was mounted aft, and four single 20mm on mountings around the superstructure. Some variants had mortars as the main armament, others rockets.

The craft were large enough to undertake sea passages, act as escorts, or even patrol offensively in the popular nocturnal pastime of "barge-busting", intercepting Japanese inshore supply barge traffic.

In addition to the 130 standard LCS (L) (3) conversions may be added 172 gun-armed LCI (G), 59 mortar-armed LCI (M) and 52 rocket-armed LCI (R).

## Landing Craft, Support, LCS (L) (3)

**Displacement:** 250 tons (light); 387 tons (full load)
**Length:** 46.67m/153ft (wl); 48.19m/158ft (oa)
**Beam:** 7.09m/23ft 3in
**Draught:** 1.45m/4ft 9in (forward); 1.98m/6ft 6in (aft, full load)
**Armament (typical):** 1 x 3in gun, 4 x 40mm (2x2), 4 x 20mm (4x1)
**Machinery:** 8 diesel engines, 2 shafts
**Power:** 1,194kW/1,600bhp for 15 knots
**Fuel:** 76 tons oil
**Endurance:** 10,120km/5,500nm at 12 knots
**Protection:** 6.35mm/0.25in steel to pilot house and gun positions
**Complement:** 70

ABOVE: **Hard-hitting miniature warships in their own right, the LCS (L) were viewed as expendable. This type of vessel was used to operate close inshore to support the landing forces.**

# Landing Vehicle, Tracked, LVT (1) to (7)

In amphibious warfare, the beach presents a difficult interface between the sea and land phases. In the late 1930s, the USMC sought a solution and approached Donald Roebling, who had developed an amphibious tractor to work in the Florida Everglades. Called an Alligator, it ran on tracks fitted with curved metal cleats. With the pontoon body afloat, the cleats acted as miniature paddles.

in 1941 despite two years of discussion with Roebling, the USMC could only fund two prototypes. Extensive trials resulted in an initial order for 200 of what would become the LVT (1). First appearing in mid-1941, the vehicle was unarmoured and had an open well for personnel or stores. The driver's position forward was fitted with a metal cab, open to the rear. The LVT was around 3m/10ft high, making it difficult for fully equipped troops to enter or leave via footholds recessed into the sides.

Usually transported in an LST, the LVT were often set afloat too far offshore. Capable of only 4 knots, they frequently suffered from swamped petrol engines. The vehicle's shortcomings were addressed by the end of 1943 with the introduction of the lightly armed LVT (2), which had 30 per cent more power and a more accessible cargo bay.

Coral atolls were frequent USMC objectives. These were fringed by reefs enclosing a shallow lagoon, a combination that could defeat conventional assault craft. The LVT was driven over the reef, across the lagoon to the beach, and then inland.

An obvious next step was to produce a fighting version to escort the troop carriers and to provide initial support ashore. The LVT (A) (1) ("A" for Armored) was better protected, with the turret and

ABOVE: **The LVT (1) entered service in 1941 and could travel at 4 knots in water and 19kph/12mph on land. The vehicle carried 24 fully equipped troops from transport ship to shore.**

37mm gun from the M5A1 tank, and two machine-guns. Based on the LVT (2), it entered service in August 1943. Early 1944 saw the arrival of the confusingly numbered LVT (4) which, with the engine mounted in front, now had a larger cargo well and a watertight rear ramp. As LVTs were used extensively to unload from cargo ships (AKA), this made for easier unloading ashore.

RIGHT: **The LVT (A) (1) was an LVT (2) modified with a 37mm gun turret and two 0.30in machine-guns. The function of the type was to come ashore with the troop-carrying LVTs and render immediate light armoured support.**

LEFT: **The LVT (2), known to the British as "Buffalo", was used during the Walcheren operation and on other river crossings in World War II.**

The delayed LVT (3) appeared later in 1944. Again, the cargo well was enlarged, this time by the use of two smaller engines, mounted in the side walls. Although petrol engines increased fire hazard, they were preferred due to an excellent power-to-weight ratio.

Battle experience demanded further improvement. The 37mm-armed LVT (A) (1) had little effect against enemy strongpoints and so, following infantry-suppression variants armed only with machine-guns, the LVT (A) (4) emerged, late in the war, mounting a short-barreled 75mm howitzer. Total production of LVTs was some 18,000 units, of which almost half were LVT (4).

LVT development slowed following World War II but was revived by the Korean War. During 1955–56, the massive LVTP (5) headed a new family of variants, including the LVTH (6) fire-support version.

Used widely in Korea and later in Vietnam, LVTs did not perform particularly satisfactorily. By the early 1960s, a replacement was required.

The LVTP (7) family (including command and recovery vehicles but none specifically for fire support)

began to enter service in early 1972. Auxiliary water jet propulsion allowed an increase in speed when afloat, while track design was optimized for speed over land. Diesel engines and an aluminium armoured body were further advantages.

## Landing Vehicle, Tracked, LVT (1) to (7)

| | Weight | | Capacity | | Speed | | Power |
|---|---|---|---|---|---|---|---|
| | Empty | Loaded | Cargo | Troops | Water | Land | (hp) |
| LVT (1) | 8.65 | 10.9 | 2.25 | 20 | 4 knots | 24kph/15mph | 150 |
| LVT (2) | 12.2 | 15.45 | 3.25 | 24 | 5.5 knots | 40kph/25mph | 200 |
| LVT (3) | 15.3 | 19 | 4 | 24 | 5 knots | 40kph/25mph | 450 |
| LVT (4) | 13.7 | 16.7 | 3.25 | 24 | 5.5 knots | 24kph/15mph | 200 |
| LVP (5) | 32.1 | 40.9 | 6 | 34 | 7 knots | 48kph/30mph | 800 |
| LVTP (7) | 18.5 | 25 | 5 | 25 | 7.5 knots | 48kph/30mph+ | 400 |

Note: Weights are expressed in US tons of 2,000lb

ABOVE: **An LVTP (5) about to land at Da Nang during the Vietnam War. The type was designed by Borg Warner Inc., and entered service in 1956.**

ABOVE: **The LVTP (7) was introduced in 1972, and underwent several upgrades. This example has reactive armour and a bow vane to improve seaworthiness.**

# Minesweeping Boats (MSB)

ABOVE: First a large minelayer, then a troop transport, then a vehicle carrier (LSV), USS *Ozark* and USS *Catskill* were converted to Mine Countermeasures and Support Ships (MCS) in the 1950s. The ships had a force of 20 minesweeping launches and carried two Sikorsky helicopters.

From the 100-fathom line to the high water mark, an amphibious force commander needs to be aware of the danger of mines and improvised explosive devices. Deep-water moored mines menace major vessels, the loss of any one of which can severely disrupt a well-executed plan. The designated anchorage needs to be guaranteed mine-free, and the necessary checks and minesweeping activities are often the first indication to an enemy of a pending invasion.

Progressing shoreward from the anchorages and embarkation areas, small craft move into increasingly shallow water, the area for bottom-laid "ground mines". From their inception, mines incorporated the highest degree of sophistication available with the technology of the time. Not adept in this direction during World War II, the Japanese generally preferred improvised devices, attached to obstructions or to coral heads located in the obvious approaches. These were removed by Underwater Demolition Teams (UDT).

The Germans, in contrast, were technically adept and ingenious, making shallow-water mine countermeasures a challenging task. By 1945, particularly in and around

ports, ship minesweeping operations had become merged with, or subordinated to, teams of skilled naval clearance divers.

In European waters the US Navy was, by 1944, experimenting with radio-controlled drone minesweepers to precede the first attack wave. Linked to a suitably equipped LCC, they were followed closely by rocket-firing LCM (3), known as "Woofus", which laid a carpet

of bombs across the beach to detonate ground mines and improvised devices.

The end of World War II saw a rapid rundown of Allied naval fleets. Mine warfare was neglected, military planners perceiving it as unimportant, prioritising the building of the carriers

ABOVE: The Korean War provided a salutary reminder that inshore mine clearance was a necessary precursor to an amphibious landing. This US Navy LCV, built in 1953, has been refitted as Minesweeping Boat, MSB-2.

LEFT: **MSB-21 in service on the Long Tau River, near Saigon, in November 1967. The river was regularly mined by the Viet Cong.**

and submarines. The Korean War suddenly reminded planners that large-scale amphibious operations were, as much as ever, dependent upon state-of-the-art mine countermeasures. War-built veteran ships were already inadequate and too few in number.

Along with its NATO partners, the USA embarked as a consequence upon building a series of wooden coastal and inshore minecraft during the 1950s. The programme produced several minor types which were to prove valuable in Vietnam.

This war was waged largely in swampy delta areas where, in the absence of roads, the highways were a tangle of sluggish, silt-laden river tributaries edged, for the most part, by dense jungle. By necessity, US troops conducted a low-level amphibious campaign in these areas.

Mines, mostly of Chinese origin, were used extensively by the enemy. Of the 57ft and 82ft Minesweeping Boats (MSB) operated by the US Navy, the smaller type was most suitable for the task.

Designated as "assault sweepers" an MSB might have preceded a column of armoured river craft. Vulnerable to ambush at close-range, however, these duties were usually subordinated to sweep-equipped LCM (6). These were equipped with excellent defensive firepower but, being steel-built, were more vulnerable to mines.

MSBs were designed to be used worldwide, often transported by ship, but they were too heavy to be handled by standard cargo lifting gear, necessitating heavy cranage. For this reason, LSDs were usually used as transport. Although diesel-propelled, many MSBs were fitted with an auxiliary gas turbine engine to generate power for the sweeps. One late hull was built from glass-reinforced plastic (GRP).

Compact, high-definition sonar was available for shallow-water mine detection while drag gear was a portable item that could be deployed by Minesweeping Launches (MSL) or even LCVPs. A 7m/23ft GRP-hulled Minesweeping Drone (MSD) was also

in service, controlled from a sweep-equipped patrol craft known as a River Minesweeper (MSR). As with so much high-technology equipment in Vietnam, however, it proved disappointing in service.

Vietnam was the severest test for inshore mine clearance. It was a war of improvisation. Territory was not held, and rivers cleared of mines one day could be re-mined by the next.

## Minesweeping Boat (MSB), 57ft type

**Displacement:** 30 tons (light); 42 tons (loaded)
**Length:** 17.42m/57ft 2in (oa)
**Beam:** 4.72m/15ft 6in
**Draught:** 1.22m/4ft
**Armament:** Officially 1 x 20mm gun; usually carried more
**Machinery:** 2 diesel engines, 2 shafts
**Power:** 448kW/6,00bhp for 10 knots
**Fuel:** Not known
**Endurance:** Not known
**Protection:** Nominal
**Complement:** 8

LEFT: **A Swift Boat, of which over 100 were abandoned when US forces withdrew from Vietnam. Note the 81mm mortar on the aft machine-gun mounting and the scrambling net for access to and from the banks of creeks and rivers.**

# Patrol Craft, Fast (PCF), Swift Boat

The United States campaign in Vietnam between 1965 and mid-1975 was conducted largely around inland waterways, for which the US Navy built up a range of specialist craft for what was probably the largest-ever "Brown Water Navy". The structure and composition of this navy have been likened to a regular, balanced fleet. The heavily armed and armoured monitors and landing craft served as capital ships and cruisers. The PCFs and PBRs (Patrol Boats, River) acted as destroyers.

PCFs, together with the WPBs (Patrol Craft, Coastguard), were deployed in October 1965, soon after the beginning of "Market Time", the blockade of the South

Vietnam coast to counter infiltration from the North. Eventually the number of PCFs deployed was over 100.

Capable of a sustained speed of 25 knots (28 maximum), they were known universally as Swift Boats, as they were called by Gulf of Mexico oil rig crews, for which the craft were originally designed as workboats. They were rugged but, being built of welded aluminium, were vulnerable to underwater obstacles.

At 15.2m/50ft in length, a PCF had a considerable draft of over 1.2m/4ft, but was sufficiently small to negotiate restricted waterways. The type was frequently used to ferry troops for

offensive shore incursions. On such operations, 20 or more fully equipped troops might be carried topside, greatly inhibiting the boat's armament.

The usual complement was one officer and four enlisted men (ratings). Standard armament comprised twin 0.50in machine-guns in a tub mounting over the wheelhouse. Aft there was a single 0.50in machine-gun with an 81mm mortar in the same mounting.

Built in Louisiana by Sewart Seacraft, the Swift Boats were completed in two large batches. The first, later termed a Mark I, had a larger superstructure than the subsequent Mark II.

ABOVE: **Formations of the "Brown Water Navy" operated in the same manner as the regular fleet. PCFs are shown here acting as a forward screen for armoured Monitors on a river in Vietnam.**

| Patrol Craft, Fast (PCF), Swift Boat |  |
| --- | --- |

**Displacement:** 22 tons
**Length:** 15.23m/50ft
**Beam:** 4.57m/15ft (oa)
**Draught:** 1.22m/4ft
**Armament:** 3 x 0.50in machine-guns (1x2, 1x1), 1 x 81mm mortar
**Machinery:** 2 diesel engines, 2 shafts
**Power:** 723kW/960bhp for 28 knots (maximum)
**Fuel:** Not known
**Endurance:** Not known
**Protection:** Nominal
**Complement:** 5

LEFT: **Over 80 Point-class cutters were built, in four closely similar but evolving groups. This is the "C" series USCGV** *Point Steele*. **In normal Coast Guard service, as can be seen, armament is restricted to two machine-guns.**

# Patrol Craft, Coast Guard (WPB)

O nly in the unique situation of Vietnam could the small Coast Guard cutter be included in a force that, in the widest sense, was "amphibious". That the US Coast Guard was there at all was due to Clause Five of its mission statement, i.e. that "in time of national emergency, or when the President so directs, the Coast Guard operates as part of the Navy".

In 1965, at the outset of the campaign, the US Army believed (incorrectly) that the major part of supplies supporting the North Vietnamese military activities was arriving by sea, either by local craft following the normal coastal traffic or by transfer-type vessels anchored offshore to unload weapons.

The resulting "Market Time" blockade divided the 1,448km/900-mile coast from 17 degrees north to the border with Cambodia into four coastal zones. These were broken down into nine patrol areas (Coast Guard), each of which controlled three to six inshore zones (Swift Boats).

The Coast Guard operated two types of small, steel-built cutter (WPB). Those chosen were the smaller 82ft Point class. Eight arrived in July 1965, and were quickly reinforced to 26.

ABOVE: **USCGV** *Point Highland* **in its earlier paint scheme. Those serving in Vietnam were painted grey, and mounted a variety of armament. Their availability relieved ships of the US Fleet from everyday surveillance duties.**

In addition to routine-patrol and surveillance duties, the WPBs gave seaward flank support to military search and destroy operations.

The 70-strong Point-class programme ran from 1960 to 1967, with stage improvements resulting in the three main groups, known as "A", "B" and "C" classes. The only major variation was in the "C" class (the final 39 craft) having engine power increased from 1,200 to 1,600bhp, with maximum speed raised from 17 to over 20 knots. Most of those assigned to Vietnam were of the slower "A" and "B" classes. All retained Coast Guard insignia.

## Patrol Craft, Coast Guard (WPB), "A" and "B" classes

**Displacement:** 67 tons (loaded)
**Length:** 23.82m/78ft 2in (wl); 25.32m/83ft (oa)
**Beam:** 5.25m/17ft 3in
**Draught:** 1.77m/5ft 10in
**Armament:** 1 x 0.50in machine-gun,
  1 x 81mm mortar
**Machinery:** 2 diesel engines, 2 shafts
**Power:** 895kW/1,200bhp for 17 knots
**Fuel:** Not known
**Endurance:** Not known
**Protection:** Nominal
**Complement:** 8–10
**Capacity:** Up to 1,900 tons distributed load
  on tank deck

LEFT: **The Armored Troop Carrier (ATC) was built on the hull of an LCM (6). This is the basic version with the troop-carrying compartment covered by a protective roof.**

A River Assault Squadron (RAS) had an establishment of two command craft (CCB), five fire support monitors, a refueller to extend endurance, and 26 ATCs. All were LCM (6) conversions. In support were 16 Assault Support Patrol Boats (ASPB), developed purely for service in Vietnam. These 50-footers could make 15 knots and carried an armament formidable enough for the type to be used as escort to a Riverine column and to guard the flanks.

# Armored Troop Carrier (ATC)

The 56ft LCM (6) was designed during World War II, but proved to be of considerable subsequent value and continued in production until 1980. Available in numbers, it was an important vessel in the Vietnam War, where it was used in a variety of roles. It was shallow in draught, manoeuvrable and had a forward ramp, qualities eminently suitable for use in the creeks of the Mekong Delta. A great disadvantage was the lack of speed, rarely better than 6 knots when loaded. When used on waterways, where the adverse current might be some 5 knots, this caused some problems.

Although also modified for the command and fire support roles, as well as "refuellers", LCM (6) were usually deployed as Armored Troop Carriers

(ATC). For this role, the tank deck was covered with a pitched metal roof. Alternatively, a flat, overhead platform was sometimes fitted, to land a helicopter for rapid evacuation of wounded troops.

Basic accommodation was for a 40-strong platoon. Three sections, each of three ATCs, were required for a company-strength operation. The superstructure was extended further forward, and featured tubs and drum-shaped turrets for a variety of defensive armament.

Some were equipped with a powerful water cannon which, in this land of mud and reed, could simply wash away an enemy position or destroy the "spider holes" that concealed Viet Cong troops.

## Armored Troop Carrier (ATC)

**Displacement:** 56 tons (loaded)
**Length:** 17.07m/56ft (oa)
**Beam:** 4.37m/14ft 4in
**Draught:** 1.2m/4ft (aft)
**Armament:** 2 x 20mm guns (2x1), 2 x 0.50in and 2 x 0.30in machine-guns
**Machinery:** 2 diesel engines, 2 shafts
**Power:** 246kW/330bhp for 10 knots
**Fuel:** Not known
**Endurance (designed):** 239km/130mm at 10 knots
**Protection:** Bullet-proof overall, Appliqué gratings to defeat shaped charges
**Complement:** 9–10
**Capacity:** 40 equipped troops, or about 4 tons cargo

ABOVE: **Some ATC vessels were fitted with a landing pad for helicopter operations.** LEFT: **ATCs of the "Brown Water Navy" alongside a headquarters ship in the Mekong Delta.**

ABOVE: **A Monitor proceeding slowly in the very shallow water of a river creek. The turret mounts a 40mm cannon and a machine-gun.** LEFT: **A "Zippo" Monitor with two flamethrowers in turret mountings. Note the blanked-off gun turret ring on the foredeck and the conventional bow replacing the ramp.**

# Monitor (MON)

The "capital ship" of the Mobile Riverine Force (MRF) was the Monitor (MON), the title of which was close in the traditional sense to those of the American Civil War – relatively heavily armed for size, well protected in an improvised way, largely modified from suitable shallow draught craft, and intended to operate on a disputed river system.

Again, an LCM (6) provided the basic hull, but as the vessel did not act as a transport, the ramp was replaced by a conventional bow, with a flat overhang as seen on lighters. The freeboard of the hull was low, seaworthiness depending

on the coaming, now continued forward where, in earlier craft, this was faired into the base ring of the forward turret. In an effort to increase speed, later craft had a spoon bow. Earlier examples had a short superstructure, leaving a section of the original tank deck, either open or roofed over. With increasing firepower the superstructure became more massive, supporting armoured vehicle-type turrets.

The original bow gun was a 40mm, in an angular mounting open at the back. This was developed to a taller gunhouse with a rear door. Late craft had a light tank turret mounting a short-barrelled 105mm

howitzer. Alternatively, some were fitted with flamethrowers, which projected a napalm stream for 150m/492ft. With grim humour, these were called "Zippo" boats.

Monitors armed with a 40mm cannon also usually carried a 20mm cannon, an 81mm mortar, two 0.50in and two 0.30in machine-guns. The 105mm variant normally carried two 20mm cannon in a single mount as secondary armament. All were fitted with both high- and low-velocity grenade launchers. All were fitted with external grills to defeat the rocket-propelled grenades (RPG).

ABOVE: **Capital ship of the "Brown Water Navy", the Monitor was heavily armed. This example has a 105mm tank turret forward and two 20mm cannon. The appliqué protection was necessary as defence against short-range weapons used by the Viet Cong.**

| Monitor (MON) |  |
| --- | --- |

**Displacement:** 90 tons (loaded)
**Length:** 18,45m/60ft 6in (oa)
**Beam:** 5.34m/17ft 6in
**Draught:** 1.07m/3ft 6in
**Armament:** 1 x 105mm gun, 2 x 20mm guns
   (2x1), 2/3 x 0.30in machine-guns (2/3x1),
   Grenade launchers
**Machinery:** 2 diesel engines, 2 shafts
**Power:** 246kW/330bhp for 10 knots
**Fuel:** Not known
**Endurance:** Not known
**Protection:** Bullet-proof overall; Appliqué gratings
   to defeat shaped charges
**Complement:** 11–12

# Landing Craft, Utility (LCU)

Designed for simplicity, capacity and economy, World War II landing craft were unavoidably slow. The Cold War saw large amphibious groupings threatened by nuclear attack, and faster craft were required. The key amphibious warfare ships were the recently completed LSDs, whose docking wells had been designed to accommodate large numbers of existing craft. Redesign would have to take this into account.

In support of an all-20-knot force, a new LST was being developed during the 1950s and, to be carried topside as in the war, a new LCT was also required. To highlight the latter's greater versatility, it became known from 1952 as a Landing Craft, Utility (LCU).

Rather confusingly, surviving war-built LCT (6) had also been recategorized LCU, the highest hull number being LCU 1465. The prototype of the new class, completed in 1953, was, therefore, numbered LCU 1466. Production of the class was completed in 1956 with LCU vessel number 4609.

The 1466 type had the same dimensions as the preceding LCTs but, oddly, was configured as a closed-stern LCU (5) rather than a drive-through LCU (6). The latter was not only for convenience in loading and discharge but also to allow the LCT to act as an in-line causeway to assist LSTs to discharge over beaches with a very shallow slope.

The reversion may have been due to load distribution associated with the exceptional lift capability of the 1466. Although the craft's displacement was only 180 tons, three 49-ton M48 Patton main battle tanks could be carried. Alternatively, there was space to carry six M41 Walker Bulldog light tanks, totalling 140 tons.

Height restrictions within an LSD demanded that a 1466 type had minimum air draught (height), the low wheelhouse accordingly being no higher than the two 20mm cannon mountings on each side. The single pole mast, with radar, had to be lowered. However, except for improved

ABOVE: **On a relatively steep beach, this 1610 type has grounded at the water's edge, permitting a dry landing for the articulated store carrier.**

lines, little had been done to increase speed, the craft having the same engine power and triple shafts ( to minimize propeller diameter) as war-built craft.

Lack of speed and drive-through capability soon became identified as a problem and, on some later hulls, propulsive efficiency was improved by fitting propeller ducts, known as Kort nozzles. By straightening the flow over the propeller these ducts augmented the thrust. In a bid to improve manoeuvrability and to reduce the tendency to broach in surf, others were

fitted with vertical-drive propellers. The latter machinery was intended to turn the craft rapidly in order to beach stern-first. The design objective was to produce a faster hull by having an after ramp and a ship-type bow section.

As the requirement for a drive-through facility remained, however, a new LCU 1610 type was developed. With length increased by 6m/20ft and beam decreased by no less than 1.5m/5ft, the type also had a 50 per cent increase in engine power, allowing a respectable 11 knots. Lift capacity was also marginally improved.

The 1610 type did have a split superstructure, however, and this was retained in the "LCU 1626" design, which

reverted to the same dimensions as the earlier 1466 type. Hull depth was increased, adding stiffness and buoyancy, improved cargo area layout and permitting the use of twin-shaft propulsion. Short, blunt hulls such as this show a distinct "hump" in the speed/power curve. Beyond this, no amount of power will show significant increase in speed. As the craft was already powered for its maximum "natural" speed, the machinery also reverted to that of a 1466 type.

For this basic design, a lower speed simply had to be accepted. Nonetheless useful, the 1626 continued to be built until the mid-1980s, terminating at LCU 1681. Alternative high-speed craft were being designed and evaluated in parallel. The air cushion type proved the most promising, leading to the design of the LCAC.

ABOVE: **An LCU 1610 type had a forward beaching draught of 1.07m/3.5ft. A 50 per cent increase in engine power allowed the top speed of the vessel to be increased to 11 knots.**

### Landing Craft, Utility (LCU) 1626 type

**Displacement:** 380 tons (beaching); 395 tons (loaded)
**Length:** 35.53m/116ft 6in (oa)
**Beam:** 10.37m/34ft
**Draught (beaching):** 1.07m/3ft 6in (forward); 1.98m/6ft 6in (aft)
**Draught (seagoing):** 2.06m/6ft 9in
**Armament:** 2 x 0.50in machine-guns
**Machinery:** 4 diesel engines, 2 shafts
**Power:** 507kW/680bhp for 8 knots
**Fuel:** Not known
**Endurance:** 2,208km/1,200nm at 6 knots
**Protection:** Nominal
**Complement:** 14

# Landing Craft, Mechanized, LCM (6) (Mods) and LCM (8)

As mentioned earlier, the original LCM (6) was an LCM (3) with 1.8m/6ft added in the mid-hull. The purpose was to carry heavier tanks – the 27-ton M3A2 Grant, then the 32-ton M4A3 General Sherman. The lengthening raised the vehicle weight limit from 30 to 34 tons, and the cargo load, some 30 tons, required care when loading. Where an armoured vehicle represented a relatively concentrated weight which could be positioned to give the LCM a favourable trim, the distribution of general cargo,

although no greater, could, without due care, result in considerable seakeeping problems, including the risk of swamping. The extra length precluded the craft from being loaded on to some earlier transports and cargo ships. The LCM (6) first appeared during 1943 and, by the end of the war, over 2,700 had been built.

Under the Lend-Lease Program, the British received over 600 LCM (2) and (3), but none of the LCM (6), as they had developed a stretched version of the LCM (3).

Known as the LCM (7), and not limited by a required compatability with transports, it had larger dimensions of 17.63 x 4.9m/57ft 10in x 16ft. The extra beam width gave the stability and extra buoyancy to carry a 35-ton tank (sufficient for a 27.5-ton Cromwell but not for a 40-ton Churchill).

Post-war, the LCM (6) remained in service but, perhaps influenced by the huge armoured fighting vehicles developed late in the war by Germany, the US Army wanted a new 50-ton limit for the capacity. BuShips was keen to improve the basic war-built LCM (6), and was looking at ways to improve beaching conditions in surf. The hull was virtually rectangular in plan, flat-bottomed but with a curved rise forward and aft. In the hands of an inexperienced coxswain, it was a difficult vessel to reverse off a beach. The LCM (6) had a tendency to broach, becoming stranded against the beach and, frequently, being wrecked. Loss rates were high.

When modified, the same 17.1m/56ft overall length had to be observed for stowage aboard AKA and APA. Beam was also limited by a requirement that the vessel be rail-transportable.

LEFT: **The LCM (8) has a lift capacity of 60 tons. Note the engines are running to keep the craft firmly head-to-beach. Only just visible is a Newport-class LST on the horizon.**

To cater for the larger dimensions of the projected 50-ton military vehicle, the cargo space was widened by reducing the width of the side walls. This narrowed the side decks outside the coamings to little more than a ledge to carry essential fittings. It also considerably reduced reserve buoyancy in the event of the cargo deck being flooded.

The ramp was increased in length, from 2.79m/9ft 2in to 3.35m/11ft. The grid-type extension enabled the new Mod. 1 to be distinguished from the earlier type. Experiments with different bottom configurations showed little advantage, and the existing arrangement was largely retained.

Series production of the LCM (6) Mod. 1 began in 1952. A later Mod. 2 was built and had reduced hoist weight from which a "high-performance" version was

developed. It had been assumed that the basic laws of hydrodynamics could be bypassed by installing sufficient power. It was expected that a 9-knot craft would make 13, if existing 450bhp engine power was increased to 1,200 bhp. The result was 10 knots and a craft so weighted down by engines that it trimmed very stern down. Nonetheless, around 100 were built.

Ever-larger loads carried in craft of fixed dimensions had the inevitable consequence of requiring a deeper beaching draught. This resulted in a larger craft, transportable on some later transport ships but most easily by LSD. This craft, the LCM (8), was built from the 1950s until 1992 for both the US Army and the US Navy. Obviously larger, the LCM (8) had a one-piece ramp mounted at a far shallower angle.

Like the LCM (6), the LCM (8) had a completely parallel cargo area, and this extra space permitted the alternative load of 150 troops, compared with 80 in the LCM (6).

---

## Landing Craft, Mechanized, LCM (8)

**Displacement:** 133 tons (loaded)
**Length:** 22.45m/73ft 8in (oa)
**Beam:** 6.4m/21ft
**Draught (beaching):** 1.35m/4ft 5in (forward); 1.47m/4ft 10in (aft)
**Armament:** None
**Machinery:** 2/4 diesel engines, 2 shafts
**Power:** Up to 806kW/1,080bhp for 9 knots (loaded)
**Fuel:** 5 tons oil
**Endurance:** 350km/190nm at 9 knots (loaded)
**Complement:** 4–5
**Capacity:** 53.6 tons (60 US tons) of vehicles, or distributed cargo weight

---

ABOVE: **Heavy armour now demands landing craft that are too large and heavy to be carried as deckloads on all but a few attack cargo ships.** LEFT: **Docking wells can become subject to water surge when the ship is at an open anchorage.**

LEFT: **An LCAC loaded with troops of the 11th Marine Expeditionary Unit during exercise "Eager Mace", September 24, 2002.**

# Landing Craft, Air Cushion (LCAC)

As already noted, the beach forms a difficult barrier between the seaborne assault force and objectives. Personnel, being adaptable, fit reasonably into a wide variety of craft. To survive an opposed landing, however, prompt, on-the-spot support and resupply is required. LVTs satisfied these various roles to a point, lifting personnel and supplies and, in armoured types, used as light tanks. The vehicle's strength was in the ability to cross the beach without trans-shipment, proceeding directly from the transport offshore to the landing area. Their capacity was, nonetheless, small and,

with the nuclear age, there came the desirability of high-speed approach from beyond the horizon. Whatever the type of craft adopted, it had to be large enough to cope with conditions over a long approach while being capable of carrying tanks and heavy equipment as well as stores which, for speed of handling, were increasingly palletized.

Studies began in the mid-1960s to define a range of high-speed craft to replace, in order of size, the LCVP, LCM (6) and LCM (8). The LCVP was effectively replaced by the helicopter. Again, the other types developed into

a proposed single design of planing craft, to be propelled at 35 knots by waterjets. The vessel would carry two 60-ton M1 Abrams main battle tanks, which had entered service in 1980. Designated the LCM (9), the craft would have been of around 37m/122ft long, drive-through and designed to fit docking wells. The craft never entered production but, in view of the high

BELOW: **The two swivelling ducts (one of which is visible above the tank) each provide 10 per cent of forward thrust and most of the directional thrust. Turning radius at speed is over 1.6km/1 mile.**

ABOVE: **The noise of an LCAC entering an empty docking well is so great that access galleries are cleared. Note the narrow clearance.** RIGHT: **The JMSDF Osumi-class LSD is designed to carry two US-built LCACs in the docking well.**

capital and through-life costs of the preferred craft, it remains a candidate as a further replacement for the LCU.

British-built hovercraft used in Vietnam, although not judged particularly successful, had demonstrated the ability to negotiate a wide variety of otherwise impassable terrain. The air cushion made the type truly amphibious and, as the tiresome laws of hydrodynamics no longer applied, it was (by vessel standards) fast. From the US Marine Corps perspective, the craft made a greater range of beaches accessible. From a holding area, some 40km/25 miles offshore, they could threaten around 161km/100 miles of coastline, thereby diluting the enemy's capacity of defence.

The size of the prototype selected for development as the LCAC needed to be around twice as long as it was wide. An M1 Abrams set the lift capacity at some 60 tons, a 25 per cent overload being

permissible. The resulting cargo deck was sufficiently spacious, at 21 x 8m/ 67 x 27ft, to allow numerous lighter vehicles to be carried.

In essence, the LCAC is built as a deep, aluminium alloy raft, bounded by flexible skirting to contain the air cushion. Flanking the cargo deck are narrow superstructures housing four gas turbine engines, of which two drive the lift fans, and two power large, ducted propellers for propulsion. The cargo deck is open, with short ramps forward and aft.

Personnel aboard are usually limited to the five operators and up to 24 vehicle crew. Heat and noise from the engines, together with the safety aspects of riding a breaking sea at 40-plus knots, makes troop-carrying dangerous. When used for this purpose (the US Marine Corps still prefer LVTs for higher on-shore mobility), a prefabricated Personnel Transport

Module (PTM) is mounted on the vehicle deck, with capacity for just 145 fully equipped troops.

Air cushion craft have a low signature for mines, and a high resistance to the explosive effects. Towed mine counter-measures sleds have been developed for leading an assault. To the US Marine Corps, the LCAC is a vital vehicle carrier. Due to the wide beam, only one could be carried on earlier LPDs and LHAs. Later-designed LHD vessels can carry three, and two are carried on an LPD-41 type.

Corrosion in the aluminium structure and high maintenance levels have caused modernization programmes to be brought forward, the opportunity also being taken to upgrade the propulsion units.

LEFT: **The noise levels and acceleration experienced aboard an LCAC are so extreme that personnel may be transported only when housed in a bolt-on-module.**

### Landing Craft, Air Cushion (LCAC)

**Displacement:** 91 tons (light); 167 tons (loaded); 182 tons (overload)
**Length:** 24.69m/81ft (wl); 26.8m/87ft 10 (oa)
**Beam:** 13.31m/43ft 8in (wl); 14.33m/47ft (oa)
**Draught:** 0.78m/2ft 6in
**Armament:** None
**Machinery:** 4 gas turbines; 2 for lift, 2 for propulsion
**Power:** 11,190kW/15,000hp total for 54 knots (light), or 40 knots (loaded)
**Fuel:** 6.2 tons kerosene
**Endurance:** 414km/225nm at 48 knots (light); 368km/200nm at 40 knots (loaded)
**Protection:** None
**Complement:** 5+ 24 vehicle crew
**Capacity:** About 70 tons of vehicles/cargo, or 145 troops

LEFT: **A flight of Sikorsky SH-3H Sea King anti-submarine warfare helicopters from HS-12 squadron, deployed on USS *America* (CV-66) in November 1994.**

# The Helicopter Force

So universal has been the deployment of the helicopter that the machine might almost be described as specially created for the amphibious planner to exploit. The impact on ship design, however, has been as great as that of minor assault craft.

Helicopters had been flown operationally for the first time late in World War II. The initial problem was one of lack of engine power and the consequently limited payload (a situation similar to that of naval aircraft in 1915). Such were the possibilities, however, that several gifted designers and major aircraft companies were urgently pursuing development.

The US Marine Corps was greatly interested. Threatened with nuclear weapons, future amphibious assault groups would need to be postioned further offshore and dispersed. Assault waves would thus require a more rapid means of transit to the beach. These would also need to be dispersed, despite experience having shown that success followed maximum concentration at the critical point. The helicopter appeared to offer a solution, the relatively high speed permitting a dispersed approach followed by rapid concentration for the assault. Indeed, the machine offered a great advantage over standard assault craft in being able to deposit troops beyond the beachhead.

A requirement for a carrier-type vessel, with a clear flight deck over a hangar, was clearly indicated. Experiments began in 1948 using a warbuilt CVE, the experience gained leading eventually to the Iwo Jima-class LPH of the late 1950s. Equipment being of equal importance, attention turned to ships which could accommodate both personnel and hardware, fitted as a helicopter carrier topside but with LCU/LCMs in a docking well. The prototypes provided valuable experience for building the LHA (1970) and the LHD (1985).

Until the introduction into front-line service of the Bell-Boeing MV-22B Osprey, the USMC helicopter inventory comprised two general-purpose types,

ABOVE: **The Westland Lynx is the fastest pure helicopter in military service. This Super Lynx Mk-21A of the Brazilian Navy is being held at the hover to drop a boarding team during an exercise.** LEFT: **The Boeing Vertol CH-46 Sea Knight was designed by a team lead by Frank Piasecki, a pioneer of the twin-rotor helicopter.**

ABOVE: **The Bell Boeing MV-22B Osprey is a tiltrotor, multi-mission aircraft with both VTOL and STOL capability. The type is in service with the US Marine Corps and the US Air Force.**

each designed almost half a century earlier. Of these, the Sikorsky CH-53E Super Stallion and CH-53D Sea Stallion could each lift 55 equipped troops to over 805km/500 miles, and the Boeing CH-46E Sea Knight could lift 25 troops over 322km/200 miles. Although vulnerable, both made the Osprey, which is heavier but faster and longer-ranged, look an expensive option. The USMC has not, however, abandoned procuring pure helicopters and will, throughout the 2020s, take delivery of 200 CH-53K King Stallion heavy lift helicopters. This evolved, thoroughly updated version of the venerable CH-53 is the largest and heaviest US military helicopter in service and can carry 12247kg/27,000 pounds for 204km/110 nautical miles.

In the assault mode, helicopters are vulnerable to ground fire from automatic weapons or ground-to-air missiles. As smaller-scale operations may well not justify the allocation of a carrier group, supporting air cover needs to be supplied by aircraft from the LH (the common generic term covering both LHA and LHD). Part of the ship's capacity must, therefore, be devoted to V/STOL strike aircraft capable of loitering over the battle area.

For close escort and pin-point support, these aircraft are supplemented by Bell AH-1Z Viper ground-attack

helicopters with wing stubs that can carry missiles such as the AIM-9 Sidewinder, 70mm/2.75 in Hydra rocket pods, or AGM-114 Hellfire quad missile launchers.

The threat posed by mines occupies a considerable amount of the planners'

attention, the US Navy having put much effort into rapidly deployable, helicopter-based countermeasures which were ultimately shelved in favour of ship-based systems that can be "flown'"underwater by remote operators.

ABOVE: **US Marine Corps AH-1Z Viper, derived from the earlier Bell AH-1 SuperCobra – note the rocket pods on the underside of the stub wing and the empty launcher for an AIM-9 Sidewinder.**

LEFT: **The US Marine Corps will take delivery of 200 CH-53K King Stallion heavy lift helicopters into the early 2030s – it is the largest and heaviest US military helicopter in service.**

LEFT: **USS *Gunston Hall* (LSD-5) has not been flooded down, the PACV being able to exit over the lowered stern gate from a dry docking well.**

# Patrol Air Cushion Vehicle (PACV)

During the Vietnam War, the "Plain of Reeds" in the Mekong Delta was something of a "no-go" area. Vast lagoons of shallow water were covered with thickly growing short reed and, as in the Bayou country in the USA, the few dry tracks and habitable locations were known only to the local population. The area quickly became a haven to the Viet Cong, as US forces experienced mobility problems. The propellers of conventional craft and the tracks of LVTs were quickly fouled by reed, which also presented a physical barrier to waterjet craft. With helicopters always in short supply, the US Army and US Navy both experimented with hovercraft, which could float over the reed without any limitations.

These vehicles, procured in the mid-1960s, were the Bell SK-5, a licence-built version of the British Hovercraft Corporation SRN-5 Warden class. While only half as fast as a helicopter, they were able to stop anywhere in the "raft" mode, and were virtually mine-proof.

In more open waters, the light aluminium structure was prone to slamming damage. The airscrew propulsion made the type extremely noisy. In the damp and humid conditions of the delta, the craft required considerable maintenance. The peripheral skirt, essential in containing the lifting air cushion, could be damaged by shingle abrasion or in the negotiation of rocky areas. (Similar experience was

encountered in Arctic exercises, where ice was the problem. Canadian forces, however, are actively pursuing the possibilities of ACVs for Arctic use.)

The US Navy's PACVs were of standard configuration, a cabin with side decks all round, and were modified to carry a heavy machine-gun position and a grenade launcher. The US Army's craft were of a flat-bed type, intended for moving equipment.

Always considered "experimental", the vehicle nonetheless inspired Bell to produce a larger type, the SK-10, which proved to be the forerunner of the LCAC now in service.

RIGHT: **In calm conditions, the air cushion vehicles have a considerable speed advantage, but this is rapidly reduced in choppy to rough sea conditions.**

---

**Patrol Air Cushion Vehicle (PACV), SRN-5**

**Weight:** 5 tons (loaded)
**Length:** 12.2m/40ft (oa)
**Breadth:** 5.79m/19ft
**Draught:** 0 (under weigh);
   0.31m/1ft (stationary)
**Armament:** 1 x 0.50in machine-gun,
   1 x grenade launcher
**Machinery:** Rolls-Royce Marine Gnome
**Power:** 597kW/800hp for 55 knots (maximum)
**Fuel:** Not known
**Endurance:** About 322km/200 miles
**Protection:** Minimal
**Complement:** 4–5
**Capacity:** 20 troops, or 2 tons cargo

ABOVE AND LEFT: **Although shallow draught might be an asset in inshore waters, the high-speed wave-piercer is actually less effective than the USS *Inchon* (MCS-12) type that it replaced.**

# Mine Countermeasures Support Ship (MCS)

Amphibious warfare vessels are "volume-critical" or, in other words, dimensions and configuration are governed by considerations of space rather than weight. For those craft that need not incorporate a docking well, a twin-hulled catamaran has much to commend it in terms of stability, seakeeping and spacious deck plan.

A conventional catamaran type has the drawback of greater wetted area and of consequent greater resistance. The Small Waterplane Area, Twin Hull (SWATH) has the same disadvantage, but offset by increased stability in a seaway. Both require considerable propulsive power and, where speed is an important consideration, a wave-piercing catamaran has a clear advantage. The

wave-piercer has become a particular speciality of Australian shipyards, where Incat designed and built the vessel that came to be known as USS *Swift* (HSV-2). The vessel has two slender outer hulls that are designed to slice through waves rather than rise in the conventional manner. A deep V-form centreline hull provides the necessary reactive buoyancy in contacting the surface on any tendency to plunging. Waterjet propulsion obviates the requirement for conventional propellers, shafts or rudders, while reducing draught and vulnerability.

Nonetheless, the choice of this vessel to 'replace' the USS *Inchon* (MCS-12) as support ship to mine countermeasures craft was criticized. USS *Inchon* could

operate a squadron of Sikorsky MH-53E minesweeping helicopters with six deck-landing spots, while USS *Swift* could house just two Sikorsky HH-60 Seahawks, with a single landing spot.

*Swift* was a high-speed commercial car ferry, modified for naval service. It was leased for a decade from 2003, and was the second catamaran the US Navy leased to test new technologies and concepts. The relatively shallow draught is thought to be an asset in the MCS role. The wide stern ramp was strengthened for heavy armoured vehicles, and in USN service it was deployed and tested in a variety of real-world scenarios.

LEFT: **The HSV is a slightly modified commercial ferry. It is in the high-speed vehicle transport role that the vessel will probably find the best usage when deployed with the amphibious fleet.**

**Mine Countermeasures Support Ship (MCS), USS *Swift*, HSV-2**

**Displacement:** 1,870 tons (loaded)
**Length:** 92m/30ft 8in (wl); 318ft 9in/97.22m (oa)
**Beam:** 87ft3in/26.6m
**Draught:** 3.43m/11ft 3in (maximum)
**Armament:** Mounting for 1 x CIWS
**Machinery:** 4 diesel engines driving 4 waterjets
**Power:** 28,348kW/38,000bhp for 47 knots (maximum), or 35 knots (loaded)
**Fuel:** 190 tons
**Endurance:** 7,360km/4,000nm at 20 knots
**Protection:** None
**Complement:** About 100
**Capacity:** 250 troops, or 500 tons cargo

# Swimmer Delivery Vehicles (LSDV)

Swimmer Delivery Vehicles (SDVs) are specialized craft designed for underwater transportation of personnel, equipment, and supplies. These vehicles play a crucial role in maritime operations, particularly in amphibious and special warfare missions. SDVs provide a means for special forces units to covertly approach enemy territory primarily submerged, conduct reconnaissance, and execute various types of operations with speed, precision, and stealth. Deployment can be from special containers fixed to the deck of large submarines, by crane from the deck of a surface ship or the well deck of an amphibious assault vessel. Some can even be dropped – unmanned – from aircraft.

Landing special service personnel from submarines was commonly practised during World War II but, although techniques have since been greatly refined, they tend not to be kept secret. Of the two main types of wartime powered craft for swimmer delivery, the midget submarine was popular with the British, Japanese and Germans. What might better be described as "delivery vehicles" were developed successfully in the Italian Maiale (pig) and copied (less successfully) by the British and Germans.

Although today's SDVs are designed to operate at various depths depending on the specific model and mission requirements, operating depths tend to range from around 30.5– 61m/100– 200ft. For propulsion, electric motors are commonly used, providing quiet operation and thereby improved stealth, while some SDVs incorporate closed-cycle diesel engines that use oxygen stored onboard, allowing for extended endurance and range. Some SDVs can travel at speeds exceeding 20 knots and have a range of several hundred miles, allowing for rapid deployment and autonomous operation over significant distances from "mother ships". Others have much shorter range and rely on the mother ships, be they surface ships or large submarines, to get them closer to the target and be on standby for recovery.

Current SDVs are typically constructed of specialized materials, such as carbon fibre or high-strength alloys, and coatings to reduce noise and detectability. These craft are equipped with advanced navigation systems and secure communication systems enabling real-time communication between the SDV and friendly forces, enhancing situational awareness and coordination during operations.

During the 1990s, the US Navy operated a number of free-flooding

ABOVE: **USS *Greenville* (SSN-772), a nuclear-powered submarine at sea, with an LSDV on deck.** RIGHT: **An LSDV being loaded into the transportation container mounted on the deck of USS *Dallas* (SSN-700).**

LEFT: **A US Navy SEAL climbs aboard a SEAL Delivery Vehicle Mk VIII before launching from the back of the Los Angeles Class Attack Submarine USS** *Philadelphia* **(SSN 690) on a training exercise, 2005.** ABOVE: **The Dry Combat Submersible (DCS) midget submarine entry into US Navy service dramatically enhanced the capability of the US Navy SEALs force.** BELOW: **The two-man wet R-2 Mala SDV was built for the Yugoslav, and later, Croatian Navy. An estimated eighteen examples were built up to the early 1990s.**

Mark VIII LSDVs which, at 6.7m/22ft in length, were accommodated within dry superstructure extensions on SSN submarines and carried four equipped swimmers. Britain's Special Boat Service operated three examples.

A more sophisticated Advanced SEAL Delivery System (ASDS), a true midget submarine connected to a modified SSN via the common escape hatch, was developed at great expense but ultimately cancelled in the early 2000s due to cost overruns, technical and reliability issues. This has been succeeded by the British-made Dry Combat Submersible (DCS) midget submarine which gets the special forces personnel to their objective bone-dry. Human divers can only operate efficiently

and safely in cold water for a limited amount of time, even with the best wetsuits and this was a significant limiting factor for operations. The 12m-/39ft-long DCS weighs 14 tons fully loaded, has a displacement of 28 tons and can be transported in a 12m/40ft shipping container on board surface ships, which then lower the DCS to the sea by crane, or via a well deck. Crewed by a pilot and co-pilot/navigator, the DCS can transport eight fully equipped SEAL personnel to their objective in the coldest water. With an endurance in excess of 24 hours and a dry environment, the DCS has extended the effective range of SEALs who can now undertake longer missions in colder water – its exact performance data is of course still classified.

Both Russia and Italy are also known to operate SDV craft for special operations.

## Swimmer Delivery Vehicle (LSDV)

**Displacement:** 55 tons (surfaced); 60 tons (submerged)
**Length:** 19.82m/65ft (oa)
**Beam:** 2.44m/8ft (oa)
**Draught:** Not applicable
**Armament:** None
**Machinery:** 1 x electric propulsion motor, 8 x electric directional thrusters
**Power:** Not known
**Endurance:** 230km/125nm at 8 knots (designed)
**Protection:** Not applicable
**Complement:** 2 crew plus 8 special forces personnel

LEFT: **A REMUS 600 being launched. The type can operate to a depth of 600m/1,969ft.**

States Navy in amphibious operations to provide surveillance, target detection, and tracking capabilities.

The RQ-2A/B Pioneer, Unmanned Aerial Vehicle (UAV), capable of ship launch and recovery, was deployed operationally not only for reconnaissance missions but also as an effective missile delivery platform. It served the United States Navy and Marine Corps deployed at sea and on land from 1986 until 2007.

In a maritime context, unmanned vehicles are broadly divided between Remotely Operated Vehicles (ROV), linked to the controller by a trailing cable carrying command signals and data, and Autonomous Underwater Vehicles (AUV), which are pre-programmed and run independently until recovered. Free of any constraint, AUVs have a future bounded only by the systems and power source that can be packed aboard. AUVs have been used widely for some time in oceanographic work and, typically, have a three-day endurance and both an Inertial Navigation System (INS) and Global Positioning System (GPS). Larger AUVs are commonly used at depths of up to 3,000m/9,843ft for scientific sampling, surveying, or search and salvage operations. Data is stored aboard for later downloading and analysis. Designed with a 2.75m x 324mm/9 x 1ft hull, such vehicles may also be launched from a torpedo tube.

# Unmanned Vehicles (UV)

Without crew and associated safety systems, fighting vehicles can be made smaller, lighter and more cheaply. They can also be used with far greater risk and, potentially, more effectively. Unmanned Vehicles (UVs) have emerged as a transformative technology in modern warfare, and their applications in amphibious operations have significantly enhanced the military capabilities of their operating forces.

The US Navy's Drone Anti-Submarine Helicopter (DASH) of the 1960s was a first bold attempt but proved to be ahead of the technology of the time. More recently the Northrop Grumman MQ-8 Fire Scout, an unmanned helicopter system, has been utilized by the United

In an amphibious warfare context, an AUV's ability to tow a high definition sonar for the remote and unobtrusive detection and location of inshore minefields is invaluable and their capabilities allow for the establishment of secure amphibious landing zones.

The REMUS (Remote Environmental Monitoring UnitS) series are autonomous underwater vehicles (AUVs) used by the US Navy and Royal Navy as well as the navies of Algeria, Croatia, Canada, Ireland, Finland, Netherlands, Japan and

LEFT: **The REMUS AUV is pre-programmed to search underwater areas independently until recovered.**

New Zealand. Versions of these torpedo-shaped vessels with reconfigurable sensors in military service include the REMUS 600 equipped with side-scanning sonar and downward-looking video camera, and can travel at speeds of up to 5 knots with an endurance of up to 70 hours at a cruising speed of 3 knots. The REMUS 100 (the numbers always denote maximum operating depth) can travel at up to 5 knots with a maximum endurance of up to 22 hours. The REMUS M3V version can also be airdropped.

The Bluefin Robotics Bluefin-9 UUV is designed for high-resolution underwater surveys and mine countermeasures and has successfully supported amphibious operation exercises to detect and neutralize underwater threats in the littoral zone. The derived Knifefish's job is to detect, avoid and identify mine threats (proud or buried) in high-clutter environments, reducing the risk to personnel by operating in the minefield as an off-board sensor, while the host ship stays outside the minefield boundaries. Knifefish also gathers environmental data to provide intelligence support for other mine warfare systems.

ABOVE: **US Navy sailors launch a REMUS 600 (designated Mk 18 Mod 2 in USN service) in the Persian Gulf.** RIGHT: **An MQ-8 Fire Scout hovers over the flight deck of the littoral combat ship USS *Fort Worth* (LCS 3).**

## Autonomous Underwater Vehicle (AUV), REMUS 100

**Manufacturer:** Hydroid LLC, Pocasset, Maine, USA
**Weight:** 37kg/81.4lb
**Length:** 1.6m/5ft 3in (oa)
**Diameter:** 190.5mm/7.5in (maximum)
**Propulsion:** Brushless DC electric motor directly driving single propeller
**Energy:** 1 kW-h lithium-ion battery
**Speed:** Variable; 0–5 knots
**Endurance:** 22 hours at 3 knots
**Maximum operation depth:** 100m/328ft

LEFT: **Vehicles from a Ready Reserve Force (RRF) being unloaded on to LASH barges from a Combat Prepositioning Ship.**

# Lighter Aboard Ship (LASH)

One logical offshoot from the "container revolution" that transformed much commercial shipping was the barge carrier, of which the best-known type was the Lighter Aboard Ship (LASH). Here, rather than 6–12m/ 20–40ft containers, the interchangeable modules were rectangular barges of 375 tons capacity. LASH ships were relevant to companies working between ports such as Rotterdam or New Orleans, which are located on major waterway systems. Barges would be taken aboard or discharged by the ship at a mooring, being moved singly or in groups by pusher tug.

Like that of an LSD, the after end on a LASH was a double-skinned, non-floodable docking well. Barges, stacked several deep, were stowed transversely and handled by a massive, 450-ton capacity gantry crane which travelled the length of the barge dock. The crane tracks were carried on beams which projected over the stern to allow a barge to be lowered into the water.

Beginning a massive acquisition of commercial tonnage during the 1980s, the Military Sealift Command took over four such ships. Following the disappearance at sea of a foreign-flagged LASH ship, the basic ship concept was abandoned.

The barge idea, however, was valid, the US Navy eventually progressing the type for second-echelon amphibious operation.

Under the label of the Improved Navy Lighterage System (INLS), an initial block of 23 dumb and six powered lighters had been acquired. All may be stacked, three deep, on a very large, flat-topped, seagoing dumb barge and towed to the operational area. Individual lighters can alternatively be transported in the docking well of an LSD or similar vessels.

On arrival, the barges are used for ship-to-shore movement of equipment (equivalent to the British "Mexeflote" system), being used as ferries, linked as causeways, or moored as pontoons for the repair of small craft.

ABOVE: **The Improved Navy Lighterage System (INLS) in operation. The US Navy ordered 23 barges and six powered lighters. Individual lighters can be carried in the docking well of an LSD-type vessel.**

## Lighter Aboard Ship (LASH), *Green Island*

**Tonnage:** 32,280 tons (gross); 46,150 tons (deadweight); 62,310 tons (displacement, loaded)
**Length:** 243.03m/796ft 10in (oa); 272.29m/892ft 9in (oa)
**Beam:** 30.5m/100ft
**Draught:** 12.45m/40ft 9in (loaded)
**Armament:** None
**Machinery:** 2 sets steam turbines, single shaft
**Power:** 23,872kW/32,000shp for 22 knots
**Fuel:** 5,800 tons oil
**Endurance:** 27,600km/150nm at 22 knots
**Protection:** None
**Complement:** 27    **Capacity:** 90 barges

LEFT: **A row of X-Lighters ("Beetles") in the harbour at "A" West Beach, Suvla Point, on December 19, 1915, loaded and ready for the evacuation of Allied forces from Gallipoli.**

# X-Lighters ("Beetles")

Early in World War I, the most cherished plan of the Royal Navy's First Sea Lord, Admiral Sir John ("Jacky") Fisher was his Baltic Project, whereby a Russian Army would be put ashore on the coast of Pomerania (divided between Germany and Poland) just 145km/90 miles from Berlin. Fisher's drive and fertile brain created many special craft, but there was overwhelming opposition from his more conservative colleagues, and he saw his "unparalleled Armada" being "diverted and perverted to the damned Dardanelles".

Among the 600-plus assorted craft of Fisher's "armada" were 200 craft built specifically to land personnel, horses,

wheeled transport and artillery on the beach. Known as X-Lighters, numbered X1 to 200, all were powered, had a shallow draught and were fitted with a ramp. As the first series-built landing craft of modern times, the type deserves to be better recognized.

Not ordered until early in 1915, all were probably always destined for the Dardanelles, for which operational planning had already begun. A basic design brief was given to the small yard of Pollock at Faversham, Kent, which, within days, produced a proposal for a flat-bottomed, shallow barge with a pointed counter stern and a spoon bow. The latter was heavily flared to provide the

necessary width for a 2m/7ft wide ramp. This was suspended around the centre of gravity by chains, attached to two manually operated pivoting beams. This characteristic feature, together with the curved cover fitted over the troop/cargo deck, brought about the craft's popular name of "Beetle". The cargo area was 18.28m/60ft in length, with a full-length centreline hatch 2.44m/8ft wide, with side decks each 1.98m/6ft 6in wide.

Unusually for the day, a diesel engine was specified, and sometimes two engines were fitted. A low coaming and short funnel covered the machinery space in the stern. Within six months, 220 had been completed.

ABOVE: **Another view of Royal Navy X-Lighters at Suvla Point, Gallipoli, awaiting evacuation.**

## X-Lighters ("Beetles"), X1–200

**Displacement:** 160 tons (light); 310 tons (loaded)
**Length:** 32.14m/105ft 6in (oa)
**Beam:** 6.4m/21ft
**Draught:** 1.07/3ft 6in (light);
1.98m/6ft 6in (loaded)
**Armament:** 1 x machine-gun
**Machinery:** 1/2 semi-diesel engines, 1/2 shafts
**Power:** 30–67kW/40–90bhp for 5–7 knots
**Fuel:** Not known
**Endurance:** Not known
**Protection:** Steering position only
**Complement:** 5

ABOVE AND LEFT: **HM Trawler** *Grimsby Town* **fitted for anti-submarine (note the depth charge racks at the stern) and anti-mine warfare. The vessel has a defensive armament of three Oerlikon cannon and a 4in naval gun.**

# Auxiliary Minesweepers

As the greatest amphibious operation to date, the Dardanelles campaign of 1915, and its failure, were hugely influential on post-World War I thinking. The main objective (to place an Allied fleet at Constantinople) was not realized primarily because of a few lines of mines. These proved to be unsweepable and impassable, which demonstrated shortcomings in the Royal Navy's attitude to mine clearance.

Despite the success of Russian mining during the 1904–05 war with Japan, the British regular minesweeping force in 1914 was made up of only a handful of converted torpedo gunboats, with the first purpose-built craft (the original Flower-class sloops) on order. The reason for the delay was that commercial trawlers had been found to be ideal for the task, and also available in large numbers, together with skilled crews.

The work of deploying, towing and recovering sweeps, together with associated equipment, was little different to trawling, while the vessels had the necessary engine power. From 1911, therefore, the minesweeping organization for British waters was established, sufficient equipment being stockpiled to equip 250 trawlers immediately. This, however, was defensive minesweeping, with skippers and crews retaining civilian status but subject to naval discipline. In the fierce currents of the Dardanelles, and under heavy shore-based fire,

such trawler-minesweepers proved inadequate, and the naval high command appeared reluctant to use available converted destroyer-minesweepers.

Only a proportion of the British trawler fleet could be requisitioned, as the population still required to be fed. Large numbers, however, together with their crews, were sunk by mines. Despite the availability of many more regular minesweepers in 1939, the fishing fleet was again raided for trawlers and personnel. Several large deep-sea trawlers served in the Falklands campaign of 1982.

ABOVE: **HM Trawler** *Ben Earn*, **one of the first of the type to be converted for anti-mine warfare. Note the minesweeping cable-winding drum mounted at the stern of the vessel.**

RIGHT: **Known popularly as the "Ellas", the distant-water trawlers of J. Marr & Company, a concern with a 100-year history in fishing based in Hull, East Yorkshire, served as minesweepers in the Falklands War, 1982.**

# Landing Craft, Assault (LCA, previously ALC)

What was then termed an ALC was defined in 1938 as a personnel assault craft hoistable by standard passenger liner davits. This limited the weight to 10 tons and defined the dimensions to accommodate crew, a 32-man platoon and five engineers/signallers. A 0.46m/18in beaching draught was specified. Cooperation between commercial interests and the Admiralty's Department of Naval Construction resulted in a strong and useful little craft.

Known after July 1942 as an LCA, the craft had virtually no rise of floor, the bottom curving upward at both ends. The double bottom gave reserve buoyancy in the event of a flooded deck area, and was very shallow. Sheltered beneath narrow side decks, troops were seated along either side. Further seating along the centreline could be screened somewhat by adding raised coamings.

Behind the hand-operated forward ramp was a protective transverse armoured bulkhead with forward-hinging doors. Much of the exposed hull was of patented bullet-proof steel. The helmsman occupied a cab on the starboard side. The cab had a lid so that the helmsman could stand on his seat to improve forward visibility. A similar port-side position was occupied by a gunner. Aft of the troop accommodation was an enclosed engine compartment containing two Ford V8 petrol engines and fuel tanks. The twin rudders and propellers were protected by rather elaborate guards.

Designed as a ship-to-shore craft (and complementary to the vehicle-carrying MLC), the LCA was often used in circumstances for which it had been neither designed nor intended (notably cross-Channel to Normandy). The resulting shortcomings attracted unreasonable criticism. In many respects, the 1,900-plus that were built were stronger and superior to the 36ft LCVP that the US forces later used and preferred.

ABOVE: **US Rangers on board a Landing Craft, Assault (LCA) in Weymouth Harbour, Dorset, on June 4, 1944. The troops sat with their equipment in three rows in what were very cramped conditions.**

## Landing Craft, Assault (LCA)

**Displacement:** 9 tons (light); 13 tons (loaded)
**Length:** 12.66m/41ft 6in (oa)
**Beam:** 3.05m/10ft
**Draught (light):** 0.33m/1ft 1in (forward); 0.53m/1ft 9in (aft)
**Draught (loaded):** 0.53m/1ft 9in (forward); 0.69m/2ft 3in (aft)
**Armament:** 1 x Bren gun, 2 x Lewis guns, 1 x 2in mortars
**Machinery:** 2 petrol engines, 2 shafts
**Power:** 97kW/130hp for 10 knots (light), or 6 knots (loaded)
**Fuel:** 64 or 98 gallons petrol
**Endurance:** Up to 147km/80mm at 7 knots (loaded)
**Protection:** 7mm/1/4in plate to vertical surfaces
**Complement:** 4
**Capacity:** 37 troops plus 364kg/800lb equipment

# Landing Craft, Tank, LCT (1) to (4)

After the Dunkirk evacuation, Churchill demanded the specification for a craft capable of landing tanks in numbers on the beaches of continental Europe. No such craft had ever existed, and designers worked from a blank sheet. A vessel of around 48.8m/160ft was specified to accommodate three 40-ton tanks and land them in 1m/3ft of water on a beach with a 1 in 35 (moderate) slope.

Production was rapid, with what became known as the LCT (1) appearing in November 1940. Major features included a tank deck, which could accommodate three 40-ton or six 25-ton vehicles. Running light, the bottom could be used for water ballast, while the side compartments could be sealed to give greater buoyancy in the event of the tank deck (which was below the load waterline) flooding. To lower the ramp, personnel had to go forward along the exposed side decks to operate the winches. A further winch, at the stern, operated a large kedge anchor, released on approach to

the beach and the cable kept taut both to maintain the craft's alignment to the beach and to facilitate reversing off.

To keep fully above the keel line, the two propellers were of small diameter. The relatively low thrust and a single rudder, combined with a shallow, beamy hull, resulted in difficult steering. The hull was built in four sections to permit transport as deck cargo.

The LCT (1) proved the principles adequately but it was apparent that a relatively small increase in dimensions would permit the loading of six 17.7-ton Valentine tanks. Mark 1 craft were, therefore, relegated to training duties in favour of the LCT (2). To achieve quantity production, this craft was assembled from modules prefabricated by non-shipbuilding companies.

Both LCT (1) and (2) were originally powered by aero-type petrol engines from World War I. Fortunately, the supply of these eventually ended, necessitating the adoption of the very

ABOVE: **A prototype LCT (2) during beaching trials. Intended to transport tanks from ship to shore, it was built to be capable of a Channel crossing.**

reliable 500bhp Paxman diesel engine. As the LCT (2) had three propellers, installed power was thus increased from 1,050 to 1,500hp, a 43 per cent increase, however this gave a speed increase of only half a knot. Fuel stowage became safer now that petrol was no longer used.

The Mark 3, or LCT (3), that followed was essentially an LCT (2) with an extra mid-hull module inserted to increase length by around 9.75m/32ft. Lines were also refined somewhat so that, even by reducing power to two engines, the type still made the same speed when loaded. This was partly by the design of the longer hull which also allowed simplified hull construction as well as saving a valuable engine. Steering remained erratic but was improved by the use of twin rudders.

LEFT: **Shorter and beamier than previous types, the LCT (4) was not designed to be covered. Note the open bridge and lack of armament.**

LEFT: **An early LCT (1), still carrying a "TLC" identifier. The vertical posts were supports for a portable metal roof. In these early craft, the whole of the open tank deck could be roofed over with a canvas cover.**

ABOVE: **An over-large funnel was a feature of the LCT (4). Camouflage shades were selected to blend with misty Channel conditions, the pattern designed to break up the vessel's outline.**

The LCT (3) could carry 11 Valentines, five Churchill tanks or 11 of the new US-built Shermans. This was satisfactory, except that the capacity to carry tanks had increased more than vessel buoyancy. Inevitably, this resulted in deeper beaching draught. French beaches, the ultimate objective, were known to have very shallow slopes, which would leave the craft grounded too far from the tideline. A shallower-draught version was obviously urgently required and allowed the chance to raise the tank deck above the load waterline for the first time, making it self-draining. The double-bottom was consequently a

generous 1.5m/5ft deep. Any improved stiffness that this gave was offset by the exceptional lightness of the construction. The hull did bend and twist quite alarmingly in a seaway.

Entering service in September 1942, the Mark 4, or LCT (4), was 1.5m/5ft shorter than the LCT (3), but 2.4m/8ft wider in beam. On these proportions, a reduction in speed had to be accepted and the craft could be beached satisfactorily on slopes of greater than 1 in 150. Vehicle-carrying capacity was again improved, while tolerable passage accommodation was provided for the crews of the vehicles carried.

ABOVE: **Note how the shallow-submerged propellers create an inefficient wash, and the large gallery that accommodates two single 2pdr "Pom-Pom" anti-aircraft guns on this LCT (3).**

### Landing Craft, Tank, LCT (4)

**Displacement:** 200 tons (light); 585 tons (loaded)
**Length:** 57.11m/187ft 3in (oa)
**Beam:** 11.79m/38ft 8in
**Draught (beaching):** 0.56m/1ft 10in (forward); 1.22m/4ft (aft)
**Draught (seagoing, full load):** 0.94m/3ft 1in (forward); 1.29m/4ft 3in (aft)
**Armament:** 2 x 20mm guns (2x1)
**Machinery:** 2 diesel engines, 2 shafts
**Power:** 746kW/1,000bhp for 8 knots (sustained), or 9.5 knots (maximum)
**Fuel:** Not known
**Endurance:** 2,024km/1,100nm at 8 knots
**Protection:** 7mm/$\frac{1}{4}$in plate to wheelhouse
**Complement:** 12
**Capacity:** 6 x 40-ton, 9 x 30-ton or 12 x 3-ton tanks, or 350 tons cargo

# Landing Craft, Tank, LCT (8)

Where British ideas much influenced early US thinking regarding amphibious vessels in general, the latter rapidly gained experience by virtue of massive construction programmes. By 1943, therefore, a reverse trickle of practical knowledge began to find its way into British design.

In the Landing Ship, Tank (LST), US forces found a most useful vessel that was particularly flexible in ballasting arrangements, which enabled safe ocean passages to be made as a cargo carrier. The vessel's draught could be differentially reduced to ground in shallow water to allow the discharge of heavy armoured vehicles.

LSTs were never available in sufficient numbers (many were "lost" in obscure military backwaters of the Pacific) and were relatively slow and vulnerable when deployed in an opposed landing. By the end of 1943,

therefore, the Landing Ship, Medium (LSM) was introduced – effectively a smaller LST but with the usefulness of a larger and faster type of LCT.

The extra speed was possible because the forward ramp was enclosed within LST-type bow doors. The raised forecastle, necessary to accommodate the length of the enclosed ramp and doors, was, to an extent, continued aft, with the resulting deep side compartments giving a higher degree of seaworthiness and, importantly, greatly improved longitudinal stiffness. There was no LST-type upper deck, so lack of torsional stiffness was still evident in rough seas.

Conceived as improved LCTs, all were in fact ordered as LCT (7), a designation that was never used in service since they were retitled LSMs. The replacement British LCT, then in the planning stage, thus became the LCT (8).

ABOVE: **The British-built LCT (4) was followed by the LCT (8), of which LCT 4001 (shown here) is an example. LCT (5), (6) and (7) were all US-built types.**

Like most British naval projects post-1943, the LCT (8) was designed with the intention of service in the Far East. Some 730 LCT (4) had been built. A number had failed structurally and required remedial strengthening. The LCT (8), therefore, had the same deep sides of the LSM, with bow doors enclosing the ramp and around an extra 12m/38ft of length. The two shafts were each powered by two Paxman diesel engines, giving a maximum speed of over 12 knots. Accommodation on this spacious landing craft was on a scale that allowed the ship's crew and the crews of the vehicles to be accommodated for seven days.

Only one LCT (8) was ever completed during hostilities, but around 24 served into the 1980s, refurbished

LEFT: **With the ramp enclosed and a longer hull, the LCM (8) was significantly faster. Increased depth gave the hull greater stiffness. HMS *Bastion* (L4040) was used during the Suez Crisis in 1956, and was sold to Zambia in 1966.**

to post-war standards and named. The names, such as HMS *Bastion* and HMS *Counterguard*, were mostly military fortification in origin, with one strangely named HMS *Arromanches*. Some remained un-named but, by the mid-1970s, all remaining craft carried battle names, commencing with the letter "A", from *Aachen* to *Audemer*.

All were now elderly, and the replacement, not on a one-to-one basis, was known as the LCT (9), although apparently not officially. It was of commercial design and, compared

with LCT (8) dimensions, it was a larger vessel. Despite engine power of 2,000bhp, the vessel could make only 10 knots. Two were built between 1977 and 1978, and were sometimes referred to as LSMs. Both could carry five 70-ton tanks, and the combined weight was equal to that transported in an LCT (8).

Operating under the Blue Ensign of the Royal Corps of Transport rather than by the Royal Navy, the craft were of novel design and ungainly appearance. The high forecastle, devoid of flare or sheer, supported the outer doors which

ABOVE: **Although built some 30 years later, the Ardennes class of the Royal Logistics Corps shows the influence of the LCT (8). Confusingly, HMS *Redoubt* (L4001) is numbered in the same series.**

protected the ramp. The tank deck ran almost to the after end of the high superstructure, which covered the deck. Deep longitudinal bulkheads flanked the tank deck, allowing headroom and improving stiffness to the hull. Externally, these formed high coamings with low, narrow side decks. The coamings could be roofed over, forming a flat centreline deck with an access hatch served by two 30-ton capacity derricks.

Most military stores were, by now, containerized. The low-density cargo containers could be conveniently carried on this forward deck. Tank crews were accommodated in the relatively spacious superstructure.

ABOVE: **The shallow draft of RASCV/HMAV *Arakan* (L4003) can here be appreciated. The high bow structure enables a maximum length of ramp to be stowed inboard. Note the sharp gradient of the ramp.**

## Landing Craft, Tank, LCT (8)

**Displacement:** 660 tons (light); 1,010 tons (loaded)
**Length:** 68.63m/225ft (bp); 70.52m/231ft 2in (oa)
**Beam:** 11.9m/39ft
**Draught (beaching):** 0.96m/3ft 2in (forward); 1.52m/5ft (aft)
**Armament:** None
**Machinery:** 4 diesel engines, 2 shafts
**Power:** 1,373kW/1,840bhp for 12.5 knots (maximum)
**Fuel:** Not known
**Endurance:** 4,600km/2,500nm at 10 knots
**Protection:** Not known
**Complement:** 22
**Capacity:** 5 heavy tanks, or 350 tons cargo

LEFT: **L3507 and L3508, two Vosper-built craft, were prototypes for the LCM (9), the first class of British minor landing craft to be built since World War II. Commissioned in 1963, they had a more steeply housed ramp.**

# Landing Craft, Medium, LCM (7) and (9)

Early Landing Craft, Medium, particularly the LCM (3) and (6), were designed to be set afloat empty using davits or cargo lifting gear, and then loaded alongside with heavy armoured vehicles. Clearances in the craft were critical across the beam while the fore-and-aft position of the load could be vital to stability. The situation was much alleviated by the introduction of the LSD, which permitted craft to be carried dry and pre-loaded before launching.

For US forces, the late introduction of the M26 Pershing tank in 1944 required a new landing craft to be designed. The British continued with medium tanks but required a craft more suitable than the LCM (3) and (6) for Far East use. Toward the end of 1944, a new LCM (7) was introduced, built of part-welded, part-riveted construction.

The LCM (7) dimensions of 18.35 x 4.87m/60ft 3in x 16ft and a weight of 28 tons did not allow it to be carried under standard davits. The beam appeared too large for the 13.42m/44ft width of the four Ashland-class LSDs being acquired through the Lend-Lease Program.

Able to carry a 35-ton tank, the LCM (7) closely followed the design principles successfully employed in the LCM (3). Externally, it lacked the distinct curve that characterized the shape of the upper edge on the coaming of the LCM (3). Only the mid-body was almost flat, with negligible rise of floor but with two shallow keels to prevent abrasion when grounding. Forward, the flat bottom was blended in a curve with the lower edge of the ramp. Aft, it swept upward to the lower edge of the square transom.

The tank deck rose in a near double curve to meet the sill of the ramp, avoiding the sharp step that characterized earlier craft, and which caused considerable problems to wheeled transport. The resulting deeper forward double bottom also counteracted tendency for the vessel to float bows-down when the vehicle deck

ABOVE: **A fully laden LCM (7) leaves the P&O liner SS *Canberra* during the Falklands campaign, with troops of the 5th Infantry Brigade destined for Blue beach on San Carlos Water.**

RIGHT: **An LCM (9) painted with "Arctic"-type camouflage during a pre-Falklands War landing exercise.**

was flooded. The crew of seven appears large but, even late in the war, manpower was cheaper than mechanization.

The LCM (7) programme was due to run to 250 craft but was cancelled in 1945. Several of these tough little craft were, nonetheless, still in service during the mid-1970s, overlapping the entry into service of the first post-war craft. Ten were built in the mid-1960s to be deployed with the two Fearless-class LPDs, and the docking wells on both could accommodate four. One was lost in the Falklands (where the type was generally referred to as Landing Craft, Utility [LCU]), but replaced by new craft built in 1986.

The LCM (9) was designed to carry a 54-ton Chieftain tank or 50 tons of cargo. During the Falklands campaign, however, LCM (9) proved to be very useful as a troop carrier. It was not meant for this usage and, following long passages in the Falklands winter, troops arrived wet, cold and very unhappy. The craft were subsequently equipped with a removable, inflatable shelter for the vehicle deck. The side coamings were also raised.

As built, all were fitted with twin propellers running in Kort nozzles to increase thrust. In the late 1990s, however, when most were approaching obsolescence, those in good condition were re-engined for waterjet propulsion. These propulsors not only removed vulnerable propeller shafts, A-brackets, propellers and rudders, but were unlikely to be clogged in shallow-water by weed. Before this, one LCM (9) was fitted with Schottel azimuth-thruster propulsion as a trials ship for a new

LCM (10) craft, under design for use with the new Albion class. Ten were built between 1999 and 2005 and, larger again at 29.8 x 7.4m/97ft x 24ft 3in, they could transport a 70-ton armoured vehicle (a Challenger 2 tank for example weighed 62.5 tons). To facilitate docking, these craft were fitted with bow thrusters. Of drive-through configuration, the craft were sufficiently different to be classed as an LCU. The LCU (10) remains in Royal Marines service at the time of writing.

ABOVE: **With the introduction of the LSD, the LCM, no longer constrained by davit limitations, became considerably larger in size. The LCM (9) weighed 115 tons.** LEFT: **The British LCM (9) dated from the mid-1960s, and was desiged to fit the docking well of the Fearless-class LPD. After 1999, the type was superseded by the larger LCU (10).**

## Landing Craft, Medium, LCM (9)

**Displacement:** 115 tons (light); 165 tons (loaded)
**Length:** 25.7m/84ft 3in (oa)
**Beam:** 6.5m/21ft 4in
**Draught:** 1.7m/5ft 6in
**Armament:** Not armed
**Machinery:** 2 diesel engines, 2 shafts
**Power:** 462kW/620bhp for 10 knots (maximum)
**Fuel:** Not known
**Endurance:** 552km/300nm at 9 knots
**Protection:** Nominal
**Complement:** 7

# Landing Craft, Gun (Large)/(Medium), LCG (L)/(M)

**B**ritish LCGs were intended to cover the few minutes between the lifting of the preliminary barrage and the vulnerable assault craft actually hitting the beach. The type would be used to lead the first wave, with fire augmented by that of armoured fighting vehicles being carried in the craft. Before touchdown, the LCGs would be manoeuvred to the side of the attack to provide enfilading support fire more accurately than offshore warships.

During 1942, a total of 23 LCT (3) and 10 LCT (4) were converted, with the bows being sealed and an upper deck added. Two 4.7in naval guns fitted with gunshields were mounted along the centreline, firing over a deep, protective bulwark. The crew was increased to 39, many being gunners from the Royal Marines.

Unavoidably, large quantities of gun ammunition were carried above the waterline and, despite some armour protection, the craft proved vulnerable to mortar fire. Forced to remain beyond mortar range, the LCG (L)s proved to be ineffective.

This resulted in the LCG (M), purpose-built with a ship-type transom stern and a spoon-type bow to allow the vessel to be held against the shore. The two main types mounted two 25pdr or 17pdr Army guns in enclosed gun positions. The mountings were arranged at angles to allow both weapons to fire both ahead and to the beam. On the LCG (M), a major feature was the "central battery", an armoured structure, enclosing gun fire control, magazine and machinery space. The LCG (M) (1) had 52mm/2in sides, 25mm/1in deck plating and transverse bulkheads. On the LCG (M) (2), this was reduced to lessen weight and improve draught.

Considerable ballast capacity was incorporated, which allowed the craft to be flooded down to lay on the sand close inshore. This reduced the exposed hull cross-section to enemy gunners and provided a more stable gun platform.

ABOVE: **The Dieppe raid showed the need for close-in naval gunfire support to deal with strongpoints and armour. LCT (3) vessels were thus modified with a variety of medium-calibre guns.** BELOW: **The LCG (M) mounted two 25pdr or 17pdr guns in enclosed gun turrets.**

## Landing Craft, Gun, LCG (M) (1)

**Displacement:** 308 tons (light); 339 tons (beaching); 381 tons (seagoing)
**Length:** 47.12m/154ft 6in (oa)
**Beam:** 6.81m/22ft 4in
**Draught (beaching):** 1.5m/4ft 11in (forward); 1.7m/5ft 7in (aft)
**Draught (seagoing):** 1.7m/5ft 7in (forward); 2.44m/8ft (aft)
**Armament:** 2 x 7pdr or 25pdr guns (2x1), 4 x 20mm guns (2x2)
**Machinery:** 2 diesel engines, 2 shafts
**Power:** 686kW/920bhp for 13.5 knots (maximum)
**Fuel:** 63 tons oil
**Endurance:** 3,183km/1,730nm at 12 knots
**Protection:** 50mm/2in vertical protection to magazines, engine room and conning tower; 25mm/1in to deck and control area deckheads; 6.5mm/¼in to gun positions and compass platform
**Complement:** 31

LEFT: **The LCS (M) (2) was around 12m/40ft in length, and powered for a slow 9-knot speed. The sides of the hull and deckhouse were protected with 6mm/¹/₄in steel plate.**

# Landing Craft, Support (Large)/(Medium), LCS (L)/(M)

The need for close-in support fire to cover the first assault waves at the point of touchdown was evident pre-war, although it was envisaged that light automatic weapons and smoke would provide adequate cover.

Dating from 1938, the LCS (M) was simply a 41ft wooden LCA fitted with some vertical and horizontal 13mm/0.5in steel plate, and a steering position protected by the same thickness plate. In the cargo well were two pedestal-mounted 0.50in heavy machine-guns and a 4in smoke mortar. In the open hull, gunners were very exposed to enemy fire, and later a 20mm cannon with gunshield was fitted.

The Mark 2, or LCS (M) (2), was an improvement in providing an armoured deckhouse amidships on which was mounted a powered turret housing twin machine-guns. The mortar remained in the same exposed position. A final version, the LCS (M) (3), was similar except for a boat-shaped, hard-chine bow, which made little improvement to the maximum speed of the craft.

Although this Mark 3 remained in production throughout the war, the Dieppe raid proved the vessels' firepower inadequate against enemy armour. Although suitable to be transported under davits, a larger, more heavily armoured craft was obviously required.

A first attempt became the LCS (L) (1), only 1.8m/6ft longer than the LCS (M) but with the beam increased by 25 per cent. In appearance, the vessel resembled a small MTB, but was capable of only 10 knots. Mounted forward was the turret from a Daimler armoured car housing a 2pdr anti-tank gun. Aft was a square-shaped turret mounting two heavy machine-guns. Amidships protection was substantial for such a small craft.

The succeeding Mark 2 had less protection but was faster. Almost twice the size, it resembled a Fairmile "D" type, and mounted a 6pdr gun in a forward turret. Two 0.50in heavy machine-guns were mounted in a aft turret, and 20mm cannon fitted in side mountings. The wooden hull and petrol engines made the vessel vulnerable to enemy fire.

ABOVE: **This early version shows little refinement, with proper protection offered only for the helmsman. Rescue ropes with foot loops were often rigged along the sides.** LEFT: **Sometimes dismissed as "Harry Tate's Navy", the inshore support craft matured into a formidable fighting force.**

---

### Landing Craft, Support, LCS (L) (2)

**Displacement:** 84 tons (light); 116 tons (loaded)
**Length:** 32.04m/105ft 1in (oa)
**Beam:** 6.54m/21ft 5in
**Draught (inshore):** 0.69m/2ft 3in (forward); 0.91m/3ft (aft)
**Draught (seagoing):** 1.12m/3ft 8in (forward); 1.02m/3ft 4in (aft)
**Armament:** 1 x 6pdr gun, 2 x 20mm guns (2x1), 2 x 0.50in machine-guns (1x2 ), 1 x 4in mortar
**Machinery:** 2 petrol engines, 2 shafts
**Power:** 373kW/500hp for 15 knots (maximum)
**Fuel:** 18 tons petrol
**Endurance:** 1,288km/700nm at 12.5 knots
**Protection:** 13mm/0.5in special steel to deck, hull sides, bridge and gun positions
**Complement:** 25

# Landing Craft, FlaK/Landing Craft, Tank (Rocket)/Landing Craft, Assault (Hedgerow), LCF/LCT (R)/LCA (HR)

Experience gained by the Royal Navy up until mid-1941 included the evacuation at Dunkirk of troops in the face of enemy air superiority. The RN had entered the war ill-prepared to meet the threat of air attack and temporary solutions were required.

The only potent long-range anti-aircraft (AA) mounting was the high-angle (HA) 4in gun which, to be effective, required director control. Air warning radar was still in its infancy and a destructive air attack often took the form of low-level passes with little or no warning. The close-range alternative, therefore, was barrage fire from numbers of automatic weapons. Excluding the ineffective 0.50in multiple-mounted heavy machine-gun, the choice was limited to

the Oerlikon 20mm cannon (in very short supply) and the readily available Vickers 2pdr "Pom-Pom" gun.

June 1941 saw the commissioning of the first two Landing Craft, FlaK (LCF) converted from an LCT (2) for close support. The tank decks were covered, the space below allocated to magazines and accommodation for the gunners.

Armed with what was available, one had a twin 4in HA mounting and three single 20mm cannon. The other had eight single "Pom-Pom" guns and four single 20mm cannon. The first vessel became the forerunner to the LCS in having the firepower to attack strongpoints or enemy armour. The LCF thus continued as a type, later based on LCT (3) and (4) hulls, and were

ABOVE: **Modified as an LCT (R), an LCT (3) carried a load of 1,064 x 5in rockets. Fired in 24 rapid salvoes, these saturated an area of 685 x 146m/ 750 x 160yd at a fixed range of 3,200m/3,500yd.**

armed with a wide variation of weapon combinations. Also during 1943, the British experimented with covering an area with salvos of 5in artillery rockets, the idea being to detonate beach mines and to stun surviving enemy forces.

Six LCT (2) were fitted with a temporary upper deck to accommodate no less than 132 rocket launchers, firing projectiles each with a 13.2kg/29lb high-explosive head. With a fixed elevation of 45 degrees, theoretical range was 3,200m/3,500yd. The craft therefore had to be positioned and aligned accurately. All rockets were

LEFT: **A full salvo of 1,064 rockets being fired from an LCT (R) 125 during trials of the type in 1943.**

LEFT: **LCT (2) conversions carried only 792 rockets. Although the crew was increased to over 70, reloading took a considerable time.**

LEFT: **A profile view of an LCF (3) shows the wide distribution of the 2pdr main armament. Two 20mm cannon are mounted at the bow, and two are mounted behind the mast.**

"ripple" fired in seconds, saturating an area of 685 x 146m/750 x 160yd. One full reload was carried on board. Following the firing of the salvo, the craft was changed back to an LCT, the temporary upper deck and launchers being discarded.

The six prototypes proved valuable during the Operation "Husky" landings on Sicily, July 1943. A further number of LCT (3) were converted. These were, of course, larger and were able to carry up to 1,080 rockets, all of which had to be manually loaded.

The US military took up the idea in late 1944, using the LSM hull. Twelve interim-built craft retained the starboard side superstructure but were fitted with an upper deck, a single 5in gun and two 40mm cannon. A full salvo of 480 rockets carried on 75 four-rail and 30 six-rail launchers could be fired in 30 seconds but it took 2$^{1}/_{2}$ hours to manually reload. Range was fixed at 3,685m/4,000yd.

Four further LSM (R) were each fitted with 85 improved 12-rail launchers. Range could be varied up to 4,801m/5,250yd by changing elevation. Firing 1,020 rockets took under a minute, but manual reloading was a lengthy operation. The "ultimate" LSM (R) arrived too late to see action (until the Korean War), but featured launchers based on powered 40mm gun mountings, capable of being trained and elevated. The launchers were also mechanically reloaded, each twin launcher firing every 4 seconds.

The British-built "Hedgerow", or LCA (R), was a standard 13m/41.5ft craft modified to carry four rows of six "Spigot" mortars of the Hedgehog type used on anti-submarine escort ships. A 24-bomb pattern, when fired, greatly stressed even a frigate with the recoil force. An LCA suffered severely, several being sunk. The function of the LCA (R) was to blast a mine-free access across a beach, but the type was not a great success on D-Day.

ABOVE: **LCF (4) 24 moored to a buoy at a Royal Navy base on the River Clyde, Scotland, in August 1943.**

## LCT (R), typical

**Displacement:** 640 tons (loaded)
**Length:** 58.56m/192ft (oa)
**Beam:** 9.46m/31ft
**Draught:** 1.04m/3ft 5in (forward);
    2.03m/6ft 8in (aft)
**Armament:** 1,080 x 5in rocket projectiles,
    2 x 2pdr or 2 x 20mm guns
**Machinery:** 2 diesel engines, 2 shafts
**Power:** 746kW/1,000bhp for 10.5 knots
    (maximum)
**Fuel:** 24 tons oil
**Endurance:** 4,968km/2,700nm at 9 knots
**Protection:** Blast reinforced wheelhouse,
    6mm/$^{1}/_{4}$in plate to bridge and gun positions
**Complement:** 51

LEFT: **Many LCI (L) built in the USA for the UK were completed as "Raiding Craft", fitted with a lower, elongated superstructure. Still retaining the portable gangways, this headquarters conversion is identified by the communications equipment.**

# Landing Craft, Control/Navigational/ Headquarters (LCC/LCN/LCH)

Despite the title, these vessels were not landing craft as such, but were developed to carry the controllers of an operation. Hundreds of assault craft required marshalling into organized waves and needed to proceed, maybe in darkness and poor conditions, to the correct part of a multi-sector beach.

Exercises quickly showed the British the ease with which blocks of assault craft could become scattered, only to land at the wrong beach, with potentially disastrous consequences.

In January 1942, therefore, a number of LCP (L), now designated LCC, were fitted with extra navigational aids and, carrying specialist personnel, were used

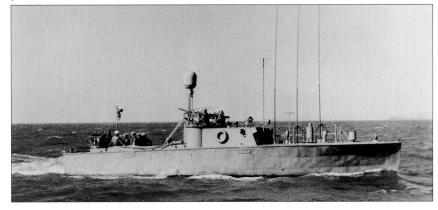

ABOVE: **Usually carried on the deck of an AKA or APA, the LCC (1) carried comprehensive communications equipment, including SO-type radar.**

to establish and mark exact start lines, as traffic control ships and to guide smaller craft. As standard Higgins boats, the LCCs quickly proved to be too small, and were replaced by the Fairmile B type, better known by the Royal Navy as Motor Launches (ML). The ML had a useful 20-knot speed and space for extra equipment, eventually including a radar "lantern" mounted on a sturdy lattice mast. The equivalent US Navy LCC, which entered service a year later, were smaller to allow transportation by AKA.

To approach close into the beach area to take a last sonar survey, act as static navigational marker or to provide smoke cover, the British Landing Craft, Navigational (LCN) was an LCP (L) conversion. The US Navy used the Landing Craft, Support (Small), or LCS (S), another modification of a Higgins boat. The Landing Craft, Headquarters (LCH) had no direct counterpart in the US inventory. Converted from an LCI (an early version with a low-

profile superstructure), they were little changed externally except for the addition of a tall tripod mast amidships. Despite the imposing designation, the LCH was intended to act as a leader ship and communications centre for groups of larger landing craft.

ABOVE: **Converted from a Fairmile B-type Motor Launch (ML), the LCH was fitted to act as a communications vessel for large groups of landing craft. Note the winch and stern anchor.**

## Landing Craft, Control (LCC), Motor Launch

**Displacement:** 75.5 tons (loaded)
**Length:** 34.16m/112ft (oa)
**Beam:** 65.64m/18ft 6in
**Draught:** 1.52m/5ft
**Armament:** 1 x 3pdr gun, 2 x 20mm guns (2x1), 2 x 0.50in machine-guns (1x2)
**Machinery:** 2 petrol engines, 2 shafts
**Power:** 836kW/1,120hp for 20 knots
**Fuel:** 10 tons petrol
**Endurance:** Not known
**Protection:** Nominal
**Complement:** Not known

LEFT: **All three of the Echo class moored alongside a jetty. The inshore minesweeper hull forms and the comprehensive electronics fits are obvious. Note the modern non-conformity in the shape of ships' crests mounted on the front of the bridge.**

# Inshore Survey Ship, Echo class

Good hydrographic intelligence is essential to the successful planning of a major amphibious operation. To available knowledge of a prospective landing area must be added detailed data on rock ledges and offshore sandbars. Then there are the less familiar variables such as the load-bearing qualities of the beach, the exact slope, and the strength and direction of the local tidal stream and currents. To such detail the postion of enemy underwater obstructions needs to be added.

The largely unknown hydrographic survey service of the Royal Navy deploys three major types of survey vessel – blue water, coastal and inshore. The last-named have hydrographic launches to extend

surveying up to the tideline, and may carry specialist teams to measure and reconnoitre the beach and beyond.

Following a landing, the service remains busy, using many techniques in common with anti-mine operations to chart obstructions in the approaches to, or in the basins of, essential ports.

World War II produced a number of improvised modifications which, by the 1950s, were being replaced by purpose-built ships. The inshore flotilla comprised three ships (HMS *Echo*, *Egeria* and *Enterprise*), which were built using the well-proven hull design of the Ham-class Inshore Minesweeper (IMS). To these were quickly added two more ships, HMS *Powderham* and HMS *Yaxham*, which later became HMS *Waterwitch* and HMS *Woodlark*

respectively, having been converted to the same high standard. All were commissioned between 1958 and 1959.

The large single-block superstructure was devoted largely to the hydrographic office. At the rear of this, two short posts supported exhausts for the diesel engines, acting also as derrick supports for the survey launch. Sweep gear for checking the depth of obstructions occupied the space in the stern.

The Echo class had an open bridge and lattice mast. The Waterwitch type had an enclosed bridge with tripod mast. All were disposed of during the 1980s in favour of chartered commercial craft.

LEFT: **The modified sweep gear aft was not for minesweeping but for checking the depth of water over obstructions. The echo-sounding launch was a valuable auxiliary close inshore.**

| Inshore Survey Ship, Echo class |  |
| --- | --- |

**Displacement:** 120 tons (standard); 160 tons (loaded)
**Length:** 32.57m/106ft 9in (oa)
**Beam:** 6.71m/22ft
**Draught:** 1.9m/6ft 3in
**Armament:** Usually unarmed; fitted with 1 x 40mm gun
**Machinery:** 2 diesel engines, 2 shafts
**Power:** 1,044kW/1,400bhp for 14 knots
**Fuel:** 15 tons oil
**Endurance:** 2,944km/1,600nm at 10 knots
**Protection:** None
**Complement:** 18–22

LEFT: **Some of the 1,000 Motor Minesweepers built were assembled in shipyards as far away as the Bahamas, Canada and Cochin (India).**

# Inshore Motor Minesweepers (MMS/BYMS/IMS/CMS)

Badly run down after 1918, the minesweeping force of the Royal Navy was in poor shape by 1939. In larger "Fleet" minesweepers, numbers were reasonably adequate, the veteran "Smokey Joe" Hunt-class ships complemented by the new Bangor and Halcyon-class ships. Of the smaller specialist craft, however, there was an absence, it being assumed that, as in the previous war, a force could be created from requisitioned commercial trawlers and skilled crews. Britain, in the event, was faced with a starvation blockade, and many trawlers were required to carry on fishing in the interests of feeding the population. The shortage of auxiliary minesweepers was so desperate that even paddle steamers, typically associated with seaside resorts, were pressed into service.

More was required. The Germans used destroyers, E-boats and aircraft to lay mines in vital coastal shipping areas. These were technically advanced types, at first magnetic, later acoustic. Unexploded examples were collected for examination by eight drifters of the Mine Recovery Flotilla.

With the secrets of the magnetic mine revealed, several important programmes were initiated. The first was to "degauss" or "wipe" steel ships to reduce the magnetic signature. A second saw several east coast colliers converted to "mine bumpers", or Mine Destructor Ships, the forward cargo space carrying enormous electro-magnets. These certainly worked, but with the probabilty of serious damage to the ship and the crew.

The long-term solution, however, was the Double L (LL) sweep, whose two parallel cables were towed by drifters. Many more ships were, nonetheless, required and, for safety, these were to be constructed from wood.

ABOVE: **The hull of the "Mickey Mouse" was built from wood in yards specializing in fishing vessels. At the bow is the Kango-type anti-acoustic mine hammer. The A-frame pivoted downward.**
LEFT: **Two "Big Mickeys" moored alongside the quay in a Royal Navy yard. The class was numbered from 1001 to 1090.**

LEFT: **Hardly had the last wood-built types of World War II been disposed of than the outbreak of the Korean War triggered a huge new building programme for Coastal and Inshore Minesweepers. Many saw little or no service. HMS *Aveley* is an IMS in Royal Navy service.**

An order for 50 "cheap" 105ft motor minesweepers was mentioned as early as January 1940, together with a larger and faster (12-knot) variant capable of sweeping ahead of convoys. These materialized as 38.4m/126ft craft but with no extra speed. Both types were termed Motor Minesweepers (MMS), differentiated popularly as "Mickey Mice" and "Big Mickeys". The essential features of both were the large LL-type cable drum abaft the superstructure and an A-frame at the bows carrying a Kango-type hammer for the anti-acoustic mine equipment.

The first and follow-up orders for the 105ft type were shared among no less than 24 home and 25 overseas

shipyards, the latter from the Bahamas to Beirut and from Canada to Cochin (India). The 126ft class had a small funnel and a raised forecastle in place of the steep bow on smaller ships.

As an example of the type's value and application to amphibious warfare, the prologue to the Normandy landings was the overnight creation of six safe cross-channel shipping lanes, each of some 80km/50 miles long, and 914–1,280m/ 1,000–1,400yd wide. Involved were 48 Fleet minesweepers, 42 MMSs and 45 trawlers, with specially fitted Motor Launches (ML) working close inshore.

The US Navy's equivalent programme was for the so-called Yard Minesweepers (YMS), which were of

very similar dimensions to the "Big Mickey", and also built of wood. Many were transferred to the Royal Navy under the Lend-Lease Progam and, when lightly modified, known as BYMS. The type had twice the engine power of the 10-knot MMS, being capable of 13 knots. The BYMS were identifiable by a single large funnel. US Navy-operated examples had two, one or no funnels.

By 1950, with only 24 various MMSs and 10 BYMSs (due to be returned to the US) in Royal Navy service, the Korean War began. This alerted the UN forces to the threat of a Soviet-backed mining campaign.

The response included programmes for building 100 Coastal Minesweepers.

ABOVE: **HMS *Brinkley* was one of nine "M2001" vessels which differed from the other 80 vessels in the class in having wood-on-aluminium frame construction. The ships were painted black when being used as special diving tenders by the Royal Navy.**

## Inshore Motor Minesweeper, 105ft MMS

**Displacement:** 163 tons (standard); 255 tons (loaded)
**Length:** 36.3m/119ft (oa)
**Beam:** 7.02m/23ft
**Draught:** 2.9m/9ft 6in
**Armament:** 2 x 20mm guns (2x1), 2 x smaller
**Machinery:** 1 diesel engine, single shaft
**Power:** Variable, between 205–373kW/ 275–500bhp for 10 knots (maximum)
**Fuel:** 22 tons oil
**Endurance:** Not known
**Protection:** None
**Complement:** 20

# Griffon Hovercraft (LCAC)

For many decades the hovercraft had been an inspired mechanical principle looking for a useful military application. A vehicle that can negotiate water, ice, swamp, foreshore or rapids, all with equal ease, must be useful. It was extensively trialled by US forces in Vietnam, where humidity and mud called for very demanding maintenance schedules. Exceedingly noisy, the general verdict was that, whatever the type was used for, a helicopter was better. The LCAC has, however, proved to be valuable, with spearhead assault being left to helicopter-borne forces.

Smaller hovercraft have been considerably quietened by using a diesel engine and slower-turning, variable pitch airscrews. British special forces operate a number of Griffon designs alongside high-speed "fast transport craft". The latter are 45-plus-knot power boats, faster than the hovercraft in most conditions, but with smaller payload and less space. 539 Assault Squadron Royal Marines (539 ASRM) operate the craft and were deployed with LCACs during operations in Iraq, where they were used to patrol marshland in the south of the country. Royal Marines Griffon 2400TD LCAC crew compartments have armour plating and bullet-proof windows, and retractable side panels allow the hovercraft to fit inside a C-130J, A400M or C-17 aircraft.

The hovercraft's advantage is that it is, essentially, a floating raft. The cabin top, enclosing accommodation for 16 troops, may be removed to leave an open platform for loads of up to 2 tons. The strength of this type of vehicle really resides in that of the imagination of the people using them.

LEFT: **Hovercraft are floating platforms that can be left open for cargo-carrying or enclosed for personnel. These are BHC (British Hovercraft Corporation) craft.**

## Griffon Hovercraft (LCAC), Type 2000 TDX (M)

**Weight/displacement:** 6.75 tons (loaded)
**Length:** 11.04m/36ft 3in
**Beam:** 4.6m/15ft 1in; 5.79m/19ft (skirt inflated)
**Draught (in rafting mode):** 0.52m/1ft 9in
**Armament:** Not usually armed
**Machinery:** 1 diesel engine
**Power:** 265kW/355bhp for 40 knots, or 25 knots in Sea State 3
**Fuel:** 0.25 ton oil
**Endurance:** 522km/300nm at 40 knots
**Protection:** None
**Complement:** 2
**Capacity:** 16 troops, or 2 tons equipment

LEFT: **Four of the later type CDIC, the "C" denoting *Chaland* (barge), were completed for the French Navy to serve with Foudre-class Landing Ship, Dock (LSD).**

# Landing Craft, Tank (EDIC/CDIC)

Until the commissioning of a French-designed class during the early 1960s, the French Navy operated LCT (4) built by the British in World War II. The new craft were of identical size to an LCT (4). The Ouragan-class LSDs, which were being constructed at the same time, were designed to carry two of the type.

Typically, the French have their own categorization, the craft being EDICs (*Engins de Débarqement d'Infanterie et de Chars*), i.e. craft for landing troops or tanks. Identified initially as EDIC 1-10, confusingly L9000 numbers were used in the series still carried by surviving British-built LCT (4).

Most EDIC vessels were flush-decked.

Masts, tetrapod or lattice were located adjacent to the funnel casing. The loading ramp folded in two sections for extra length and appeared to be assisted in operation by a set of light sheerlegs.

From the mid-1970s, the class was reduced by scrappings and sales abroad, the retirements heralding the construction of a new type, again of similar dimensions. Only four, however, were completed for the French Navy. Two in 1988, later taking the names FS *Rapière* and FS *Hallebarde*, were designed specifically to fit in the docking well of the Foudre-class LSD, then under construction. Of orthodox Landing Craft, Tank (EDIC/CDIC) layout, the new craft had a low superstructure and

folding mast. Although of similar size and function to the earlier type, all were termed CDIC, "C" representing Chaland (barge).

The two sister ships, completed first, were of modified layout, differing externally in a higher superstructure and a hydraulic crane forward. Later named FS *Sabre* and FS *Dague*, both were fitted for tropical service, and deployed to Tahiti and Djibouti respectively. Known perversely as EDIC II, or EDIC 700s, the type also attracted export orders from Senegal and Lebanon. *Rapière* was sold to Chile in 2011 (becoming *Canave*) and *Hallebarde* was put on reserve in 2014.

ABOVE: **An *Engin de Débarquement d'Infanterie et de Chars* (EDIC) could carry 350 tons of cargo. Here, in ideal conditions, the vessel is beached in a light swell.**

**Landing Craft, Tank (CDIC)**

**Displacement:** 750 tons (loaded)
**Length:** 59.4m/195ft (oa)
**Beam:** 11.9m/39ft
**Draught (beaching):** 1.1m/3ft 7in (forward); 1.76m/5ft 9in (aft)
**Armament:** 2 x 20mm guns (2x1)
**Machinery:** 2 diesel engines, 2 shafts
**Power:** 806kW/1,080bhp for 11 knots (maximum)
**Fuel:** 20 tons oil
**Endurance:** Provisions for 15 days, or 5,960km/3,250nm at 9 knots
**Protection:** Nominal
**Complement:** 18

LEFT: **CTM 1, the first of the type, was built from steel and entered service in 1965. On March 31, 1982, the vessel was scrapped after 17 years usage with the French Navy. CTM 29, _Nué Dho_, built from aluminium alloy, was delivered on June 23, 1988, and remains in service.**

# Landing Craft, Medium, CTM/LCM (8)

The general-purpose LCM (8) began to enter US service around 1949. Because the steel-built Mod. 1 weighed 56 tons unloaded, it was complemented by the 34-ton aluminium-alloy hulled Mod. 2, light enough to be carried aboard some AKAs.

For such an apparently simple craft, the LCM (8) caused considerable design problems. The 22.4m/73ft 6in length was quite critical to safe trim, the designed working load being that of a main battle tank of the time. To reduce resistance, the ramp was stowed at the unusually shallow angle

of 35 degrees to the horizontal. Further variants showed the difficulty of deciding between the economy and robustness of steel (Mods. 1, 3 and 5) and the lightness, greater expense and relative fragility of aluminium alloy (Mods. 2 and 4).

The French built 16 steel-hulled LCM (8) under licence during 1965 and 1967. Known as CTM (Chalands de Transport de Matériel), they were reportedly capable of carrying 90 tons. This corresponded to a full load of around 150 tons, whereas the US Navy rated Landing Craft, Medium, CTM/LCM (8) their craft, both steel and alloy, at around 60 tons, with full-load

figures of 116 and 121 tons respectively. A further identical 15 CTMs were built between 1982 and 1992, during which time the earlier craft were disposed of mainly by transfer to friendly states. Numbered CTM 17 to 31, many of the later production craft have since been given Vietnamese-themed names commemorating the French involvement in Indo-China.

The CTMs, although with limited remaining service life, are the preferred craft for the Mistral-class LH which, alternatively, can carry a single CDIC. No less than ten CTMs could be loaded on a Foudre class LSD. The docking well on the Mistral class was designed to carry two US-built LCACs and can only carry four CTMs.

ABOVE: **Designated _Chalands de Transport de Matériel_ (CTM), the type first entered service in 1965. CTM 21 _Guéréo_ is one of the second series built between 1982 and 1992.**

## Landing Craft, Medium, CTM/LCM (8)

**Displacement:** 150 tons (loaded)
**Length:** 23.4m/73ft 6in (oa)
**Beam:** 6.35m/20ft 10in
**Draught:** 1.25m/4ft 1in (beaching)
**Armament:** 2 x single 0.50in machine-guns can be fitted
**Machinery:** 2 diesel engines, 2 shafts
**Power:** 336kW/450bhp for 9.5 knots (maximum)
**Fuel:** 3.4 tons oil
**Endurance:** 736km/400nm at 8 knots
**Protection:** Nominal
**Complement:** 4
**Capacity:** 90 tons

ABOVE AND LEFT: **Ever more sophisticated, mines are increasingly required to be identified and destroyed manually. The Vulcain-class tenders were designed to support 12 clearance divers and two medical personnel.**

# Mine Countermeasures Divers' Tenders, Vulcain class

To create and maintain a mine-free route, it is necessary first to conduct a thorough survey, followed by the removal of all obstructions. A final survey then provides a datum condition, recorded by a combination of high-definition sonar backed by considerable computer capacity. All remaining features being thus accurately defined, it is a relatively simple task to keep the route open, with electronics immediately indicating any new obstructions on the seabed.

Before any major operation, such procedures would be followed only as far as practicality allowed. The operations

BELOW: **FS *Vulcain* has a clear afterdeck with a 5-ton capacity crane. The gap between the funnels suggests the location of the decompression chamber.**

are now conducted on a regular basis to guarantee safe routes for ballistic missile submarines needing to transit the relatively shallow continental shelf waters separating their base from the open sea. In addition to mines, active or passive, uninvestigated objects en route might also comprise devices to monitor ship movements and to record the radiated noise characteristics of a specific craft.

Clearance work is demanding, involving teams of divers or specialist Unmanned Underwater Vehicles (UUV) to investigate and, probably, remove each unknown object. Diving teams and their equipment are too space-consuming to be accommodated aboard a standard MCSO. The first vessels modified for the task were ex-US Navy MSCs.

In 1980, a thorough trial conversion was made of the French auxiliary vessel FS *Isard*. This defined the necessary accommodation required, including a decompression chamber, lifting gear, ROV, small craft and helicopter spot.

The requirements established the design for the four Vulcain-class ships ordered in 1984 and based on the hull of *Isard*. This features a short, raised forecastle and a long amidships block incorporating accommodation. A two-man decompression chamber, rated to a 150m/492ft depth, is carried. The clear afterdeck has a 5-ton SWL hydraulic crane, used for recovery work or handling small craft and ROV/AUVs.

## Mine Countermeasures Divers' Tenders, Vulcain class

**Displacement:** 409 tons (standard); 490 tons (loaded)
**Length:** 36.96m/121ft 4in (bp); 41.6m/136ft 6in (oa)
**Beam:** 7.5m/24ft 7in
**Draught:** 3.2m/10ft 6in
**Armament:** 1/2 x 0.50in machine-guns can be fitted
**Machinery:** 2 diesel engines, 2 shafts
**Power:** 1,641kW/2,200bhp for 13.5 knots (maximum)
**Fuel:** 90 tons oil
**Endurance:** 5,244km/2,850nm at 13.5 knots
**Protection:** Nominal
**Complement:** 15 plus 12 divers and 2 medical personnel

LEFT: **Working with a Eurocopter Panther, the dayshapes for a vessel with restricted manoeuvrability are carried on the mast of FS** *Antarès*. **Note the two sonar towfish stowed on the starboard side of the afterdeck, with two Oropesa floats to port.**

# Mine route survey craft, Antarès class

The three ships in this class complement the Vulcain-class diving tender in being the vessels used to survey proposed mine-free routes. For this role they are equipped with a comprehensive range of aids and, for the size of the vessel, a large crew.

Adequate working space was a design requisite, solved by the adoption of a trawler-style hull already used successfully for the Glycine-class navigational training vessel. The high-freeboard hull has a long forecastle and a low working deck aft, largely enclosed by high bulwarks. The large deckhouse incorporates a wheelhouse and navigation facilities.

The main electronics system is currently a DUBM-41B sidescan sonar, a high-frequency, high-definition, short-range set operating at 500 kHz. The towfish can be utlized at up to 10 knots and will scan up to 200m/656ft either side of the ship's track, in depths of up to 80m/262ft. Unusually, the towfish is stabilized using Oropesa-type floats more often associated with "traditional" minesweeping. The vessels are also fitted for the very similar task of streaming a sweep wire to define water depth over large obstructions. The stern carries two light cranes, floats and sweep gear, standard fitments on a minehunter.

Search results are input to a specialized Syledis route-recording system, which produces the baseline route condition against which all subsequent scans are compared. The ships have inherited the deep draught and relatively large-diameter propeller of the trawler. A bow thruster is fitted, but such a device is primarily an aid to low-speed manoeuvring, having little effect when a ship has significant forward speed. The ships are also used for offshore patrol.

## Mine route survey craft, Antarès class

**Displacement:** 295 tons (standard); 340 tons (loaded)
**Length:** 28.3m/92ft 9in (oa)
**Beam:** 7.7m/25ft 3in
**Draught:** 3.8m/12ft 6in (maximum)
**Armament:** 1 x 0.50in machine-gun
**Machinery:** 1 diesel engine, single shaft
**Power:** 597kW/800bhp for 10 knots
**Fuel:** 50 tons oil
**Endurance:** 6,624km/3,600nm at 10 knots
**Protection:** None
**Complement:** 24

RIGHT: **The hull of the FS** *Altair* **shows a distinctive trawler origin. The same trawler-style hull was successfully used on the Glycine-class navigational training ships.**

ABOVE: A Lida-class inshore minesweeper, known to the Russian Navy as the Sapfir class. The glass-reinforced plastic (GRP) hull has a slightly arched appearance aft. The usual degaussing girdle is not fitted.

# Inshore Minesweepers (IMS), Yevgenya/Lida class

Although expert in mine warfare, the Russian Navy is vulnerable, and has produced many types of countermeasures vessel for both defensive and offensive operations.

With Inshore Minesweepers (IMS), the then Soviet Union followed the West in adopting glass-reinforced plastic (GRP) as a non-magnetic and easily repairable building material. The first product of a new facility at Kolpino, near Leningrad, was a series of some 90 Korund-class minehunters, built between 1969 and 1985, and known in the West as Yevgenya.

The hull had a pleasing sheerline, with a low-forward bulwark to improve dryness. A single-block superstructure had accommodation for the entire crew. The relatively spacious afterdeck allowed deployment of sweep gear for all usual types of mine. Several crew members were clearance divers, and used follow-up markers dropped by a television-guided ROV.

Designated as Roadstead Minesweepers, the Yevgenya class was equipped with a small high-frequency dipping sonar for the detection of hostile Unmanned Underwater Vehicles (UUV). Explosive charges were carried to attack such types.

All the Yevgenya class were retired by 2005, having been superseded by the Sapfir type (codenamed Lida).

Similar in layout and appearance to the earlier craft, the Lida class are, nonetheless, almost 9m/29ft longer and proportionately wider. The earlier pole mast was replaced by a tripod type, but the major external difference is the helmet-type mounting for a 30mm Gatling-type gun in place of the original twin 25mm weapon mount.

On-board equipment is largely updated versions of those on the Yevgenya class, with the addition of removable rails for inshore minelaying. Intended mainly for export, limited production appears to have occurred since 1996.

ABOVE: This Sapfir class (codenamed Lida) is fitted with the normal degaussing girdle around the deck edge. The common practice of painting the after hull to disguise exhaust stains has been used.

### Inshore Minesweepers (IMS), Lida class

**Displacement:** 135 tons (loaded)
**Length:** 31.45m/103ft 1in (oa)
**Beam:** 6.5m/18ft 7in
**Draught:** 1.58m/5ft 2in
**Armament:** 1 x 30mm Gatling-type gun, shoulder-launched SAMs, mines
**Machinery:** 3 diesel engines, 3 shafts
**Power:** 671kW/900bhp for 12.5 knots
**Fuel:** Not known
**Endurance:** 736km/400nm at 10 knots
**Protection:** Nominal
**Complement:** 14

# Landing Craft, Air Cushion (LCAC)

The Russian equivalent to Marines are the Naval Infantry. During World War II, the force were shown to be adept at using the sea for outflanking movements or conducting numerous raids. Post-war, the amphibious element of the Soviet Navy was, for long, somewhat neglected, as the emphasis was placed on defensive measures. This was mainly to counter the threat of major landings by the West's powerful amphibious fleets covered by battle-tested carrier and surface support groups. Hundreds of missile-armed minor warships of numerous classes were built over the years, the aim being to swamp the defences of an amphibious attack with sheer numbers. Most of these types had conventional planing or semi-planing hulls, but hydrofoils were also used. The more recent is the Dergach, a rigid sidewall surface effect vessel.

Air cushion craft go back rather further in the amphibious force, which saw much improved funding from the late 1960s. Innovation produced three major similar designs during the 1970s: the Gus, Aist and Lebed. Since then, however, the only significant new design has been the Zubr class (NATO codename Pomornik) of the early 1990s.

Similar to an enlarged British-built SRN6, the 27-ton (loaded) Gus is capable of transporting 24 equipped troops at around 50 knots, and equates

to a personnel-only assault landing craft. A canopy may or may not be fitted over the personnel section. In having to uses ladders to disembark, troops are vulnerable. Around 32 Gus types were reportedly built between 1969 and 1976. Any craft remaining in service are most likely to be used in the training role.

The Aist class, of which 18 are believed to have entered service between 1970 and 1985, is similar to the British-built BH7, but again larger. The class

ABOVE: **The Zubr class (NATO reporting name Pomornik) is a joint Russian and Ukranian design, and is the largest LCAC in operational use.**

was tested extensively for use in mine countermeasures, and proved not only to have an almost undectable signature but also to be relatively immune to mine explosion. Large, the type is fitted with a ramp at each end and has a 74-ton cargo capacity. Alternatively, around 220 troops can be

ABOVE: **The Zubr class is powered by five Kuznetsov MT-70 gas-turbine engines, two for lift and three for propulsion. The type has been in service with the navies of Russia, Ukraine and Greece.**

LEFT: **In the same class as a US Navy LCAC, the Lebed type entered service in 1975. The 20 built were powered by MT-70 gas-turbine engines for lift and to drive the two four-bladed variable-pitch propellors. By 2005, only three remained in service with the Russian Navy.**

transported for over 322km/200 miles at 40 knots. A small number of the Aist class are belived to remain operational.

A Lebed class, dating from 1982 to 1985, is half the size of an Aist class and has a bow ramp only. More compact in appearance, four pylon-mounted, open airscrews have been changed to two quieter ducted units. Although capable of transporting 35 tons of cargo or 120 troops at 45 knots, all of the class have been retired.

At more than 550 tons loaded, the Zubr class is by far the largest air

cushion assault craft in the Russian inventory, and is currently the world's largest hovercraft. Some ten examples remain in service with Russia, Greece and China's PLAN.

The Zubr class has a flat-topped, rectangular-section central hull with a ramp at each end. This "cargo compartment" is bordered by two low side , which form the tops of the wing compartments. The very spacious upper surfaces appear under-used due to limiting weight restrictions. The solid, two-level bridge structure supports the

fire directors for two 30mm Gatling-type guns. Near the bow, two multi-rail rocket barrage launchers are mounted. The major feature on the Zubr, however, is the row of three ducted airscrews which produce directional thrust for steering, rather than conventional rudders.

None of the other current Russian designs appear to have progressed beyond the experimental stage, being deemed unsuitable for series production. From the design aspect, the capacious box-shaped hulls offer little inherent stiffness and are very liable to vibration problems. Weight was critical, requiring the use of aluminium alloy hull components.

ABOVE: **Russian Naval Infantry coming ashore from a Zubr-class LCAC during an exercise on the Baltic coast.**
BELOW: **With ramps forward and aft, the Aist class superficially resembles the earlier British-built BH7.**

## Landing Craft, Air Cushion (LCAC), Zubr class

**Displacement:** 340 tons (light); 550 tons (loaded)
**Length:** 57.3m/187ft 10in (oa)
**Width:** 25.6m/83ft 11in
**Draught:** N/A
**Armament:** 2 x quadruple SA-N-8 ("Gremlin") SAM launchers, 2 x 30mm Gatling-type guns, 2 x 22-round barrage rocket launchers
**Machinery:** 5 gas turbines; 2 for lift fans, 3 for propulsion
**Power:** 45,133kW/60,500hp for 63 knots (maximum); 37,300kW/50,000hp for 55 knots (sustained)
**Fuel:** 56 tons kerosene
**Endurance:** 552km/300nm at 55 knots (loaded)
**Protection:** Nominal    **Complement:** 31
**Capacity:** Up to 36 troops, or 10 LVTs, or 3 main battle tanks

# Landing Craft, Medium (LCM), Ondatra/Serna class

ABOVE: Twenty-nine Ondatra-class LCMs are known to have been built from 1979, to serve with Ivan Rogov-class LSDs.

Around 80 T-4-type LCMs were built between 1968 and 1974. Pre-dating LSDs in the then Soviet fleet, their dimensions of 20.4 x 5.4m/66ft 10in x 17ft 8in were based on lifting 50 tons. The size was somewhat less than that of the LCM (8) in US Navy service, which could carry 60 tons on 22.43 x 6.43m/ 73ft 6in x 21ft 1in. Reportedly, the T-4 could make 10 knots in light condition with an installed power of only 300bhp. This speed is unattainable by an LCM (8) with 1,080bhp.

The T-4s were starkly rectangular, lacking sheer or flare, but the Ondatra class that superseded the T-4 between 1979 and 1991 has a slight forward sheer, emphasized by the deeper coamings, which also acts as an upper support for the longer ramp. Dimensions of the T-4 allow six to be carried in the docking well of an Ivan Rogov class vessel.

After long-term evaluation, the Serna-type fast LCM, a private venture craft available on the open market, entered Russian Navy service from 1994. With a 50-ton load capacity, this 25.65m/84ft craft has a semi-planing, wave-piercing hull the underside of which is an air cavity, a principle similar to that which the US military proposed for the fast LCU 1682 class, which was cancelled in 2006. The contained air cushion may provide some upthrust, but is primarily to reduce suction between hull and water, permitting the craft to plane with relatively low engine power. Once on the plane, wave-making resistance drops considerably, while the significant decrease in draught (some 14 percent) reduces wetted area and lowers skin resistance.

Also of light alloy construction, the craft is claimed to be able to make 30 knots with only 2,462kW/3,300bhp of engine power. Speed is emphasized by the raked-back styling, the hull sides being full depth and lacking the usual narrow side decks outside a deep coaming.

ABOVE: The Serna class fast LCM, following Russian Navy evaluation, entered service from 1994. The vessel, which was developed as a private venture, is capable of 30 knots when loaded.

---

### Landing Craft, Medium (LCM), Ondatra class

**Displacement:** 107 tons (loaded)
**Length:** 24.5m/80ft 4in (oa)
**Beam:** 6m/19ft 8in
**Draught:** 1.55m/5ft 1in
**Armament:** None
**Machinery:** 2 diesel engines, 2 shafts
**Power:** 448kW/600bhp at 11 knots
**Fuel:** Not known
**Endurance:** 505km/275mm at 10 knots
**Protection:** Nominal
**Complement:** 5
**Capacity:** 1 x 40-ton vehicle, or 50 tons distributed cargo

ABOVE: **The 10m Shohatsu type could accommodate 35 troops.** LEFT: **Attrition rates in small assault craft were always high. A stranded steel-built 14m Daihatsu shows the main features. Note the characteristic continuous sheerline.**

# Landing Craft, Tank (LCT), Daihatsu types

Extended operations in China during the 1930s saw the Imperial Japanese Army identify the need for a craft capable of landing personnel, artillery and vehicles "over the beach". Certainly uninfluenced by early British trials in this direction, the Daihatsu was produced to serve as the landing craft aboard the *Shinshu Maru*. Such craft appeared subsequently aboard a range of Japanese merchant vessels which had been converted to transport and attack cargo ships.

"Daihatsu" refers incorrectly but conveniently to a series of craft. Built in vast numbers, most were 14m and 17m craft. With the shortage of steel from 1944, the wooden 15m craft was built. More rarely 10m and 13m craft were encountered.

The design owed much to traditional Japanese working craft, and was completely open except for a protective shield in front of the helmsman. The hull had a continuous sheerline, with a flat cargo/vehicle deck, a short forward ramp and rounded stern. Usually loaded alongside larger vessels, the sides were protected by heavy rubbing strakes. The Daihatsu type was powered by a variety of engines and proved to be the lifeline of Japanese island garrisons, particularly in the bitterly disputed Solomons.

Only the 14m and 17m vessels can really be considered LCTs. The Pacific theatre was ill-suited to tank warfare, the Japanese using mainly the manoeuvrable Type 95 KE-GO light tank, which was easily transported on the 14m craft. With the arrival of the US-built Sherman, the Type 97 CHI-HA became more common. A medium tank, it was transportable only on a 17m Daihatsu.

Also worth mentioning was the so-named Umpoto-powered pontoon, a three-sectioned raft supported on two longitudinal submerged metal buoyancy tanks fitted with de-rated torpedo motors. The 21 x 4m/70 x 14ft craft carried 15 tons of cargo, was virtually silent and had a low silhouette.

ABOVE: **So uncoordinated were Allied forces opposing them that the Japanese were able to rapidly overrun much of the Far East. Recapturing the taken land and islands would take a long time.**

## Landing Craft, Tank (LCT), Daihatsu types ●

| | Displacement (light) tons | Length (oa) | Beam | Draught (mean) | Speed (knots) |
|---|---|---|---|---|---|
| 10m type | 6.5 | 10.6m/34ft 9in | 2.44m/8ft | 0.58m/1ft 11in | 7.5 |
| 13m type | 16 | 13m/42ft 8in | 2.9m/9ft 6in | 0.79m/2ft 7in | 8 |
| 14m type | 21/22 | 14.57m/47ft 10in | 3.36m/11ft | 0.76m/2ft 6in | 7.5–8.5 |
| 15m type | 17.5 | 15m/49ft 2in | 3.63m/11ft 10in | 0.53m/1ft 9in | 8 |
| 17m type | 33/38 | 17.61m/57ft 9in | 3.71m/21ft 2in | 1m/3ft 3in | 8–10 |

# Mine Countermeasures Drones and Control Ship

Because of the increasing intelligence and lethality of modern mines, techniques for surveying by Autonomous Underwater Vehicles (AUV) and investigation/demolition by Remotely Controlled Vehicles (ROV) are evolving continuously. Swept channels, or areas designated for search, can be marked inconspicuously with transponders laid by swimmers. Such devices transmit only when signalled, and will be used only when simpler means do not suit the nature of the operation. By "simpler means" it would usually imply visual markers, i.e. moored buoys. Most visual among these is the simple Dan buoy, as used on fishing craft over the centuries.

In the suspected presence of mines, Dan buoy-laying is as hazardous as any activity and, during the early 1980s, the Swedish Navy developed the Self-propelled Acoustic, Magnetic (SAM) craft to both sweep and mark clear channels under remote control. Japan acquired six SAMs, which are used in pairs from the converted Hatsushima-class minehunters *Kamishima* (MCL 724) and *Himeshima* (MCL 725). In calm conditions at least, paired drones are transported to the area of operation by being secured alongside the parent ship, rather than being towed.

The drones comprise a rectangular, non-magnetic platform which is supported clear of the surface by two longitudinal, cylindrical buoyancy tanks. The tanks are inflated and, being flexible, are virtually immune to mine explosions. The shock wave of an explosion will expend much of its energy by momentarily deforming the cylinders, little being transmitted to the platform.

TOP AND ABOVE: **Designed and built in Sweden, these Self-propelled Acoustic, Magnetic (SAM) drones are in service with the Japanese Navy.**

A rectangular cabin on the raft houses acoustic equipment, power generators and the diesel engine which drives the single Schottel azimuth unit. The shrouded propeller may be swivelled through almost 360 degrees.

Thirteen SAM units have been operated by four navies around the world and this experience has led to the improved SAM 3, a third generation USV.

ABOVE: **A Hatsushima-class minehunter operating as control ship for SAM drones, which are used in pairs to sweep and clear channels.**

## Mine Countermeasures Drones and Control Ship

**Displacement:** 20 tons (loaded)
**Length:** 18m/59ft 1in (oa)
**Beam:** 6.1m/20ft
**Draught:** 0.7m/2ft 3in; propeller extends to 1.6m/5ft 3in
**Armament:** None
**Machinery:** 1 diesel engine driving Schottel azimuth thruster
**Power:** 157kW/210bhp for 8 knots
**Fuel:** Not known
**Endurance:** 607km/330nm at 7 knots
**Protection:** None
**Complement:** None

# Landing Craft, Utility (LCU), Yura and 1-go class

Landing Craft, Utility (LCU) have replaced the older Landing Craft, Tank (LCT), the different designation reflecting greater flexibility. War-designed craft are intended for cheap and rapid series production, where parameters hold higher priority than hydrodynamic efficiency. Peacetime standards, however, allow for hulls of improved shape, but at the expense of more components requiring complex curvature. This, coupled with higher power, enables current Japanese LCUs to make 12 knots. This may not appear a very impressive increase over the 10–10.5 knots of the original LCTs but, for this type of hull, it represents considerable improvement.

The JMSDF currently operates just three LCUs out of four built. The first

two, ambitiously labelled Landing Ship, Utility (LSU), also took landing ships' 4,000-series numbers. Of a late 1970s design, they were the *Yura* (4171) and *Noto* (4172). Despite being classed as "ships" (as opposed to "craft"), both featured an open vehicle deck and are single-ended. The usual high forecastle supports the ramp and two clamshell-type outer doors. Although there is no upper deck, accommodation is provided for 70 troops. This does necessitate a relatively large superstructure. The Osumi class LSDs, designed to carry two LCACs, thus cannot accept a Yura-type LCU, which is some 4m/13ft longer in total, and has too much height.

The new 1-go class, designated LCU 2001 and LCU 2002, were built between 1988 and 1992, and are more compact

ABOVE: **LCU 2002, a 1-go class of the JMSDF about to land during an earthquake relief exercise at Yokosuka on September 1, 2008. In the background is USS *Essex* (LHD-2), which was also involved in the same exercise.**

than the Yura class vessel. Some 6m/20ft shorter overall, the type has no forecastle, the ramp being stowed at a much shallower angle and without outer doors. A permanent light full-width gantry is used when operating the ramp. Without accommodation for troops, the superstructure on the vessel is one level lower. Air draught is reduced further by folding masts.

## Landing Craft, Utility (LCU), 1-go class

**Displacement:** 420 tons
**Length:** 52m/170ft 8in (oa)
**Beam:** 8.7m/28ft 6in
**Draught:** 1.6m/5ft 3in (aft, beaching)
**Armament:** 1 x 20mm Gatling-type gun
**Machinery:** 2 diesel engines, 2 shafts
**Power:** 2,238kW/3,000bhp for 12 knots
**Fuel:** Not known
**Endurance:** Not known
**Protection:** Nominal
**Complement:** 28

ABOVE: **The Japanese Maritime Self-Defence Force JS *Yura* (4171), the first to be built. Note that the clamshell-type bow doors are open and the landing ramp lowered.**

# Siebel Ferries and F-lighters (MFP)

Until the surprise demand to mount the eventually aborted Operation "Sealion", the *Wehrmacht* had been concerned only with water crossings no larger than those of the major European rivers. Assault crossings were spearheaded in *Sturmboote* (assault boats), propelled by an outboard motor and transported by road. On the assumption that bridges would be either destroyed or outflanked, powered pontoons were developed to follow up with vehicles and heavy equipment. These broke down into road-transportable modules, and were assembled on site.

The "Sealion" exercise had graphically demonstrated the need for specialist craft if larger-scale operations were ever to be considered. If the Germans had any knowledge of British experiments with assault landing craft, it is not obvious by their response, which was highly individual. As a matter of some urgency, two types of craft were produced, both of which were subject to much variation.

The first, the Siebel Ferry, was credited to Wilhelm Siebel, a future aircraft designer who, at that time, served as a major in the *Luftwaffe* reserve. Like most good ideas, his

ABOVE: **Note the very shallow vehicle deck on the MFP, the upswept sheerline and the lack of means by which troops could leave the upper deck.**
BELOW: **A damaged and disarmed F-lighter. The long arch of the coamings stiffened the shallow hull with minimum addition to weight. The bow ramp is in the closed position.**

was simple, using two sets of existing pontoons in parallel, and bridging both with a flat vehicle deck to form a large and very stable catamaran. Simplicity was everything, and the ramps were removable, to be attached by man-power for loading and discharge, a weak point in the face of an opposed landing. A wide ramp gave forward access for larger vehicles. Smaller vehicles could pass either side of the aft-located superstructure to use quarter ramps. The superstructure was no more than a protected wheelhouse flanked by platforms, usually for quadruple 20mm FlaK mountings.

Called a *Heeres-Transport-Fähre*, the Siebel Ferry could lift around 230 tons. When assembled, the vessel measured 32.3m x 14.7m/106ft x 48ft. The ungainly shaped vessel could travel at a creditable 10 knots, powered by four 620hp diesel engines. Readily transportable, the Siebel Ferry was deployed on coastal and inland waters anywhere from Lake Ladoga, near St. Petersburg, to the Caspian Sea. Defensive firepower, augmented by that of vehicles and artillery carried on deck, could be formidable.

The name *Marinefahrprähme* (MFP) indicated the role of a seagoing lighter, but the Allied forces that regularly encountered the type referred to them

simply as "F", or "FlaK" Lighters. The type resembled an LCT, but with an enclosed vehicle deck and unobstructed side decks fitted with minelaying rails. The hull was, of course, shallow and, to achieve the required headroom on the vehicle deck, high coamings to the hull were necessary. The line of these sloped down at the forward end, meeting at the bows with the upswept forward sheer of the hull. The overall effect was to give the vessel a strange humped profile. The square bows supported protective doors and a short ramp that, when in use, usually required an extension. During load and discharge of vehicles, the forward sections of deck roof needed to be removed.

The control position was a small three-level, open-bridge tower. As the type was used more in combat situations, the bridge structure became flanked with various arrangements of platform to support whatever armament was available. Typically a single 8.8cm (the much-respected "88") would be mounted, and also one 3.7cm high-angle gun and twin or quadruple 2cm FlaK mountings.

Where the early craft (hull numbers to 626) had a mean draught of only 1.8m/5ft 10in, which made them virtually immune to torpedo attack, additions in

ABOVE: **Simply a deck overlaying two sets of rectangular pontoon hulls, the Siebel Ferry was treated with respect by Allied light forces owing to the firepower frequently transported. This example has an 8.8cm FlaK at each corner.**

armament and 25mm/1in protective plate gradually increased the draught to 2.7m/8ft 11in. Standard MFPs were 49.8 x 6.6m/163ft 6in x 21ft 8in, and displaced some 200 tons. There were shorter and beamier variants, the *Marinenachschubleichter* (MNL) "supply lighter" of 280 tons and, smaller but wider again, the purpose-built *Marineartillerieleichter* (MAL). The latter was intended as an escort for the MFP which were, unlike Siebel Ferries, unable to rely on the armament of vehicles carried on the deck.

| MAL |  |
|---|---|

**Displacement:** 180 tons (loaded)
**Length:** 35.5m/116ft 6in (oa)
**Beam:** 8.6m/28ft 3in
**Draught:** 1.80m/5ft 10in
**Armament:** 2 x 7.5cm Army guns (2x1), 6 x 2cm guns (1x2/4x1), 1 x 8.6cm mortar
**Machinery:** 2 diesel engines, 2 shafts
**Power:** 403kW/540bhp for 8 knots
**Fuel:** 4.2 tons oil
**Endurance:** About 920km/500nm at 6.5 knots
**Protection:** 25mm/1in
**Complement:** 28

ABOVE: **During the run-up to Operation "Sealion", nearly 1,300 barges were collected in Channel ports, over 80 being visible in this group alone.**
LEFT: **At the top of the picture it can be seen that the bows of these barges have been removed and replaced by ramps.**

# Inland Waterway Barges

Operation *Seelöwe* (Sealion), the projected German invasion of Britain in 1940, was ordered at short notice and without specialist assault craft. In order to land 16 divisions over three days, it was thought that 1,277 inland waterway barges would be needed. Towage was common on European waterways, so many of these were unpowered, requiring a total of 471 tugs to be requisitioned.

A typical Rhein *Schleppkahn* (literally "towbarge") was little different to the powered craft so familiar today. When loaded, the sidedecks were just above the water, with the hatch cover supported on high coamings. Forward freeboard was low, there being no forecastle. Ground tackle was primitive and usually hand-powered. Most carried stern anchors,

which would have been used to prevent broaching in surf. The protruding barn-door-type rudder was highly vulnerable.

Never intended to operate far from a river bank, few safety features were incorporated. To maximize carrying capacity, the double bottomed hull was very shallow. Depth of hull at the sides was some 3m/10ft, while headroom under hatches at centreline was around 4.5m/15ft. High-sided transport would have required open hatches.

The hull being long and shallow, designed for the distributed load of a bulk cargo, would have had to be loaded carefully. In the absence of ballast capacity, this would have been exacerbated by the need to achieve a low forward-beaching draught.

Modification to the vessels was extremely basic, the bows being cut away to the width of the coamings and to a level just above the load waterline. The resulting gap was filled by a flap which was lowered to permit a ramp to be manually run out (under fire).

ABOVE RIGHT: **Unsuitably clad German troops manhandling a 75mm field gun into a converted barge that lacks even basics such as a winch.**
LEFT: **Fast assault craft for river crossings made good propaganda material. The helmsmen and the early outboard motor appear vulnerable.**

| Inland Waterway Barges |  |
|---|---|

**Displacement:** 3,630 tons (loaded); 3,000 tons (cargo deadweight, maximum)
**Length:** 105m/344ft 8in (oa)
**Beam:** 13m/42ft 8in
**Draught:** 3m/9ft 10in
**Armament:** None
**Machinery:** None
**Power:** N/A
**Fuel:** N/A
**Endurance:** N/A
**Protection:** None
**Complement:** 3–4

ABOVE: **Type 393** *Nixe* **at anchor with others of the class. The Ariadne class were named after cruisers that had served with the German Imperial Navy (1871–1919).**

LEFT: *Perseus* **of the Type 340/341 group has a different style of bridge structure.**

# Inshore Minesweepers (IMS), Types 340 and 394

With origins going back to the 1920s, the R-boat (*Raumboot*) was developed rapidly during World War II. The vessel had excellent seakeeping qualities and served variously as minesweeper, minelayer, convoy escort or light gunboat. Variants ranged from 26–41m/85–136ft in length, with a displacement of 60–175 tons. The design of the largest, the so-called "GR" type, took the multi-purpose ethic just too far, being criticized as being "too costly for minesweeping, too slow for an MTB, too

lightly armed for an MGB of her size, and too fast for a pure convoy vessel". Restricted by what could be built in the early post-war era, however, the German Navy contracted the original shipyard, Abeking & Rasmussen, to produce a coastal and inshore minesweeper design that could be used in other roles with minimum alteration.

Differing only in the type of propulsion, the design of the larger 340 and 341 types was clearly based on the R-boat. Abeking & Rasmussen built 21 of the total of 28

"patrol minesweepers" between 1959 and 1963. Built of wood, the type had similar operational capabilities to the R-boat but was slower and, at 47.5m/156ft overall, somewhat larger. Unusually, the vessel was fitted with two cycloidal propellers.

More truly inshore minesweepers were the 18, again very similar, Type 393 and 394, between 1961 and 1968. These, also constructed of wood, were built by Krögerwerft of Rendsburg. The hulls, with a pronounced chine and near full-length rubbing strake, again echoed their origin. The relatively large superstructures were similar to those on the defensively orientated craft which, as IMSs, were also deployed as patrol boats. All the crew could thus be more safely accommodated above the upper deck when engaged in mine clearance.

Abeking & Rasmussen completed a smaller version in 1966. It was intended as the first ship for a series of 20 which was, however, cancelled.

ABOVE: *Gemma* **was fitted for minesweeping rather than as a patrol craft. The T-shaped davit for handling Oropesa-type floats was very distinctive.**

LEFT: **The Type 340's R-boat origins are clearly visible here. This is** *Jupiter*, **fitted out as a fast minesweeper.**

## Inshore Minesweeper (IMS), Type 394

**Displacement:** 238 tons (standard); 246 tons (loaded)
**Length:** 38.01m/124ft 9in (oa)
**Beam:** 8.03m/26ft 4in
**Draught:** 2.1m/6ft 11in
**Armament:** 1 x 40mm gun
**Machinery:** 2 diesel engines, 2 shafts
**Power:** 1,492kW/2,000bhp for 14.5 knots
**Fuel:** 30 tons oil
**Endurance:** 1,196km/650nm at 14 knots
**Protection:** Nominal
**Complement:** 24

# Landing Craft, Medium/Mechanized (LCM), Yuqing/Yuchai and Yunan class

These useful craft have been produced in very large numbers, however in the absence of LPD-type ships for transportation in a pre-loaded condition, all appear not to have been used for conventional amphibious warfare but rather for the day-to-day policing and control of a nation with a long coastline and vast internal river system. The nation's coastal waters are uniformly shallow, while those inland waterways not yet canalized are subject to great seasonal fluctuations in depth.

For all practical purposes, the Yuqing class (1960s) and the improved Yuchai type (1980s) are identical and a number are believed to remain in service. The design is reportedly based on that of the Soviet-built T4, with the same beam but with length increased by 44m/14ft 6in. As the cargo deck is an identical 9.5 x 3.9m/31ft 2in x 12ft 10in, the extra length is in the larger two-level accommodation

ABOVE: **A total of some 250 of the Type 067 Yunan class LCMs were built by the early 1990s. Since then, many have been withdrawn from service and placed in reserve by the People's Liberation Army.**

superstructure, which accommodates more than 20 crew and vehicle personnel.

Either type is designed to carry a medium tank, the vehicle deck being accessed via a bow ramp. Unusually, the vehicle deck is covered, with flat roller-type hatch covers that stack at the rear during loading, or to accommodate high vehicles. The coamings are proportionately lower than on a T4,

LEFT: **A Type 068 Yuqing-class LCM at a naval base in China.** BELOW: **Marines of the People's Liberation Army embarking on a Type 068 Yuqing LCM during an amphibious landing exercise.**

but headroom has been maintained internally through the higher freeboard of the hull.

Built in parallel with these classes for more than two decades, was the somewhat larger Yunan type, of which production ceased only in the early 1990s. Of an estimated 280 built, the great majority are surplus to requirements and maintained in reserve. With an extra 2.7m/9ft of length overall, the vehicle deck is considerably increased to 15 x 4m/49ft 3in x 13ft 1in. This results in a smaller accommodation superstructure carried a little further aft.

## Landing Craft, Medium/ Mechanized (LCM), Yunan class

**Displacement:** 133 tons (loaded)
**Length:** 27.50m /90ft 3in (oa)
**Beam:** 5.4m/17ft 9in
**Draught:** 1.4m/4ft 7in (seagoing)
**Armament:** 2/4 x 14.5mm machine-guns  (1/2x2)
**Machinery:** 2 diesel engines, 3 shafts
**Power:** 448kW/600bhp for 10.5 knots
**Fuel:** Not known
**Endurance:** 920km/500nm at 10 knots
**Protection:** Nominal
**Complement:** 6
**Capacity:** 1 heavy tank, or 46 tons distributed cargo

# Coastal Minesweepers and Drones (MSC and MSD), Wosao and Futi class

TOP: **The Wosao class was a Chinese-built replacement for the Sasha class.** ABOVE: **Based on Western practice, the Wonzang class is the latest Coastal Minesweeper (MSC) of the People's Liberation Army (Navy).**

The Chinese Navy does not operate Inshore Minesweepers (IMS) for shallow-water countermeaures, preferring to deploy larger Coastal Minesweepers (MSC), standing off and controlling drone craft. Despite a great tradition of small-craft construction, Chinese-built MSCs are not wooden-built, surprisingly. Western practice, adopted by the then Soviet Union, favoured wooden MSCs with high forecastles and low working decks aft (typified by the British-built Ton class and Soviet-built Sonya class). As a model, however, the Chinese Navy preferred the 45.1m/148ft steel-built Sasha, a design dating from the mid-1950s and already being phased out in the 1980s when the

Wosao class entered service.

The Wosao I class is flush-decked, with sheer at either end but what appears to be inadequate freeboard. Unusually, from the survivability aspect, there is a row of large open scuttles, around 1m/3.3ft above the normal waterline. The type lacks the 57mm gun as mounted on the Sasha class. There is no funnel, this being replaced by a large compact superstructure. A larger version of the class was dubbed Wosao II by NATO.

The clear afterdeck is fitted for sweeping the common range of mines. Surveying to establish clear routes involves the ship deploying boom-mounted towfish, which carry side-scan sonar, and this increasingly hazardous

practice led to the development of purpose-designed drone craft. Details of these, known as the Futi class, are uncertain but, at 21m/61ft overall, the type is smaller than a German-built Troika and larger than a Swedish-built SAM. The 47-ton displacement, however, suggests a hull of orthodox shape. Fabricated in GRP, the type can, like the Troika, be manually controlled, but they are intended to be remotely operated from a distance of around 4.8km/3 miles. On passage, the Futi class is powered by two diesel engines but, when minesweeping, electric power is used.

ABOVE: **The Soviet-built Sasha class minesweeper was constructed on a steel hull.** LEFT: **Seen on the left are Futi Type 312 drones in service with the Pakistani Navy. The type can be manually or remotely controlled from a command vessel.**

## Coastal Minesweeper (MSC), Wosao class

**Displacement:** 310 tons (loaded)
**Length:** 44.8m/147ft (oa)
**Beam:** 6.2m/20ft 4in
**Draught:** 2.27m/7ft 6in
**Armament:** 4 x 25mm guns (2x2)
**Machinery:** 2 diesel engines, 2 shafts
**Power:** 1,492kW/2,000bhp for 15.5 knots
**Fuel:** Not known
**Endurance:** 920km/500nm at 13 knots
**Protection:** Nominal
**Complement:** Not known

# Landing Platform, Dock (LPD), Type 071

In 2007, China completed an LPD-type vessel with an estimated 25,000-ton fully loaded displacement, making it significantly larger than the Dutch MV *Rotterdam* and its derivatives.

The practice is to size docking wells to suit multiple stowage of large air cushion craft or LCUs. Existing craft in these categories appeared to be unsuitable. Chinese-built LCAC-type craft were tried but, presumably unsatisfactory, were

quickly scrapped. The largest deployable air cushion craft at the time, the so-called Payi type, was tailored to LSTs and had a capacity of just 10 troops. Eight Russian-built LCACs, classified LCUA, were acquired but had four times the footprint of US forces equivalent, in addition to having too great an air draught to be LPD-transportable.

Existing LCUs were also unsuitable. The category can vary widely, for instance the standard US Navy LCU 1610 class is around 41m/135ft in length, and the British LCU (10) is only 30m/98ft. The *Yuling*, a design dating to the 1970s,

ABOVE LEFT: **A Type 071 LPD still at the fitting out stage, with the stern gate lowered and opening to the cavernous interior. It was uncertain as to what type of LCAC or LCU would be embarked.** ABOVE: **Conforming to what has become a near-standard international pattern, the Type 071 resisted a Chinese trend to over-arm their warships. The transition from wide forecastle deck to narrow waterline results in an interesting knuckle line.**

however, was over 56.5m/185ft long.

The form of this Type 071 intrigued Western analysts for some time as they tried to determine its performance and all-round capabilities. Eight were ultimately delivered for PLAN service and one for the Thai Navy.

BELOW: **This helicopter deck appears to have temporary markings. The small crane does not appear to have a hatch connection to the docking well.**

## Landing Platform, Dock (LPD), Type 071

**Displacement:** 20,800 tons (estimated)
**Length:** 210m/680ft (oa)
**Beam:** 26.5m/86ft
**Draught:** 7m/23ft
**Armament:** 1 x 76mm DP gun,
    4 x 30mm CIWS,
    4 x 120mm rocket launchers
**Speed:** 20 knots
**Capacity:** 500 troops, 15 EFV, 2 LCAC
    (estimated)
**Aircraft:** 2–4 helicopters
**Complement:** Not known

# Inshore Minesweepers (IMS), Bay class

Coastal, as opposed to ocean, minesweeping was not specifically addressed by the Royal Australian Navy (RAN) until the mid-1950s, when a projected domestically built class of ships was rejected in favour of

acquiring six British-built Ton-class vessels. Purchased in 1961, these served through to the 1980s and were replaced only at the turn of the century by six Italian licence-built Gaeta class, significantly larger vessels.

ABOVE AND BELOW: **The high superstructure of the Bay class results from all power generation and accommodation being located topside. Catamarans require careful hydrodynamic design to avoid interaction between the hulls. A retractable sonar is mounted in the port hull. A hydraulic crane is mounted aft to handle towfish.**

Inshore mine countermeasures, essential to any intervention warfare, were addressed in 1980. Two prototype craft, to be followed by a class of six, were ordered. The type selected was a catamaran which, for the size of the craft, gave the largest useful upper deck working area.

Known as the Bay class, the first two (HMAS *Rushcutter* and HMAS *Shoalwater*) were constructed of glass-reinforced plastic (GRP), an expensive choice. The further six vessels were cancelled.

The superstructure included a diesel generator compartment, supplying power to the propulsion motors located in each hull, which drove Schottel-type azimuth thrusters. Between the hulls, the upper deck extended down in a boat shape, designed to reduce pitch by entering the water and momentarily increasing forward buoyant upthrust. For rigidity, the hulls were linked at keel level by a faired transverse strap, probably far enough aft to limit emergence and slamming in head sea conditions. Of note was the demountable operations/control room, located at the rear of the superstructure.

Apparently unsatisfactory, the two vessels had a relatively short service life, both being decommissioned in 2001. Since then, the RAN has favoured reliance on Craft Of Opportunity (COOP), and acquired a number of commercial fishing vessels to evaluate their suitablity for inshore mine countermeasures.

## Inshore Minesweepers (IMS), Bay class

**Displacement:** 100 tons (standard); 170 tons (loaded)
**Length:** 31m/101ft 9in (oa)
**Beam:** 9m/29ft 6in
**Draught:** 1.8m/5ft 10in (mean)
**Armament:** 2 x machine-guns
**Machinery:** 2 diesel engines, 2 electrically driven azimuth thrusters
**Power:** 134kW/180hp for 10 knots
**Fuel:** Not known
**Endurance:** 2,208km/1,200nm at 10 knots
**Protection:** Nominal
**Complement:** 13

# Glossary

**AGC** Amphibious Command Ship (US); LCC from 1969.

**AKA** Attack Cargo Ship (US); LKA from 1969.

**ALC** Earlier designation of LCA.

**"Amtrac"** Popular term for LVT.

**APA** Attack Transport (US); LPA from 1969.

**APD** Auxiliary Personnel Destroyer (US); later High-Speed Transport Destroyer.

**ARG** Amphibious Ready Group (US).

**ATG** Amphibious Task Group.

**AUV** Autonomous Underwater Vehicle.

**ballast** Additional weight taken aboard to improve stability, to correct trim or to modify ship movement.

**bandstand** Raised island platform for gun mounting.

**beam** Width of hull at waterline at Standard Displacement.

**bhp** Brake horsepower. Power available at output of a diesel engine.

**bunkers** In the modern sense, fuel, rather than the compartments in which it is stored.

**BYMS** British Yard Minesweeper Variant on YMS (US).

**C3 (C-3)** US Marine Commission designation for a cargo ship of between 137–152m/450–500ft waterline length and carrying less than 100 passengers. Note also

the "C" referred to standard cargo vessels of under 122m/400ft, C2 of 122–137m/400–450ft, and C4 of 152–168m/500–550ft.

**camber** Transverse curvature of a ship's deck.

**cantilever** Overhung structure supported at only one side or end.

**casing (funnel)** Outer plating surrounding exhaust end of uptakes.

**CATF** Commander, Amphibious Task Force (Naval).

**chine** Line of intersection between sides and bottom of a flat-bottomed or planing craft.

**CIWS** Close-In Weapon System. Close-range, anti-missile defence of automatic guns and/or missiles on single mounting.

**CLF** Commander, Landing Force (Marine).

**CTOL** Conventional Take-Off and Land.

**Daihatsu** Common name for a range of Japanese landing craft.

**DASH** Drone Anti-Submarine Helicopter.

**DD tank** Duplex-Drive amphibious tank.

**deadweight (tonnage)** Actual carrying capacity of a cargo ship, expressed usually in tons of 2,240lb. Abbreviated to "dwt".

**derrick** Pivoted spar, fitted with winches, for lifting loads. In US, a "cargo boom".

**displacement, full load or "deep"** Weight of ship (in tons of 2,240lb) when fully equipped, stored and fuelled.

**displacement, standard** Weight of ship less fuel and other deductions allowed by treaty.

**draught (or draft)** Mean depth of water in which a ship may float freely.

**DUKW** Amphibious truck, commonly known as a "Duck".

**ECM** Electronic Countermeasures.

**ELINT** Electronic Intelligence.

**endurance** Usually equal to twice the operational radius.

**EOD** Explosive Ordnance Disposal.

**ESM** Electronic Support Measures.

**flare** Outward curvature of hull plating.

**freeboard** Correctly, the vertical height between the waterline and the lowest watertight deck. Commonly, the vertical height of the shell plating from the waterline at any particular point.

**gross registered tons** Measure of volumetric capacity of a merchant ship. One gross ton equals 100cu ft (2.83m$^3$) of reckonable space. Abbreviated to "grt".

**"Hedgerow"** "Hedgehog"-type anti-submarine spigot mortar adapted for beach mine clearance.

**HMT** Her Majesty's Transport.

**horsepower (hp)** Unit of power equal to 746 watts.

**ihp** Indicated horsepower. Specifically, the power delivered by the pistons of a reciprocating steam engine.

**IMS** Inshore Minesweeper.

**knuckle** Line of change in direction of shell plating. Usually a signature-reduction measure, but also reduces excessive width of upper deck in hulls of pronounced flare.

**LAMPS** Light Airborne Multi-Purpose System.

**LASH** Lighter Aboard Ship.

**LCA** Landing Craft, Assault.

**LCA (HR)** Landing Craft, Assault (Hedgerow).

**LCAC** Landing Craft, Air Cushion.

**LCC** Landing Craft, Control (UK); AGC after 1969 (US).

ABOVE: **The Royal Navy aircraft carrier HMS *Ark Royal* conducting a Replenishment at Sea (RAS) with the Royal Fleet Auxiliary supply vessel RFA *Wave Knight* in the North Sea. HMS *Ark Royal* was withdrawn from Royal Navy service in October 2010.**

LCF  Landing Craft, FlaK.

LCG (L)/(M)  Landing Craft, Gun (Large)/ (Medium).

LCH  Landing Craft, Headquarters (UK); British equivalent of AGC/LCC (US).

LCI (L)/(S)  Landing Craft, Infantry (Large)/(Small).

LCI (R)  Landing Craft, Infantry (Rocket).

LCM  Landing Craft, Mechanized.

LCN  Landing Craft, Navigation (UK).

LCP (L)/(M)/(S)  Landing Craft, Personnel (Large)/(Medium)/(Small).

LCP (R)  Landing Craft, Personnel (Ramped).

LCS (L)/(M)/(S)  Landing Craft, Support (Large)/(Medium)/(Small).

LCS (R)  Landing Craft, Support (Rocket) (UK).

LCT  Landing Craft, Tank.

LCU  Landing Craft, Utility.

LCV  Landing Craft, Vehicle.

LCVP  Landing Craft, Vehicle, Personnel.

length (bp)  Length between perpendiculars. Customarily the distance between forward extremity of waterline at standard displacement and forward side of rudder post. For US warships, lengths on designed waterline and between perpendiculars are synonymous.

length (oa)  Length, overall.

length (wl)  Length, waterline. Measured at standard displacement

littoral zone  The area of a sea or lake close to the shore.

LSC  Landing Ship, Carrier (Derrick Hoistings) (UK).

LSD  Landing Ship, Dock.

LSDV  Swimmer Delivery Vehicle.

LSF  Landing Ship, Fighter Direction.

LSG  Landing Ship, Gantry (UK).

LSH  Landing Ship, Headquarters (UK).

LSI (L)/(M)/(S)  Landing Ship, Infantry (Large)/(Medium)/(Small) (UK).

LSM  Landing Ship, Medium.

LSM (R)  Landing Ship, Medium (Rocket).

LSS  Landing Ship, Sternchute (UK).

LST  Landing Ship, Tank.

LVT  Landing Vehicle, Tracked.

MAB  Marine Amphibious Brigade (US).

MAF  Marine Amphibious Force (US).

MAU  Marine Amphibious Unit (US).

MCMV  Mine Countermeasures Vessel (UK).

ABOVE: **A Landing Craft, Air Cushion (LCAC) from USS *Bonhomme Richard* (LHD-6) of Expeditionary Strike Group Five (ESG-5) supporting Operation Unified Assistance, the humanitarian operation effort in the wake of the tsunami on Sumatra, Indonesia, January 10, 2005.**

"Mexeflote"  Powered pontoon used also as causeway unit (UK).

MGB  Motor Gun Boat (UK).

ML  Motor Launch (UK).

MLC  Early designation of LCM.

MMS  Motor Minesweeper (UK).

Monitor  Shallow-draught vessel with heavy armament.

MSC  Military Sealift Command (US).

MSB  Minesweeping Boat (US).

MTB  Motor Torpedo Boat (UK); US equivalent PT.

NATO  North Atlantic Treaty Organization.

NGS  Naval Gunfire Support.

OTH  Over The Horizon.

PCF  *see* Swift Boat.

PDMS  Point Defence Missile System. Rapid-response, close-range anti-air missile system.

Plan Orange  US plan for war against Japan.

protection  In this context, usually only splinter-proof, but variable.

RAF  Royal Air Force.

RCT  Royal Corps of Transport.

RFA  Royal Fleet Auxiliary.

ROV  Remotely Operated Vehicle. Usually with umbilical.

SAM  Surface-to-Air Missile.

sheer  Curvature of deckline in fore-and-aft direction, usually upward toward either end.

shp  Shaft horsepower. Power at point in shaft ahead of stern gland. Does not include frictional losses in stern gland and A-bracket.

sided  Situated at sides of ship, usually as opposed to centerline location.

SIGINT  Signal Intelligence.

ski jump  Pronounced upward curvature at forward end of flightdeck, to enhance effect of short take-off run.

SSM  Surface-to-Surface Missile.

stability range  Total range through which, from a position of equilibrium, a vessel is stable in the static condition.

STUFT  Ships Taken Up From Trade.

SWATH  Small Waterplane Area, Twin Hull.

Swift Boat  Otherwise PCF; 50ft coastal surveillance boat (Vietnam).

TF  Task Force.

TG  Task Group.

trim  Amount by which a vessel deviates, in the fore-and-aft axis, from the designed draught.

TU  Task Unit.

turbo-electric  Propulsion system in which a steam turbine drives an electrical generator. This supplies energy via a cable to a propulsion motor coupled to the propeller shaft.

UAV  Unmanned Aerial Vehicle.

uptake  Conduit exhausting products of combustion to the funnel.

volume critical  Vessel whose design is driven by space rather than weight considerations.

V/STOL  Vertical or Short Take-Off and Land.

Warsaw Pact  Eastern military bloc, essentially a counter to NATO.

weight critical  Vessel whose design is driven by weight rather than space considerations.

# Index

RIGHT: **US Rangers on board a British-manned LCA waiting to be taken to a transport ship in preparation for the assault on Pointe du Hoc (Normandy) on June 6, 1944.**

BELOW: **A Type 072-II (Yuting II) during an exercise for the amphibious forces of the People's Liberation Army in China.**

BELOW: HMS *Fearless* and HMS *Intrepid* were both in service with the Royal Navy for 40 years.

# Picture Acknowledgements

Picture research for this book was carried out by Jasper Spencer-Smith, who has selected images from the following sources: JSS Collection, Cody Images, Imperial War Museum, US Navy Archive, Topfoto, Italian Navy, UK MoD, and Wikimedia.
(l=left, r=right, t=top, b=bottom, m=middle):

Cody Images: 3, 6b, 7bl, 7br, 8t, 8b, 9t, 12t, 13b, 16–17, 18–19, 20b, 24–5, 26, 27t, 29b, 30m, 30b, 31m, 31b, 36t, 36mr, 36br, 37br, 38b, 39b, 41, 44t, 47t, 48t, 48bl, 53b, 54, 56tl, 56br, 57t, 58t, 61, 64–5b, 66mr, 67t, 68b, 72, 74b, 75b, 77, 80b, 81b, 84mr, 85tl, 85ml, 88tr, 88mr, 90, 99b, 100t, 101b, 111b, 115b, 116b, 134t, 136t, 148b, 149t, 158t, 159t, 165, 166t, 168t, 169t, 172b, 173tl, 175, 187t, 194, 195t, 196, 198t, 200t, 202tl, 202b, 206t, 212t, 213, 214b, 215, 217, 230t, 231t, 231m, 232–33, 234t, 235b, 238t, 239t, 240, 244b, 245b, 253, 256, 258–59.
Italian Navy: 184 both, 185 both.
Topfoto: 21t, 22tl, 23b, 76tl, 86b.
US Navy (public domain): 37t, 38t, 40t, 40bl, 49t, 49b, 50–1, 62b, 73br, 75t, 78tl, 96t, 96b, 97t, 197, 206b.
UK MoD Crown Copyright: 1, 2, 6t, 94–5, 148t, 150b, 151t, 152b, 153, 154t, 156 both, 157 both, 235m, 244t, 264b.
Wikimedia Images: 219m, b, 130 all, 131 all, 161 both, 163 both, 180 both, 181 both, 188 both, 189 both, 190 both, 191 both, 223 all, 2256.

Every effort has been made to acknowledge photographs correctly, however we apologize for any unintentional omissions. These will be corrected in future editions.

# Key to flags

The nationality of each vessel is identified in the relevant specification box by the national flag that was in use at the time of service.

 Australia

 China

 East Germany

 France

 Germany – World War II

 Germany post-World War II

 Greece

 Italy

 Japan

 Netherlands

 Spain

 Soviet Union

 United Kingdom

 United States of America

This edition is published by Lorenz Books an imprint of Anness Publishing Ltd
info@anness.com
www.lorenzbooks.com
www.annesspublishing.com

© Anness Publishing Ltd 2023

Publisher: Joanna Lorenz
Editorial Director: Helen Sudell
Editorial: Felicity Forster, Jonathan North
Book Design: Nigel Pell
Cover Design: Nigel Partridge
Production Controller: Ben Worley

PAGE 1: An LVTP (7) launching from the docking well of a US Navy LPD.
PAGE 2: HMS Albion and a combat boat from the Royal Norwegian Navy.
PAGE 3: Russian naval infantry coming ashore from a Rubr class LCAC during an exercise on the Baltic coast.

ABOVE: **French military personnel offloading heavy equipment on January 25, 2010, in the main seaport of Port-au-Prince, Haiti. This was part of Operation "United Response", a multinational humanitarian and disaster relief effort to assist Haiti in the aftermath of the earthquake on January 12, 2010.**